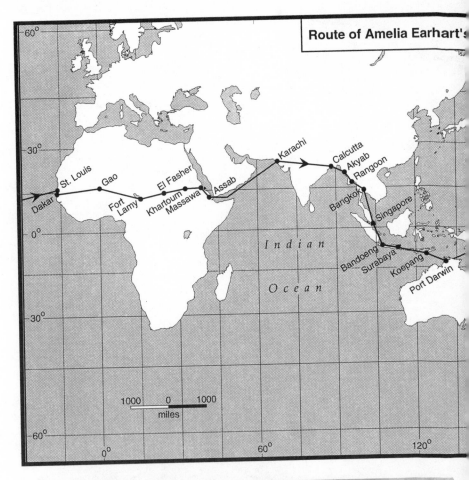

Route of Amelia Earhart's

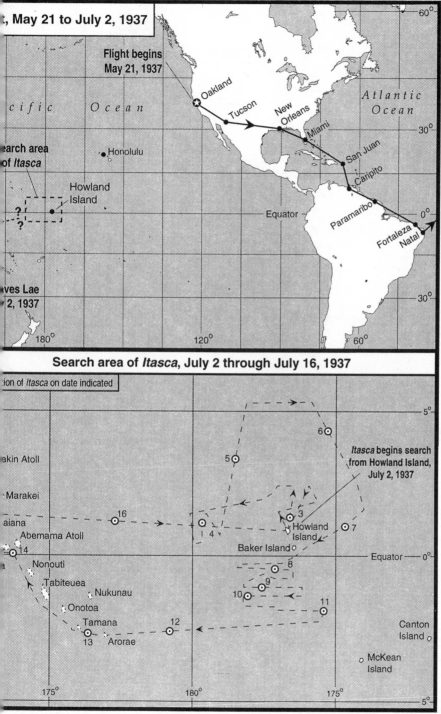

, May 21 to July 2, 1937

Flight begins
May 21, 1937

*A t l a n t i c
O c e a n*

cific O c e a n

Oakland

Tucson

New
Orleans

Miami

San Juan

Caripito

Honolulu

earch area
of *Itasca*

Howland
Island

Equator

Paramaribo

Fortaleza
Natal

? ?

ves Lae
2, 1937

60°

30°

0°

30°

180°   120°   60°

Search area of *Itasca*, July 2 through July 16, 1937

ion of *Itasca* on date indicated

akin Atoll

Marakei

aiana

Abemama Atoll

Nonouti

Tabiteuea

Nukunau

Onotoa

Tamana

Arorae

13

14

16

5

6

4

3

Howland
Island

Itasca begins search
from Howland Island,
July 2, 1937

7

Baker Island

8

9

10

11

12

Canton
Island

McKean
Island

Equator

5°

0°

5°

175°   180°   175°

Jack Hopper

Amelia

ALSO BY THE AUTHORS

BY DONALD M. GOLDSTEIN AND KATHERINE V. DILLON:
The Williwaw War (1992)
The Pearl Harbor Papers: Inside the Japanese Plans (1993)

BY THE AUTHORS WITH J. MICHAEL WENGER:
The Way It Was: Pearl Harbor, The Original Photographs (1991)
D-Day Normandy: The Story and Photographs (1993)
"Nuts!": The Battle of the Bulge (1994)
Rain of Ruin: The Hiroshima and Nagasaki Atomic Bombs (1995)
The Vietnam War: The Story and Photographs (1997)

BY THE AUTHORS WITH GORDON W. PRANGE:
At Dawn We Slept: The Untold Story of Pearl Harbor (1981)
Miracle at Midway (1982)
Target Tokyo: The Story of the Sorge Spy Ring (1984)
Pearl Harbor: The Verdict of History (1987)
December 7, 1941: The Day the Japanese Attacked Pearl Harbor (1988)
God's Samurai: Lead Pilot at Pearl Harbor (1990)

BY THE AUTHORS WITH MASATAKA CHIHAYA:
Fading Victory: The Diary of Admiral Matome Ugaki (1991)

BY DONALD M. GOLDSTEIN, PHIL WILLIAMS, AND J. M. SHAFRITZ:
Classic Readings of International Relations (1994)

BY DONALD M. GOLDSTEIN, PHIL WILLIAMS, AND HANK ANDREWS:
Security in Korea: War, Stalemate and Negation (1994)

Amelia
A Life of the
Aviation Legend

Donald M. Goldstein
and
Katherine V. Dillon

BRASSEY'S
An imprint of Batsford Brassey, Inc.
Washington • London

Library of Congress Cataloging-in-Publication Data

Goldstein, Donald M.
    Amelia : A life of the aviation legend / Donald M. Goldstein and
Katherine V. Dillon.
      p. cm.
    Includes bibliographical references and index.
    ISBN 1-57488-199-X (alk. paper)
    1. Earhart, Amelia, 1897–1937.   2. Women air pilots—United States—Biography.
I. Dillon, Katherine V.   II. Title.
TL540.E3G63   1997
629.13'092—dc21
  [B]   96-37902
                                                    CIP

10 9 8 7 6 5 4 3 2 1
Printed in the United States of America

TABLE OF CONTENTS

PREFACE

*A*melia Earhart has become a mythic figure, and the books and articles about her are legion. They range from serious biographies to books written for children and even fiction. Many are very good indeed and deserve respect. Others, in particular some of those concerned primarily with her disappearance, were frankly written to support a preconceived theory and show little interest in or understanding of Amelia as a person.

With so many volumes to choose from, why another? Oddly enough, the very extent of the published material suggested the possibility of a book that would draw from and consolidate some points from a number of the major existing volumes.

We also turned to the main newspapers of the day for coverage of this very public figure. They proved to be a prime source of both facts and atmosphere, the latter more immediate than any secondary source could provide.

Above all, we have profited by the work of two remarkable men—the late Captain Laurence F. Safford, USN (Ret.), and John F. Luttrell, a Georgia businessman—who gave us much previously unpublished material.

Safford's contribution is indirectly a part of the late Gordon W. Prange's legacy to us. During his researches on Pearl Harbor, he interviewed and corresponded with Safford, who in 1941 had been chief of Naval Communications Security. Although they disagreed on some points, they liked and respected each other and kept in touch. Eventually Safford sent Prange a copy of a manuscript concerning Amelia Earhart for comments and suggestions, as he did to several others.

Prange was interested, but his current commitments precluded his taking an active part in the project. So the manuscript remained in the Prange files until, after his death, we completed and saw published the projects that he had initiated. Then we were free to consider Safford's text.

Like so many others, Safford had followed Amelia's career in the newspapers since her *Friendship* flight in 1928. Then came the tragic end of her round-the-world flight in 1937. Safford's direct interest in the subject came about in the 1960s, when he read at least two books that referred to a Navy high-frequency direction finder installed on Howland Island in 1937. This type of equipment had come under Safford's cognizance, but he could not remember the Navy's having authorized any such installation. He determined to find out, with a view to writing a technical article for the *U.S. Naval Institute Proceedings*.

With the dedication, intelligence, and devotion to detail that had made him a towering figure in the field of cryptanalysis, Safford set upon his quest. He found an amazing amount of data available, and the inevitable happened. His project moved beyond an article into a book, and then he found himself having to discard material to keep the manuscript in bounds.

As we went deeper and deeper into Safford's work, we realized that if we simply edited it, the result would be primarily of interest to radio and communications experts and to other technicians. His chapters on Amelia up to her final loss, while containing many fresh insights, did not give a fully dimensioned picture of this remarkable woman. Clearly, if we wished to fill this void, we had to find out more about her as a person and as a flier, her family, her education, her public life, and her personality. Thus this book began to shape itself.

The next adjustment in our thinking came when John F. Luttrell contacted Goldstein. His approach to the Earhart puzzle could not have been more different from Safford's. The latter was practical. He attempted to solve the mystery of what happened to Amelia on the basis of such factors as radio wavelengths, fuel capacity, the aircraft's capabilities, air routes, strip maps, weather, and preparations for the project. In contrast, Luttrell was and is a romantic, fascinated by the mysterious, the bizarre. It was not in his nature to accept the idea of a simple if regrettable accident. He plunged deep into the various theories—some of them indeed weird—as to what might have been Amelia's fate. Like Safford, he gathered an enormous amount of material, much of it unpublished.

Luttrell's interest was not primarily in helping to write a book but in finding the Earhart plane, which he believed had come down on land. His initial choice was Winslow Reef, but he later switched to Mili Atoll, a site several other Earhart buffs also selected. He believed that she had been on some sort of government mission. Luttrell sent us a large carton of material, full of enlightening correspondence and other papers to and from various writers and enthusiasts, many of the Amelia-was-a-spy persuasion. We could by no means accept this theory, but Luttrell's material forced us to face the fact that we would have to deal with this aspect of the Earhart case because it had become a part of American mythology.

In developing the book, it fell naturally into three sections. Part I, "Takeoff" (chapters 1 through 8), covers Amelia's background, girlhood, discovery of aviation, selection to participate in the *Friendship* project, the fame that accrued to her in consequence, and her marriage to George P. Putnam. Part II, "High Flight" (chapters 9 through 17), opens with her solo crossing of the Atlantic, the feat that sealed her fame. In the following years, Amelia kept up a very full lecture program and established several flying records. A notable exploit was her solo flight from Hawaii to California, the first successful attempt by either man or woman. She established her relationship with Purdue University, which resulted in the university's furnishing her with the new aircraft in which she would attempt to circle the globe. Part III, "Flight into Mystery" (chapters 18 through 31), covers the last months of Amelia's life: her preparation for the round-the-world flight, her unsuccessful first attempt, the arrangements for a second try, the various stages of her journey, the final takeoff from Lae, and her disappearance. This section also discusses the communications problems, attempts at rescue, and the flood of theories that continued for years.

The reader may note some oddities of grammar in the quotations from Amelia's writings. They do not arise from ignorance; she had a very good command of the language. But she liked to play with it. This was in keeping with her personality, and we believe it would be a mistake to change her words or insert an apologetic "*sic.*" Also, we have kept the geographic names in use in Amelia's time.

We have tried to give a balanced picture of a fascinating personality, her life, and her final flight, using in many instances her own words to tell her story. We do not claim to have solved the mystery of her disappearance, although we have our opinion, but we believe we have contributed to an understanding of what happened and why. The longer we worked on this book, however, the more interested we became in Amelia's life rather than her death. It is good to remember that such people have lived—men and women, willing to break new ground, who do so not with grim endurance but with grace and good nature.

We wish to express our thanks to the family of our mentor, Gordon W. Prange, for their support and patient cooperation over the years. We also wish to express appreciation to our research assistants, Leah Campos and Rob Mullins; and a special thanks to our typist and editorial assistant, Kendall Stanley; and, of course, to our friends and editors at Brassey's, Inc.—Don McKeon, Kathleen Graham, and Frank Margiotta—for helping us to bring this ten-year odyssey to completion. We acknowledge with thanks the permission of the Edgar Cayce Foundation, Virginia Beach, Virginia, to quote from the Cayce Readings.

In gratitude and admiration, we dedicate this book to John F. Luttrell, to the memory of Laurence F. Safford, and to all who have followed the Earhart trail in a sincere search for the truth.

DONALD M. GOLDSTEIN, Ph.D.
Professor of Public and
International Affairs
University of Pittsburgh
Pittsburgh, Pennsylvania

KATHERINE V. DILLON
C.W.O., USAF (Ret.)
Arlington, Virginia

INTRODUCTION

As we write this, in September of 1996, Amelia Earhart would have been ninety-nine years old. Had it not been for a cruel twist of fate, she might still be with us, for she came of a long-lived strain. Her great-grandmother lived to be ninety-eight—this in a century when sixty was considered a ripe old age—and her mother to be ninety-five. Although never robust, Amelia followed a sensible regimen; she ate lightly, drank no alcohol, and estimated her annual cigarette intake at about three—cigarettes, not cartons. This abstinence required a certain amount of self-discipline and self-assurance because, at the height of her career in the 1930s, not to smoke marked one as hopelessly not with it.

But although Amelia never deliberately flouted public opinion, she never allowed it to influence her. She simply went her own way in her own way. As a later generation would put it, she did her own thing—courteously, good-naturedly, but firmly.

Today it is difficult to realize just how much of a pioneer she was. We doubt if she saw herself in that light. She took up flying, not in defiance or rebellion, but "for the fun of it"—a favorite phrase of hers. She lacked the competitive instinct that drove many other fliers and did not particularly care whether she won or lost a race. What she did care about, ardently, was the future of aviation.

She was also a champion of equal opportunities for women, without being in the least antagonistic toward men as such. Instead, she directed her impatience at the social systems and especially the educational systems of her day, which divided male and female into neat compartments without regard for the wishes or aptitudes of the individuals. In her chosen field she achieved the delicate feat of excelling in a predominantly male profession without antagonizing her colleagues, at least those whose opinion she valued. A number of the great men of aviation befriended and helped her.

What effect Amelia's writings and lectures, delivered in her soft voice, had on the thinking and mores of her day is impossible to assess; however, she had one supreme advantage—an audience. Her two transatlantic flights had given her a unique cachet. This was not a woman knocking ineffectually on a closed door; this was a woman who had coolly picked the lock.

Of course, some disapproved of or felt threatened by Amelia's activities and hinted that she was a lesbian. This is almost certainly untrue, at the time the standard putdown of any woman seeking entry into a traditional male field. The euphemism was "unwomanly." In general, however, Amelia was a prime public favorite. It was virtually impossible to dislike this slender young woman, intelligent, humorous, and attractive without being beautiful. With the exception of Charles A. Lindbergh, Amelia was the most popular figure in American aviation. And while Lindbergh could sorely try his fans' loyalty by avoiding them or being downright rude, Amelia was sensible enough to realize that, having embraced a public career, she must accept the public's interest and praise with good grace and appreciation.

Why did the American people of her day choose Amelia Earhart as their particular favorite? Hers was one of the most inexplicable of human attributes that can be summed up only by that overworked word "charisma." There were other women pilots contemporary with her, some of whom may have been better fliers, and some who were undoubtedly prettier. But her face would remain in memory long after the beauties of the day had been forgotten. In the 1980s, one Amelia fan, Dan Wade, said that he "fell in love" with her picture on the eight-cent U.S. airmail stamp. "There's just something about the way she looks. She's the all-American girl, the girl next door. You can't help but fall in love with her."[1]

Yet these are superficialities. Beneath them lay the bedrock of character that the public instinctively sensed and saluted. Anne Morrow Lindbergh called Amelia "the most amazing person—just as tremendous as C., I think. It startles me how much alike they are in breadth. . . . She has the clarity of mind, impersonal eye, coolness of temperament, balance of a scientist."[2]

Our century is the poorer because Amelia Earhart was lost shortly before her fortieth birthday. Whatever second career she chose, it surely would have been productive and useful. As it is, she remains a valid historical figure, typical of the best of her era, and in a sense she has become a part of the American collective unconscious.

PART

1

Takeoff

Chapter 1
Childhood Idyll

*A*melia Mary Earhart was the product of an almost incredibly "Norman Rockwell" background. On both sides, her family had been American since before the Revolution. Her great-grandmother, born Maria Grace, remembered that when she was a little girl her father had hoisted her to his shoulder so that she could see George Washington ride by.[1]

While Maria was growing up, a German boy named Gebhard Harres was struggling his way to freedom. Faced with military conscription in his native Brunswick, he escaped to the Netherlands, where he shipped aboard a Dutch freighter. After two years and seven months at sea, he reached Philadelphia and settled there. He became a toolmaker, and by the age of twenty had been made a junior partner in the business. That same year, 1818, he married Maria Grace.[2]

They had seven children; the youngest, Amelia Josephine, was born in 1840. Twenty-one years later, she married Alfred Otis, a native New Yorker who was descended from James Otis, the orator credited with coining the phrase "taxation without representation," and whose speeches were an important part of the momentum toward the American Revolution.[3]

Alfred Otis had pushed west early, entered the brand-new University of Michigan at Ann Arbor, and became the first honor graduate in its first class. He and a few other ambitious young men decided to settle in Atchison, Kansas.[4] When Alfred brought his bride to Atchison, it was still typically frontier, with unpaved streets providing convenient wallows for pigs. Indians frequently visited the town, friendly but slightly scary to the young eastern woman. The Atchison milieu was fine for a man like Alfred, bent upon becoming a big fish while the pond was still small. Considerations other than ambition dictated his choice of locale, however, one being his desire to help keep Kansas an antislavery state.[5]

Shortly after the Otises established their home, the Civil War broke out. Like most of the men in town, Alfred enlisted in a Kansas regiment. After an abortive expedition into Mississippi, the Kansas men returned home for guard duty at Fort Leavenworth. Alfred was still there when mustered out.

Over the next decade or so, Atchison grew to be a prosperous railroad terminus, and as the town's star rose, so did that of the Otis family. Alfred's law practice and canny real estate investments made him wealthy by the standards of the day; his presidency of a bank and election as judge of the U.S. District Court attested to the regard of his fellow citizens. He and Amelia produced six children—four boys and two girls—and Maria Harres made her home with them. She was in her seventies, a very old age for the time, but still active.[6]

Meanwhile—a long meanwhile—another family stream was converging upon Atchison. Anthony Altman, formerly of Hesse, and his wife, Miriah Josephs, of a noble French family, settled in America in the 1760s. Among their descendants four generations later was a Lutheran minister, David Earhart.[7]

In his way, David Earhart was as remarkable as Alfred Otis, but his ambition ran on a different track. He asked only to be a good servant of God. To prepare for his calling, he attended an academy at Indiana, Pennsylvania, where he studied English, Latin, Greek, and mathematics. In Wooster, Ohio, he studied theology and was ordained in the Evangelical Lutheran Church in 1844.[8]

Three years earlier, David had married Mary Wells Patton. The couple had twelve children, evenly divided between boys and girls. They did not rear their brood without tragedy; four of their daughters died in childhood.

During these early years of his ministry, David preached to congregations just beginning to use English rather than German as their tongue of worship. In later years, David wrote a vivid, touching description of the grim, never-ending labor of clearing, tilling, and farming the land in those days in western Pennsylvania. He paid especial tribute to the pioneer women, whose lives were exhausting drudgery. David was proud of these brave folk, and of his own family. "There was not a drunkard among the whole of our kin. Nor do I know of any bearing our name to have been arrested for crimes of any kind."[9]

In the spring of 1860, the Earharts moved to Sumner, Kansas, a small town some three miles south of Atchison. Ill fortune dogged them, and the family was "often put to great straits." To help make ends meet, David taught Hebrew and Greek at Midland College near Atchison.[10]

During this period there occurred an incident destined to be a favorite family tale for years to come. The youngest boy, Edwin, took advantage of his father's absence one Sunday, went fishing, and brought home six large river catfish. David, having returned, demanded of Edwin "how it happened that he had desecrated the Lord's Day by fishing."

Edwin, age seven, replied with ready wit, "Sir, you know fish always bite better when you are preaching!"

Concealing his amusement with some difficulty, David "reproved him for his levity" and "declared that, of course, we must not eat the fish caught in defiance of the Fourth Commandment."

This was too much for Mary Earhart. It was she, not her unworldly husband, who had to cope three times a day with feeding a large family on a preacher-cum-teacher's salary. "Husband, let us consider Edwin's fishing a work of necessity which is permitted by Holy Writ," she interposed firmly, "for I think the children need the nourishment. You and I will abstain, but it seems wrong to refuse the gifts of nature because of the day."

David retired, bested. As he wrote, "Truly there is no answer to an upright woman's plea for her children's welfare."[11]

After a brief return to Pennsylvania, the Earharts settled in Atchison. There David "lived in comparative retirement," teaching a Bible class and occasionally preaching. A photograph of him during these later years of his life shows a face of spiritual strength and gentleness. Hints of his future granddaughter appear in the molding of the bones and the slender, ascetic hands.

For all the hardships of his life, he must have been happy, for he earnestly hoped that Edwin would follow him in the ministry. With this thought in mind, he sent Edwin to Thiel College in Greenville, Pennsylvania. There the boy made an excellent record and graduated with honors. Years later his eldest daughter visited Thiel and discovered that "his record for scholarship, i.e., age of graduation, has never been equalled. He was fourteen when he entered college and only eighteen when he got his degree."[12]

To his father's disappointment, Edwin had no call to the pulpit and wanted to study law. David could give him no more financial help, so Edwin worked his way through by tending furnaces, assisting professors, and "tutoring slower but more affluent students." His future son-in-law would describe him thus: "Handsome, brilliant but irresponsible, and almost spectacularly poor in pocket."[13]

While Edwin was thus scratching to prepare himself for his profession, Alfred Otis and his family lived with the grace and comfort possible only with money and social position. One of Amelia's sisters, Mary, had entered into a highly satisfactory marriage with the equally well-to-do Dr. Paul Challis. They resided in a mansion he built amid extensive acreage overlooking the Missouri River.

There seems little doubt that Alfred Otis had evolved into something of a stuffed shirt, but that was only to be expected of a prosperous Victorian paterfamilias. He was public-spirited and a leader in founding a small private institution, the Latin School, to which he sent his children, daughters included. The trustees were lucky enough to find an inspired teacher, a mathematician who spoke six languages and possessed the knack of drawing out his pupils. Alfred's daughter Amy did so well that she was accepted at Vassar College, proof in itself that her father had some advanced notions; higher education for women was by no means taken for granted in the 1880s.[14]

Unfortunately, Amy had been delicate since she was sixteen, when a bout of typhoid impaired her hearing. Her beautiful long hair was sacrificed to the common conviction that a woman's hair sapped her strength. Then, the same year that she should have entered Vassar, Amy came down with diphtheria. Maria Harres, ninety-two years old but still going strong, installed Amy in her own room and forbade anyone else in the family to come near the patient, lest they, too, catch this dread disease. Her devoted nursing plus the skill of a local doctor and especially of his student-doctor son pulled Amy through.

Her long convalescence ruled out Vassar, but she kept busy teaching Sunday school, helping organize a (Charles) Dickens club, going to balls and cotillions, and riding horseback.[15] She was at full bloom for her presentation ball that June. Amy was not a beauty, but she had a gentle prettiness and, more important, an appealing charm she would never lose, and she lived to be ninety-five. As might be expected, Alfred Otis pulled out all the stops to ensure that his daughter was properly launched into society. To take advantage of the beautiful weather, the ball was held outdoors. A carpenter built a floor over the lawn. He had to work around a big, wrought-iron Stag-at-Eve, which looked quite jaunty when Amy hung a necklace of red roses around its neck and a lantern on one antler. The family handyman strung wires between the trees and affixed a Japanese lantern about every ten feet.

As Amy stood by the porch steps with her parents, greeting their guests, she had the satisfaction of knowing that the setting was perfect and that she herself was looking her prettiest. At that moment, as if arranged by a clever stage director, her brother Mark came up with a strange young man in tow. "This is Edwin Earhart," he said, "the law student who has pulled me through this year's examinations!"

Edwin looked at Amy, Amy looked at Edwin, and whatever matrimonial hopes Alfred and Amelia may have cherished for their daughter sank without a trace. Years later Amy told her daughters, "I liked him right away and I soon knew that he liked me."

From a city full of eligible potential husbands, Amy had set her heart on the penniless son of an equally penniless preacher, and the boy had not even graduated from law school! Four years would elapse before he took his degree. And even then, how could he support any wife, much less Atchison's leading debutante?

Alfred was too smart to forbid the match flat out or to forbid the couple to meet. But he issued a stern proviso: "I expect any gentleman who marries my daughter to be able to show an income of at least fifty dollars a month, with the prospect of increasing that considerably as time goes on."[16]

Today, when $50 just might buy a pair of shoes or dinner at a good restaurant, it is difficult to visualize what a staggerer this must have been to Edwin. In the late years of the nineteenth century, Edwin could have rented a "five-room house, in firstclass repair" for $10 a month and bought a couch for $6.98. The same money could have purchased a good suit, with shirts at 69¢. Shoes ran from $1 to $3. He could have read his *New York Times*—$9 a year—while sipping his breakfast coffee at 14¢ a pound.[17]

So fifty dollars a month was by no means starvation wages, and Alfred had set Edwin no small task. Perhaps he wanted to discover whether Edwin was a fortune hunter, and it is quite possible, as Edwin's future son-in-law thought, that Alfred did not believe his daughter's admirer could ever make it. There was always the possibility that over the years the young people would drift apart.

But they did not change their minds. Although it took him five years, Edwin rose to the challenge. He and Amy were married on October 18, 1895. It was a quiet ceremony in Trinity Church, for the family feared that a full-scale society wedding would be too much for Maria Harres, now ninety-eight. Amy wore a brown going-away costume instead of bridal white; the groom wore the traditional black broadcloth suit with Prince Albert tails.[18] Immediately after the ceremony, Edwin and Amy boarded a train for Kansas City, Kansas, where Edwin had found employment and where a fully furnished house awaited them—the gift of Alfred Otis.

Later Amy's daughter Muriel acknowledged that her mother did not make "the transition from pampered debutante to poor man's wife" without some heartache and frustration. Like most young women of her class and generation, Amy would have been instructed in the household arts; however, in the Otis home there was no need to skimp. Many small economies that would have been second nature to her deceased mother-in-law, Mary Earhart, were outside Amy's frame of reference. But the young couple were too intelligent, too well-bred, and too much in love to let their marriage dissolve in tears, sulks, and recriminations. They soon settled down, happy in their marriage and each other.

Real tragedy struck them the August following the wedding. An accident to a cable car sent Amy into premature labor, and the baby, a girl, died. Edwin took the tiny corpse to Atchison, where Alfred met him at the railroad station, whatever animosity that lay between them swallowed in grief. The faithful Otis handyman dug a grave in a corner of the Otis lot, and there the baby was buried.[19]

Amy recovered with all the resilience of youth, and a little over a year later she was overjoyed to be pregnant again. Her mother urged that Amy return to Atchison to have the baby, lest complications develop. Thus it happened that this second girl was born very much alive in the home of her maternal grandparents on July 24, 1897. In accordance with family custom, she was named for her two grandmothers—Amelia Mary. It soon became evident that the Earharts had produced what her French many-greats-grandmother might have called *une originale*. Her first word was "Papa" rather than the customary "Mama."[20]

About three years after Amelia, the Earharts rounded out their family with another daughter, named Grace Muriel. The "Muriel" was just because her parents liked the sound of it; the "Grace" was for Amy's favorite sister-in-law. It is pleasant to reflect that, even if unintended, "Grace" also honored the indomitable Maria Grace Harres, who had died about a year before Amelia's birth. This new baby was more conventional than her sister; her first word was "Mama."

If the two girls suffered from that formidable condition, sibling rivalry, it is not evident from any of their later writings. Muriel adored her big sister "Meely," as she called her because her tongue could not quite manage "Amelia." The latter called Muriel "Pidge," for no good reason. The nicknames stuck, and the Earhart girls answered to Meely and Pidge well into adulthood.[21]

The girls had an unusually happy childhood, for Edwin and Amy had the knack of parenting. They shielded the girls from any realization of their money problems, although they could not entirely conceal those of others. Blacks were constantly seeking employment with little or no success. After all those years, there was still an irrational tendency to blame them for the Civil War. But when one stopped at the Earhart door, Amy always gave him something to eat and a handout. Her generosity was one of her most endearing traits, one, however, destined to worry and irritate Amelia in later days, when Amy's openhandedness would be unleavened with common sense.

Edwin permitted the girls to watch, fascinated, while he worked on an invention to hold signal flags on trains. In May of 1903 he went to Washington to patent his gadget, only to find that he was two years too late—another man already held a patent on an identical device.

Some months after his return, a city tax collector showed up on the Earhart doorstep with a delinquency notice. Having given her husband the necessary forty-one dollars she had saved to pay the tax well before the April deadline, Amy assured the collector that he must be mistaken, and he agreed to check the files. That night Amy mentioned the incident at the dinner table. The conscious guilt on Edwin's face made his admission almost superfluous. He had used the tax money toward securing his patent, sure that he could sell the invention to the railroad and pay the tax with the proceeds.

Amy, to whom "debt" was a dirty four-letter word, was genuinely shocked and dismayed. Her husband made light of the incident; he could find the money. This he did by collecting some overdue fees and blithely selling some valuable law books that his father-in-law had given him. He paid the delinquent tax, and that would have been that, except that a lawyer who had bought three of the books mentioned the purchase to Judge Otis. Alfred was hurt, shamed, and furious. Muriel dated from this incident the crack in family solidarity that would lead to much bitterness in the future.[22]

There can be no doubt that Edwin was irresponsible. When he received a hundred dollars for some legal work, he took his family for a week at the World's Fair in St. Louis and blew every cent of it. Of course, his daughters had no idea of finances and thought their father was wonderful. He was never too busy or too tired to play with them, read to them, and make up long, blood-and-thunder serial stories. Amelia and Muriel recognized and enjoyed these yarns as fiction, but at times he severely shook pop-eyed neighborhood children when— hale, hearty, and whole—he claimed to have lost an arm or a leg or even been killed in fights with outlaws or Indians.[23]

Shortly after their return from St. Louis, the spirit moved Amelia, then seven years old, to build a roller coaster with the help of Muriel, a neighbor boy, and their uncle Carl Otis, who was visiting the Earharts. With several planks, a wooden box, and an eight-foot tool-shed as a takeoff point, they constructed a workable if rickety track. They greased it with lard, and Amelia took the first ride. Box and passenger hit the trestle their uncle had helped put in place, spilling Amelia out. Her lip was bruised and her dress torn, but her eyes were blazing with joy and excitement. "Oh, Pidge, it's just like flying!" she exclaimed. She wanted to extend the track and straighten the trestle, but Amy ordered the dangerous contraption destroyed.[24]

Not that Amy was an overcautious mother. She did not attempt to force her daughters into the conventional mold of "nice little girls." The pastimes considered suitable for "nice little girls" were largely static— dolls, dollhouses, tea parties with real or imaginary playmates, board games, and the like—all of which interested the Earhart girls not at all. They craved action.

Amy's only sister, Margaret, was a disciple of clothes reformer Amelia Jenks Bloomer, so Amy was aware of those surpassingly ugly but practical garments known as "bloomers." She had a seamstress run up dark blue flannel gym suits for the girls to play in on Saturdays. These were the first such garments in town and caused some mild disapproval from the neighboring housewives.

Amy allowed her daughters to experience any unusual event that came their way, such as staying up to the unheard-of hour of 11 P.M. to watch an eclipse of the moon. And the whole family, plus some neighbors, perched on a shed roof to watch the 1908 appearance of Halley's comet. Indeed, Amy had the gift of using everything as an opportunity to teach. Even the distasteful job of cleaning chickens she transformed into a little lecture on the wonders of nature: "See, girls, how neatly this hen's little lungs fit here, just above her tiny heart."[25]

Naturally the girls had a dog, a large black animal of uncertain ancestry and even more uncertain disposition. Amelia and Muriel could do anything with James Ferocious, but he had no use for outsiders. One day some boys invaded the backyard and teased the dog, which was chained, until it broke free and went for them. His barking brought Amelia to investigate. Instinctively she did the right thing— stood absolutely still and spoke in a calm, soothing voice: "James Ferocious, you naughty dog, you've tipped over your water dish again. Come along into the kitchen and I'll get you some more." He trotted after her obediently; Amy ordered the boys to leave. She praised Amelia for her bravery. "I wasn't brave, mother," she replied. "I just didn't have time to be scared."[26]

Amelia's love for animals occasioned her only direct revolt on record against parental authority. A neighbor had a beautiful little mare named Nellie, which he neglected and abused to the point where one day she broke free, jumped a railing into the river, and was drowned. Her owner had injured himself in pursuit, and in the neighborly tradition of the time, Amy told Amelia to take him a piece of cake and inquire after him.

Amelia clasped her hands behind her back and shook her head. "Mother, I won't take cake or anything else to that horrid man. After the way he treated Nellie, I'm glad he got hurt. Spank me if you want to: I just won't do it." Herself an accomplished horsewoman with a tender heart, Amy could not insist.[27]

The girls inhabited another world beyond that of healthy outdoor games—the world of books. They read to themselves; they read to each other; their parents read to them. Judge Otis had given Amy a set of Dickens, an inexhaustible source of delights. Sunday evenings were reserved for Bible stories and *Pilgrim's Progress*. Edwin had a comic talent that made such works as *Pickwick Papers* really fun. To Amelia it seemed that her father "must have read everything and, of course, therefore knew everything. He could define the hardest words as well as the dictionary and we used to try to trap him and he to bewilder us."

Frequently, when Amy assigned them household chores, instead of dividing the tasks, one read aloud while the other worked. Amelia was especially drawn to poetry, and the girls would wash dishes or dust while chanting from *Horatius at the Bridge* or *Sohrab and Rustum*.[28]

The Earhart fortunes seemed to take an upward turn when George MacCaughan, leading attorney for the Rock Island Railroad, offered Edwin a job in the legal claim department. Edwin and Amy decided to leave the girls with the Otises while they looked for a suitable house in Des Moines. On the train trip to Atchison, heavy rains caused flooding and some of the passengers almost panicked. "Meely, are you afraid?" asked Muriel. Her sister answered with all the lofty annoyance of eight years, "Of course not, silly. There are no bears here." The passengers' tension exploded in laughter.

What had been planned as at most a two-months' stay extended to almost a year. Although the girls missed their parents, they loved their grandparents, and there were congenial companions of their own age, particularly their cousins, Lucy and Katherine Challis, called, respectively, Toot and Katch.[29]

While life in the Otis household was much more formal than in the Earhart ménage, it had compensations. For instance, the never-ending fascination of the judge's handmade shoes, which creaked when he walked. Above all, there was the Otis library. On its well-stocked shelves were bound copies of such magazines as the *Youth's Companion, Harper's Weekly,* and *Puck,* going back a good ten years. A new world opened to the girls with the discovery of the collected works of Victor Hugo and Alexandre Dumas. Sir Walter Scott, George Eliot, Thackeray—all were grist for their mill. Amelia later wrote that she was "a horrid little girl" and wondered how her grandmother had put up with her, adding, "Perhaps the fact that I was exceedingly fond of reading made me endurable." In the library she got in no one's way.[30]

The Otises enrolled their granddaughters in a private school. Amelia loved it, although never qualifying as a "teacher's pet." At least one teacher, Sarah Walton, recognized her quicksilver qualities: "Amelia's mind is brilliant, but she refuses to do the plodding necessary to win honor prizes. She deduces the correct answers to complete arithmetic problems, but hates to put down the steps by which she arrived at the results." Thus a less bright but more careful classmate won the arithmetic prize. This did not upset Amelia at all. She could do the sums, and Miss Walton knew she could, so what did the medal matter?[31]

Amelia and Muriel never forgot that Christmas at Atchison. Their parents arrived, loaded down with packages. Questions about the contents elicited the classic response, "Layovers for meddlers and crutches for lame ducks." Christmas morning solved the mystery, for the two largest packages contained sleds. And what sleds! Girls' sleds of the day were short and lightweight, meant to be ridden sitting bolt upright, pulled by an adult or at best coasting down a gentle incline. These which the Earhart girls unpacked were boys' sleds, long and strong for "bellywhopping." The youngsters were incoherent with joy, and Grandmother Otis was horrified.

Edwin's second gift came in answer to a hint. The girls had possessed a little BB popgun long enough to become fairly proficient, and they had written their father asking for a "real" gun. He obliged with a .22-caliber Hamilton rifle. This was even worse than the sleds, in Mrs. Otis's eyes. "Edwin, you're not giving a nine-year-old child a gun, I hope!" she exclaimed. He assured her that the recipients knew and would obey firearm regulations, and the girls eagerly chorused agreement.

On another occasion, Amelia asked for footballs for herself and her sister, and her father was glad to oblige. The suspicion arises that Edwin was enjoying a vicarious childhood, bestowing on his daughters the gifts he had wanted as a boy that his father had been too poor to afford. Fortunately the girls were as happy to receive these presents as he was to give them.

Eventually Mrs. Otis impounded the rifle, but the sleds were another matter. Amelia's skill at "bellywhopping" saved her life. She was zipping down a very steep hill when a junkman's cart pulled out of a side road directly in her path. Huge blinders prevented the horse from seeing danger approaching, and the junkman did not hear Amelia's cries of warning. The hill was too icy to allow her to turn. With amazing presence of mind, she held her course, ducked her head, and flashed under the horse between its front and hind legs. Had she been sitting up like a proper little girl, a collision would have been inevitable.[32]

In the schoolgirl Amelia, many traits had already manifested themselves that would characterize Amelia the woman: intelligence, kindness, coolness under pressure, love of the outdoors, originality, a certain impatience with details, and, by no means least, charm and a gift for friendship. Many years later, her cousin "Toot" Challis wrote to Amelia's husband that "children don't analyze one another. All I knew was that Amelia was more fun to play with than anyone else—I admired her ability, stood in awe of her information and intelligence, adored her imagination, and loved her for herself—and it held true always."[33]

Chapter 2

Shadow on the Sun

F inally Edwin and Amy found suitable housing in Des Moines, and their daughters joined them. The girls went through a period of adjustment. In Des Moines they had no secure spot in the city's aristocracy. Much worse, in their eyes, they had no spreading lawns and huge barn as their playground, no playmates to compare with their Challis cousins.

Amy had planned on enrolling her daughters in public school. A neighbor advised her to cut off Amelia's braids, because every child got head lice during the first week, and short hair was easier to clean. Amy's enthusiasm for public education dropped to zero. For twenty-five dollars a month she engaged a governess from Atchison, a young widow, Mrs. Florence Gardiner, whose husband had drowned while on their honeymoon. She "wore an expression of resigned sadness," to quote Muriel, and tended to burst into tears at any mention of the ocean.

Her gloomy presence cast something of a pall over the cheerful Earhart dining table, and she did not understand Edwin's teasing humor. She turned rigid with shock when he presented Amy with a long box, telling her it was a new saw for her to use on the cordwood. Amy went along with the joke, answering in her gentle way, "Oh, Edwin, that will be so nice. I did have a hard time with those last logs!" The box actually held the complete works of Rudyard Kipling, bought on the installment plan. Payment was typical: Edwin paid the first installment; Amy had to scrounge the rest out of household funds.

Gardiner considered Edwin an "undermining influence" on the girls, what with encouraging their tomboy games and giving them a football instead of sewing baskets. But in her lachrymose way, she was not a bad teacher. The girls disliked the sewing and music lessons she insisted upon, but loved the poetry she read to and with them—readings far in advance of the school program. And she taught them the rudiments of French, which they spoke with an uncompromising Midwestern accent. Still, when at Christmas Mrs. Gardiner wanted to go home to Atchison, Amy decided to make the break permanent.[1]

She realized that the time had come to brave head lice and send her daughters to public school, where they could study a broader range of subjects and make friends of their own age. The girls enjoyed both their classes and playmates, Amelia in the seventh grade, Muriel the fourth.

One morning they set forth in blue and white store-bought gingham dresses. Arriving at school, Muriel was discomfited to see that a black classmate named Lulu May wore an identical dress. Some latent snobbery arose in Muriel. Why, everyone would think that her father, a lawyer for the railroad, could not afford to clothe his daughters any better than could Lulu May's, a porter at the railroad station! At recess Muriel persuaded Amelia that they should hurry home and change.

They explained the problem to Amy. She was too wise to issue a flat veto. They could change if they really wanted to, but, "I'm just wondering . . . how Lulu May will feel when you tell her you think she isn't nice enough to wear the same kind of dress that you do."

"Why, Mother, we won't *tell* her," Muriel assured her.

"Not with your tongues, but by your actions, surely," Amy answered.

Suddenly the girls understood that their projected action would be "mean." There was no pettiness in the Earhart girls. Convinced of error, they hurried back to the playground and sought out Lulu May. Amelia took her hand and said, "Look, Lulu May, we're all three just alike."

Muriel never forgot the expression on the little brown face as Lulu May said, "You know, I thought for a while you all had gone home to change your dresses so you wouldn't be like me."

Wincing inwardly, Amelia laughed, "Why, what a crazy notion! Come on, I've got a ball. . . . Lu bats first!"[2]

About this time, at an Iowa State Fair held in Des Moines, Amelia had her first look at an airplane, "a thing of rusty wire and wood." A nearby adult pointed it out to her, saying, "Look, dear, it flies." But it left ten-year-old Amelia cold. She was much more interested in a hat made from an inverted peach basket that she had just bought for fifteen cents. The incident had its ironic aspects. The adult Amelia Earhart hated hats, and the latest Paris creation could not have kept her away from any aircraft.[3]

The Earharts had been in Des Moines for about a year when Edwin became head of the railroad's Claim Department at an almost doubled salary, with privileges that included use of a private car. Whenever he had to make a long trip, he took the family along. Amelia did not believe that their periodic pullouts from school hindered their progress. She thought she "gained as much from travel as from curricula." All this jaunting about was as free as the sunshine. Amelia was sixteen before she bought a rail ticket, and paying for rail fare never did "seem quite right" to her.

To Amy's delight they could move into a larger house, and once more she could afford a cook and a maid. On the grounds of the new house was a vegetable plot, and Amy agreed to purchase at market prices whatever crops the girls could raise. Muriel tended her garden by the rules and in due time could harvest fresh vegetables for the family table. In Amelia's section the weeds flourished along with the crops. She wanted to see which survived. And who knew, she might produce a new vegetable. Amelia disliked orthodox cooking but enjoyed experimentation, so an occasional weird dish appeared in the Earhart kitchen.[4]

For four summers the Earharts were able to enjoy real vacations at Worthington, Minnesota, a small town on the shores of Lake Okabena. At last Amelia could ride, for the family from whom they rented the house permitted the girls to use their Indian pony, Prince. For some reason which Amelia never understood, her grandmother had taken a firm stand against Amelia riding horseback, although Amy had been "a beautiful and enthusiastic horsewoman."[5]

During the remaining months of the year, more intellectual pursuits were available. National and world events were discussed at the Earhart dinner table and carefully explained to the girls. Season subscriptions enabled them to hear such great artists as Amelita Galli-Curci, Ernestine Schumann-Heink, Rosa Ponselle, and Fritz Kreisler. There were semiannual art exhibits with works on loan from museums and dealers. Muriel preferred pictures of horses and dogs, Amelia "misty" landscapes. Muriel conceded that their artistic judgments were trite, but at least they appreciated those capable of depicting beauty. A number of families clubbed together and subscribed to magazines, passing them around among themselves.[6]

Does it all sound too good to be true—the brilliant, amusing husband and father, the serene, caring wife and mother, the healthy, happy little girls? There is a cynical saying, "If it sounds too good to be true, it probably is." In this case, the words were all too accurate. The Earharts had experienced their last unshadowed days as a family unit.

Amelia's writings contain no hint of the trouble. She would share with her public the details of her exploits, pleasant recollections, and happy incidents, but her sorrows and the depths of her emotions she kept to herself. Her husband later wrote ambiguously: "Finally this period of exacting work and irregular hours broke Mr. Earhart nervously, and he was ordered to give up all activity. Reluctantly he resigned from the Rock Island, and for the first time in fifteen years tried to take a vacation."[7]

Perhaps Putnam was respecting his wife's wishes, yet it is quite possible that she never confided the details to him. It was Muriel who aired the family skeleton. She and Amelia first knew that something was wrong with their father when, running to meet him one Saturday, they saw that he was walking slowly, putting each foot down with exaggerated care. Summoning up a pallid smile, he told his daughters and their friends waiting to play "Indians" with him, "Dad can't play today, kiddies, doesn't feel good." He stumbled up the steps to the front door. His wife's usual welcoming smile changed to a mask of disbelieving shock as she saw his condition.

At breakfast the next morning, he confined himself to black coffee. "I guess we better go to church this morning," he suggested. While Amelia and Muriel were changing into their Sunday best, Amy gave them the explanation which was their due: "Every once in a while, girls, some of the men in Dad's office ask him to drink with them, and often, he says, he can't refuse without seeming very rude. That's what happened yesterday. We must try to keep him from doing it again because it's bad for his health and for his work for the railroad."

In fact, as they learned later, Edwin would already have been in serious trouble with the railroad had it not been for Rose, his loyal stenographer. When under the influence, he dictated belligerent letters that Rose suppressed until he was sober enough to handle his correspondence in his usual capable way.

On this particular Sunday, Edwin, who was a warden of the church, behaved so well that Saturday seemed like a fading nightmare. He promised to "walk the straight and narrow path from now on."[8]

But he didn't. A number of factors probably led Edwin to turn to the bottle. The Peter Principle may have been involved: Edwin had risen in the railroad above his level of competence. This could only add to the sense of inferiority his Otis in-laws had always imposed upon him. In his drinking buddies, he found acceptance and approval. Muriel believed that his recent release from poverty played its part, enabling him to savor a "pleasure" he could not previously afford. She also believed that in the early stages he was not a true alcoholic; a novice at drinking, he could not hold his liquor with his cronies who were accustomed to several drinks at the end of the workday.

Edwin reeled home two or three times a week, and the drink brought out a nasty side of his character the girls had never seen before. He raged against the household costs, the Otises, the railroad, or anything else that came to mind. The girls learned to keep out of his way, a hard lesson indeed, as hitherto he had been the sort of father every child deserves and all too few have. It hurt them cruelly to see that apparently he no longer cared about them.[9]

Edwin's father had written years before that the Earhart family had never produced a criminal or a drunkard. The linkage is significant; a drunkard was not a criminal but was equally undesirable on the family tree. In those turn-of-the-century years, society had little or no concept of alcoholism as a disease. A drunk was a drunk, a disgrace to be concealed as far as possible. This treatment—a judgmental attitude allied to enabling cover-up—was probably the worst possible way of handling the situation. Certainly it was in the Earhart household, where the more Edwin drank, the more disgusted his womenfolk grew, and the further they withdrew, the more he turned to his drinking companions.

At the office, even Rose could not catch all of Edwin's errors. A letter of reprimand from Mr. MacCaughan, who had sponsored Edwin's upward path, provoked the latter to an irascible reply. MacCaughan went to Des Moines, found Edwin drinking at his desk, and sent him home. That evening MacCaughan visited Edwin and Amy, insisting that the former take "the Keeley cure," in which the patient received a drug to induce violent illness if one drank. Edwin resisted at first, with the predictable comment that he could stop drinking whenever he wanted to. Tactfully MacCaughan stated that Edwin's body as well as his willpower needed strengthening. Another man would take over his job, but Edwin would be reinstated as soon as he proved himself.

The next morning Amy greeted the girls radiant with hope. Their father was going to a hospital for a month, and when he came out he would be "our own dear Dad again." When he came home, clear-eyed and healthy-looking, to waltz his wife down the hall while his daughters laughed and applauded, it seemed that Amy's optimism was justified.[10]

Within a few days, however, he began drinking again. At that inauspicious moment, Mrs. Otis died, leaving an estate to be divided equally among her two daughters and two sons, one of whom, Theodore, was feebleminded. Somehow Mrs. Otis had learned of Edwin's drinking and, fearful that he would waste Amy's inheritance, left her share in trust for twenty years or until Edwin died.

Furious at this insult, Edwin returned to the bottle at full power. His rage at his mother-in-law was all the more violent because he was intelligent enough to know that he had earned her distrust. Inevitably his work suffered, and the Rock Island never reinstated him. The reason for his release spread through the close-knit world of railroading; as a result, he could not find work until the spring of 1913, when he was offered the position of a minor clerk in the Great Northern Railway's freight office in St. Paul. This was a distinct comedown, both in prestige and salary, but it was better than nothing and might offer a base upon which to build anew.[11]

The trip to St. Paul was lugubrious. They were traveling in what all of them knew was a downward direction. Their accommodation no longer was a private car but a packed day coach. Edwin sat slouched in a corner. His wife turned her head away from the girls, but could not conceal her tears.

Amelia and Muriel were less unhappy. Although they were sorry to leave Des Moines and the many friendships they had made, the move had the interest of a new experience. Nevertheless, the memory of her father's discouragement and her mother's tears went to bed with Muriel. She whispered the Lord's Prayer, and when she came to "forgive us our trespasses as we forgive those who trespass against us," she added an emphatic rider: "except I'll never, never forgive saloon keepers, all of them, everywhere!"[12]

In St. Paul, Edwin rented a large house that had been vacant for two years. They soon found out why. The house was impossible to heat, although it swallowed coal by the ton. The rent plus fuel absorbed every bit of Edwin's salary. The girls entered Central High School, Amelia as a junior and Muriel a freshman. Amelia's favorite subject was physics, with Latin a close second, thanks to a teacher who treated it like a living language and insisted that his pupils speak it in class. They also attended St. Clement's, a nearby Episcopal church, where Amelia joined the Altar Guild and Muriel sang in the junior choir.

Some three months after their arrival in St. Paul, Edwin came home very happy. The railroad was sending him to check out a freight train wreck and look after the company's interests. The girls hurried to pack his suitcase as they had done so often in the past. During dinner Amelia was unusually silent. In the kitchen, clearing up after the meal, she showed Muriel an unopened bottle of whiskey she had found among Edwin's socks. Just as she began to pour it down the sink, her father entered the kitchen and shouted, "Stop that, you meddling little fools! I must have that!"

He was about to strike Amelia when Amy appeared and clutched his arm. His anger subsided as suddenly as it had arisen. Indeed, he appeared dazed when he realized what was happening. "I nearly hit you, Meely, and I've never done such a thing in all my life." He admitted that he would be better off without the bottle.

The girls bore no malice and helped him into his overcoat, chanting excerpts from "Horatius at the Bridge" by way of encouragement. He promised to return the next night cold sober. This he did; further, he handled the assignment well and received a commendation from the railroad. But within three weeks he had spoiled everything. In a drunken haze during an investigation, he involved the railroad in considerable embarrassment. So instead of a promotion, he stayed in his low-level job and indeed may be counted fortunate to have retained that.[13]

Social life for the Earharts was almost nil. Amy had a wealthy uncle living in St. Paul who, with his family, paid a duty call, then dismissed his niece and her family from his scheme of things. Never before had Judge Otis's daughter been treated so contemptuously. Equally hard to accept was the fact that even if the uncle had taken them under his wing, Edwin could not have afforded fees for junior clubs and assemblies.

Amelia and Muriel eagerly anticipated a Twelfth Night party to be held at their church. Two boys from the congregation were sufficiently taken with the Earhart girls to urge them to be sure to attend. In those days, fathers escorted their daughters to functions and called for them at the appointed hour, never later than midnight. Edwin agreed to take the girls and to stay long enough for a waltz with each. He promised to be home by 5:30 P.M. That would give them ample time to dine, dress, and be off by 8 P.M.

Time ticked by; the clock struck six, then seven, then eight, and still no Edwin. He did not appear for another hour, and then in no condition to escort anyone anywhere. Muriel dashed upstairs, flung herself sobbing on her bed, and pounded her pillow in disappointment and frustration. This fresh proof that she and her sister came in a poor second to his bottle in Edwin's priorities was almost more than she could take.

Tears and poundings were not Amelia's style. With a set face she stripped the living room of the Christmas decorations and preparations for postparty hot cocoa. Then she read herself to sleep. She cared no less than the more demonstrative Muriel; her emotion went too deep for tears. In her adult life, she would never drink alcohol in any form. As for Muriel, she added to her prayers, "God bless Carrie Nation!"[14]

Poverty challenged their ingenuity. One evening Edwin dropped off a streetcar, lurched across the sidewalk, and was knocked down by a car. He was not badly injured, and his hospital charges totaled only ten dollars. Today a ten-dollar hospital bill seems like a dream of far-off paradise, but for the Earharts it meant no spring clothes for the girls.

Amelia rummaged in the attic and came down with her arms full of silk pongee curtains made for the home in St. Paul. "You may not know it now, Pidge," she declared, "but those beautiful Earhart girls are wearing the latest thing in pongee dresses for the Easter parade."

Neither of them liked to sew, and they had no idea of how to use a pattern. But the fashions of the day were simple, and Amelia had an instinctive style sense. Somehow she managed to produce two wearable outfits, Muriel's dyed green and Amelia's, brown.

Later that spring Edwin was offered a place in the claims office of the Burlington Railroad at Springfield, Missouri. So once more the Earharts broke up housekeeping and traveled to a new location. Staggering disappointment awaited them. The man whose job Edwin had been promised had decided against retiring, and he produced a letter from the Kansas City office agreeing that he could stay another two years. This man notified the main office of the mix-up and asked for funds to reimburse the Earharts for their trip. The company agreed and also hired Edwin for a month to clear back cases.

Faced with hanging fire for a month, Amy made a suggestion. In Des Moines they had befriended a family named Shedd. Edwin had helped Mr. Shedd to find a good job, and, while househunting, the Shedds had lived with the Earharts. The Shedds now lived in Chicago and once before had invited their benefactors to live with them until settled satisfactorily. Amy decided to take them up on their generous offer.

Edwin protested against his family, as he saw it, abandoning him, but Amy stood firm. In fact, her health demanded a major change. The last three years had played havoc with her nervous system. Her hearing had deteriorated badly; she jumped at any unexpected sound; at times her legs refused to support her. Their doctor in St. Paul warned Amelia that these were signs of a possible nervous breakdown. Mrs. Earhart must stop worrying and must have three hours of daily bed rest; otherwise, her condition would become much worse.[15]

The Shedds telegraphed, "Our home is your home now until next year or longer." So it was decided that Edwin would serve out his month in Springfield, then move to Kansas City to open a law office, while his wife and daughters visited the Shedds. Amy had no intention of sponging on her friends and planned to take a tiny apartment near them. Muriel entered the local high school, but Amelia wanted no part of it, protesting that the chemistry lab was "a kitchen sink." She settled upon Hyde Park High School, which necessitated Amy's moving to the Hyde Park district.[16]

In those years graft was rampant in Chicago and affected the school system. For the first time the Earhart sisters found themselves saddled with teachers who could not teach. Amelia suffered especially under a thoroughly incompetent English teacher, deaf as a post, whom the other students openly mocked. With incredible naïveté, she asked them to join her in a petition for a good instructor. Not surprisingly, this suggestion went over like the proverbial lead balloon.

Amelia endured the chaos for two weeks and then obtained permission to spend her English period in the school library. There she read about four times the required number of books, but her self-chosen isolation did not help her popularity. When she graduated in 1916, the caption under her picture read, "The girl in brown who walks alone." It was typical of Amelia that, having graduated, she skipped the graduation exercises. Mayor Anton J. Cermack of Chicago presented her diploma to her some sixteen years later. Shortly thereafter,

Cermack would be killed by an assassin's bullet intended for Franklin D. Roosevelt.[17]

Amelia had attended six high schools in four years, a procedure not commonly recommended for good education; however, she believed, "What we missed in continuous contacts over a long period, we gained by becoming adapted to new surroundings quickly." Her husband went further: "Perhaps it was this very frequent uprooting . . . that developed in her the ease of manner, the flair for making acquaintances which stood her in such good stead later on."[18]

The Chicago period was brief—not longer than ten months. Then Amy decided that the time was ripe to join Edwin in Kansas City, where he had been living with his sister and her family. Edwin was delighted to have his womenfolk back, and they settled down in a small house.

Soon Edwin persuaded Amy to try to break her mother's will. This was not entirely selfishness on his part. Her brother Mark, who had charge of the funds, had mismanaged them. Amy detested the idea of washing the family's dirty linen in a courtroom, but it was now a question of saving money destined for her daughters' higher education. The will was set aside, and Mark was ordered to turn over all funds. Then it was discovered that the sixty thousand dollars he had received had shrunk to forty-five thousand dollars in less than four years.[19]

Now Amy could send Amelia to the school of her choice, Ogontz School in Rydal, Pennsylvania. Tuition and board totaled six hundred dollars for half a year; textbooks, concerts, operas, medicine, and postage were extra. Amelia attended Ogontz from October 3, 1916, into the spring of 1918. In her published writings she barely mentioned this period. Her letters, however, reveal a growing maturity and independent mentality.

Headmistress Abby Sutherland and Amelia seem to have developed a rather wary mutual respect. In a letter to Amy written soon after arriving at Ogontz, Amelia described Sutherland thus in her unorthodox style: "She is a very brilliant woman, very impressive as she is taller than I and large. When I first saw her I thot she was come up from the depths as her cheekbones are high and her face seemed hard somehow." In due time she found the headmistress charming as well as brilliant.[20]

Sutherland later wrote to George Putnam, "Amelia was always pushing into unknown seas in her reading.

"The look in her straightforward, eager eyes was most fascinating in those days. Her most characteristic charm was her poise, her reserve, her curiosity."[21]

Some of Amelia's letters home are strictly schoolgirl. In the same missive that described Sutherland, she wrote, "I played hockey yesterday and made two goals, the only ones made."[22] In March 1917 she described a "lovely feast. . . . We played the ukeleles at twelve o'clock and sang." Some of the girls contributed sandwiches, cakes, pastry, ice cream, and hot chocolate with marshmallow, which they drank from trophy cups.

Yet this same letter, with its description of a "feast" that only a teenage stomach could love, showed a budding interest in the outside world: "What do you think of the railroad strike and the abdication of the Tzar? There seems to be no public sentiment back of the unions as there was in the beginning which will make their demands harder of attainment. They have gone too far."[23]

She was selected for one of the three sororities and enjoyed it very much until she discovered that some girls belonged to none. Firmly believing "every girl ought to have the fun of belonging to a sorority if she wants to," she urged Sutherland to authorize a fourth. As with her high school campaign for a good English teacher, Amelia's motives were excellent, her practical psychology faulty. She did not take into account that for many of the girls the sororities' exclusiveness was a large part of their appeal.

Her crusading spirit disliked some of the academic restrictions. Already well read, she was disgusted because the class reading Ibsen's plays discussed *A Doll's House,* but not *Ghosts* and *Hedda Gabler.* Sutherland might well have considered it quite advanced to permit study of a play in which the heroine walked out on her husband to escape not ill treatment but his smothering protectiveness. Venereal disease and abnormal psychology, however, were beyond the pale.[24]

Amelia's religious convictions were beginning to show signs of independent thinking. After the distinguished Indian poet, Sir Rabindranath Tagore, had lectured at the school, one of the girls mentioned her hope that he might become a Christian. "Why should he?" asked Amelia. Before the ensuing argument wore itself out, she was accused of atheism, a charge she denied. "I do believe in God, but not in many of the tenets in the catechism I had to learn when I was little. God, to me, is a power that helps me to be good."[25]

About this time Amelia began a scrapbook devoted to magazine and newspaper items about women who were succeeding in unconventional occupations. She pasted in an article about proposed antidiscrimination legislation, but wrote alongside it: "This method is not sound. Women will gain economic justice by proving themselves in all lines of endeavor, not by having laws passed for them."[26]

After her summer vacation in 1917, Amelia returned for her senior year at Ogontz, which had moved to a new location. Never one for half measures, she signed on for a murderous academic schedule. In addition, she was vice president of her class, secretary of the school's Red

Cross chapter, secretary and treasurer of Christian Endeavor, and a leader of the glee club.

Reading of all these activities, Amy feared that the school was allowing her daughter to overwork and wrote to the headmistress protesting. Amelia reacted with all the embarrassment of youth confronted with parental fussing: "Dear hen, don't write Miss S. letters of advice and warning. They go thru the whole faculty and come to me and I just shrivel. I am not overdoing."[27]

In later days, the faculty of Ogontz were astounded to learn that Amelia had turned to aviation instead of literature. Her teachers recalled that "her rooms were filled with books, which she avidly perused during the day and half the night." But the only volumes on scientific subjects were those required for her courses.[28]

In November 1917 Ogontz installed the honor system, and Amelia was on the governing board. In that capacity she became sorely disillusioned with the headmistress, writing to Amy, "Miss S. wanted faculty members on the board but we declined it so she is raging about mob rule and claiming we are all 'blackguards,' so called and putting every failure to us."[29]

Muriel had graduated from Westport High School in Kansas City and was attending St. Margaret's College in Toronto. Amelia spent the Christmas holidays with her and returned to Ogontz to finish her senior term. She did not graduate, however. A diploma from Ogontz meant no more to her than had a diploma from Hyde Park High School. She had absorbed all that Ogontz had to teach her and, more important, she had had an experience in Toronto that convinced her she must put away childish things.[30]

Chapter 3
Amelia Finds Wings

*W*orld War I raged throughout Amelia's time at Ogontz without seeming to make much impact there. Her letters barely mention the conflict. In November 1917 she heard *Aida* with Giovanni Martinelli as Rhadames, and wrote Amy dryly, "The audience was stunning in consistent evening dress and showing no signs of war stress."[1]

Strolling down King Street in Toronto with Muriel, Amelia was thus psychologically unprepared to see walking toward them four one-legged men painfully swinging along on crutches. For anyone with a spark of compassion, the sight would have been painful; for Amelia it "changed the course of existence." She loved dancing and outdoor sports; here were four young men who would never dance again, never kick a football, never serve a tennis ball, never hike in the woods.

For Amelia, aching pity was not enough; she had to do something constructive. This she could not do by returning to graduate from an exclusive girls' school. Amy understood her daughter and put no obstacle in her way. Accordingly, Amelia took a crash Red Cross course in first aid and joined the Volunteer Aid Detachment. After finishing the course, she was assigned to Canada's Spadina Military Hospital.[2]

In her future writing Amelia stressed the amusing side of her hospital experience. Neither her generation nor her character permitted her to spread her deepest emotions on a counter for the world to see. So she wrote in a light vein, "Of course one of the jobs of a V.A.D. was to be a merry sunshine." Her job entailed much more than that. She scrubbed floors, emptied bedpans, washed trays, and performed any other menial but necessary task the nurses might require of her. Her hours were 7 A.M. until 7 P.M., with a two-hour break in the afternoon.[3]

She was in great demand for backrubs. Her hands were memorable. In later days she would deprecate any suggestion that she was attractive, but no one could deny that she had one positive beauty—her long, tapering hands. These suffering men, however, were more interested in the strength and skill of her fingers than in their beauty.

Soon the director of nurses discovered that Sister Amelia knew enough chemistry to work in the dispensary and the diet kitchen. Of the former assignment, Amelia decided, "Probably the fact that I could be trusted not to drink up the medical supply of whisky counted more than the chemistry."

The kitchen offered her the greatest opportunity and challenge. The monotony of hospital food appalled her. Vegetables were a dispiriting alternation of turnips and parsnips. A quick bit of research proved that stewed tomatoes would cost less than a cent a serving more than the usual vegetables. Armed with these facts and the argument that "tomatoes are so much cheerfuller," Amelia persuaded the head dietitian to add canned tomatoes to the menu.

Next she took dead aim on the desserts, which never varied from day to day. Ten years later she still was "unable to look a jelly-roll in the eye." That had been the inevitable sweet in the officers' mess. What inspired her to action, however, was the rice pudding inflicted daily upon the enlisted men. They hated it to the point where two men in adjoining beds buried a spoon in a mound of rice pudding and on it spelled out in matchsticks "R.I.P."

Amelia volunteered to make blancmange. When the ingredients arrived, the whole staff pitched in with contributions including fancy molds, candied cherries, and orange slices. It did not take long for the word to spread that Sister Amelia was responsible for this most welcome break in routine. The two matchstick wielders expressed their sentiments by spelling out on their tray:

▶ RAY, RAY
   U.S.A.![4]

Amelia might choose to record only such incidents as these, but the fact remains that she was in daily contact with hideous pain. She was confronted with it her first day on the job. Someone, either by accident or as a particularly unfunny joke, set off the fire alarm. The noise and confusion almost devastated the shell shock patients. Some screamed, some wept, others begged for an end to their sufferings. Such agony was all the more difficult to witness because it was not the unavoidable result of disease or accident, but of man's inhumanity to man. It is not surprising that Amelia emerged from her hospital experience a confirmed pacifist.[5]

Some weekends, Amelia's day off coincided with Muriel's, and the sisters went horseback riding. A horse named Dynamite had suffered under his previous owner and, profoundly suspicious of humans, threw anyone who tried to ride him. After a month of apples, gentle talk, and petting, he accepted Amelia. The stable owner was so grateful to her for transforming the bucking fury into a good mount that he always let her ride Dynamite free.

Dynamite was indirectly responsible for Amelia's first real introduction to aircraft. One of the girls' occasional riding companions was a Royal Flying Corps officer who admired Amelia's skill and courage. He invited her and Muriel to visit his airfield. The planes fascinated Amelia, but their friend could not give the girls a ride, as civilian passengers were against regulations. "But I hung around in spare time and absorbed all I could," Amelia wrote. "I remember the sting of the snow on my face as it was blown back from the propellers when the training planes took off on skis."[6]

The influenza epidemic of 1918 struck Toronto. This was one of history's major disasters, claiming twenty million lives worldwide. Sister Amelia was one of the few permitted on night duty, and she served in a pneumonia ward where she "helped to ladle out medicine from buckets." She stayed well throughout the epidemic that killed so many and then took seriously ill with what she diagnosed as "a case of too much nursing, perhaps with too long hours." She suffered from "pain and pressure around one eye and copious drainage via the nostrils and throat." Today a doctor would probably prescribe antibiotics, but these had not been discovered in 1918, so Amelia had to endure several minor operations and a long convalescence.[7]

Meanwhile Muriel had transferred from St. Margaret's to Miss Capen's School at Northampton, Massachusetts, preparatory to entering Smith College. As soon as Amelia was well enough to travel, she joined Muriel in her small apartment. There Muriel took care of her sister until Amelia could get about on her own. Then the girls spent much time strolling through the countryside or exploring the town. On one such occasion Amelia spotted a banjo in a pawnshop window and bought it for twenty-five dollars. The girls knew the purchase would put a dent in their budget; however, Muriel was happy at this sign that once more Amelia was interested in something "just for fun."

Amelia loved music, had taught herself to sight read, and also played on the piano by ear many popular classics and operatic numbers. Now she found someone to teach her banjo technique. She also took a five-week course in automobile mechanics, which she credited with laying the foundation for her later knowledge of motors.

That first postwar spring—1919—Amy came to Northampton bearing tidings for which her letters had already prepared her daughters. Edwin was on the move again, this time to California. Amy was to spend the summer with the girls while Edwin sought a place to live. It was Amelia who located the perfect cottage on Lake George, where the three spent an idyllic summer. At its end they were ready to face major changes—Amy to join Edwin, Muriel to enter Smith College, and Amelia to enroll as a premedical student at Columbia University.[8]

Her experience at Spadina had given her an interest in medicine, and her summer by the lake had brought back her strength and upbeat disposition. Amy had certain misgivings about her daughter's choice of a career. Amelia wrote her reassuringly:

▶ Don't worry about meals or mentality. I didn't realize how the pipings of doubt had impressed you until you mentioned your worries today. Don't think for an instant I would ever become an atheist or even a doubter nor lose faith in the [Episcopalian] church's teachings as a whole. That is impossible. But you must admit there is a great deal radically wrong in methods and teachings and results today. Probably no more than yesterday, but the present stands up and waves its paws at me and I see—I can't help it.[9]

Amelia took what she called "all the 'ologies'" that would prepare her to practice medicine, and threw in a course in French literature just "for fun." A letter that her friend Marian Stabler wrote to George Putnam years later reveals that in fact Amelia was seriously overdoing it:

▶ This course she was taking was really a three-man job, with the full quota of lectures and lab courses at Columbia, and another full quota at Barnard, and listening courses elsewhere. Apparently Columbia and Barnard didn't compare notes, as she wouldn't have been permitted to carry a load like that if anyone had known.[10]

Despite this strenuous schedule and her shortage of money, Amelia managed to have some of the "fun" so essential to her nature. The steps of Carnegie Hall's "peanut heaven" were not too uncomfortable if one was young and loved music. "Forbidden underground passageways" connected the various university buildings; Amelia explored them with the zest of a child. She persuaded the custodian to tell her the location of the key to the door leading to the library dome. "And more than once we climbed the endless steps, and up over the roof on our hands and knees to the very top of the dome," recalled Louise de Schweinitz, Amelia's closest college chum. While on their lofty perch, inevitably the two young women talked of marriage. Louise eagerly looked forward to a career as a doctor but could not help wondering if anyone would ever propose to her. She need not have worried. As Dr.

Louise deS. Darrow, she would have both marriage and a successful career. "I can think of lots of things worse than never getting married," Amelia answered, "and one of the worst is being married to a man who tied you down."[11]

By the end of the year, Amelia realized that she lacked the temperament to practice medicine. She enjoyed medical research, however, and thought she might follow that line. Her biology professor, James MacGregor, found Amelia "a most stimulating student" who with Louise made "a remarkable team." Amelia, he remembered, "grasped the significance of an experiment, mentally assayed the results, and drew conclusions while I was still lecturing about setting up the experimental machinery."[12]

Had matters progressed smoothly with her family, Amelia might have remained in that line of work. But at this point her story took another turn. Her parents urged her to join them in California; she could take up her studies there if she so desired. Amy's daughters read between the lines that relations were strained between their parents. Amelia did not want to go, but a strong sense of personal responsibility had been hammered into her. As Muriel, who would remain in the East that year, saw Amelia off on her transcontinental train journey, the latter said, "I'll see what I can do to keep Mother and Dad together until you finish college, Pidge, but after that I'm going to come back here and live my own life."

Amelia reached the house Edwin had rented to find that a miracle had taken place: Edwin had stopped drinking. Before Amy's arrival, a businessman, a Christian Scientist, had invited Edwin to his home for dinner and to church meetings every Wednesday. Using principles and methods similar to those of the not-yet-extant Alcoholics Anonymous, these good people brought him back to sobriety and self-respect. "Everybody seemed to care about helping me," he said wonderingly. "I can't begin to tell you the trouble those people took to put me back on my feet." He formally became a Christian Scientist, and his new friends put so much legal business in his way that by the time first Amy, then Amelia, joined him, he was once more a respected claims lawyer and working his way toward prosperity.[13]

Edwin's long enslavement to the bottle and his final emancipation had a profound psychological effect upon Amelia. As mentioned, she never drank alcohol in any form. Quite possibly she feared the taint might be in the blood, in which case a single drink could trigger a disastrous chain reaction. But, stern with herself, she would be amazingly patient and compassionate with others. She had living proof that an alcoholic could be gifted, likable, and, when sober, good at his job.

For the moment, Edwin's sobriety seemed to ensure a "happy ending"—rehabilitated husband, faithful wife, delighted daughters. But real life is not quite so pat. The threat of eruption had subsided temporarily, but the underground rumblings were still there.

The Earhart home was larger than the family needs, so to ease the financial strain they rented two rooms to three young men. One of them was Samuel Chapman, a darkly handsome, rather serious-looking chemical engineer, a graduate of Tufts University. He and Amelia were mutually attracted. They played tennis, swam together, and enjoyed long discussions about books and plays. Both were sympathetic toward those less fortunate than themselves and dabbled a bit in socialist ideas, although disapproving of violence and destruction of property.

One night Amelia and Sam donned shabby clothes and slipped into an illegal meeting of the Industrial Workers of the World. They joined some thirty others sitting on the floor of a vacant store. Before proceedings were well under way, the rattle of a nightstick on the door heralded the advent of four policemen. Someone had tipped off the authorities. "All you boys go home to bed now," said the sergeant with a grin, "so's you can do a good day's work tomorrow!" This was a not-too-subtle crack at the reputation of the IWW, whose initials, in common parlance, stood for "I Won't Work." Both the policemen and the dismissed audience were good-natured. Still, Amelia remarked to Sam as they walked home, "I think they should have had the right to talk it out tonight instead of being sent home like naughty children."[14]

Meanwhile, the Earhart funds were dwindling alarmingly. After Muriel's junior year at Smith, Amy's nest egg had shrunk to about twenty thousand dollars. Something would have to be done to build up capital. Sam introduced the Earharts to Peter Barnes, who with his partner Bill Chambers owned gypsum mining rights near the Moapa Indian Reservation, and who needed capital. It looked like a solid investment. The construction trade offered a steady market; the Indian reservation provided a convenient source of labor at seventy-five cents per day; Edwin verified that Barnes and Chambers had a contract with a cement company. The young men were of excellent character and hard workers. Peter became one of the family circle to the extent of calling Amy "Mother E." He was jubilant when she told him she would put some twenty thousand dollars into his project, and he spent about half that sum on two trucks to haul the gypsum.

One day early in 1922 Edwin and Amelia went to inspect the site. On this particular day an unexpected hitch developed. Although the sky was cloudless, the Indians were moving to higher ground. "No work," they told Mr. Wilkes, the local government Indian agent, laconically. "Big rains come soon."

Amelia and Mrs. Wilkes shoveled gypsum into buckets that Edwin and Mr. Wilkes emptied into a truck. Suddenly it became evident that

they should have heeded the Indians with their centuries-long expertise in reading nature's warning signs. Clouds appeared; soon the gul-
lies would be awash in flash floods. Wilkes rode his horse across the
bridge, under which water was already boiling. The bridge held, and
Wilkes signaled for Bill Chambers to drive the truck across with
Edwin, Amelia, and Mrs. Wilkes. It was a heart-stopping ride; however, they crossed safely. But the weakened bridge broke under the
gypsum-laden truck with Peter Barnes at the wheel. Bill risked his life
trying to rescue Peter, but he had been killed instantly.

On the mundane level, the floods had also washed away Muriel's
senior year at Smith, Amelia's plans for further study, and Amy's assurance of a secure old age. Amelia wrote a sad note to Muriel: "There
is no way that I can soften the blow for you. We have to take these
things as they come. Peter is drowned, the mine seems irreparably
flooded, and all of Mother's investment is gone. We are still reeling
from the blow. If Dad and I had not witnessed the tragedy, we would
find it hard to believe."[15]

The fact that the Earharts were broke again, hence further formal
education was out of the question for the girls, bothered Amelia much
less than it might have in other circumstances. Some time prior to
the disaster at Moapa River, she had found the love of her life, and it
wasn't Sam Chapman.

The aviation bug that first bit Amelia in Toronto had never worked
out of her system. She began to haunt air circuses, often with her
father. These events were fairly common in those days, held in the
attempt to sell aviation to a still largely dubious public. They featured
stunt flying and tries at altitude and speed records.

At one such meet at Long Beach, Amelia pointed out a young man in
flying gear. "Dad, please ask that officer how long it takes to fly," she
requested. Edwin conversed with the man for a few minutes and reported, "Apparently it differs with different people, though the average
seems to be from five to ten hours."

Amelia had another question: "Please find out how much lessons
cost." Obligingly Edwin again consulted with the flier and advised:
"The answer to that is a thousand dollars. But why did you want to
know?" Amelia later wrote that she wasn't quite sure.[16]

Shortly thereafter, Edwin made an appointment for Amelia to go up
for a trial flight. "I am sure he thought one ride would be enough for
me, and he might as well cure me promptly," she wrote.

The field was no more than "an open space on Wilshire Boulevard,
surrounded by oil wells." By chance the pilot on this first flight was
Frank Hawks, then just "a barnstorming pilot on the west coast," but
destined to smash many a speed record. To Amelia's mingled exasperation and amusement, she found that a third person must go along.
When she asked why, Hawks and his companion exchanged grins. No

remarkable degree of extrasensory perception was necessary to read their minds. "I was a girl—a 'nervous lady.' I might jump out. There had to be somebody on hand to grab my ankle as I went over. It was no use to explain I had seen aeroplanes before and wasn't excitable."

To a fortunate few there comes a moment when they know, beyond doubt or question, what they want to do—no, what they *must* do—with their lives. As soon as the propeller seized the air and the little aircraft lifted skyward, Amelia knew that she had to fly.[17]

That evening she announced to her parents, "I think I'd like to learn to fly." Neither Edwin nor Amy took her seriously. "Not a bad idea," Edwin replied lightly. "When do you start?"

She would have to look into the matter, she told him, but would let him know soon.

No flying schools existed at that time; most flight instructors were World War I veterans. Amelia thought she would be self-conscious taking lessons from a man of such immense experience, so she decided to wait until she could find a woman instructor. Surprisingly, she succeeded, arranged for lessons, and broke the news to her family "with the proposition that somebody pay for them."

Edwin bluntly told her that he couldn't afford it. Amelia thought that he believed that if he couldn't, or wouldn't, pay, that would be the end of it. He should have known his Amelia better than that. She found a job as unskilled labor with the local telephone company so that she could pay her own way. It took her a long time to reach her goal; full-time, low-paying employment left her with little opportunity for lessons.[18]

Amelia's first teacher was Neta Snook, called "Snooky," a real character in a field rife with characters. An old-time flier, Waldo Waterman, described her to George Putnam:

▶ In those days we were not quite sure as to whether "Snooky" was a man or woman, as few of us saw her except in a pair of dirty coveralls, her reddish hair closely cropped, and her freckled face usually made up with the assistance of airport dust and a dash of grease. . . . She was one of the first women to take up flying after the War.

Amelia wrote to Muriel of Snooky:

▶ She dresses and talks like a man and can do everything around a plane that a man can do. I'm lucky that she'll teach me, not only because she will give me lessons on credit, but because she is a top-notch flier and one of the first women to get a pilot's license in Canada.

Snooky's aircraft was a little yellow Canadian Curtiss "Canuck," a training plane similar to the American JN 4 Jenny, but easier to handle. Stunt pilot Frank Clark noticed that there were no drift wires inside the wings and asked her, "Who covered the wings?"

"I did," she replied disconcertingly.

"And would you believe it," Clark told Putnam, "she never did put in those wires—or worry about 'em either. And somehow the crate held together!"[19]

Once Snooky crashed with Amelia in a cabbage patch. Amelia charged this up to "carelessness in not refueling"; however, such accidents were common in the current state of the art. "Pilots just naturally expected to have to set down once every so often because of engine failure."

Amelia adopted the style of dress favored by the other fliers. Any woman engaged in flying had no choice but to wear "breeks and leather coats." The fields were dirty and dusty; planes had to be scrambled into, and engines worked on. A dress or skirt would be impossible. Cautiously, she began shortening her long blond hair, but had not yet bobbed it, not wanting to appear "eccentric."[20]

Muriel had returned to California in June and, one week after her arrival, stood with Snooky to watch Amelia's solo flight. Amelia was unhappy with her "exceptionally poor landing." But, as another pilot told her, at least she came down with gas still in her tank. Fledgling pilots had been known to panic on their first solos and circle the field until an empty gas tank forced them down.[21]

On December 15, 1921, at Los Angeles, Amelia took and passed her qualification trial for an international license from the Fédération Aéronautique Internationale, issued by the National Aeronautic Association in Washington, D.C. For some reason the license did not come through until May 19, 1923. License numbers started at 6000, and Amelia's was 6017. Thus she was the seventeenth person—and the first woman—to be so licensed.[22] Actually, as Amelia explained later, "it wasn't really necessary to have any license at that period. . . . People just flew, when and if they could, in anything which could get off the ground."[23]

Inevitably Amelia wanted a plane of her own. She had soloed in a Model K Kinner Airstar biplane and decided to purchase a secondhand one from its designer, William Kinner. The price ate up all of Amelia's and Muriel's savings, plus a few hundred dollars from Amy. Amelia took possession on her twenty-fifth birthday, July 24, 1922. As Kinner had only one plane, Amelia let him use it for demonstrations in exchange for free hangar space. Its motor vibrated so hard that Amelia's feet "went to sleep after more than a few minutes on the rudder bar." To give some idea of Amelia Earhart's first plane, fully loaded it weighed a thousand pounds. Its range at full speed with one passenger was 500 miles, with two passengers, 200 miles. Its maximum speed was eighty to eighty-five miles per hour.[24]

The owner of a plane had to look the part. So Amelia took the money she had earmarked for a raincoat and bought a leather coat, helmet, and goggles. The coat looked so pristine that it would immediately proclaim her a greenhorn, so, braving the family's amusement, she wore it around the house and even slept in it one night to break it in properly.

The summer of 1922 was a period of happiness for the Earhart sisters. Every Sunday morning they filled a market basket with sandwiches and one of Amy's chocolate cakes and set out for the airfield. There the pilots tried to earn a few dollars taking passengers aloft— Frank Hawks charged one dollar for a ten-minute flight. Muriel enjoyed being around aircraft and the "slightly crazy" pilots. Sometimes she worked on Snooky's plane, shellacking the canvas wings or replacing rusty guide wires.

When passenger fares did not cover the cost of gasoline, the pilots sat around and talked shop. Occasionally the mantle of prophesy descended upon Amelia: "Some day we're going to have planes with cockpits enclosed, so a pilot won't have to be blown to pieces. Some day I'm sure we'll have planes large enough to carry ten or a dozen passengers and they'll go on regular schedules like trains."

To which Snooky replied, "Well, Meely, a lot more people are going to have to get over being scared to fly before there'll be that kind of business."[25]

Muriel found congenial work as a teacher in the fourth grade of a Los Angeles school. Amelia needed employment to pay for her flying. She took a course in commercial art at the University of Southern California and enjoyed securing unusual effects with ordinary objects: "I can't name all the moods of which a garbage can is capable." She also took moving pictures, selling the film of an oil well's first gush to an enterprising real estate agent, who told her, "I'd like to show my prospects what might happen any day in their own yard."

An offer of "easy money" she rejected firmly, although it tickled her ready sense of humor. A man approached her to smuggle liquor out of Mexico. "A woman can get by where a man can't," he assured her earnestly. "No one would ever suspect you. There's not a thing to be afraid of. You could do it easy."

One day in October Amelia gave Edwin and Muriel tickets to an air circus at Rogers Air Field in Los Angeles, remarking that she would not be able to sit with them. This clued them in that something was up, so they were not really surprised at the announcement that a young lady would attempt an altitude record. Always practical, Amelia asked representatives of the Aero Club of Southern California to seal her barograph so that no one could claim that she had tampered with it. She was climbing when the spark control lever became disconnected. The engine vibrated and knocked alarmingly, so she came down. But she had established a record. It held only a few weeks until Ruth Nichols, destined to be her good friend, broke it. But however temporary, it was Amelia Earhart's first aviation record.[26]

Like most pilots of her generation, she had her share of accidents and near-accidents. Perhaps her narrowest squeak of this early period came when she was attempting to better the women's altitude record again. She plunged into a bank of clouds that turned out to be full of snow and sleet that coated her goggles and disoriented her. Knowing that she had to get down before the sleet weighed down the fragile wings, she put the plane into a spin and was fortunate enough to come into the clear with several thousand feet still to go.

The men at the field scolded her roundly. "Suppose the clouds had closed in until they touched the ground. We'd have had to dig you out in pieces."

"Yes, I suppose you would," she agreed briefly.[27]

For all Amelia's joy in the sky and Muriel's contentment in teaching her fourth-graders, the situation between their parents caused the sisters much sorrow. Edwin and Amy agreed that their marriage was beyond repair, and Edwin filed for divorce. Amy did not contest.

Amy and Muriel preferred the East to California, so the Earhart women decided to return to the Boston area. Amelia would have liked to fly across country but could not afford the gasoline. Reluctantly she sold her aircraft and bought a Kissel sports car, painted canary yellow. At least one person, Sam Chapman, was pleased to see the last of the aircraft, and soon he followed Amelia east. It looked like Amelia's aviation phase had died a natural death, in which case Sam's devotion might finally pay off.

Muriel traveled by train to be in time for summer classes at Harvard. She settled in Medford, a Boston suburb, and taught at a junior high school. Amelia drove Amy in the new car and, typically, made an adventure of the trip. She headed north, treating herself and her mother to the beauties of Sequoia, Yosemite, and Crater Lake national parks, and then continued into Canada, visiting Banff National Park and Lake Louise.

Outside Calgary came one of those incidents that for Amelia added a spice of humor to life. Somehow they had lost their way and stopped to inquire of the only human being in sight, a blanketed Indian. "Where is the main road?" Amelia asked.

"Unh, papoose," he grunted, not very helpfully. This same exchange continued until he pointed to a little stuffed monkey in the car. Deducing that he wanted it for his child, Amelia gave it to him. This transaction miraculously endowed the Indian with the King's English. "You made the wrong turn five miles back," he said, and gave the necessary directions with flawless diction.

The two women cut back into the United States to visit Yellowstone. Amelia spotted many air mail beacons as they traveled east. Upon reaching Boston, she was surprised to find her car the center of much attention. A yellow automobile had not been too conspicuous in California; in Boston it definitely made a statement.

Within a week of joining Muriel, Amelia was in the hospital. The breakup of her parents' marriage had coincided with a severe attack of her old sinus problem, an ailment that throughout her life flared up during periods of stress. In Massachusetts General Hospital a small piece of bone was removed to permit drainage. Upon discharge she declared that for the first time in four years she was free of headache and nasal pain.

She returned to Columbia to take up those subjects, including physics, that interested her, with no thought of a degree. In those days, a college sheepskin was not the virtual necessity it would become later, so Amelia could take what courses she wanted without being bound by a mandatory curriculum.[28]

Muriel, who loved teaching, was sure that her sister, too, could be happy teaching English or science, and Amelia wanted to try it. She spent the summer of 1925 at Harvard Summer School with the view to qualifying as a teacher. For some time thereafter, she taught foreign students in the extension program of the University of Massachusetts. There were no fixed classrooms; classes might be scheduled anywhere within thirty miles of Boston in the late afternoons and evenings. Salary and transportation allowance were both so basic that often she barely made expenses. Amelia stuck it out for a number of months, but obviously she had encountered a dead end.

She had found a way to keep up her flying, joining the American Aeronautical Society. William Kinner had moved east to establish a sales agency. Amelia demonstrated the Kinner plane, and in return he allowed her to use it to put in flying time when no prospective customers were in the offing.

The other pilots in the area soon assessed her not only as a skilled flier but also as one who understood the mechanics of her craft. She loved a smooth-running engine almost as much as the act of flight and did not in the least mind getting her slender hands greasy in the maintenance of the aircraft.

In that respect, her male associates treated her as one of themselves; however, they recognized in her a girl of character and breeding, and respected her accordingly. As Paul Mantz, later a good friend and colleague, recalled, "I never knew any man who would try to 'pull anything' with Amelia. If she came into the hangar when someone happened to be telling an off-color story, that person would get a kicked shin or a stepped-on toe to indicate to him that he had better continue his story later."[29]

Chapter 4

"Ask for Amelia Earhart"

*B*y the autumn of 1926, Amelia was thoroughly dissatisfied with her teaching job. On an impulse she answered a newspaper advertisement for a part-time English teacher to foreign-born pupils at Denison House, the second oldest social center in Boston. She located the place in "a little island of residences surrounded by warehouses and other buildings." The stone fronts and fine detailing of the tenements proclaimed that the neighborhood had seen better days.

Marion Perkins, head of Denison House, had no hesitation in hiring Amelia at sixty dollars a month. "She had poise and charm. I liked her quiet sense of humor, the frank direct look in her grey eyes." Perkins soon found in Amelia "an unusual mixture of the artist and the practical person." She put her to work directing the evening classes for the foreign born. Little teaching was involved; her principal task was to follow up the classes by visits to the pupils' homes.

The neighborhood was predominantly Chinese and Syrian, with an admixture of Irish and Italian. She was intrigued to see clay cooking utensils of a type in use in the Near East for centuries sitting on American gas stoves. Occasionally she shared a meal with her "clients," and some of the dishes reminded her of her own girlhood experiments.

Perkins had enough experience and native intelligence to understand that the only way to handle Amelia was to keep her on a very loose rein. Amelia responded with eager enthusiasm. To Amy and

Muriel it seemed that at last she had found her niche. To her the neighborhood people were not "cases" but friends with pleasures to share, sorrows to comfort. Often she brought a small gift—a ball for a child, ivy for an old Chinese. She would fill her car, dubbed "the Yellow Peril," with teenage girls and drive them to her home for a picnic or marshmallow roast. The only part of her job she disliked was the paperwork.[1]

Within a year she had become a full-time worker, in charge of the prekindergarten tots and directing the teaching of girls from five to fourteen years old. To be available at all hours, she moved into a top floor apartment in Denison House.

The move distressed Sam Chapman. Why should Amelia be content to pour out her affection and devote her time to some fifty settlement house children when he wanted nothing more than to marry her and give her children of her own? Such a marriage, on the surface, had much to commend it. Sam had a fine position as an engineer with the Boston Edison Company, and he owned a beautiful home at Marblehead, a location both he and Amelia loved. What is more, Muriel was certain that Amelia truly loved Sam.

But Amelia instinctively knew that the time was not ripe for marriage, certainly not the kind of marriage Sam wanted, with him as the sole breadwinner and a stay-at-home wife totally devoted to him and their children. Sam was not being unreasonable; this was the normal pattern of marriage in the 1920s. Seeking reasons for her, to him, incomprehensible reluctance, he wondered if the irregular hours his job demanded were an obstacle. "Meely, I'll be whatever you want me to be," he told her. "I will get other work tomorrow if you say so."

Many women might have found this a touching avowal of devotion; it was exactly the wrong thing to say to Amelia. "I don't want to tell Sam what he should do," she told Muriel irritably. "He ought to know what makes him happiest, and then do it, no matter what other people say. I know what I want to do, and I expect to do it, married or single."

What Muriel called their "tenuous engagement" was broken with no ill feelings on either side. Sam and Amelia continued to be the best of friends.[2]

About this time, at one of the staff meetings at Denison House, the discussion turned to "the cowardice of refusing to make decisions." A few days later, Amelia asked her sister's opinion of a poem she had written. Muriel suggested a minor change, which Amelia accepted. Shortly thereafter she showed the poem to Perkins. In those few lines Amelia had crystallized her personal creed:

▶   Courage is the price that Life exacts for granting peace.
The soul that knows it not, knows no release
From little things:
Knows not the livid loneliness of fear,
Nor mountain heights where bitter joy can hear
The sound of wings.

How can Life grant us boon of living, compensate
For dull gray ugliness and pregnant hate
Unless we dare
The soul's dominion? Each time we make a choice, we pay
With courage to behold resistless day,
And count it fair.

While at Denison House she wrote other verses, by no means great poetry, but demonstrating an understanding of and sympathy with the child mind, as well as the poetic side of Amelia's nature.

At times the practical part of her character lost out to the artistic. Muriel gave Amelia forty dollars to pay the coal bill. Amelia gave the coal company twenty dollars and spent the rest on a carved bird she discovered in a Chinese shop.[3]

This was another happy time for the Earhart girls. They were earning their livelihood at congenial work. Amy lived with Muriel and kept house for them. Her deafness had increased to the point where she depended on a hearing aid. She seldom ventured out except to shop or go to church, where she made new friends, and kept up with old ones by a steady stream of correspondence. Later she admitted to being at times "too tired and nervous" to sleep. Perhaps she was having difficulty adjusting to this strange new world where women earned their own living and rode around in automobiles with their men friends without a chaperon. Perhaps, too, the fact that Edwin had married again seemed to break the last link with her youth.

Amelia's college chum Louise de Schweinitz was interning at a Boston hospital. Often she and her fiancé, Daniel Darrow, with Amelia, Sam, Muriel, and Albert Morrissey, would pile into the Yellow Peril and drive to Marblehead to swim or dig clams and then picnic around a driftwood fire. Morrissey had served in the Navy during World War I; soon he and Muriel were engaged.

Louise's presence reactivated some of Amelia's interest in the field of medicine. Once she talked her friend into introducing her as a visiting intern to witness a childbirth. On another occasion, Louise had to lance a carbuncle on a man's neck, and the ward nurse passed out cold. Amelia took over, coolly following her friend's whispered instructions until Louise had finished the unpleasant chore.

Amelia did not have time to fly as much as she would have liked, but she got together with a young architect, Harold T. Dennison, who was planning to build an airport. Amelia rounded up "a few dollars" and became one of five incorporators of the concern. She was in touch with Ruth Nichols with the view to organizing women fliers. Ruth had begun to fly while a student at Wellesley. Unlike Amelia, she was photogenic. This, combined with the social register status of the Nichols family, piqued the public interest. But she was no mere "glamor girl" pilot and in the next decade would establish impressive altitude records.

Amelia was delighted when the National Playground Association asked her to be a member of the Boston committee of judges in a model airplane tournament. As she wrote, "None of this was what you could call important—except to me. It was sheer fun."[4]

Afternoon was Amelia's busy time, when the schools released swarms of children who converged upon Denison House. Amelia had to see that they reached their assigned classes and that leaders and instructors were ready. Complications always arose: A volunteer worker was unable to come or several children wanted to do anything except that for which they had been scheduled.

So when a telephone call came for her one afternoon in April 1928, at first she refused to take it. "I'm too busy to answer just now. Ask whoever is calling to try again later."

The youngster who brought the message persisted. "But he says it's important to speak with you."

Reluctantly, Amelia went to the phone. "Hello. You don't know me, but my name is Railey—Captain H. H. Railey." The caller asked if she would be interested "in doing something for aviation which might be hazardous." Although at first Amelia thought the call was a joke, the fact that Railey frankly admitted the venture might be dangerous interested her. Still, she asked for references, which he gave. "They were good references, too!"[5]

Behind this call was another. Shortly before, George Palmer Putnam of the long-established publishing firm, G. P. Putnam's Sons, had informed Railey that the explorer, Commander Richard E. Byrd, had sold his trimotor Fokker "to a wealthy woman who plans to fly the Atlantic." He had heard that "floats are being fitted to the plane at the East Boston airport." He suggested that Railey join him in taking a look.

"'Hell!' said he. 'If it's true we'll crash the gates. It'd be amusing to manage a stunt like that, wouldn't it?'" He asked Railey to check up and telephone him if the story proved true.

Railey had no trouble in finding the projected pilot, Wilmer L. Stultz, and the mechanic, Louis "Slim" Gordon, at the Copley Plaza Hotel in Boston. Stultz had been drinking—no unusual circumstance—and admitted that he was preparing for a transatlantic flight. He let slip the name of the backer's lawyer, David T. Layman.

In New York a few days later, Railey contacted Layman, who told him that the mysterious sponsor was Mrs. Frederick S. Guest, the former Amy Phipps of Pittsburgh, now of London and New York. Her husband had been secretary of state for air under British Prime Minister David Lloyd George. Amy Guest had planned to fly from the United States to England in the former Byrd plane, which she had renamed *Friendship* as a symbol of the amity between her native land and her adopted country.

The Guest family, however, protested so vociferously that she agreed not to participate herself. But she insisted that the flight go forward with a woman aboard—a woman who could represent the United States with charm, intelligence, and ability. Hence it came about that Layman deputized Railey to find the "right sort of girl" for the venture.[6]

It was typical of Putnam and Railey's brashness that they thus butted into a project that was none of their business. It was equally typical of the confidence they inspired that instead of being kicked out they were welcomed and their aid sought.

Railey returned to Boston where, on a hunch, he telephoned a friend, Rear Admiral Reginald K. Belknap, USN (Ret.), and put the problem to him. "'Why, yes,' said he. 'I know a young social worker who flies. I'm not sure how many hours she's had, but I do know that she's deeply interested in aviation—and a thoroughly fine person. Call Denison House and ask for Amelia Earhart.'"

Later Railey waxed reflective about this set of circumstances: "On the slight pivot of my casual conversation with George Putnam turned the whole career of Amelia Earhart—her transformation from an obscure social worker, absorbed in the lives of polyglot gamins at a Boston settlement house, to a world figure in aviation and the honored guest of kings and queens." But in any case, he mused, she would probably "have become a constructive factor in the industry to which she was so passionately devoted."[7]

Satisfied with Railey's references, Amelia agreed to an appointment at his office that afternoon. Evidently considering that a witness would not come amiss, she brought Perkins along. Amelia made an immediate favorable impression on Railey. "How would you like to be the first woman to fly the Atlantic?" he asked.

Amelia could not possibly "refuse such a shining adventure." But, ever practical, she requested such details as Railey was free to give. She did not relish the idea of going along merely as a passenger and expressed the hope that she might take the controls at least for a short time, weather permitting. Evidently Railey gave her little if any encouragement in this hope because, as he later wrote, "at the time . . . she was unable to fly with the aid of instruments alone, and her experience with tri-motored ships had been inconsequential."[8]

Railey saw in Amelia an "extraordinary" resemblance to Charles A. Lindbergh, the first person ever to fly solo across the Atlantic, and all the publicity expert in him jumped to attention. He asked her to re-move her hat, which she did, "brushing back her naturally tousled, wind-swept hair, and her laugh was infectious." The name "Lady Lindy" sprang into Railey's mind. He knew enough of human nature to realize that Amelia would relish this publicity angle even less than would Lindbergh, but the newspapers would eat it up.

That "Lady Lindy" business plagued Amelia for the rest of her life. She had enormous respect for Lindbergh and cringed to think that he might believe her to be willingly cashing in so crassly on his reputa-tion. One hopes that she never learned that this stunt was not a spon-taneous newspaper creation but deliberately started by Railey.

With every passing moment, Railey was more and more convinced that he had hit the jackpot and was greatly impressed by Amelia's poise, warmth, and dignity. Amy Guest had stipulated someone "rep-resentative" of American women. In Amelia, Railey felt that he had discovered "not their norm but their sublimation."[9]

Having secured Railey's approval, Amelia went to New York for in-terviews with Putnam, Layman, and John S. Phipps, who represented his sister, Amy Guest. They talked for about an hour, more about her education, work, and interests than her flying. Amelia found a certain humor in her position: "If I were found wanting in too many ways I would be counted out. On the other hand, if I were just too fascinating, the gallant gentlemen might be loath to risk drowning me." Reporting the experience to Perkins, under promise of secrecy, Amelia told her, "I realized that they were making me talk to see whether I dropped my 'g's' or used 'ain't,' which I am sure would have disqualified me as ef-fectively as failing to produce a pilot's license. Mediocrity seemed to be my cue, so that's what they got."

"Mediocre, eh?" responded Perkins with gloomy skepticism. "They're crazy, if they don't take you for being anything but mediocre."[10]

Perkins could foresee that however this adventure ended, Denison House would have lost this vivid, intelligent woman she valued as an assistant and loved as a person. If the expedition failed, on the one hand, the odds were against survival. Other women had attempted the Atlantic crossing and only one, Ruth Elder, had lived through the experience.

On the other hand, if all went well, Amelia would be lionized more than any private citizen since Lindbergh flew the Atlantic solo in 1927. Even if Amelia wished, could she escape the consequences of her fame and settle down again as an obscure social worker?

Apparently untroubled by such thoughts, Amelia chatted happily about her New York visit. She had found George Putnam fascinating. After the interview he took her to Grand Central Station in a taxi. "I wish the ride might have been longer because he was such an interesting talker," she said to Perkins. But he hustled her on the Boston train without ceremony and without offering to pay her fare.[11]

Putnam was indeed an interesting man, but not everyone's cup of tea. One author described him as "a promoter, a gifted writer, a bit of a con man. . . . Brash, complex, irritating, driven. . . . I've met dozens of people who knew him, and not one who liked him."[12]

Putnam was born in 1887 into a setting of wealth and bustling gentility. His father and two uncles comprised G. P. Putnam's Sons. When George was born, the Putnam roster of authors had long read like a who's who in American letters: Washington Irving, James Fenimore Cooper, and others of equal stature. George revealed early that he was not destined to be merely an upper-class desk jockey. He left his studies at Harvard in favor of the University of California at Berkeley. He moved to Bend, Oregon, at the age of twenty-three, with a total capital of three hundred dollars, and in an amazingly short time he was mayor of the town, elected when the incumbent fell out of a bawdy house onto his head. George lived in Bend for seven years, editing the local newspaper. In 1911, socialite Dorothy Binney came out from New York to marry him, and their son David was born there.

After serving in World War I, George returned to New York with his family to take over the family firm. He added to its stature by signing on some of the most prominent names of the day: Walter Damrosch, Ignace Jan Paderewski, Robert Benchley, and the like. He was partial to explorers and published, among others, Byrd, Roy Chapman Andrews, and Sir (George) Hubert Wilkins. George's lions were real lions, as opposed to the merely notorious. Probably his most brilliant coup was persuading the publicity-shy Lindbergh to write the story of his flight, entitled simply *We*.

George sought the limelight and lapped up personal publicity. In one area he was reticent—his acts of kindness to those in distress. In the course of his lifetime he wrote ten books, and in 1925 he organized and led an expedition to Greenland for the American Museum of Natural History. His eldest son, David, went along and later wrote *David Goes to Greenland*, a successful children's book.

A tall man, George was good-looking in an intellectual way. He could fly into a tantrum when someone's density triggered his temper.[13] It was typical of him to take over a project like the *Friendship* flight, which promised reams of favorable publicity, and then to work on it hard and well. But had the project been scratched, Amelia probably would never have heard from him again.

Two days after returning to Boston, Amelia received a gracious note from Amy Guest and a formal agreement from her lawyer. The position was hers if she wanted it. The contract stipulated that Amelia would be in charge while airborne, and her decisions would be final. Amy Guest would pay all expenses. Amelia would receive no pay; moreover, any royalties or other payments she might receive as a result of the flight would go into the expense fund. This was fine with Amelia, who felt that participation was its own reward. The pilot, Stultz, would receive twenty thousand dollars and the mechanic, Gordon, five thousand dollars. Louis Gower was selected as a standby pilot in case Stultz could not serve.[14] Commander Byrd had recommended the two pilots, and Stultz chose Gordon as the mechanic.

Amelia was happy with the crew, whom she considered "the best in the way of flying ability." Both Stultz and Gordon had years of experience in their respective fields. In addition, Stultz was a skilled radio operator. As Amelia wrote, it was unusual "to find a man who is a great pilot, an instrument flier, navigator, and a really good radio operator all in one."[15]

Stultz was twenty-eight years old, a native of Williamsburg, Pennsylvania. From 1917 to 1919 he was with the Army Air Service. Then he moved to the Naval Air Service, where he spent three years, completing his training at Pensacola, Florida. After "extensive work in commercial aviation," Stultz became pilot to Mrs. Frances Grayson on her first attempt at an Atlantic crossing. But the aircraft, *Dawn,* developed engine trouble, and Stultz safely nursed it for "500 miles of perilous flying" back to Maine. With another pilot, Grayson tried again. She and her two companions were lost when *Dawn* disappeared.[16]

The selection of Stultz was not without risk. He had a serious drinking problem. Sober, there was no better pilot, but he was quite capable of going on a bender that would totally incapacitate him.[17]

Slim Gordon came from San Antonio, Texas, where he was born in 1901. Like Stultz, he was a veteran of the Army Air Service, in which he served from 1919 to 1926. Since then he had been a flight mechanic for Reynolds Airways.[18]

As public relations officer, Railey had an unusual task—not to spread the word but to contain it. Premature publicity, in Amelia's words, would have "swamped all concerned with thrill writers and curiosity seekers." This secrecy was very much to Amelia's liking. All throughout her flying career she would demonstrate an aversion to the public counting of unhatched chickens, and she kept her plans confined to a close circle as long as possible. She did not tell even Amy and Muriel of her *Friendship* project; however, she confided in Sam Chapman and told him where to locate her will in case of her death. To George Putnam she entrusted letters to Edwin and Amy, to be opened only if she perished. George kept those letters until after her death years later. The note to Edwin read in part:

▷ Hooray for the last grand adventure! I wish I had won, but it was worthwhile anyway. You know that.

I have no faith that we'll meet anywhere again, but I wish we might.

Obviously Amelia had no belief in an afterlife.[19]

The *Friendship* was kept at an obscure field in East Boston. If anyone became inquisitive, the cover story was that it was being readied for Byrd's second Antarctic expedition. The field was strictly "off limits" to Amelia, who was well known to many fliers in the Boston area. She spent much time with Stultz, Railey, Putnam, and Byrd, who was the project's technical adviser. She had become acquainted with Railey's wife, Julie, who urged her "to back out if she felt the slightest degree uneasy."

"No," Amelia answered, "this is the way I look at it; my family's insured, there's only myself to think about. And when a great adventure's offered you—you don't refuse it, that's all." Moreover, Amelia wrote to Railey, taking him off the hook: "You have done nothing more than present the facts of the case to me. I appreciate your forbearance in not trying to 'sell' the idea, and should like you to know that I assume all responsibility for any risk involved."[20]

Dorothy Putnam liked Amelia. "She is a lady in the very best sense of the word," she told the press later, "an educated and cultivated person with a fine, healthy sense of humor. And a girl easy to look at, too." For Amelia's part, when she wrote her account of the flight, she dedicated the book to Dorothy Putnam.

Dorothy mentioned that Amelia's resemblance to Lindbergh was "almost uncanny." Others noted the likeness. "She looks more like Lindbergh than Lindbergh himself," said Norwegian artist Brynjulf Strandenaes, who had painted Lindbergh and sketched Amelia.[21] The likeness was most noticeable when Amelia wore her flight helmet and lifted her head in a certain way. It was not so evident when she wore her usual quietly stylish garb.

Most preflight discussions took place at the Byrd home, where the commander's wife, Marie, was a calming influence. More than once her quiet tact kept George or Stultz from stalking off in a huff.

"How do you do it, Mrs. Byrd?" Amelia asked.

Marie Byrd laughed. "Oh, Meely, I've had lots of practice." She went through a similar exercise every time her husband prepared for an expedition.[22]

The *Friendship* group had a brief but sharp cliffhanger. Mabel Boll, an aviatrix nicknamed the "Diamond queen" because of her large collection of jewels, wanted the honor of being the first woman to fly the Atlantic, and she wanted Bill Stultz as her pilot. Stultz had flown her and Charles A. Levine, veteran of an unsuccessful attempt at an

Atlantic crossing, from New York to Havana. According to Boll, while they were still in Havana, Stultz "promised to be her pilot on a flight across to Europe." She still cherished the ambition to fly the Atlantic in Levine's aircraft, *Columbia.*

Not yet having signed a formal contract for the *Friendship* flight, Stultz was legally free to honor his previous oral arrangement if he so chose. He went to visit Boll in New York but did not commit himself, nor did he inform her of the *Friendship* project. As he had told none of his colleagues why he had gone, they were exceedingly upset, fearing that he had gone off to "hang one on." The next day, however, he returned to Boston, safe and sober, and asked for Byrd's advice. He recommended that Stultz "stay with Amelia," which Stultz agreed to do.

One can only conclude that Stultz was keeping a foot in both camps. Boll clearly considered him committed to her, while Muriel's account indicates that he had received Boll's offer after informally joining the *Friendship* crew. Certainly it is difficult to imagine Byrd's recommending to anyone that he break a valid contract.

By early June, the *Friendship* was ready to go, mechanically speaking. A trimotor Fokker with a wingspread of seventy-one feet, it was designed to carry up to one thousand gallons of fuel. Its equipment included "a 600-meter sending and receiving radio apparatus" plus emergency equipment, should the plane make a forced landing and the primary set go dead. The *Friendship* had been modified into a seaplane by replacing the wheels with pontoons. These would offer a good chance of landing safely on fairly smooth seas, but added appreciably to the plane's weight. The cabin space was almost completely filled by two large gas tanks, in addition to the wing tanks. There was barely room between these tanks for the crew to squeeze through. "Fortunately the physical architecture of all three members of the *Friendship*'s crew was distinctly Gothic," Amelia remembered.

A small table for the navigation instruments was the sole furniture. For seats the crew used a five-gallon water can or their flying suits rolled into pillows. From the exterior the plane was a cheery sight, painted orange and gold. This color scheme was not dictated by artistic motives but because orange could be seen farther away than any other color. This color could save the crew's lives if they came down in the Atlantic.[23]

The only factor now to consider was the weather, and Amelia came to value the advice and friendship of Dr. James H. Kimball of the U.S. Weather Bureau in New York. "Doc," as he was known to an entire generation of aviators, could predict and report the weather, but not produce it to order. And the weather refused to cooperate.[24]

The situation was so frustrating that Putnam told Byrd, "I'm almost ready for a binge myself." George admitted that Amelia stood the enforced waiting better than anyone else in the group. She greeted each unfavorable weather report with a vigorous "Damn!" then went to Denison House, where she was carrying on her duties as best she could.

Three times Doc Kimball gave the green light; three times Stultz could not get the heavy plane off Boston Harbor. No one could charge Amelia with appreciably contributing to the weight of the plane. Setting the pattern for her future flights, she traveled light. "Toilet articles began with a toothbrush and ended with a comb. The only extras were some fresh handkerchiefs and a tube of cold cream." She recognized that the modifications to the aircraft were largely to blame. "Never again will I fly the Atlantic with pontoons on my plane," she fumed.

On June 3, 1928, they tried again: once more, no liftoff. They realized that drastic measures were necessary. Lou Gower's weight might make the difference, so Stultz taxied to the float where Putnam and Railey were waiting for the takeoff, and the standby pilot joined them. "I didn't want him to go," Amelia wrote in her log, "but of course realized he was the only one to leave and a sacrifice of something was necessary. . . .

"For the first time I then felt the *Friendship* really lighten on the water and knew the difference of a few pounds had made her a bird."[25]

Amelia had delegated Sam Chapman to break the news of the venture to Amy and Muriel, but several newspapers got the word early, so the two women learned of the takeoff from the papers. Sam Chapman and Albert Morrissey were soon on hand to help Amy and Muriel deal with the swarming reporters. This was a completely new experience for the Earhart women. "In my day," said Amy tartly, "nice people had their names in the paper only when they were born, married and died."[26]

In painful contrast, the press, having learned that a transatlantic flight had begun with—gasp!—a woman on board, broke out in a rash of print guaranteed to dismay the publicity-shy. Most of the articles were favorable. A sour note in this chorus was Mabel Boll. She broke into tears of fury and frustration while phoning the *New York Times:* "I can't understand it," she sobbed. "Wilmer was down here only a few days ago and I asked him when he was coming back to fly the *Columbia.* He said in just a few days, and that he would be here today sure. . . . I depended on him." She declared angrily that if possible she would take off immediately with another pilot. But the plane was not ready and she had to wait, simmering.[27]

Meanwhile, the *Friendship* had left Boston behind, with Slim Gordon at the controls, Bill Stultz on the radio, and Amelia sitting on the floor. She tried to take a picture of the harbor but had to devote all her attention to the cabin door. The spring lock broke just before takeoff, and Amelia had to hold the door closed until Gordon could move back to repair it. She narrowly averted being pulled out, and when Gordon appeared he, too, "came within inches of falling out when the door suddenly slid open. . . . However, a string tied through the leather thong in the door itself and fastened to a brace inside the cabin held it shut fairly securely."

After this scare, Amelia settled down for a nap, in her ears the small rubber plugs Marie Byrd had given her, saying that the commander had used them on his own transatlantic flight and, as a result, was the only member of the crew who could hear when they landed. Amelia awoke to find her colleagues preparing to land at Halifax. Nibbling on an orange, she waited in the plane while Stultz and Gordon went ashore to seek accommodations. They had planned to continue the flight immediately, but fog held them overnight. At their hotel, reporters and cameramen invaded the men's room and tried to persuade them to dress and pose. This lack of consideration angered Amelia.

They were able to take off at about 10 A.M., after loading one hundred gallons of gasoline. The weather was perfect, and Amelia reflected that had this refueling not been necessary, they could have bypassed Newfoundland and headed for Europe.[28] In the ensuing thirteen days, they had good cause to wish that this had been possible.

Chapter 5
The Flight of the Friendship

*A*rrival at Trepassey, Newfoundland, resembled a cross between a rodeo and a farce. The project had arranged for a mooring, and the crew wanted to be directed to it. Instead, about a dozen small boats circled the plane, in the bow of each a "maritime cowboy" trying to cast a rope to the aircraft, obviously in the hope that whoever succeeded could tow the *Friendship* to his own mooring. Gordon stood on a pontoon trying to keep the plane clear and warding off these opportunists with frantic yells. The noise of the *Friendship*'s idling motors, the launches' engines, and the shouts made an indescribable din. Amelia was helpless with laughter. "In the cockpit, Stultz, I fear, was talking to God about it." Finally they reached their own mooring and were able to proceed to their quarters in the home of a Mrs. Deveraux. She seemed to be in some doubt that Amelia was real and touched her to be sure she was "present in the flesh."[1]

As soon as possible, Amelia telegraphed to Amy: "Know you will understand why I could not tell you plans of flight. Don't worry. No matter what happens it will have been worth the trying. Love, A." Amy dispatched a truly gallant reply: "We are not worrying. Wish I were with you. Good luck and cheerio. Love, Mother."[2]

The *Friendship* crew hoped to leave Trepassey on June 5, but "a howling gale" kept them stranded. Gordon took advantage of the delay to repair a crack in the oil tank "with cement and adhesive tape." For three days "the wind blew briskly from the northwest." Had they been airborne, this would have been ideal, but it made the sea too choppy to load the gasoline.[3]

For almost two weeks they remained prisoners of fog, waves, or both. As the days dragged by, certain elements of the press turned against the venture and seemed to believe that the delay was due to Amelia's reluctance to continue the flight. This criticism did nothing for the crew's sinking morale. Somehow the papers got hold of Amelia's telegram to Amy. Rightly or wrongly, she blamed Muriel for the leak and wrote her "a blistering letter."[4]

There was nothing to do but wait, and Trepassey did not offer much in the way of entertainment, although Amelia never forgot the New-foundlanders' hospitality. She read one of Deveraux's six books and played endless games of rummy with Gordon. She was interested in examining Deveraux's many hooked rugs, "some made from cotton washed ashore twenty years ago from a wreck." By June 11, Amelia's state of mind was reflected in her log: "Oh, if only we can get away soon. It is hard indeed to remain sans books, sans contact with one's interests and withal on a terrific strain."[5]

The "terrific strain" was Stultz, who had turned to the bottle to relieve his frustration and boredom. The situation became extremely serious, for this was no case of a drink or two to relax tension. Stultz drank by the bottle until he had befuddled his brain. Amelia and Gordon tried to keep him occupied with hikes or fishing, but after an hour or so, Stultz would either produce a bottle or turn back to the village.

This might have been marginally endurable had Stultz simply sent himself into a stupor, but the liquor made him belligerent and irra-tional. Once he ordered Gordon to row him out to the *Friendship,* which he proceeded to taxi around the harbor, seriously endangering the fishing craft moored in the path of his blind rage. On several occa-sions he gave Gordon useless and dangerous orders. The mechanic told Amelia furiously that he was fed up with being ordered around by "a drunken so-an-so." It took all of Amelia's tact to soothe him down.

The situation worried Amelia no end and placed upon her a heavy burden of responsibility. Putnam later wrote, "I suppose no more ironic difficulty could have risen up to plague a girl who never drank herself, hence knew little about drinkers and the technique—if any—of han-dling them." Obviously George did not know that Amelia was all too well acquainted with the vagaries of alcoholics. The immediate prob-lem at Trepassey, however, was whether she should replace Stultz. Lou Gower was still standing by in Boston. Amelia could inform Putnam by telegram of the state of affairs and ask that Gower be flown up to take over. She hesitated to take this drastic step for two reasons: First, she and Gordon knew that, when sober, Stultz was a better pilot than Gower. Second, with her hard-won compassion for alcoholics, she hated to take action so potentially damaging to Stultz. Once the word spread that the *Friendship* project had jettisoned Bill Stultz for drunkenness, it would be most unlikely that he would be entrusted ever again with a responsible flying job.[6]

Meanwhile, after a series of delays, Mabel Boll in *Columbia* with a new crew reached Halifax on June 12. There she planned to refuel the aircraft and "take off as soon as the weather permits." The trip from New York had been exceedingly rough, however, and it seemed possible that the crew would be "too exhausted to begin a transatlantic hop the next day." Although pleased to learn that the *Friendship* had not yet taken off, Boll denied that *Columbia* was racing the *Friendship*. "I wish Miss Earhart and her companions the best of luck."

That same day, the weather at Trepassey looked favorable, but the *Friendship*'s eight attempts to take off were unsuccessful. After still other futile tries the next day, Amelia and her crew had to ask themselves if takeoff would require leaving behind a substantial quantity of fuel. This would mean that they could not fly directly to England but must use the Azores-Lisbon route. According to the press, "The Portuguese Consul at St. John's was asked last night to arrange the necessary landing facilities at the Azores and Lisbon."[7]

This was the situation when, at 11 P.M. on June 16, Amelia received a telegram from George: Doc Kimball had predicted favorable weather for about forty-eight hours as far out as the mid-Atlantic. This would swing the project away from the Azores-Lisbon plan to the North Atlantic route.

Doc Kimball's prediction also effectively resolved Amelia's dilemma about Stultz. It was too late to send for Gower; they must take advantage of the good weather, and that meant sticking with Stultz. Nevertheless, it was touch and go. When Amelia knocked on the men's door the next morning, Stultz was out cold. Stern measures involving cold water and hot black coffee roused him enough that he could navigate to the dock with Amelia and Gordon holding him up.[8]

One of Amelia's last actions at Trepassey was arranging with "Pop," the village storekeeper-postmaster-telegraph operator, to send a message to George Putnam half an hour after Pop saw the plane lift off. The message was "Violet"—the prearranged code announcing that the flight was on its way.

After one false start, *Friendship* finally took to the air at 11:40 A.M. on June 17, with a hungover pilot and a depleted gas supply. On one of their previous trials they had determined that the plane could not rise carrying the planned nine hundred gallons, so two hundred had been removed. This cut down the margin of safety but could not be helped.[9]

Amelia established herself at the chart table to begin her log when she spotted a whiskey bottle, about three-quarters full. Preparing to drop it overboard, she hesitated. If Stultz found it missing, he might go into one of his violent spells. She decided to leave it alone and hope for the best. Most fortunately, somewhere aloft Stultz the pilot conquered Stultz the alcoholic. He still had not touched the bottle when, toward the end of their journey, Amelia thankfully let it slip into the Irish Sea.[10]

After the initial excitement of takeoff, the crew of the *Friendship* settled down to business. Amelia had hoped to take a turn at the controls but had to content herself with keeping the flight log. She was not trained in instrument flying, and it became evident that this technique would be the order of the day. Either Doc Kimball's weather report had been overly optimistic, or else the weather had shifted rapidly. Soon the plane encountered a head wind and heavy rain, then ran into snow. After emerging from this, they had a brief bit of sunshine and radioed George their first message: "Out of fog now; clear weather." Cape Race forwarded this at 1:19 P.M. EDT. At 2 P.M. the steamer *Concordia* reported sighting the *Friendship* "heading seaward at high speed over the Grand Banks." About this time, Mrs. Stultz at her home in Hempstead, Long Island, received a message from her husband: "Passed through banks of snow, fog and hail; clear weather now; everything going fine."[11]

In this sunny interval, Gordon took over the controls from Stultz, who slept for an hour and then went back on the job. At 4:45 P.M. EDT the British steamship *Rexmore* reported that the *Friendship* had asked for and received bearings. "Signals from *Friendship* were loud but plane was not sighted." The bearings indicated the plane was about 500 miles from Newfoundland and 1,165 miles out of Ireland. Stultz asked that this information be relayed to New York. Looking out the window, Amelia saw "a true rainbow—I mean the famous circle. . . . I have heard of color circles in Hawaii."

Almost two hours later, *Rexmore* again reported, "Further signals received from seaplane *Friendship* . . . ; apparently still going strong. Signals good." Keeping her log, Amelia was almost mesmerized by the glory of the sky: "The view is too vast and lovely for words. I think I am happy—sad admission of scant intellectual equipment.

"I am getting housemaid's knee kneeling here at the table gulping beauty."[12]

At that time of year and the latitude of the *Friendship*'s course, night fell late. It was not until about 10 P.M. that Amelia noted, "Darkness complete. Stultz sits alone, every muscle and nerve alert. Gordon sleeps. There are many hours to go."

The cabin was bitter cold, and Amelia was thankful for the fur-lined flying suit she had almost rejected. When Major Charles Wooley of Boston offered it to her, she had hesitated. But Byrd had recommended that she take it, and now she was glad she had.

At midnight she woke Gordon, who ate a sandwich and four chocolate bars. Amelia remembered, however, that they were not really hungry. At Trepassey they had taken aboard scrambled egg sandwiches, oranges, malted milk tablets, and five gallons of water. Also, in case they were forced down, they carried pemmican, "a very concentrated food used by explorers," supposedly chockful of nutrition but highly unpalatable. The men had coffee; Amelia never drank it unless she had no other choice, but somehow the cocoa she had been promised did not appear. She did not miss it; all she ate or wanted was three oranges and some of the malted milk tablets.

Gordon took over while Stultz dozed, and Amelia stretched out on the floor for her first sleep of the flight. She awoke in time to record, "A mountain of cloud. The North Star on our wing tip. My watch says 3:15. I can see dawn to the left."[13]

By this time news had spread that the *Friendship* was under way, and people on both sides of the Atlantic eagerly followed the story. The news came as a great surprise and disappointment to the crew of the *Columbia*. Some urged that they follow immediately, but they decided to wait at least several hours until certain factors had been resolved: Was this just a test flight? What was the route? If the *Friendship* disappeared, *Columbia* could make the attempt. But if *Friendship* reached England safely, the race was lost.

That the *Friendship* might indeed disappear was a distinct possibility, based on the track record. Up to this point, the Atlantic had been unforgiving of women who attempted the crossing by air. Ruth Elder had been lucky. In October 1927, she and George W. Waldeman were forced down near the Azores, where a Dutch tanker rescued them. As mentioned, Frances W. Grayson and three crew members had been lost in December 1937. European women attempting the east-west flight were no more successful. With two crew members, Princess Ludwig Lowenstein-Wertheim left Upavon, England, for Canada in August 1927. That was the last anyone saw of them. More recently, in March 1928, the Honorable Elsie Mackay and Captain Walter Hinchcliffe were lost after leaving England's Cranwell Airdrome.[14]

That last morning the *Friendship* climbed to its highest elevation, eleven thousand feet, to lift over clouds "which reared their heads like dragons." In addition to shapes of various beasties in the fog, which all three noted, "there were recurrent mountains and valleys and countless landscapes amazingly realistic."[15]

They now entered upon the tensest part of the flight. The radio had been dead all night; fuel was running low; the port motor was coughing. By Stultz's calculations, they should be near some part of the British Isles, but so far they had seen no land. Suddenly, at about 6 A.M. EDT, they spotted a liner. It was the USS *America*, although they did not know this until later. At this time *Friendship* had only an hour's gas left and had passed the estimated time for reaching Ireland.

In fact, they had flown over the southern tip of Ireland without seeing the land below; plane and liner were both off the east coast. Stultz wrote a note asking their position, which they placed in a bag, weighed with an orange and tied with a silver cord. Amelia tried to drop this through the hatchway onto the liner's deck, but missed. A second attempt was no more successful. Captain George H. Fried of the *America* saw the plane, which was low enough for him to read the name and other markings. He had his radio operator try to make contact but, of course, he could not reach the *Friendship*. This was 10:30 A.M. local time.

What should they do? Should the *Friendship* crew admit themselves lost, land beside the liner, and be hauled aboard, or stick to their course? Tacitly they agreed to continue. Half an hour later, *Friendship* overflew some fishing boats, a good sign that land was near. Amelia recorded the climactic moment:

> ▶ Bill, of course, was at the controls. Slim, gnawing a sandwich, sat beside him, when out of the mists there grew a blue shadow, in appearance no more solid than hundreds of other "landscapes" we had sighted before. . . . *It was land!*
>
> I think Slim yelled. I know the sandwich went flying out the window. Bill permitted himself a smile.

They skirted the coast looking for a likely landing site. At a small bay near a little town, Stultz set the plane on the water. Amelia recorded: "20 hrs., 40 min. out of Trepassey *Friendship* down safely in harbor of———," leaving a blank to be filled in when she found out the name of their landfall.[16]

They had touched down on Loughor estuary, off Burry Port, Carmarthenshire, Wales. For a while it seemed that Stultz had chosen the one town in the United Kingdom that had never heard of the *Friendship*. The only signs of life were three men working on a nearby railroad track. The fliers waved frantically and Gordon yelled, hoping to get across that they needed a mooring. The Welshmen paused in their labors and even walked down to the shore. Then, their curiosity evidently appeased, they turned their backs and returned to work.

A few more people appeared, and Gordon scrambled down to a pontoon and called out for a boat. Either those ashore could not hear him, or else his American accent defeated their Welsh ears. Amelia waved a white towel out the window as a distress signal. One man on shore "pulled off his coat and waved back."

This was friendly but not very helpful. Nearly an hour passed before a harbor policeman, Norman Fisher, rowed out to the plane to see what this was all about. He rowed Stultz ashore to telephone Southampton. The word came at 2:45 P.M.[17]

Waiting for action, Gordon snatched a nap. He had plenty of time; several hours passed with nothing further happening. Meanwhile, Railey at Southampton had procured a seaplane and was hurrying to the scene, accompanied by Allen Raymond of the *New York Times* and a Captain Bailey of Imperial Airways. They landed within a few hundred yards of the *Friendship,* and Railey caught sight of Amelia "seated Indian fashion in the doorway of the fuselage and with Indian composure indifferent to the clamor ashore." Railey and his party procured a dory, and as they pulled near he called, "Congratulations! How does it feel to be the first woman to fly the Atlantic?"

Her reply was a listless lift of her hand and the single word, "Hello!"

Greeting Stultz and Gordon, Railey scrambled aboard. Obviously all the crew were "dog tired," but he sensed in Amelia something else—"disappointment." He dropped down beside her and asked, "What's the matter? Aren't you excited?"

"Excited? No," she replied. In fact, Amelia was prey to emotions that Railey, to whom publicity was the breath of life, was quite incapable of understanding. This was the same young woman who, not so many years ago, had not bothered to pick up her diplomas from high school and finishing school. She had acquired the necessary learning; the symbols thereof and the accompanying ceremonies and congratulations of graduation meant nothing to her. Now she faced a situation in which she would be praised and admired for something she had not done. She had not "flown the Atlantic"; she *had been* flown—a horse of a very different hue. She burst out to Railey, "It was a grand experience but all I did was lie on my tummy and take pictures of the clouds. We didn't see much of the ocean. Stultz did all the flying—had to. I was just baggage, like a sack of potatoes."

Railey replied bracingly, "What of it? You're still the first woman to fly the Atlantic, and what's more the first woman pilot."

Evidently realizing that Railey could not share her feelings, Amelia summoned up a smile. "Oh, well, maybe some day I'll try it alone."[18]

The group had planned to leave immediately for Southampton, but the tide was racing, so they decided to stay at Burry Port overnight. Railey arranged for moorings, and at last the fliers could deplane. They were rowed ashore, where for the first time Amelia experienced the full impact of becoming a public figure. The inhabitants of Burry Port had finally realized who their visitors were and more than made up for their initial indifference.

Today, when anyone with the inclination and the fare travels across the Atlantic by air with no more qualms than when taking the New York–Washington shuttle, it is difficult to visualize the interest and enthusiasm these early flights generated. And on this adventure, for the first time, a woman had participated. No wonder the six policemen assigned to escort the fliers barely got them through the crowd. Indeed, to reporter Raymond it seemed briefly "that she would not outlive her triumph." Amelia remembered, "In the enthusiasm of their greeting those hospitable people nearly tore our clothes off."

The group surged to the nearby factory of the Frickers Metal Company, where Amelia received a bouquet from the mayor, and the three visitors stood on the steps to be photographed and sign autographs until the foreman's wife called a halt. "This poor lamb needs her tea . . . all of you come back later on if you want." She led the three Americans inside and regaled them with tea and hot buttered scones. "Now I know I'm in Great Britain," Amelia smiled gratefully, "thanks to you and this."[19]

This early in her public experience Amelia had to deal with her purported resemblance to Lindbergh. At Burry Port one of the first questions reporters asked her was whether she knew Lindbergh and did she think she looked like him. They added that she was being called "Lady Lindy." Amelia explained with some asperity "that I had never had the honor of meeting Colonel Lindbergh, that I was sure I looked like no one (and, just then, nothing) in the world, and that I would grasp the first opportunity to apologize to him for innocently inflicting the idiotic comparison."

Later, in less hectic circumstances, she would reply to similar questions with a laugh and the comment, "Oh, I've got the kind of face that looks like everybody." About a year later, after she had met Anne Morrow Lindbergh, Amelia wrote to her:

▶ I had no chance at the banquet of the Ohio Federation of Women's Clubs to thank you for your graciousness in absolving me from blame in the ridiculous "Lady Lindy" publicity.

I believe I have never apologized so widely and so consistently for anything in my life, excepting possibly having been born. The title was given me, I believe, probably because one or the other of us wasn't a swarthy runt. . . .

The overexuberance of the public gave Amelia a certain sympathy for Lindbergh, who could be very aloof and sometimes downright rude to the press and his fans. "It's no fun to have one's clothes torn," she would say, in later days. "It's simply ghastly to be *pinched*. There's a mania to manhandle Lindbergh. No man has ever been treated as he has, though even I have had things literally stolen off my back."[20]

Although Amelia could understand how distasteful such incidents could be to an introvert like Lindbergh, she did not follow his example. She had too much common sense to embark upon a course certain to draw public attention and then resent that attention.

That night at the hotel in Burry Port, dinner was late, served at about 10 P.M. Railey escorted Amelia to her room, and before returning she asked him to send two cables, one to Amy, the other to Perkins. They said simply, "Love, Amelia."[21]

Muriel was "close to collapse" after sharing an "all-night vigil" with her mother and warding off inquisitive reporters, but Amy was "rigidly erect of carriage, determinedly unmoved of feature," when they were told of Amelia's safe arrival. A well-bred woman of Amy's generation did not air her emotions in public. "Well, now that it's all over, I'll have a chance to catch up on my mending," was her overt public reaction.[22]

That night Amelia sank into her tub for her first hot bath since leaving Boston, then crawled into bed. She could not sleep in, however, for they had to take off early in the morning to reach Southampton on schedule. On this flight across the Bristol Channel and the Devonshire hills, at last Amelia had the chance to pilot the *Friendship* before Stultz took over for the landing. They settled down on Southampton water to siren wails, foghorn moans, tugboat whistles, and the cheers of a welcoming crowd. An official launch, bearing among others Amy Guest, came out to bring the *Friendship* crew to shore, so Amelia had the opportunity to meet and thank the woman whose generosity and vision had made it all possible.[23]

That was the last Amelia saw of the *Friendship*. Later she learned that after passing through several hands the plane had become "the air force of a band of revolutionists in South America." It was also the last the fliers saw of "the charts and other paraphernalia" they had used on the flight and would have cherished as remembrances. But evidently the British souvenir hunters were as swift as they were light-fingered.

On shore they were welcomed by Mrs. Foster Welch, the lady mayor of Southampton, who to Amelia's surprise was addressed as "Mister Mayor." Then Amelia, Amy Guest, and Mr. and Mrs. Hubert Scott Pain (Payne?) of Imperial Airways were ushered to a yellow Rolls Royce for the drive to London. As they passed through Winchester, Amelia asked to see the famed cathedral where King Alfred had been crowned and King Canute was entombed. Time permitted only a fifteen-minute stop, then off again on the road to London.[24]

Amelia had hoped that the next day, June 21, would be reserved for rest, but it proved to be hectic beyond belief. The assault on the *Friendship* headquarters at the Hyde Park Hotel began before dawn. Allen Raymond, tongue in cheek, characterized this as Amelia's "day of opportunity to make money, accept luxurious gifts, aid struggling unrecognized geniuses, appear at numerous public and private functions, sign autograph books, and even acquire a husband."

The latter was a farmer from Kent, who seemed to think he was conferring a favor upon Amelia. He offered her marriage provided "she is well-off financially." Among the "unrecognized geniuses" was an inventor with a device he claimed would make transatlantic flights completely safe. "He never passed the outer ramparts." Would-be poets popped up, one hailing Amelia as "Sweet Eve of the Air," another as "Venus of the Ethereal Blue," which must have amused Amelia, who never could see herself as attractive, let alone like Venus.

Some of the odder epistles elicited from Amelia a plaintive "Why are people like that?" She firmly rejected offers to appear on the screen or stage and declined a limousine. One writer expressed resentment that she, "a mere woman passenger," was receiving all the attention and praise that properly belonged to the pilots. In this sentiment Amelia heartily concurred. By afternoon she was "visibly wilting." She was realistic enough to expect a fair amount of publicity, but "never dreamed how great a hubbub" her trip would raise.

So far as they could, Stultz and Gordon escaped the "hubbub." Just as Amelia referred all public credit to them, they praised her as "a good shipmate" and were more than willing to let her have the dubious pleasures of the limelight. Gordon accepted the offer of a car, and the two men drove around seeing the sights, encountering a few old friends, and making new acquaintances. Caught in a stream of traffic returning from the races at Ascot, Gordon saw his first top hat and, even more exotic, a gray topper, something he had never heard of.

After a long, relaxing automobile ride seeing the sights of London, Amelia recovered her vigor and enjoyed dinner at Amy Guest's home, chatting pleasantly with "the numerous notables" present.[25]

On all such occasions Railey was her escort, and throughout the London period he increasingly admired her serious, forthright manner, "warmed . . . by humor and grace." He saw in this unassuming young woman the seeds of greatness: "her simplicity would capture people everywhere; her strength of character would hold her on her course."

During their London stay, Railey turned down more than twenty thousand pounds in offers "to cash in on the flight." Each evening he would report to Amelia on the day's crop, and they would laugh. But Railey soon realized that "Amelia's affairs required precious little management"—she could trust her own "unfailing good taste and good sense."[26]

Meanwhile, reactions were coming in from many quarters. In Paris, a member of the *New York Times* staff happened to call upon Marshal Foch. The old soldier's first question was, "What is the news from Miss Earhart?" He was delighted to learn of her success and at once passed on the good word to Madame Foch.

Ruth Elder, visiting in Paris, was one of the first to send congratulations. She, who had failed in her own attempt, wired warmly, "I was with you every minute in spirit and thought. I know only too well what a grand exploit it was."

Mabel Boll and her pilots sent a message with "warmest congratulations" on the feat that had "brought great glory to the American nation." Boll still planned to fly to Europe, but a few days later she was frustrated when Levine insisted that she return the *Columbia* to Curtiss Field on Long Island.

President Calvin Coolidge broke his traditional silence to send greetings: "I wish to express to you, the first woman successfully to span the North Atlantic by air, the great admiration of myself and the people of the United States for your splendid flight. Our pride in this accomplishment of our countrywoman is equalled only by our joy in your safe arrival. The courageous collaboration of the co-pilot, Mr. Wilmer Stultz, and Mr. Gordon likewise merit our cordial congratulations."

This message, mentioning Stultz as "co-pilot" and apparently as an afterthought, bothered Amelia more than it pleased her. She hastened to reply, "SUCCESS ENTIRELY DUE GREAT SKILL OF MR. STULTZ STOP HE WAS ONLY ONE MILE OFF COURSE AT VALENTIA AFTER FLYING BLIND FOR TWO THOUSAND TWO HUNDRED FORTY-SIX MILES AT AVERAGE SPEED ONE HUNDRED THIRTEEN M.P.H."

At Stultz's hometown, Williamsburg, Pennsylvania, his mother had collapsed upon learning of his safe arrival but recovered in time to join in an old-fashioned celebration, beginning with factory whistles and ringing bells and culminating in a street parade and fireworks. A steady downpour of rain failed to dampen the fête.[27]

Most of the British press comments were favorable and congratulatory, but Amelia found the brickbats more interesting than the bouquets. One paper referred to her superciliously as a "pleasant young woman who should be capable of spending her time to better advantage on her own side of the water." Someone sent her a clipping from the *Church Times* expressing its disapproval in no uncertain terms. One part of this editorial was notable for its unconscious irony: "The voyage itself, for nearly all the way through fog, is a remarkable achievement made possible by the skill and courage of the pilot. But his anxiety must have been vastly increased by the fact that he was carrying a woman passenger." If only the writer knew the anxiety the pilot had caused the woman passenger—and, indeed, was still causing her! For Stultz was hitting the bottle again. Often he did not keep appointments or showed up decidedly the worse for wear.[28]

Amelia's first order of business was clothes; she had arrived in London with nothing but those on her back. Under the guidance of Amy

Guest, and wearing a borrowed outfit, she went shopping at the famous Selfridge department store. Still unused to her fame, she was surprised when the owner, Gordon Selfridge, greeted her and refused to accept payment for the clothes she selected. When she emerged clad in a stylish gray outfit with a "perky" black hat, she looked so different from newspaper pictures of her in her bulky flying suit that nobody recognized her, and she could walk about London's streets without being besieged.

She visited Toynbee Hall, the pattern for Denison House, and Lady Nancy Astor at her country home. Her outspoken hostess delighted Amelia by saying bluntly, "I'm not interested in you a bit because you crossed the Atlantic by air. I want to hear about your settlement work." Someone, then, still regarded her "as a human being."

Amelia also met Lady Mary Heath, the Irish flier who had recently completed a record flight from Capetown to London. Lady Mary allowed Amelia to pilot her little Avion, and Amelia was so pleased with it that she bought it.

Gordon had a moment in the limelight when he revealed that he had telephoned Ann Bruce in Brookline, Massachusetts, and she had promised to marry him soon after he returned.

Amelia had a surprising sample of British press originality. At a group interview with reporters, the first question was "Should you like to meet the Prince of Wales?"

Amelia said nothing, leaving the reply to an American official, who answered, "That depends on His Highness' wishes."

Evidently this well-behaved, soft-spoken young woman did not fit someone's preconceived notions of American womanhood, for the next day Amelia was dumbfounded to find herself quoted as saying, "Wal, I sure am glad to be here, and gosh, I sure do hope I'll meet the Prince of Wales."

Fortunately this fictitious example of stage-cowgirlese tickled Amelia's sense of humor, and she kept the clipping as a prized souvenir. She reflected ruefully that if the prince read this alleged quotation, no wonder he did not ask to meet her![29]

Chapter 6
Ticker Tape and Travel

*T*he *Friendship* trio left England on June 28, sailing on the USS *President Roosevelt*. For all three, this was their first ocean voyage, and they were impressed with just how much water they had overflown. They loved these long days of total relaxation. Captain Harry Manning, the ship's skipper, gave them the freedom of the bridge, where they could enjoy privacy. Almost every day, one or the other asked him jokingly, "Can't you take us to South America instead of New York?" As Amelia wrote, "all three of us dreaded the inevitable receptions." Between the seasoned sailor and the young aviatrix, a firm friendship sprang up. Daily she watched as he plotted the ship's course in the chart room, and from him she learned much-needed lessons in navigation.

On the day before landing, Amelia received a radiogram from George Putnam listing a formidable week's schedule. Foreseeing difficulties, she took Captain Manning into her confidence about Stultz. "It was bad enough in London where people are tolerant, as you know, Captain, but what will happen if I can't keep him sober for the New York and Boston affairs?" she asked despairingly.

Of course, Manning could not guarantee Stultz's good behavior for the duration, but he promised to have him at the gangplank the next day in a sober condition.

For more than one reason, Amelia exclaimed, "The next time I fly anywhere, I shall do it alone!" The captain reassured her that she would make many flights in the future, and perhaps some day he would help her plan a solo flight.

The next morning Amelia felt somewhat apologetic to discover that the passengers, who had arisen early and breakfasted at 6 A.M., had to wait several hours for the mayor's official yacht, *Macon,* to arrive to take the celebrities ashore. If the other passengers resented the delay, they did not show it, and sent up a cheer when Amelia, Stultz, and Gordon appeared with Manning on the bridge.[1]

A sharp wind was stirring up heavy waves, and *Macon*'s skipper had some difficulty in coming alongside so that the liner's gangway could touch down on the boat's deck. Looking "trim" in blue silk crepe with touches of white and a close-fitting black-and-white feather hat, Amelia watched the maneuver until it was time to transfer.

The trip from liner to dock was a reception in itself. None of Amelia's family was present, but Stultz's mother was aboard, as was Gordon's fiancée, Ann Bruce, "a striking brunette." Among others present were John B. Phipps Amy Guest's brother), Ruth Nichols, and the ubiquitous Grover C. Whalen, chairman of the mayor's committee of welcome. Reporters and cameramen crowded around Amelia. Stultz and Gordon were almost lost in the shuffle, but George and Dorothy Putnam rounded them up. George urged Stultz to participate in the interview, but he only smiled and took refuge behind the bouquet of roses Amelia had placed on a chair.

Amelia proved a pleasant, cooperative interviewee, but she deftly fielded a question about Sam Chapman, and that subject "was promptly dropped." She stated that she planned to continue in aviation, might write a book, but would accept no movie contracts. Reporters persuaded Stultz to say a few words, and as he was describing the technical aspects of the flight, the boat pulled into the Battery among whistles and the traditional stream of water from fireboats.[2]

The celebrities were perched upon the backs of convertibles and driven through downtown New York to City Hall. They waved and smiled their thanks to the enthusiastic spectators, while ticker tape and the pages of telephone books showered down. As usual, Amelia found a leavening of humor: "Riding up Main Street while people throw telephone books at you is an amusing modern version of a triumphal march."

Joseph V. McKee, acting mayor in the absence of "Jimmy" Walker, received the *Friendship* crew on the steps of City Hall and presented each with a scroll of appreciation. Then they were off to a luncheon at the Biltmore Hotel hosted by Byrd, with many notables such as Bernt Balchen and Sir Hubert Wilkins. After a few social events, the *Friendship* group moved on to Boston.

Invitations to similar honors in other cities had rained upon them, but it had been decided that apart from New York, celebrations should be confined to Boston, Medford, and Chicago. At the Boston airport,

Amelia snatched a few moments with Amy, Muriel, and Perkins. As photographers snapped, several spectators, eager for a glimpse of the famous bob, sang out, "Take off your hat, Amelia!" She made a little face, but obligingly removed her modish straw cloche. Tossing it to Muriel, she remarked ruefully, "Here's where I get sixty more freckles on my poor nose, I guess!"

An endearing feature of the procession to Boston City Hall was the piping cries from windowsills or wherever else a child could sit—"Miss Earhart! It's me!"—as the car moved past various Denison House regulars. For each Amelia had a warm smile and "Hi, there!" of recognition that made the youngster's day.[3]

The Boston celebration was what one newspaper called "a real homecoming." New York had greeted newsworthy figures; Boston welcomed back one of its own. The weather in New York had been threatening; in Boston it was perfect. Crowds estimated at between 250,000 and 300,000 lined the streets as the three fliers, with Commander Byrd, drove to City Hall.

There the three fliers received the keys to the city and the usual ordeal by oratory, mercifully brief. They had a few hours' rest, then a banquet with more speeches, including brief remarks by the three new celebrities and a question-and-answer period. Commander Byrd, who was conducting the program, finally brought it to an end.[4]

Amelia and Muriel were waiting for a taxi outside the hotel when George Putnam drove up behind the wheel of the good old Yellow Peril and turned it over to its owner. It was thoughtful of Putnam to realize that by this time Amelia would have had her fill of public vehicles and would enjoy nothing so much as driving her own car in peace for some private time with Muriel.

As the two women bowled along past Massachusetts General Hospital, Amelia observed, "Those are the people who are doing really worthwhile things. What I have done is important to me, but ninety-nine out of a hundred people who come out to see the boys and me don't know or care what contributions we have made to aviation. Sometimes I'm inclined to laugh at the whole parades and reception bunk." Muriel consoled her that she had only two more parades to get through, Medford's hometown one and Chicago's, which no doubt would be the "brass-band-red-carpet treatment to end them all."

Aside from her dislike of public hoopla, Amelia wanted to start work on the book for which Putnam's firm had her under contract. George had arranged for her to write it while a guest in his home at Rye, New York. He offered her a secretary, which she accepted gladly, and a ghost writer, which she refused. Like Amy and Muriel, she was disappointed not to be writing it at Denison House. But she told Muriel realistically, "I'm afraid my value as a social worker is nil while this hullabaloo keeps up." Then, too, she needed money, and George had assured her that upon publication of the book she could earn several thousand dollars on the lecture circuit, although, as she remarked to Muriel, "why people should want to listen to me talking about being a passenger in the *Friendship* I can't imagine."[5]

No doubt George did want to provide Amelia with all possible assistance. Then again, he could be forgiven if he felt a bit like Pygmalion. Persuading a goddess to breathe life into a statue was a feat only a little more impressive than transforming a thirty-five-dollar-a-week social worker into a national heroine. Here was the ticket to the limelight he craved, and he was not about to let her leave his orbit. He never did, to the point where reporters would complain about his invincible pushiness. All too often a short comment from Amelia came wrapped in a speech from George.

This, however, was a problem for the future. Meanwhile, two more receptions loomed. Amelia enjoyed the parade and ceremonies at Medford, which had a very hometown flavor. She and Muriel had a good laugh at the reporters who were eager to find Sam Chapman and exploit him as Amelia's fiancé. They never found him, for he was in the fifth row of the grandstand making himself inconspicuous. After the ceremonies, he took Amelia to Marblehead for a brief beach picnic.[6]

The group returned to New York, where on July 11 the three fliers were guests at a dinner at the Biltmore, given by Chrysler Sales Corporation. Later that evening, at Madison Square Garden, several hundred people saw Amelia presented with a blue roadster. On that occasion, she made a radio broadcast in which she tried to set a few things straight. "I did not go into the flight to make my fortune," she emphasized. "Flying is a sporting business and the *Friendship* flight was a sporting proposition. The one big reward is our thrill in having succeeded." As she lost no opportunity to do, she referred the credit to Stultz and Gordon.

The two men spoke briefly, too, both praising the work of the weather experts. Stultz commented slyly that one of his favorite circumstances about flying was that the noise of the engines precluded talking. "It will be a long time before anyone has to make a speech in an airplane."[7]

On July 17, Amelia and Dorothy Putnam went shopping for hats. Even engaged in this time-honored feminine occupation, Amelia was recognized, and an official of the store gave her three hats. That night the three fliers, Mrs. Stultz, Miss Bruce, and the Putnams flew to Altoona, Pennsylvania, for a brief visit to Williamsburg.

The party moved on to Chicago by private railcar attached to the Broadway Limited. A quick nose-count before the start of the drive to City Hall revealed that Stultz had disappeared. After half an hour,

Amelia and Gordon were so upset that they wanted to telephone the mayor to cancel the program. George persuaded them that this would be rude and damaging to Amelia's reputation. Then he had a brainstorm—he would be Bill Stultz for the day. In preparation he took off his glasses and put on Stultz's helmet. The resemblance left much to be desired, for George towered a good five inches over Stultz. They could only hope that no one along the line of march knew Stultz by sight.

They got away with it, although perforce George as George had to disappear. At the luncheon the mayor noted his absence and expressed regret; he would have liked to meet him. "I hope he has not met with an accident."

"Oh, I don't think you need to worry about an accident," said Amelia demurely. "Mr. Putnam is a most ingenious person, I have heard."

But she was uneasy until safely on her way out of Chicago headed back to New York. George sent the mayor a note of apology; a sudden indisposition had kept him away. Gordon stayed behind, promising to find Stultz and get him headed in the right direction.[8]

That summer's mail was a revelation to Amelia, who had never realized just what a target, for good or ill, a "public character" could be. Two hundred letters a day were normal. Many were from children, and these she tried to answer, but for routine requests for an autograph she sent a postcard. Some of her adult fans were kindly, expressing admiration and encouragement; for these she was grateful.

Some of her mail was definitely of the crank variety. One woman wrote, "Please send me $150; it will just pay for my divorce which I must have." She was writing because "I know you believe in women's freedom." Another woman asked for one of her formal gowns. "I am just about your size and I know you will not wear an evening dress twice." The mail also brought, in Amelia words, "diverse proposals of marriage, and approximations thereof." Most bewildering to her were the many offers of employment. "The psychology of inferring that flying the Atlantic equips one for an advertising managership or banking, leaves me puzzled."[9]

In addition to these glimpses of the American public, she learned something about the reliability of the press: "It appeared that I was a demi-orphan; my father, I learned, had been dead four years—I saved that clipping for him. One day I read that I was wealthy, the next that the sole purpose of my flight was to lift the mortgage from the old homestead—which there isn't any—I mean homestead."[10]

Inevitably, Amelia's family drew press attention, and in a letter dated August 28, 1928, she dropped Amy a hint or two: "Perhaps you'd better not talk my intimate details of salary and business with Pidge. I don't want her to spread the news and always fear she will." She added some advice on how to handle the press: "When and if the reporters come to you, please refer them to Mr. Putnam. Don't even say yes or no if you don't want to. Just say you can add nothing to their tales and to ask me or GPP. Tell 'em you know many of my plans but are not divulging."[11]

Sometime in August the Avian Moth she had purchased from Lady Mary Heath reached Amelia, and she could pursue a cherished plan to indulge herself in a cross-country vacation. On the first leg she took George along for "a little jaunt." At Pittsburgh's Rodgers Field they came to grief. George explained to the press, "Miss Earhart had made a perfect landing and was taxiing to a stop when the plane struck an unmarked ditch in the field and went into it. The plane made what is called a ground loop and nearly turned over." Neither Amelia nor George was injured, but the little aircraft sustained a "smashed landing gear, a cracked-up left lower wing and a splintered propeller." Parts would have to be brought from New York, which could take several days. As soon as repairs were completed, Amelia went on, dropping George off at Dayton, Ohio.[12]

Amelia still had no definite plans for her future. "For the moment all I wished to do in the world was to be a vagabond—in the air."

Incidents of Amelia's vacation flight are worth recording as examples of the problems attendant upon solo flying in a small craft in the 1920s. Amelia usually kept her map open on her knee, fastened to her clothes with a safety pin. West of Fort Worth, the map tore off and blew away. There were no visible landmarks, so she followed her previous course. Soon, a bit to the north, she saw a busy highway. "So many cars must be going somewhere," she reasoned. She followed the road out of Texas into New Mexico, where the highway "and its traveling population simply oozed away."

Spotting "a small cluster of houses," she landed at one end of the town's only street. The population turned out and helped her fold the plane's wings. After sending off some telegrams by the town's only telephone, she ate at the Owl Café and enjoyed "the luxury of a real bed." She was grateful for the cool night, for she was severely sunburned. Her goggles had left her eyes surrounded by white rings of untanned skin, and she very much feared that by the time she reached Los Angeles she would "resemble a horned toad."[13]

At her next landing, back on course, in Pecos, Texas, when a tire proved to be flat, she "sat down gingerly" with no problem. But she had to stay in Pecos until needed engine parts arrived from El Paso. There, in Pecos, on September 8, a copy of her book *20 Hrs., 40 Min.: Our Flight in the Friendship,* caught up with her.

Another misadventure came to Amelia in Arizona. An overheated motor forced a landing "on a lonely ranch." Then, as the plane had proved unable to reach enough altitude to cross Arizona's mountains, she headed for the Mexican border and "followed the Southern Pacific

Railroad tracks through the lower country." At Yuma, Amelia asked "several residents" to help her tow the plane "to the end of the field for the takeoff." The overenthusiastic helpers pushed too hard, and the aircraft fell on its nose, bending the propeller. Amelia hammered it into position and took off, reaching Glendale, California, that afternoon.

At Los Angeles she visited Edwin and attended the National Air Races, renewing acquaintance with friends, some of whom she had not seen since she was a flight student. She disclaimed any intention of participating in the races. "I don't profess or pretend to be a flier. I am just an amateur, a dub," she told the press. Soon she returned to New York, making her the first woman to fly solo round-trip across the continent. Amelia, however, was not out to establish any records on this trip. She just wanted an interlude of fun before plunging into the next chapter of her life.[14]

She discovered that her mind had more or less been made up for her. Putnam had already lined up a formidable lecture tour. No persuasion was needed to find audiences—clubs, colleges, civic groups, all wanted to hear Amelia. Such celebrity lectures were a popular form of entertainment in those pretelevision days, and Amelia was just right for the times. In appearance, the female ideal of the day was slender, long-waisted, topped with a small bobbed head. Amelia could have been tailored to fit these specifications. Moreover, she was attractive enough to make looking at her a pleasure, while not so beautiful as to be a threat to the women in her audiences. Her public loved her for her honesty, her courage, her gentle humor. She seemed to typify the best of the Roaring Twenties with none of their vices—the gallant breaking with tradition, the eager acceptance of life, unspoiled by boozing, doping, and frenetic jazzing.

Amelia liked people and enjoyed talking about aviation, but George had overscheduled her. By the end of winter, she was a very tired young woman and happy to accept an offer to join *McCall's Magazine* as aviation editor. This job fell through because, before she could start work, an advertisement appeared for Lucky Strike cigarettes reading, "This is the brand that the crew of the *Friendship* carried."

When the tobacco firm first offered her $1,000, she had refused. To all intents and purposes she was a nonsmoker, with an annual intake of about three cigarettes. The firm upped the price to $1,500 and promised that she would not be asked to say that she personally smoked, only that the *Friendship* crew did. Amelia reluctantly agreed, not because of the money, which she promptly gave to Byrd for his second Antarctic expedition, or the promise, which at best was an evasion. She capitulated because Stultz and Gordon, who happened to smoke Luckies, had been offered $750 each, and the company would not accept the two men without Amelia.

Her loyalty cost her the *McCall's* job. The magazine wrote stiffly to Putnam as Amelia's agent, "We feel Miss Earhart's usefulness to *McCall's Magazine* is now questionable, in view of her recent sponsorship of a brand of cigarettes." The problem was not one of public health; the physical dangers of smoking were little, if at all, understood at that time. It was a question of image. While many women smoked, it was still considered not quite ladylike.

It all worked out for the best. Ray Long, editor of *Cosmopolitan Magazine,* offered her the post of an associate editor, committed to write at least eight articles that year. She accepted with pleasure and plunged into a series of articles that were immediately popular. Her writing was straightforward, authoritative, and spiced with her characteristic light style.[15]

If Amelia had hoped that this job would give her the daily semiprivacy of a small office, she was way off base. The lecture circuit continued unabated; she had to write her magazine articles in snatched moments aboard trains or in hotel rooms. It was not unusual for twenty-seven engagements to be scheduled in one month, with barely time for travel, and none at all for rest.

This pattern, which continued for years, may well have contributed to her untimely death. For all her wholesome, outdoor image, Amelia was not physically robust. George should have arranged—indeed, insisted upon—regular breaks in her schedule. Then, too, flying, like any other art, requires constant honing. She should have been spending several days a week sharpening her techniques and mastering such invaluable skills as Morse code and radio operation.

Not even his plentiful enemies ever accused George Putnam of being stupid, so he should have been well aware of these considerations. But if he had scruples, they went down like ninepins before the bowling ball of his ferocious craving for publicity. As for Amelia, at this time she still considered herself a "dub," an amateur, and lacked the true professional's drive toward perfection. Possibly she leaned overmuch on George's judgment. Having made him her manager, she let him manage—not a bad principle in most cases. George, however, definitely needed a restraining hand, which Amelia did not exert.

Flying was not a cheap hobby; she needed the money her engagements brought in. Nevertheless, a schedule of two well-placed lectures a week, three days of working seriously at her profession, with weekends of rest and recreation, would have been enough to keep Amelia's name before the public, and made her a better pilot and a healthier woman.

Amy worried about the strain her daughter was under but consoled herself that Amelia had inherited a valuable quality from her father—"when she reached a certain stage of exhaustion she was able to lie down and go right to sleep."

From the Missouri Pacific train Sunshine Special, Amelia wrote Amy on March 7, 1929, remembering her birthday and promising to "bring a sprize" when she returned east. "It seems funny to be riding on the M.P. without a pass. The same old bumps are in the road-bed."[16] She did not mention to Amy that four days before she had had another accident. While landing at Curtiss Field, her Avian "nosed over in the mud. . . . The propeller was wrenched and damaged." Amelia left the plane in the care of mechanics from Air Associates, who promptly installed a new propeller.[17]

Then on March 25 a severe thunder and hail storm forced her down in a cornfield near Utica, New York. Wading through ankle-deep mud, she turned the Avian away from the main force of the gale, then proceeded to a nearby farmhouse to telephone for help. Soon a truck came to move the plane to the Utica airport, and Amelia was free to pursue her purpose in flying to Utica—to surprise Muriel, who was teaching in that city, and to discuss plans for Muriel's wedding to Albert Morrissey. A pilot, Marwin K. Hart, and his wife invited the sisters to visit them overnight. The next morning, Amelia continued on her way to Buffalo, where she was scheduled to speak at an air show.[18]

A few days later, she was in Brownsville, Texas, where she took and passed "with flying colors" her tests for a transport license, which she received on March 28, 1929. This feat proves that while Amelia's expertise may never have quite caught up with her fame, she was far from a "dub." A transport license was the highest accreditation possible, and Amelia was only the fourth woman to achieve it. Her predecessors were Ruth Nichols, Lady Mary Heath, and Phoebe Fairgrave Omlie of Mono Aircraft Company.[19] Both before and after her marriage to Vernon Omlie, Phoebe had been a true daredevil, engaging in such feats as wing-walking, and her stunts had been featured in that silent film cliff-hanger, *The Perils of Pauline*. But the Omlies were also committed to aviation in a serious way, and in later years Phoebe would serve as an adviser in that field in the Roosevelt administration.[20]

In addition to Amelia's scheduled lectures and her magazine articles, she found herself adviser and confidante to a generation of airstruck youngsters, many suffering from the generation gap. "My mother won't let me fly" was a common wail of frustration. A good second on the complaint list was the conservatism of many colleges, some even forbidding air travel between the students' homes and the campus, on pain of expulsion.

Amelia knew very well that these young men and women were going to get into the air somehow, come hell, high water, mothers, or deans. She worried about the youngsters who haunted every airfield, accepting any free ride offered them with total disregard for the plane's condition or the pilot's qualifications.

Some mothers did not issue a flat ban but tried to postpone the inevitable. "I shall let my daughter fly when she is sixteen"—or some other arbitrary figure reached who knows how.

"Why not now?" Amelia would reply amiably, a query that brought forth some amusing but seldom rational answers. And, as Amelia wrote dryly, "Sometimes I knew Daughter had already been up, so the explanation did not matter anyway."[21]

Amelia was not a belligerent feminist, but her logical mind found absurd the current culture pattern that forced individuals into pigeonholes according to their sex rather than in accordance with their talents and wishes. In token of these feelings, she presented a trophy to be awarded to the girl making the best record in a model airplane tournament being held in late May. "Girls have had few opportunities to express their mechanical bent," she stated. "Yet some of them would prove better carpenters than cooks, just as some boys would make better pies than machines. . . . Model making gives a background in aeronautics that women as well as men will need tomorrow."[22]

Chapter 7

Gain and Loss

*I*n June, Muriel was in a flurry of last-minute preparations for her marriage that month. Of course, Amelia was to be maid of honor. She had promised to be in Medford in time to attend a rehearsal and party the night before the ceremony. Time passed and no Amelia. Muriel hovered between worry and resentment at her sister's "seeming indifference." Just as the party was setting out for the church, Amelia phoned. "Pidge, I'm terribly sorry—I'm fog-bound in New Jersey. Don't worry; I'll be down tomorrow morning, even if I have to take (heaven forbid!) a train."

She was as good as her word and supported her sister with charm and dignity. Sam Chapman was an usher, and the ever-hopeful cupids of the press noted that his eyes seldom left Amelia.

After the ceremony the minister, the Reverend Dwight Hadley, asked Amelia something about her sensations on the Atlantic flight. Amelia replied, "I think what Pidge has just done today took more courage than my flying did." He could not accept this without a gentle rebuttal: "When you meet the man whom you deeply love and respect and who feels the same toward you, marriage is the happiest and most natural thing in the world." Amelia merely nodded in reply.[1]

In 1929 Amelia had her first direct experience in the business world. In July she joined the traffic department of Transcontinental Air Transport (TAT) to operate a plane-and-train service from New York to Los Angeles. From the perspective of today, the schedule sounds most peculiar. One left New York City on a Monday evening by train to Columbus, Ohio; changed to a plane as far as Waynoka, Kansas; took the train there to Clovis, New Mexico; and there finally emplaned for Los Angeles, arriving Wednesday evening.[2]

Lindbergh flew the first east-bound plane, changing to the first west-bound one, aboard which Amelia was a passenger, and piloted it to the West Coast. Anne Lindbergh accompanied him, and under these circumstances Amelia met her for the first time. Amelia took an immediate liking to this "extremely gentle person, essentially modest, totally lacking mannerisms, pretenses and superiorities."[3]

Anne Lindbergh was equally impressed with Amelia. She immediately realized that Amelia's likeness to her husband went far beyond a mere physical resemblance. She remarked on how alike the two pilots were in breadth and how intelligent and well-balanced Amelia was.[4]

Two of Amelia's associates at TAT were Paul "Dog" Collins and Eugene Vidal. Collins, the superintendent of operations, was a former airmail pilot with some eight thousand hours of flying time. As Amelia wrote, "A great pilot himself, he understood the background of airplanes and other pilots." He was a member of the Caterpillar Club, composed of those who had saved their lives by parachuting from their planes, and Amelia loved to hear him tell of "hitting the silk" over a wilderness section of Pennsylvania, less worried about possibly landing in a tree than about encountering a bear.

Gene Vidal was a member of the technical staff, involved in most analysis and passenger problems. A former Army pilot, he had been an All-American football player and track star at West Point and "a member of several Olympic teams."[5]

Amelia helped arrange schedules, but her principal task was "to sell flying to women." Air ticket sellers claimed that many more men would fly but for the fears of their wives. How much of this was valid, and how much a face-saving device on the part of men themselves hesitant to fly, is anybody's guess, but TAT took it seriously enough to send Amelia far and wide to combat it. She had the use of TAT's planes whenever she preferred not to use her own. In her missionary work her best "teaching aid" was Amy, who often flew with her. In fact, Amy grew so blasé about air travel that it rather bored her, and she usually took along a detective story to keep from falling asleep. Thus, in the most impressive way possible, Amelia "put her money where her mouth was" by entrusting to the air not only her own life but the life of the person she loved best.[6]

Toward the end of July the Putnams and Amelia took a brief vacation to Block Island, Rhode Island, to enjoy some water sports. Both women were excellent swimmers. After a morning of spearfishing, on July 22 Amelia attempted a deep-sea dive from the demonstration submarine *Defender*. Frank Crilly, a noted deep-sea diver, fastened Amelia into his own suit, and she slipped over the side. Just before her helmet disappeared beneath the surface, Crilly and Commander Sloan Danenhower, skipper of the sub, unceremoniously hauled her out, "much to her surprise and without any signal from her." The men had noticed that the suit was leaking, Amelia's slim wrists being too small for the suit's rubber wrist fasteners.

Unfortunately, newspaper accounts of the incident gave the impression that Amelia had lost her nerve. Understandably annoyed, Amelia went down the next day, accompanied by Crilly, and remained on the bottom for some twelve minutes. It was no big deal to Amelia: "Plenty of women have been deeper and stayed longer."[7]

August found Amelia and her mother in Los Angeles, but Amy took a train back to New York the day after their arrival. On August 14, Amelia wired her: "OKAY VISIT MURIEL. SENDING CHECK FOR HER. DON'T WORRY ABOUT RACE."[8]

The race in question was the Women's Air Derby from California to Cleveland, the first such event. Amelia had sold her Avian and bought a Lockheed Vega to enter the race. The Vega was a monoplane largely of wooden construction. She admitted that her acquisition "was a third hand clunk but to me a heavenly chariot." Thinking that "possibly there might be a few adjustments necessary" before she entered the race, she flew the Vega from New York to check it out with the Lockheed factory in California.

There for the first time she met Wiley Post, then "a routine check pilot" for Lockheed. He took up the Vega and came down "to tell everyone within earshot that my lovely airplane was the foulest he had ever flown," as Amelia later recorded. Of course, the more Post disparaged the plane, the better pilot Amelia seemed to be, to have been "able to herd such a hopeless piece of mechanism across the continent successfully." The upshot was, in Amelia's words, "Finally Lockheed officials were so impressed by my prowess (or so sorry for me) that they traded me a brand new plane. The clunk was never flown again."[9]

There were only some sixty licensed women pilots in the United States, and nineteen of them started, despite widespread predictions that at the last minute nobody would show up. Moreover, Amelia later remarked in a radio talk, "I had been assured confidentially by various fliers along the route that they all had their dustpans ready to sweep up the two or three women who might start, and their airplanes, for they considered it inevitable that wreckage of the Derby would be scattered all the way across the continent."[10]

Will Rogers presided over the start, and for once his humor was not appreciated, being of the heavy-handed, cutesy type guaranteed to inspire any woman with thoughts of murder. The press took its cue from Rogers and named the race "the Powder Puff Derby" and the contestants such names as "Angels" and "Lady birds."

All nineteen completed the first lap, from Santa Monica to San Bernardino, except Mary Elizabeth von Mack. The field was too crowded for her heavy plane and she turned back to Montbello; however, she may have rejoined, because the *New York Times* of August 27, 1929, lists her among the finishers. Margaret Perry had to pull out early when she developed typhoid fever. Several accidents marred the race and one fatality: Marvel Crosson of San Diego, who held the current women's altitude record, did not reach the control stop at Phoenix. A search party the next day found her body. She had been forced to bail out, and her parachute did not open.

Advice poured in to stop the race, some even claiming that it had been proved conclusively that women could not fly. The contestants voted unanimously to continue. "It was all the more necessary that we keep on flying," Amelia told the press. "We all felt terribly, but we knew that now we had to finish."[11]

At Yuma Amelia crashed into a sandbank, damaging a propeller although not herself. Her colleagues voted to wait until her Vega was repaired, a gesture of good sportsmanship she much appreciated. Fortunately her fellow fliers did not suffer by it, because flying time scored did not include time spent in repairs.[12]

At various stops autograph hounds surged around the planes. A cigarette tossed away casually landed in the cockpit of Blanche Noyes's aircraft. She did not discover it until airborne, when the butt ignited a fire and Blanche had to land. She was soon back in the air.

At a food-and-fuel stop at Pecos, Florence "Pancho" Barnes overshot the runway and peeled the top off a car parked too close to it. She was pulled out of her plane unhurt and would become a legend as a stunt flier and racer.

Rumors of sabotage started. At the end of the race, however, the finishers, with one exception, agreed that the rumors were groundless. The exception was Thea Rasche of Germany, who "declared that her fuel line had been fouled by dirt and that she hoped to find out how it happened."[13]

The fifth stop was at Wichita, the sixth at St. Louis. At Columbus, the final break before Cleveland, sixteen of the original nineteen were still in the race. Amelia landed two minutes ahead of Ruth Nichols. When time came for Nichols's takeoff, she left the ground and her right wing dipped, striking a tractor. The plane somersaulted three times before screeching to a halt. It seemed impossible that anyone could have survived such a horrendous crash. Amelia cut off her engine, vaulted out of the Vega, and sped to the scene. Miraculously, Ruth was unhurt except for bruises, but perforce out of the race.[14]

The other Ruth—Elder—had to land and ask directions when the wind ripped her map from her hand. No sooner had she landed than her bright red aircraft attracted the interested attention of a herd of cattle. "Oh God, let them all be cows!" she prayed. She got off safely and came in fifth in the heavy plane division.[15]

Louise Thaden won in that division, although since the first leg she had had to breathe bending forward to get oxygen from a four-inch tube to avoid carbon monoxide from the exhaust pipe. Gladys O'Donnel, a mother of two from Long Beach, placed second. Amelia came in third with Blanche Noyes close behind.[16]

Well now! Evidently the Fates were sadly lacking in a sense of dramatic inevitability. Here was the most famous woman pilot in the country, flying a brand-new aircraft—and she came in third. Did that mean Amelia was a poor flier? By no means. To come in third against such competition was no disgrace. In a modest article, Louise Thaden credited her victory, not to herself but to her aircraft. "I won because I had a faster ship. And even then I had to fly wide open."

Muriel averred that "winning was immaterial" to Amelia. What mattered was that the race proved that women could fly, and fly well.[17] The women had also demonstrated that they had the courage to persevere in the face of adversity, and the sort of good sportsmanship toward one another of which women were commonly believed incapable.

As an indirect result of the derby, four pilots—Margery Brown, Fay Gillis, Frances Harrell, and Neva Paris—wrote to all licensed American women pilots, proposing that they form an organization. Twenty-six women, including Amelia, met at Curtiss Airport to initiate the group. Some of the names proposed as the title were so ridiculous that finally Amelia proposed that it be called by the number of charter members. Thus was born the famous Ninety-Nines, with Amelia as first president.[18]

Much of the autumn of 1929 Amelia spent in California. On November 22 she scribbled a pencil note to Amy that she was "having a lovely time here flying a great deal." She was also working hard and had her secretary, Nora Alstulund, with her on the West Coast.

Amelia visited her father and his new wife, Helen, whom Muriel described as "a mature and kindly woman whom he had met in the Christian Science congregation." Edwin had made a down payment on a small cabin in Eagle Rock, a little north of Los Angeles. He was happy with his "cheerful and understanding" wife, but far from well. Amelia wrote to Muriel, "I'm afraid Dad may not enjoy his little cabin too long, Pidge. . . . He looks thinner than I've ever seen him, and Helen says he has no appetite at all and tires very quickly now."

Helen had a steady but small income as a saleswoman for a jewelry firm, but Edwin could not bring himself to send bills to the friends to whom he had given expert advice. As a result he was worried about mortgage payments. Amelia paid off the mortgage, some two thousand dollars, arranging "a life tenancy freehold" first for Edwin, then Helen, for their lifetimes. She retained title in her own name, designating Amy, then Muriel, as her heirs to the property.

Apparently all was not moonlight and roses for the Morrisseys. About this time Amelia wrote to her mother about Muriel, who was pregnant with her first child: "By all means stay with Pidge. I think she needs you and apparently Albert is no judge. Keep out of his way and disappear when he is about. Poor old Sis, I'm sorry she's having so much rotten luck."

On December 10 she wrote Amy, "Hooray for Chrizmuzz. Here's something for you and Pidge." She hoped to be with them for the holiday but could not be sure. She added, "Let me know when you are short and I'll send along some cash."[19]

These two letters mark a change in Amelia's standing in the family. Her father was dying, Albert Morrissey was showing signs of being in his way as irresponsible as Edwin, Muriel was tied down by her pregnancy and later by the care of two small children, and by neither temperament nor training was Amy suited to take the helm. By default Amelia became head of the family.

Another family also had been having its problems. George and Dorothy Putnam had drifted apart and agreed upon divorce, which became final on December 20, 1929. Dorothy moved to Florida with the two boys, and on January 12, 1930, in the West Indies, married Frank Monroe Upton of New York. George promptly proposed to Amelia, who just as promptly turned him down. George proposed no less than five times over the ensuing year, receiving five friendly but definite rejections.[20]

Amelia was involved with another airline. Collins and Vidal left TAT and, financed by Townsend and Nicholas Ludington of Philadelphia, established the New York, Philadelphia, and Washington Airway, sometimes called "the Ludington Line," offering ten round trips daily between the three cities. Amelia went with them. This was the sort of pioneering challenge she enjoyed. There were a number of strikes against the line. The New York–Washington corridor had frequent and excellent train and bus service, so no one really had to fly to get from one city to another. The line had no government airmail contract, considered a financial sine qua non. Moreover, Collins and Vidal offered their passengers no special luxuries, cutting such expenses to the bone. To the surprise of everyone but the founders, the line was a success. In its first year, the line carried 66,279 passengers and flew 1,523,400 miles. The daily totals exceeded "the combined totals of the various lines flying from London to Paris."

Amelia's duties were reeling in passengers and keeping them satisfied. This involved "endless letters" and equally endless speech schedules. She soon learned that the happy passenger seldom said so: "It is the disgruntled one who takes pen in hand and writes and writes and writes." Those unused to air travel could not understand why their amount of baggage was limited when no such restriction existed on railroads. The line carried some express items, which resulted in occasional oddities. Amelia personally "chaperoned a canary from New York to Washington." A pony was transported from Philadelphia to Washington, occupying two seats.

Officially pets were prohibited, but at the end of each flight a surprising number of "demi-tasse dogs" emerged from coats and furs. The line granted an exception to one woman who begged to take her pet along. "It's a lap dog, my dearest possession," she pleaded. At the appointed hour she showed up with something the size of "a young heifer." The airline had its revenge. She had specified a lap dog, and she must hold him on her lap or leave him behind. The discomfited women chose the first alternative.

Eventually the owners sold the line to a competing company. Gene Vidal shortly joined the Department of Commerce as assistant secretary for air, and Paul Collins went to the Boston & Maine Airway, where Amelia joined him for a short time.[21]

The year 1930 opened with Amelia and Nora Alstulund sharing "a large double room" to enable her to live on her earnings and help Amy financially. She wrote her mother on February 3 from New York enclosing a check for a hundred dollars, adding, "Hereafter you will receive it monthly from the Fifth Avenue Bank. I have put all my earnings into stocks and bonds and the yearly income in your name." At that time, one hundred dollars a month was a very acceptable income; many were working full time for considerably less.

Through much of 1930, however, Amelia's main concern was for her father. When Muriel's son David was born, Amy wrote to Edwin, who replied pleasantly. He was happy to be a grandfather. He did not see much of Amelia but followed her in the newspapers. Mendaciously, he added that he was very much better.[22]

On June 25, Amelia was in Detroit where she established two speed records in her Lockheed Vega, with its Pratt and Whitney Wasp engines of 420 hp, one for 100 kilometers at 174.89 mph, the other at 171.49 mph for the same distance with a payload of 500 kilograms.[23] Three days later, she wrote to Amy that Edwin would have to have an operation. "Of course I'll have to stand the expense and will gladly but I wish I knew who the physician is and something about him." She had written to Helen Earhart for more details.

Back in New York, Amelia found a letter from Edwin dated June 27. He was too weak to undergo the recommended operation, and his physician, C. M. Hensley, had advised him to go to a sanitarium to build up his strength and gain some weight. He weighed only 105 pounds. Rather wistfully, he mentioned his hope of soon realizing some money on one of his cases. Amelia made a quick trip west to see for herself what the situation was. Then, once more in New York, she wrote Amy on August 8. Edwin was "desperately ill—starving to death. There is a stricture of some kind which prevents his taking much nourishment." His mind was clear and he insisted he was better, but Helen was "almost breaking under the strain," so Amelia offered to help with "monthly payments so she could rest."[24]

About a month later, Muriel wrote to Dr. Hensley asking about her father's condition. He replied on September 3 that Edwin had stomach cancer and an operation would only hasten his death. The outlook was grave with "little hope for his recovery." That same day the doctor wired Amelia: Would she guarantee $175 to cover the cost of an "absolutely necessary" blood transfusion? This she did immediately.

After about two weeks, Dr. Hensley wired again that she must come to Eagle Rock soon. Helen also wired: Edwin was "perfectly rational" and eager to see Amelia. Amelia had been under a heavy financial strain and the idea of another trip to the West Coast "almost staggered" her; however, she could not do other than grant her father's wish. Yet, because Edwin was not suffering, she could not believe he really had cancer. She spent about a week with her father and stepmother, during which she had to face the facts. For a time Edwin had shown such "marked improvement" that Helen, too, was unable to believe the diagnosis. Edwin himself did not know what his problem was.[25]

The daughter whose first word was "Papa" and his second wife conspired lovingly to make Edwin's last days as happy as possible. He lost the "big case" he had hoped would bring him some money; Helen and Amelia told him he had won it. Amelia "paid the hundred little debts he always had." He frequently asked about Amy and Muriel, and Amelia faked telegrams from them to him.

Believing that Edwin was showing improvement, she left for New York on Tuesday, September 23. She got no farther than Tucson when a wire from Helen reached her: Edwin had died about eight hours after Amelia left. So she hurried back to California and stayed for the funeral, then returned to New York. She wrote Amy on October 2, "He was an aristocrat as he went—all the weaknesses gone with a little boy's brown puzzled eyes."[26]

In addition to the ordeal of Edwin's passing, Amelia was fretting about Amy and Muriel. The Morrisseys were living in quarters not at all to Amelia's liking. She wrote Amy in mid-September: "I do hope Pidge moves out of her hole. I feel as you do it's bad for health and morale. All the middleclassness of the family heritage bursts into bloom in such surroundings. All the fineness—for there's some—is squashed. It would be unless you were around."

Amelia knew her mother's impulsive generosity, and a letter written in mid-October reveals her worry that Amy would give her money "to Pidge and the Balises." Amy's niece, Nancy Balis, was a favorite with her. "However," Amelia continued, "I am not working to support either. Little things are all right but I don't want any large proportion to get out of your hands—borrowed or given."[27]

The loss of her much-loved father, worry about her mother and sister, and the year's heavy financial drain, along with her regular schedule of work and lectures, were enough to make the most altar-shy of women have second thoughts about marriage. Would it not be pleasant if there were someone with whom one came first, someone of one's own generation with whom one could talk about something beyond trivialities, someone with whom to share a civilized social life?

Such thoughts might have occurred to any single woman in Amelia's circumstances. In her case, however, for marriage to have a chance her husband must have certain qualifications. First, he must recognize that for Amelia freedom and a certain amount of solitude were as essential as food and drink. Of course, in the larger sense she was not free—no one is really free who has gainful employment, family ties, and high public visibility. Second, he must be supportive of her flying. Third, he must be sufficiently well established in his own field, and have a strong enough ego, not to be jealous and resentful of her fame. Fourth—really implicit in the other three—he must have plenty of money. To put it brutally, Amelia could not afford to marry a poor man. She was not mercenary; the things money meant to many women—jewels, furs, designer clothes, expensive cars, being seen in the right place at the right time—meant nothing to her. But she needed funds for her flying, and she knew she would always have to support her mother.

Waiting in the wings was a man who fulfilled all of these conditions, and who had already proposed to Amelia five times. So it is not too surprising that when George popped the question for the sixth time, Amelia accepted. The site was not romantic—a Lockheed hangar at Burbank, where they were waiting for Amelia's Vega to warm up, surrounded by roaring motors and scurrying mechanics. Amelia nodded, gave George's arm a friendly pat, and scrambled aboard. The last George saw of her for several days was a fluttering scarf.[28]

Amy was not at all happy with the engagement. The not very logical reasons she set forth were that George was twelve years older than Amelia and divorced. The age gap was not too broad for two people no longer in their first youth, and Amy herself was divorced. Very likely she found distressing the realization that she would no longer come first with Amelia. At times one senses a coolness between Amy and George. He called her "Mrs. Earhart" until Amelia's disappearance, when he began to call her "Mother Earhart."[29]

He and Amelia were married on February 7, 1931, at the home of his mother, Frances Putnam, in Noank, Connecticut. For once, George had restrained his public relations instincts, and no one knew about the event until it was over. Even his mother did not know until the sixth that the seventh would be the day. Probate Judge Arthur Anderson of Groton performed the five-minute ceremony. The only witnesses were Frances Putnam; Judge Anderson's son, Robert; George's uncle, Charles Faulkner; "and twin black cats." Once again Amelia was "the girl in brown"—she wore a brown suit, brown crepe blouse, brown shoes.[30]

Just before the judge, a family friend, arrived, Amelia slipped a letter into George's hand—"a sad little letter, brutal in its frankness, but beautiful in its honesty":

▶ There are some things which should be writ before we are married. Things we have talked over before—most of them.

You must know again my reluctance to marry, my feeling that I shatter thereby chances in work which means so much to me. I feel the move just now as foolish as anything I could do. I know there may be compensations, but have no heart to look ahead.

In our life together I shall not hold you to any medieval code of faithfulness to me, nor shall I consider myself bound to you similarly. If we can be honest I think the difficulties which arise may best be avoided. . . .

Please let us not interfere with the other's work or play, nor let the world see our private joys or disagreements. In this connection I may have to keep some place where I can go to be myself now and then, for I cannot guarantee to endure at all times the confinement of even an attractive cage.

I must exact a cruel promise, and that is you will let me go in a year if we find no happiness together.

I will try to do my best in every way. . . .[31]

This vote of no confidence failed to deter George. Perhaps he was insightful enough to see in this letter less a declaration of independence than an appeal for understanding. In any case, Amelia was the bright particular star to which he had hitched his wagon. He had no intention of bowing out. So he smiled at her, nodded agreement, took her hand, and led her to the ceremony.

One of Amelia's first acts as Mrs. George Putnam was to wire Muriel: "Over the broomstick with GP today. Break the news gently to mother." Muriel and Alfred wired their best wishes, closing with a Gypsy blessing: "May the floods never reach your cooking pots."

Naturally the wedding of Amelia Earhart and George Putnam was a nine days' wonder, and the press did full justice to it. Many friends of both parties feared that the marriage could not last.[32] Certainly it did not follow the standard pattern of the day. But there is no real reason to believe that the Putnams were not well content with themselves.

How sexually compatible they were or were not we do not know and doubt if anyone else does. In these days of "kiss and tell" it is sometimes difficult to remember that there was a time when no one with any pretensions to good breeding would have dreamed of airing the intimacies of their marriage.

Muriel, who knew Amelia perhaps better than anyone else, pointed out that they had much in common. Both loved good books, the theater, classical music, fine painting. Amelia admired people of real accomplishment and enjoyed meeting such friends of George as explorer Roy Chapman Andrews, artist Rockwell Kent, and actress Cornelia Otis Skinner. With the last Amelia felt a special rapport, delighting in her gentle wit and gift for seeing the absurd.

On February 22, 1931, Amelia wrote to her mother praising Amy's handling of an interview she had given in Philadelphia. She continued, "I am much happier than I expected I could ever be in that state. I believe the whole thing was for the best." She invited Amy to come see their apartment. "I have two canaries and you know I've wanted one for ever so long."

George made certain changes in his life to free himself to devote almost all of his time to managing Amelia's career. He sold his interest in G. P. Putnam's Sons and signed on as chief of the editorial department at Paramount Pictures.[33]

Possibly the best indication that the marriage was sound was the fact that at the end of a year Amelia did not exercise her option to call it a day.

She had been married only two months when the opportunity arose to break new ground. As she wrote later, "Just then the autogiro was the very newest thing in aviation, and so naturally enough I found myself drawn to it." The autogiro had an unpowered rotating propeller above the fuselage for lift; a conventional propeller gave forward movement. The autogiro has been almost entirely superseded by the helicopter with its engine-powered rotating blades.

Her first flight in this type of craft came "near Philadelphia on a bright spring day" when veteran autogiro pilot James B. "Jim" Ray took her up for "fifteen or twenty minutes. . . . He made a couple of landings and then brought his giro to a stop." Demonstrating a touching faith in his passenger, he climbed out, saying, "Now you take it up." Despite her misgivings, for Ray had given her no instructions, she took off, feeling "a novice again, with all of the uncertainty of a beginner." This impromptu solo made Amelia "the only woman to have flown alone in an autogiro."

No one knew how high a stock model autogiro could climb, so later she was given the chance to "take one upstairs and keep on going until it would go no farther."[34] Some newspapers pointed out that she could not "help but establish a record," for no other woman had attempted it. Rain and fog canceled her first trip, scheduled for April 7, 1931, at Pitcairn Field near Willow Grove, Pennsylvania.[35] The next day was sunny and pleasant, so she tried again. The whistles at the Pitcairn factory had just blown for noon when she took off. Among the five hundred or so spectators were the plant's three hundred employees, who had formed a pool. Each held a numbered slip, the one nearest the altitude achieved to be the winner.

This was not strictly an attempt at a record for a record's sake; this was a test of the craft's capability. The autogiro she had purchased was not ready for delivery, so she flew a standard model with no special modifications. To record the result, a sealed barograph was placed on board, as well as "a simple oxygen outfit" in case Amelia should need it.[36]

At 18,500 feet the giro was still climbing, and Amelia was sure she could have reached 22,000 feet, despite occasional strong winds. She used only "a few whiffs" of the oxygen and was too well bundled up and too interested to feel the cold, but the gasoline was dangerously low. She promptly came down, and had the giro refueled for a second attempt. She took off again at 6:04 P.M. At that hour the crowd had thinned out considerably, and only a scattering of spectators, including George, were present when she landed the second time, having added 500 feet to her first mark.[37]

Chapter 8

Daughter, Sister, Wife

pproximately two weeks after her autogiro altitude record,
Amelia went to the hospital for minor surgery. From a letter to Amy dated April 27, 1931, it appears she had a ton-
sillectomy. "I'm home now but almost inarticulate. Also the
knees are a bit wobbly."

At this time Amelia was less concerned with her own painful throat
and shaky knees than with her sister. Earlier in the year she had lent
Muriel twenty-five hundred dollars—a very substantial sum in the
1930s—to enable the Morrisseys to make a down payment on "a decent
house." This they did, moving into a home large enough to provide a
bedroom for Amy, and another for David and whatever children might
follow him.

Warm-hearted, family-oriented Muriel could not understand that
such a loan was a business proposition, not a casual favor between sisters. In the same letter telling Amy of her operation, Amelia wrote
with some exasperation: "Please have Muriel send me a properly
drawn second mortgage. I suppose it is impossible to impress upon her
the fact that [a] businesslike relationship between relatives is not an
unfriendly act. . . . I'm no Scrooge to ask that some acknowledgment of
a twentyfive hundred dollar loan should be given me. . . . You understand but I think she never will. . . ."[1]

Muriel knew well that Amelia was no "Scrooge." In addition to the
financial support she gave her family, there were such incidents as
Uncle Theodore and the white horse. On a visit to Atchison, "Cousin
Jim" Challis took Amelia to visit her uncle Theodore Otis, her mother's
brother who had been slightly retarded from birth. He had a little

chicken farm, where Amelia and Jim found him devastated by the recent death of his old horse, Whitey, who had been his partner in delivering eggs for some twenty years. "He was my whole family to me," her uncle, in tears, told Amelia.

She conferred hastily with Jim, then turned back to Theodore and told him gently that Whitey had gone "to the good horses' heaven" and they couldn't bring him back, but Jim would get him another white horse right away. Theodore was so grateful and delighted that, as they left the farm, Amelia remarked to Jim, "I never spent a happier fifty dollars, I'm sure."

One of her friends in the Ninety-Nines had an alcoholic husband; Amelia paid for his treatment, which lasted six months. Later she helped one of her former mechanics, who was tubercular, to establish a date farm in Arizona. And, Muriel noted, "There were many other similar 'little lifts,' as Amelia called her deeds of kindness, known only to herself and her checkbook."[2]

No, it was not parsimony that prompted Amelia to put the loan on a businesslike basis. The problem was Albert. On the surface, the Morrisseys' was a conventional marriage. Albert left for work every day; Muriel earned four or five dollars a week teaching at Grace Church Day School, while Amy baby-sat with little David.

Muriel kept up a good front, and her neighbors would have been astonished to learn how uncomfortable was her home life. Albert took spells when he would not speak to Muriel "for weeks on end," he paid no attention to David, he refused to help his own mother in any way, and he gave Muriel seventy-five dollars a month from which he expected her to pay all the household and personal expenses. By deft financial juggling, Muriel kept the household going and in a neat condition, although she feared to invite visitors because she never knew what mood her husband would be in.

Probably she could not have managed without the extra income from her church work. Fortunately, she enjoyed teaching, so her job gave her much-needed pleasure as well as a few extra dollars. Amy was no drain on the household—far from it. She had her monthly check from Amelia and slipped Muriel an occasional few dollars, not to mention acting as unpaid baby tender. To top it all off, Muriel was pregnant with her second child.

As for Albert, his only interest seemed to be the local American Legion post, of which he was a pillar. No matter how many corners Muriel had to cut, he always had funds to pay his dues, contribute to various Legion-sponsored drives, and keep his uniform spruce.[3] The impression is that Albert was one of those individuals perpetually stuck at the adolescent level, pleasant as long as they are not called upon to accept mature responsibility, and unfit for the inevitable stresses of marriage.

Early in May, having recovered from her surgery, Amelia addressed the Athletic Association at Barnard College, with a typical balance of optimism and realism. There was no physical reason why women should not enter aviation, she stressed; they just had to work twice as hard as a man to get the same recognition. This was the fault of the educational system, which was based "on sex, not on aptitude." This was a favorite theme of Amelia's, and to espouse it publicly took almost as much courage as to fly the Atlantic. At that time, and for years to come, airing such notions left one open to the deadly charge of being "unwomanly."[4]

Accompanied by mechanic Eddie McVaugh, she left Newark, New Jersey, in her autogiro on May 28, 1931. A large sign on the fuselage read "Beech-Nut Packing Company," the firm that financed the venture for the advertising. Amelia was glad of the chance to test the craft "on a long trip, under all kinds of weather conditions." She followed the northern mail route and experienced only one delay. The fuel tank developed a leak, and she had to remain overnight at Battle Field, Mc-Keesport, Pennsylvania. She reached Oakland on June 6, the first woman to cross the country by giro, and, indeed, hers was only the second such craft to reach the West Coast.[5]

On June 12, on her way back east, Amelia had a crack-up at Abilene, Texas. Newspaper accounts stated that "by skillful operation of her autogiro" she escaped serious injury "when the ship failed to rise quickly on a takeoff." Amelia remarked that she "did not take a long enough run on the takeoff." The news report added that "a whirlwind, common this season of the year in West Texas, developed under the giro, resulting in a decrease in the pressure that caused the plane to fall with greater force."[6]

On June 20 it was announced that the Department of Commerce would reprimand Amelia for "carelessness and poor judgment" because of her accident that had "wrecked several automobiles." Amelia protested that she had brought the giro down "in the only space available to prevent hitting any cars or hurting any people." She added that the rotor struck one car, but she did not believe any serious damage resulted. Evidently someone in authority had second thoughts, for the reprimand, when it came, "wasn't one really," as Amelia wrote Amy. "I am not a careless pilot and the letter doesn't say so."[7]

Home in late June, she wrote to invite Amy to visit her and George. "I think Pidge could spare you for a lil while and mebbe you need the rest before the second coming, if I may put it that way." But Amy could not leave Muriel with her baby due shortly. Amelia wrote to her mother in July, "I didn't realize Pidge was so near. I certainly hope she makes it as easily as possible. Also that she has learned enough about anatomy to prevent further trials for a while."[8]

On one level, this was crass impertinence; Muriel and Albert's sex life was none of Amelia's business. Nevertheless, one can imagine that this was her slightly panicky reaction to a vision of little Morrisseys arriving in an annual procession for Amelia to support and Amy to wear herself out tending.

Muriel's daughter was born on July 31 and named Amy for her grandmother. About two weeks later, Amelia visited Muriel to pay her respects to her new niece. As always, Muriel and Amy were delighted to see Amelia. For all their problems, this was a loving and united family.[9]

Amy's future was a constant worry to Amelia. Granted the family record of longevity, her mother might well live to be one hundred, and if she persisted in giving her money to Muriel she could end up in poverty. In view of Albert's attitude toward his own mother, it was un-likely that he would support his mother-in-law, and Amelia might not always be around to take up the slack. She knew that someday there might come an accident she did not survive.

In fact, she did have another crack-up, three months to the day following her misadventure of June 12. This took place in Detroit, when she was ferrying her giro from the airport to the state fairgrounds. As she explained to Amy, "The landing gear gave way from a defect and I ground-looped only. The rotors were smashed as usual with giros, but there wasn't even a jar."[10]

George witnessed the crash, "vaulted the rail and raced for the wreck on the wings of fear." A guy wire caught his legs at the ankles. He "did a complete outside loop, up into the air and over," landing full on his back. He sustained three cracked ribs; Amelia "had not a scratch." As he limped toward his wife, she hurried forward, impul-sively crying out, "It's all my fault!" Seeing that he was not seriously injured, she regained her poise and grinned at him, saying, "So flying is the safest, after all. If you'd been with me, you wouldn't have been hurt."[11]

Somehow the newspapers got hold of Amelia's involuntary "It's all my fault!" and decided that she was blaming the crack-up entirely on herself, although she had meant only that George's injury was her fault. Once more she was forcibly reminded of the imbalance in news-paper coverage of a plane crash involving a male pilot and one involv-ing a female. In fact, one aircraft manufacturer told her frankly that this was why he "couldn't risk hiring woman pilots," despite their capability. "A man can damage a plane and hardly a word be said," he explained to Amelia, "but that doesn't apply when sister stubs her toe." Amelia could do nothing but accept the publicity as best she could. Another giro was rushed out from Philadelphia in time for her to meet her next appointment in a midwestern city.[12]

Throughout her busy schedule, Amelia continued to strive mightily to instill some financial sense into her delightful but impractical mother, which occasionally made Amelia sound unpleasantly penny-pinching. In the same letter to Amy describing her second giro accident, written on September 17, 1931, she asked Amy to remind Muriel that she had received only "the first notation of the mortgage arrangements." She wanted "a certified copy accompanied with notes which could be handled by a bank if desirable. These can be just for the record." Muriel did not respond, leaving one to wonder if Amy ever delivered the message.

Sometime in the fall of 1931, Amelia wrote a letter to Amy worth quoting as revealing the depth of her worry and irritation over her mother's financial situation:

> I am enclosing a check for $33. This plus the $17 I sent last month makes $50. I am depositing the rest of the amount to your credit here. I am very much displeased at the use you have put what I hoped you would save. I am not working to help Albert, or Pidge much as I care for her. If they had not had that money perhaps they would have found means to economize before.
>
> I do not mean to be harsh, but I know the family failing about money. As for your paying board, such a thing is unthinkable as you have done all the housekeeping which more than compensates. . . .
>
> It is true that I have a home and food but what I send you is what I myself earn and it does not come from GP. I feel the church gets some of what should go to living expenses and I have no wish to continue that to Pidge's loss. . . .[13]

George and Amelia had worked out an unusual but practical financial arrangement. They divided expenses into exact halves; anything left over went into a fund they called "¿Quien sabe?" They divided their time between George's house in Rye and "a small hotel apartment" in New York City. Amelia had, as George put it, "no special flair for housekeeping . . . and spent no time torturing herself with a conventional longing to be expert." But she liked an orderly, well-run home, and every morning she was in residence she started the day with a visit to the kitchen to be sure that the day's needs would be met and the household staff satisfied. As she had in girlhood, she did a bit of gardening, especially enjoying her harvest of "little kumquat-shaped yellow tomatoes" that she placed in bowls strategically located for nibbling.

She considered her independence not a hazard to the marriage but a strength. She suspected that all too many women regarded matrimony as a social storm shelter. In contrast, she believed "that the effect of having other interests beyond those exclusively domestic works well. The more one does and sees and feels, the more one is able to do, and the more genuine may be one's appreciation of fundamental things like home, and love and understanding companionship."

She continued to use her maiden name, and George thought this only reasonable. As "Amelia Earhart" she was known and indeed loved all across the United States. Sometimes newspapers referred to her as "Mrs. Putnam"; George never did.[14]

That "Amelia Earhart" meant something far beyond the United States is evidenced by a Japanese girl, Mizno Iriye Yamada, who sent her a scrapbook full of pictures of and stories about Amelia, with the modest request that she inscribe it. Instead, Amelia wrote her a charming letter. This thoughtful gesture represented some sacrifice in time, for her correspondence was so huge that she and her excellent secretary could scarcely keep abreast of it.

With her sense of humor, she got a certain amount of amusement from the task. She kept two special files, the first labeled "Cousins," where she stashed away all the letters from those who claimed to be relatives. The second file, "Bunk," was the repository of songs, poems, and flowery compliments. On one particularly fulsome telegram she noted for her secretary, tongue in cheek, "Show this to GP so he may appreciate me."[15]

As was inevitable with two people of such forceful character, George and Amelia had their differences. One matter over which they crossed swords was the children's hat incident. On her return from the *Friendship* flight, Amelia had worn a tan cloche. On one of her trips to California, George arranged with a manufacturer of children's hats to put out small replicas, to be decorated with a brown ribbon bearing Amelia's signature. They were to sell for what was then the goodly sum of three dollars, of which Amelia would receive fifty cents. When she returned, George showed her the sample, beaming with pride in his brainchild.

Amelia blew up. "GP, I can't ever go along with this. It's terrible. You must cancel whatever contract you have made at once!"

George had a gentleman's upbringing, but he was first and foremost a promoter. The vulgarity that had struck Amelia like a slap in the face sailed over his head. He could see nothing objectionable in sending forth thousands, maybe millions, of little girls with his wife's name on their hatbands as if she were a commodity or a comic strip character. What was wrong with turning an honest dollar—in fact, a lot of honest dollars—in any way one could dream up, a way that, not too incidentally, would keep Amelia's name before the public?

Truly uncomprehending and somewhat angry, he rejoined, "But why? Meely, why? The hats have already been shown around and they are a sure money-maker with youngsters. Why do you object?"

"Because, first, I don't like the idea of everybody who has three dollars advertising my name; second, I don't think they are worth three dollars and lots of kids would be cheated. Call up the man who has the contract right now," she demanded. "I won't have it!"

Recognizing that his wife was adamant, however unaccountably, George arranged that production be stopped.[16]

Amelia did not object to commercial ventures as long as they made sense and did not exceed the bounds of good taste. The lightweight luggage bearing her name proved so practical for air travel that it sold for years. She pioneered the lounging pajamas so popular in the 1930s. For a year or so her line of women's clothes sold well. This included shirts of parachute silk that she insisted be made with tails. Women's blouses had been tailless, and she knew how exasperating it was to raise her arms and have her blouse ride up out of her skirt or slacks. Her creations were mostly tailored and featured novel buttons shaped like silver screws, oil cups, bolts, and twisted wires. Business and professional women liked these wearable, stylish clothes. Unfortunately, the venture had to end, thanks to Amelia's own integrity. She would only use the best of materials, which eventually priced her line out of the market.[17]

The year 1932 opened with Amelia tired out from a "strenuous southern trip" on the lecture circuit. When she returned in December 1931, she had to plunge into the manuscript of her book *The Fun of It,* which kept her housebound to a large extent. In January she had a visit from "Toot" Challis, her cousin, whom she had not seen for some five years. This was somewhat unusual; the Putnams' guests usually were mutual acquaintances, mostly celebrities in one field or another.

Amy and Muriel never came, but they were never far from Amelia's thoughts. In mid-February she wrote to Amy, who had been hospitalized, a letter revealing several facets of her complex character: "I think it would have been better to let me know than let things get so bad." She was writing to Muriel for the name of the doctor and other details: "I will see to hospital expenses. Don't worry about that end. . . . I should prefer to pay the bills direct if you will have them forwarded here."

There were the generosity and the sense of family responsibility; Amelia would foot the bills as a matter of course. There, too, was the realism that preferred to pay the bills direct rather than have the money filter through Amy's far-from-sticky fingers.

Another paragraph in this same letter is much less admirable: "About Pidge. Why don't you suggest to her that Albert . . . go to Dr. Pecici and get a little information? Surely if Pidge can't manage things it is important for him to do so. Anyway I think he should share the mechanics of being a husband, as one [partner] should not bear the whole responsibility."[18]

This was a truly outrageous invasion of her sister's privacy. As Amelia would scarcely have written thus out of the blue, it seems likely that Muriel had had a pregnancy "scare" with little Amy not yet seven months old. In any case, on occasion Amelia had a regrettable tendency to address Amy as if she and Muriel were children, and not very bright children at that.

An unusual experience enlivened the early spring. On February 28, Amelia became "the first woman to address the Sunday afternoon lecture audience at the workhouse on Welfare Island." Her listeners must have been genuinely interested, but they bombarded her with questions that, if unsophisticated, were intelligent: Were gliders and autogiros practical? Why did airplane radios seem to break down more than others? What was an air pocket? What was the safest plane made?[19]

This brief encounter with men who could not escape into the sky may have reminded Amelia that there was another world out there beckoning to her, a world beyond family responsibilities, endless lectures, letters, and books to be written. It was time for another adventure in Amelia's real world—the realm of beauty, space, and blessed solitude.

PART

2

High Flight

A young Amelia with her mother, Amy, during the 1920s—before her days as an aviatrix.

Amelia in her flight suit before the famous 1929 *Friendship* flight, when she became the first woman to fly across the Atlantic.

The *Friendship* arrives in Southampton, England, after landing at Burry Port, Wales, following the flight from Newfoundland. The plane was a Fokker F-7 originally flown by the explorer Richard E. Byrd.

Amelia and Captain A. H. White after a June 1928 flight from Croydon to Northolt, England.

Amelia with Orville Wright (*left of plaque*) and Senator Bingham (*right*) at the Wright Memorial in Kitty Hawk, North Carolina, in December 1928.

With Bill Stultz, who piloted the *Friendship* across the Atlantic, in June 1928. Stultz would die a year later in a crash at Roosevelt Field, New York.

At home with her husband George Putnam, Amelia's promoter and a well-known publisher.

Amelia with famous aviatrix Ruth Nichols.

With polar flier Bernt Balchen in front of their plane in Teterboro, New Jersey.
Balchen outfitted Amelia's Lockheed Vega for her solo crossing of the Atlanttic.

Arriving at Culmore Field in Northern Ireland after her transatlantic solo flight in May 1932. Amelia had proved her skills as a pilot and gained even more fame.

Leaving Buckingham Palace after a visit with the Prince of Wales.

(*Right*) Greeted by Andrew Mellon, the American ambassador to Great Britain, upon her arrival in London on May 22.

(*Below*) A triumphant Amelia waves to the New York crowd during a parade celebrating her transatlantic flight.

Amelia and her husband in flight suits, January 1935.

Chapter 9
Vindication

*F*or the past four years, underlying all of Amelia's fame, her personal joys and sorrows, had been a nagging sense of unworthiness. This was what Muriel called "the stigma she felt at being only a passenger on the *Friendship*."[1]

Actually, Amelia had nothing with which to reproach herself in that connection. No fraud had been involved. She had insisted that all credit belonged to the two men who flew the plane. Still, there it was—logical or not, she felt an urgent need to vindicate herself.

One morning early in the spring of 1932, she and George were breakfasting when Amelia lowered the newspaper she was reading and asked slowly, "Would you *mind* if I flew the Atlantic?" George was conscious of twin reactions—a heart-lurch of fear and "something akin to elation, in the presence of so adventurous a spirit." But he was not surprised; they had discussed the project "casually from time to time." Certainly he did not mind, if that meant trying to hold her back.

The first person she and George drew into the project was Bernt Balchen, whom George called "one of those incredibly wise persons." This great Norwegian flier had been with Roald Amundsen in 1926 on his flight to the North Pole and with Byrd at the South Pole in 1929. In addition, he had crossed the Atlantic as one of Byrd's transocean party in 1927.

Balchen came to the Putnams' home one Sunday in April. After lunch, the three played croquet. Suddenly Amelia put down her mallet and began, "I want to tell you, Bernt—" She broke off, and the three sat down on a nearby rock. She told Balchen of her desire to solo across the Atlantic. "Am I ready to do it?" she asked. "Is the ship ready? Will you help me?"

With his usual direct simplicity, Balchen replied to each question in turn. "Yes. You can do it. The ship—when we are through with it—will be O.K. And—I'll help."

Toot Challis was staying with the Putnams. The three were in the kitchen that night when Amelia, busy slicing bread, told her cousin, "I'm—I'm going to fly the Atlantic again. Alone." Toot froze in position, and the cocoa she was watching boiled over. All three pitched in to mop up and make more cocoa. Knowing that Amelia wanted privacy, Toot kept the secret.[2]

This was in accordance with Amelia's usual policy of preflight secrecy. She chartered her Vega to Balchen, who was planning to fly to the South Pole with Lincoln Ellsworth. Balchen flew the plane to "the old Fokker factory" at Teterboro, New Jersey, where he joined forces with Eddie Gorski, an expert mechanic from Lockheed. Together they considerably modified the Vega, installing a new fuel system, placing "a large gas tank in the fuselage," replacing the ailerons, and adding "a drift indicator, two compasses, and a directional gyrocompass" to the instrument panel. In accordance with Amelia's vow taken just before the *Friendship* flight, there would be no pontoons. As she said to George, "I'll just have to keep on going until I get to land." She added a light touch: "You know I hate to get my hair wet!"[3]

While the Vega was being readied, Amelia worked hard honing her skills, especially instrument flying and ground training, and kept in close touch with Doc Kimball concerning weather conditions around Newfoundland and well into the Atlantic. "We never talked definitely of my plans and I don't know that he was aware exactly what was up until the last minute," Amelia wrote. Kimball would have been stupid had he not guessed what was afoot, but he, too, kept the secret. Amelia did not even tell her family of her plans.[4]

Preparing plane and pilot for this adventure took well over a month, and, as always, everything depended upon the weather. On the morning of May 19, Amelia drove to Teterboro to talk with Balchen and Gorski and perhaps get in a little flying time. But about 11:30 George telephoned. Doc Kimball had reported conditions were favorable to reach Newfoundland.

Abandoning all thought of lunch, Amelia drove back to Rye and changed into jodhpurs and windbreaker. Five minutes sufficed to collect such necessities as her maps, a toothbrush, and a comb. For food she took only a can of tomato juice and a thermos to be filled with soup because, as she wrote later, "A pilot whose land plane falls into the Atlantic is not consoled by caviar sandwiches."

For a few moments she allowed her love of beauty to take over. "Beside and below our bedroom windows were dogwood trees, their blossoms in luxuriant full flower, unbelievable bouquets of white and pink flecked with the sunshine of spring." Then, pausing only to tell the housekeeper she need not prepare dinner that night, Amelia sped back to Teterboro.

There, briefly and unknowingly, she touched the future of flight. Her fuel and oil tanks were filled "under the guidance of Major Edwin Aldrin, an accomplished flier." His son, Colonel Edwin E. "Buzz" Aldrin Jr., would be the second man to set foot on the moon.[5]

George had reached Teterboro in time to send Amelia off. He handed her a twenty-dollar bill with the request that she call him as soon as she landed in Europe. The Vega took off at 3 P.M. EDT, with Balchen at the controls and Amelia and Gorski taking their ease for the flight to St. John. George later disclaimed responsibility for the leak, but somehow the newspapers got word that the attempt was under way.

At 6:46 P.M. Balchen made "a splendid landing" at St. John, where they stayed overnight. To the press Balchen expressed optimism. "Mrs. Putnam has ninety-nine chances out of a hundred to cross the Atlantic if she gets an even break. She is probably the greatest woman pilot of today." Considering the source, this was truly a compliment to be cherished.

At 8:23 the next morning they moved on to Harbour Grace, the point of departure, landing at 12:23. After a brief rest, Amelia read the telegrams that awaited her, including one from George promising to join her in France and the latest weather report from Doc Kimball. On the way to the airfield, she paused at a restaurant long enough to have her thermos filled with tomato soup.

Doc Kimball had confirmed that good weather would prevail but warned that she might run into trouble south of the normal crossing lines. As Amelia noted, "The outlook wasn't perfect but it was promising."[6]

It was all so different from her first Atlantic crossing: no long wait in an agony of boredom for favorable weather, no heavy pontoons to cut down speed and necessitate a water landing, no alcoholic colleague to keep her in a constant state of anxiety. Perhaps best of all, she was alone. This venture was hers to win or lose.

The Vega had been refueled and stood ready. Balchen described the takeoff:

▶ She arrives at the field in jodhpurs and leather flying jacket, her close-cropped blond hair tousled, quiet and unobtrusive as a young Lindbergh. She listens calmly, only biting her lip a little, as I go over with her the

course to hold, and tell her what weather she can expect on the way across
the ocean. She looks at me with a small lonely smile and said, "Do you
think I can make it?" and I grin back: "You bet." She crawls calmly into
the cockpit of the big empty airplane, starts the engine, runs it up, checks
the mags, and nods her head. We pull the chocks, and she is off.[7]

The time of takeoff was 5:50 P.M., Friday, May 20, 1932. Amelia had
a little while to savor the joy of flight and the peace of solitude. Then
two things became abundantly clear: (1) Not even the best of weather
forecasters can be totally reliable and (2) the most expertly modified
and maintained of mechanical devices can develop problems at the
most disconcerting times.

First, the predicted fair skies disappeared. Fog set in, and as she
nosed the Vega up to avoid the fog, ice began to form on the wings.
Later she told George that "weather reports from both sides of the
ocean were '100 per cent wrong.'" Next, the altimeter failed, something that had never happened to her in all her years of flying. Shortly
thereafter, the plane ran into "rather a severe storm with lightning,"
so that Amelia had difficulty in maintaining her course. This situation
endured for about an hour. Then, as she told a reporter for the *New
York Times* the next day, "The gasoline gauge in the cockpit broke and
I was getting gas all down the back of my neck. Then the exhaust manifold burned out." Small blue flames were licking around it, and she
knew the danger could only increase, but she hoped the heavy metal
would last for the rest of the flight. She remembered "wondering, in a
detached way, whether one would prefer drowning to incineration."[8]

At this point, she could have turned back to Newfoundland but
decided to keep on toward Europe. With a brief break in the weather,
she nosed up again, but the slow climb indicated that once more she
was taking on a dangerous load of ice, weighing down the wings and
curtaining the windows with slush. Moreover, it so coated the air
speed indicator that it did not register accurately on the panel.

She had no choice but to go down until she could see the whitecaps,
although she had no way of telling exactly how far she was over them.
After she landed, it was found that the barograph "recorded an almost
vertical drop of three thousand feet" at one point.

The fog pursued her down so low she had to go higher, seeking "middle ground" between ocean and ice. Having no way of gauging her
height, this was more difficult than it sounds. Lacking both reliable
altimeter and speed indicator, she had only the gyrocompass with
which to navigate. Balchen's foresight in installing that instrument
may well have saved Amelia's life.[9]

She was conscious of neither hunger nor fatigue, taking no nourishment except a can of tomato juice sipped through a straw. As for being

tired, George commented to the press, "You're not going to get sleepy while flying blind with a sick plane over the ocean."

Dawn found her still with ice on the wings, flying through tightly packed white clouds. After about an hour, she ventured down into a sunny opening between layers of clouds, but the glare was so dazzling, even with her dark glasses, that she had to drop through the bottom layer "to fly in the shade, as it were."

The last two hours of the flight were the most difficult. Her planned destination was Paris, but this was no longer possible. Gas was leaking, the damaged manifold was "vibrating very badly," and the weather had delayed her. So she changed course to due east, heading for Ireland. She feared that she might have veered southward and if so might miss the southern tip of Ireland; actually, she was right on course. When she spotted land, it was a little north of the Irish Atlantic coast's midpoint.

She had no idea where the nearest airport might be, but sighting a railroad she decided to follow it, hoping it would lead to a city with an airport. The railroad took her to Londonderry, where she circled in search of a landing field. Instead, all she could find were beautiful green pastures. "I succeeded in frightening all the cattle in the county, I think, as I came down low several times before finally landing in a long, sloping meadow," she described the scene later. "I couldn't have asked for better landing facilities." The time was 14 hours 56 minutes from takeoff.[10]

Back in the United States, Amy and Muriel had not permitted Amelia's flight to disturb the household routine, and they retired at the usual time. Amy claimed she was sure her daughter would complete the mission safely. Still, she was visibly shaken when a false report came in that Amelia had crashed near Paris's Le Bourget airport and been injured.

The same report frightened George, who sat up all night in his office with a few friends, including Captain Railey. The error was corrected within twelve minutes, but to George those minutes were "interminable," and he never forgot them.[11]

For a brief spell Amelia sat quietly in the cockpit, and who can doubt that in those moments she was a perfectly happy woman. At last she had exorcised the sense of unworthiness. She had flown 2,026 miles solo across the Atlantic, to land at Culmore on the outskirts of Londonderry five years to the day after Lindbergh's historic flight to Paris. "I've done it!" she said aloud.[12]

She taxied to a nearby farm cottage, "from which emerged a couple of surprised dairy maids, and a farm hand," Dan McCallon. At first he couldn't tell whether his unexpected visitor was a man or woman, but he asked courteously, "Have you flown far?" "From America," Amelia replied, "all calm-like."

Dan was "all stunned and didn't know what to say."

Amelia's version of her landing, given with her characteristic blend of grace and humor to a crowd of newsmen and photographers the next day, explained:

> I was never in Ireland before, but the sight of the thatched cottages and the marvelous green grass and trees left me no doubt that I had actually made the Emerald Island. I was still surer when I heard the brogue of my friend Dan McCallon. I had my first experience of Irish hospitality in a much-needed glass of water from Dan's little cottage, and there I washed some of the grease from my face. All the while my poor plane was lying in the field near by, scaring Dan's cattle to death.

The owner of the farm, Robert Gallagher, appeared almost immediately. The Gallaghers knew about Amelia and made her welcome. Mrs. Gallagher served her tea, while Mr. Gallagher sent for police constables to guard the Vega.[13] The farm had no telephone, but Mr. Gallagher drove Amelia the five or six miles to Londonderry to the home of Mrs. Francis McClure. There at last Amelia could call her husband. This was about 4 P.M. EDT. It was quite a long chat. Amelia told George about the problems she had encountered but assured him that the engine itself gave no trouble. She asked him to convey her special appreciation to Balchen and to let Amy and Muriel know that she had landed safely.

At 4:45 George was on the air over Columbia Broadcasting's WABC. "I have just had the pleasure and the thrill and the fun and the joy of talking to my wife by telephone as she sits in the home of a hospitable couple in the far north of Ireland," he burbled. Then he settled down to relay the substance of their conversation, paying tribute to Balchen as Amelia wished.

Amelia returned to the Gallaghers' farm, but that night came back to Londonderry, to the Northern Counties Hotel, to "answer a stream of telephone calls from the United States and England." A crowd gathered at the hotel and cheered "with real Irish enthusiasm" when she emerged. The mayor of Londonderry was among her new fans. "You have done an amazing thing," he said as he grasped her hand.

Dozens of Londonderry's citizens vied for the privilege of having her as their overnight guest, but she chose to spend the night with the Gallaghers to be near her plane. There again interviewers besieged her with questions, which she answered "willingly and good-naturedly." Soon, however, nature demanded repairs. She could not conceal her yawns and had to excuse herself. "Now for a bath and some sleep," she said with her friendly smile.[14]

All told, she had been fortunate to land in this charming locale off the beaten track. The circumstance gave her a much-needed respite before facing the enthusiastic but rather overwhelming hospitality awaiting her in London and elsewhere in Europe.

Well before Amelia retired at the Gallagher farm, messages began to pour in. President Hoover was among the first to express "the pride of the nation. . . . You have demonstrated not only your own dauntless courage, but also the capacity of women to match the skill of men in carrying through the most difficult feats of high adventure."

Mayor James M. Curley of Boston began to plan a mammoth celebration. He sent Amelia a telegram of the type she filed under "Bunk": "Boston, your home town, congratulates her heroine and queen of the air. We proudly await your homecoming."[15]

The brotherhood—and sisterhood—of the air reacted to Amelia's victory with warm generosity. Elinor Smith had been glued to her radio for the final hours of Amelia's flight. Elinor had been flying with her father since childhood, soloing at the age of fifteen, and winning her transport license three years later. Unlike Amelia, Elinor was a bit of a swashbuckler, early nicknamed "the Flying Flapper of Freeport," and had once flown under the four East River bridges. But she was also a solid professional with several altitude and endurance records to her credit. Although she herself was planning a transatlantic flight, she mentally followed Amelia's course with affectionate concern. When the news flashed over the air that Amelia had landed safely, Elinor flung her arms in the air, leaped over a chair, and shouted, "Gee, that's great!"[16]

Commander Richard E. Byrd, who had been such a good friend to Amelia, was really enthusiastic, although there is no record of his leaping over furniture. "Simply great!" he exclaimed. "Amelia Putnam is an extraordinary person. I know of no man who has more courage than she."[17]

Amelia's neighbor at Rye, Ruth Nichols, was, like Elinor Smith, planning a transocean flight, as she had been before Amelia's first crossing. She wired cordially, "You beat me to it for the second time, but it was a splendid job. My greatest admiration for your planning and skill in carrying out the hop."[18]

Perhaps most treasured was a message from the Lindberghs. In the midst of their grief and horror at the kidnapping and murder of their first son and the consequent Walpurgis Night of publicity, they cabled Amelia, "We do congratulate you. Your flight is a splendid success."

A message that touched and amused Amelia came from Phil Cooper, who owned the dry cleaning establishment the Putnams patronized: "Knew you would do it. I never lose a customer."[19]

The British added their voices, one of the first being the secretary of state for air, who by coincidence happened to be the Marquess of Londonderry. He followed the official wire with a phone call, telling her "that from the viewpoint of aviation everybody was proud of her and that we were anxious to welcome her."

The *Sunday Times* called her flight "one of the most spectacular in the history of aviation," observing, "Not America only, nor women only, but the whole world is proud of her." The *Sunday Express* hailed her as "a great girl. . . . She takes her place high on the pinnacle beside the immortal Lindbergh. Her glory sheds its luster on all womanhood."[20]

Of course, there were the usual killjoys and those who seemed to feel threatened in the presence of female accomplishment. One columnist disdainfully called the exploit "a useless display of courage"; another disapproved of Amelia as "unwomanly."[21]

It is likely, however, that nothing short of an assassination threat could have marred Amelia's joy and satisfaction as she made ready to return to London, the city that had been so kind to her when, as she believed, she did not deserve it. Now she could look her public in the eye.

Chapter **10**
Europe Welcomes Amelia

*D*uring their first telephone conversation of May 21, George asked, "Do you want me to come over?"

"I don't know whether you need to—you're busy," replied Amelia. "Let's see what happens in the next forty-eight hours." By that evening, however, the crowds at Londonderry, the press attention, and the pileup of messages suggested that her husband's public relations expertise might be very useful, so in her second call to him she asked that he catch the next liner to Europe.[1]

Before leaving on the *Olympic,* George wrote an extraordinary letter to Amy. He would take letters from her to Amelia. If Amy and Muriel would like to meet him and Amelia in New York when they returned, his secretary would arrange accommodations for them. But he anticipated a "hectic" arrival; perhaps they would rather "keep out of things and come later to visit at Rye." Needless to say, after this none-too-gentle hint, Amy and Muriel were not at the dock to greet Amelia.[2]

Meanwhile, on May 22, Paramount News flew Amelia to London. After her Vega was repaired, it would be taken to London also, to be exhibited at Selfridge's department store. Lady Astor had wired her, "Come to us, and I will lend you a nightgown," but Amelia accepted Ambassador Andrew W. Mellon's invitation to stay at the U.S. Embassy.

He met her when she landed at Nanworth Air Park in Middlesex. He, too, was a newcomer to England and reacted with mild astonishment to the antics of the newsreel cameramen, some of whom were literally fighting for position. "Do you suppose they really mean it?" he asked Amelia.

Someone in the party mentioned that Amelia would have to borrow some clothes. "Oh, that will be all right," Mellon assured her, "because my daughter, Mrs. David Bruce, is staying at the Embassy too and—yes, I would think things of hers will be sure to fit you—at least, pretty well."[3]

The next morning, clad in a borrowed outfit, Amelia set out for Selfridge's to renew old acquaintance and purchase a wardrobe. While she waited for a selection to be shown to her, she was asked to sign her name, using a diamond-point pen, on the plate glass window the Selfridges used as an autograph album. That day began her friendship with Gordon Selfridge.[4]

One of Amelia's first actions in London was to make an international broadcast, which Amy and Muriel heard in Medford. They both enjoyed it very much, but Muriel added, "None of us thought that the voice we heard was Amelia's, although it came over very clearly and distinctly. It didn't sound like her and it wasn't until she used several pet expressions and phrases that we woke up to the realization that it was Amelia we were listening to."[5] In the early 1930s, reproduction of the human voice was not yet flawless. This may help to explain why Amelia's voice on old newsreel tracks sounds high and shrill, whereas many who knew her agreed that she had a soft, beautiful voice.

The London District of the Institute of Journalists had scheduled a luncheon at the Criterion Restaurant on May 22 to welcome Ambassador Mellon. They hastily included Amelia in the invitation. The London *Times* faithfully reported the courteous if lengthy exchange of toasts, but it is evident that Amelia stole the show. When her turn came to be toasted, the entire company sang, "For she's a jolly good fellow."

In her response, Amelia expressed her pleasure in being in England and "hoped to explore London." She stressed that she "came over with no plans and no special purpose. I felt my trip should be a justification of myself, and a satisfaction. I have enjoyed myself very much, despite the Press"—here the newsmen broke into laughter—and she added that they had been "very kind."

She recounted a bit about her exploit, adding, "My flight adds nothing to aviation. It has no significance at all." She did not anticipate making another such trip to London. "I think it would take more than four years to sell the idea to my husband." Again the audience laughed appreciatively. Cheers greeted her as she ceased speaking.[6]

The *Manchester Guardian*'s reporter was impressed by the fact that Amelia "showed no trace of nervousness, not even when she was speaking . . . there was no hesitation, no break or change of tone in the soft, drawling voice. Experienced public men there may well have prayed for her nonchalance before an audience."

Editorially, however, while conceding Amelia's courage, the *Guardian* deprecated such flights as hers as "a gamble, a sporting feat, and little more. . . . The future of transocean flying seems to lie with the large flying boat, or conceivably, with the airship." This statement demonstrates the danger in leaving the safe harbor of fair comment for the choppy waters of prophecy.[7]

A much appreciated tribute came to Amelia from the British Guild of Air Pilots and Navigators. Learning that Gordon Selfridge was an experienced pilot, Amelia asked him to fly her to Brooklands to receive the organization's Certificate of Honorary Membership. Prior to Amelia, only one foreigner had received it—Dr. Hugo Eckener of dirigible fame.[8]

On May 24, Amelia was away from the embassy when a call came for her—the Prince of Wales wanted to meet her. The embassy soon tracked her down and she hustled back. After pausing for lunch, she drove to York House, where the prince received her in his private rooms. They spent more than half an hour together, and Amelia discovered that her host was a flying enthusiast, genuinely interested in the details of her flight.

As she left, he said rather wistfully and with obvious sincerity, "I envy you your freedom in flying, Mrs. Putnam. I should so like to have my own plane and license, but British tradition is hard to circumvent." He added more formally, "We are indeed happy that your second flight also had its successful termination in the United Kingdom. We hope you will come again!"

The press was waiting as Amelia left York House "The Prince was just as I expected to find him, charming and delightful," she told the reporters. "We talked shop, discussing airplanes and flying in general."[9]

Such acceptance and praise as Great Britain heaped upon Amelia could easily have inflated a head less level than hers. But she continued to insist that her flight meant nothing beyond her personal satisfaction. At a luncheon given by London's American correspondents and their wives on May 25, she described her venture as "purely personal, to justify my *Friendship* flight, where I did none of the flying."

The next evening, May 26, she attended a council dinner of the Royal Aeronautical Society as its first woman guest. After dinner, at a reception held in the great hall of the South Kensington Science Museum, Amelia stood near the Wright brothers' historic biplane and declared, "My flight contributed nothing except the fact that it brought me here in a Wright machine."[10]

On May 31, Amelia, attired in a shimmering green gown, attended a Derby charity ball at Grosvenor House. Her escort, Ambassador Mellon's son-in-law, David Bruce, led her to the Prince of Wales's table to pay their respects. The prince promptly asked Amelia to dance. That this was not just a courtesy is evident from the fact that twice more that evening the heir to the throne led Amelia out on the floor, where "the two were seen dancing happily together."[11]

It was one of those arresting moments when two diverse streams of history touch momentarily, leaving an unforgettable picture: Edward Prince of Wales dancing with Amelia Earhart Putnam before the shadows fell.

Another encounter with a celebrity did not go nearly so well. On June 2, the day Amelia was to leave England for France, she wrote to Amy, "G. B. Shaw is being towed in to meet me or I him." Her old acquaintance, Lady Nancy Astor, would introduce them.

This idea should have been strangled at birth. A meeting between Shaw and Amelia could only give the playwright a chance to exercise his malice at the expense of a young woman who was too polite to give him as good as he sent.

After their meeting, he informed a newspaper reporter that he had told Amelia, "just what I thought of her, and you had better ask her about it." Told that she was on the way to France, he chuckled, in high glee in having upheld his reputation for rudeness, "That's just as well."[12]

Probably Amelia did not let his barbs sting too much. In having incurred his displeasure, she was in good company, from Shakespeare to Sherlock Holmes.

That evening Amelia left England as the guest of C. R. Fairways, president of the Royal Aeronautical Society, and his wife, aboard their yacht *Evadne*. The yacht reached Cherbourg at 5:45 A.M. on June 3, an hour and a quarter before the liner *Olympic* docked with George aboard. At 7 A.M., U.S. Consul Horatio R. Mooers and the Vicomte Jacques de Sibour, Selfridge's son-in-law, reached the yacht by tug to convey greetings. At 8:30 George arrived by another tug to join his wife. "I'm terribly proud of her," he told the press, "but I hope transatlantic flying won't become a habit with her."[13]

Over breakfast, she told him the saga of the twenty-dollar bill he had given her at Teterboro. She had used it to pay for her first cable to him, but "being American money, it rattled round in the cable office" and Amelia was able to redeem it with English money borrowed from "one of the Paramount boys," whereupon she autographed the bill and returned it to her husband, who kept it as one of his "most treasured souvenirs."

On the way to Paris, Amelia told George about her London shopping spree. "It was fun to have to start right in and buy *everything!*" she finished in very feminine style.[14]

Paris was eager to do Amelia honor. When her train arrived at the Gare St. Lazare on the afternoon of June 3, hundreds so overflowed the tracks that the train had to stop fifty feet from the end of the track. Enthusiastic spectators "broke through police lines, swarmed behind her and literally pushed her out to where her auto was waiting."

The rest of the day was full, and if this was a fair sample, she could expect to see little of "the real Paris," as she hoped to do. That afternoon the Aero Club of France awarded her its coveted gold medal, "reserved for signal accomplishments." The Paris chapter of the National Aeronautic Association of the United States gave her a dinner, and the American Legion entertained her at a reception.

Through it all, those she met found her "quiet, charming and modest," protesting, "It wasn't a big flight, just a gesture for my personal satisfaction. And if it took courage, I wouldn't have been able to do it."[15]

On that last point the Parisians knew better and took her to their hearts to a truly unusual degree. At the American Embassy, Minister of Air Paul Painlevé presented her with the Cross of Knight of the Legion of Honor. "Five years ago," he said, "I had the great pleasure to decorate Colonel Lindbergh after his remarkable flight. And now I have the honor to bestow this cross upon the Colonel's charming image."[16]

Amelia laid the customary wreaths upon the Tomb of the Unknown Soldier and the Lafayette Escadrille monument. A certain amount of purely social activity took place, including attendance at the air races and meeting such hardy perennials of the society pages as Lady Mendl and Elsa Maxwell. Always there were the crowds of people eager to touch her or pull at her clothes, as if they hoped some of her charisma might rub off on them. Amelia never grew accustomed to this manifestation but bore it stoically, knowing it to be the inevitable concomitant of fame.[17]

On June 7, Amelia became the first foreign woman to be received officially by the French Senate. After listening "with no little amazement" to speech after speech loaded with compliments, she made her reply with a few details about her flight. She enchanted them by finishing, in her soft voice, "But after all, Messieurs, it is far more difficult and important to make good laws than to fly the Atlantic."

The president of the senate capped this compliment with quick Gallic wit: "But, Madame, when you fly the ocean, what you do is a danger only to yourself, while we make laws which are a danger to so many!"[18]

In Rome, a meeting of most pilots who had flown the Atlantic had been under way, under the auspices of the Italian government. Amelia was invited; however, her commitments precluded going to Rome in time to participate. The invitation to visit Italy was renewed, so she and George decided to accept. They traveled from Paris by the Simplon Express in the company of Vicomte de Sibour and his wife, Violette. At Milan a representative of the Italian Air Force flew them to Rome.

Each of the Putnams posed a problem for the Italians. George was, as he put it, "as welcome as a plague." His firm had published a book entitled *Escape*, by Francesco Nitti, telling of his escape from the Lipari Islands, Mussolini's Siberia. Naturally the book was exceedingly anti-Fascist.

When they met, Mussolini's eyes had a "sly, almost twinkling" expression as they looked into George's. He said, "I am glad to see for myself a distinguished American who—publishes books about Italy!"

In Amelia's case the difficulty was not politics; she was of the wrong sex. All the attendees at the recent gathering of transatlantic fliers had received decorations from the Italian government. As one who had flown across the ocean solo and the only one to have crossed it twice by air, Amelia deserved official recognition if anyone did. But she was a woman, and Mussolini's Italy was deeply committed to the principle that women belonged at home producing babies on an assembly-line scale. So there was no Italian medal for Amelia, which bothered her not at all; she took a detached interest in the sociological aspects of the situation.[19]

To anticipate a bit, some three years later there was an odd little aftermath. Guiseppe Castruccio, Italian consul-general at Chicago, presented Amelia with a "Balbo" medal. About two weeks later, Castruccio wrote Amelia that the medal was not, in fact, from his government, just "his own gift of personal devotion," this despite the fact that the decoration's leather case bore the inscription, "Conferred on Amelia Earhart by the Italian Government, May 23, 1935." Amelia promptly sent it back.[20]

That same "Balbo"—General Italo Balbo, commanding the Italian Air Force—had charge of the Putnams during their stay in Italy. A likable personality, he took Amelia for a hair-raising spin in his racing car from Rome to Ostia. "That's the fastest I've every traveled—close to the ground," she said as he braked to a halt. Later Balbo took her and George for a hop in his flying boat.[21]

But if the Italians were officially ambivalent, personally they were cordial. At the airport the crowd "brushed aside the policemen, pushed past the authorities gathered at the airport, clapped and cheered and otherwise displayed its admiration." Even Mussolini, despite his veiled crack at George, was friendly when the Putnams met with Il Duce on June 10. He had sent Amelia roses when she landed in Rome and now chatted with her in English about her flight.[22]

Amelia's next VIP was a man of a very different stamp from Mussolini. Albert, King of the Belgians, was the hero who had led his people in their gallant but doomed resistance to the Germans in World War I. He and the queen, with one of the young princes, entertained the Putnams at an informal lunch on June 13. All three royals spoke fluent English and made their guests feel right at home. To Amelia, Albert seemed all that a king should be. He and Amelia talked mostly of aviation, about which he seemed quite knowledgeable. "We had a grand time just 'ground flying.'"

After lunch they went into the garden, where the queen took some snaps, using "an ancient little camera." When she had finished, King Albert accepted the inevitable by saying, "Now I think we must let the press photographers in." They grouped themselves in accordance with the photographers' wishes. "You see, they have to get these pictures," the king explained. "It's their job. The least one can do is cooperate."

Before this pleasant visit ended, King Albert conferred upon Amelia the Cross of Chevalier of the Order of Leopold.[23]

George had been cobbled together for the occasion. In his haste to catch the *Olympic,* he had just flung a few clothes into a suitcase, and therefore he had nothing suitable to wear in the presence of reigning royalty. His costume for the day represented "the friendly pooling of the Legation's resources"—one diplomat's striped trousers, another's vest, still another's coat. Amelia fastened the trousers to the vest with safety pins. Someone produced a silk hat, but it didn't fit, so George had to hold it, hoping to achieve "the bland and eventful look of one who has either just doffed his hat grandly or is just about to put it on."

The Putnams could not leave Belgium without visiting Auguste Picard, famed balloonist of the stratosphere. The three took to one another immediately. Picard had been eager to meet Amelia. He was planning to come to the United States and hoped to go ballooning with her. This came to nothing, but Picard later visited the Putnams in Rye.[24]

Much as they enjoyed Europe, they were beginning to feel the tug of "work and responsibilities" at home. So on June 15 they embarked upon the *Île de France.* Three French aircraft hovered overhead, finally dropping flowers on the liner's deck in a gesture of farewell. As Amelia stood at the rail with George, she laid her hand over his. "GP, thank you for this wonderful three weeks," she said. "I shouldn't be here now, you know, if you hadn't helped me with so many things."[25]

Chapter 11

The White House and Elsewhere

*P*ress coverage for the last few days of the Putnams' homeward voyage centered around plans for receptions and ceremonies scheduled in Amelia's honor. Although both she and Mayor "Jimmy" Walker of New York City had asked that the festivities be modified in view of the times, New York would give her the traditional ticker tape parade.[1]

The decision was wise politically and psychologically. In that year of deep economic depression, Americans had little cause to cheer, and such a prideful, happy occasion could give spirits a much-needed lift. This was only one of many honors being planned, adding up to the sort of public relations coverage that was meat and drink to George and that Amelia accepted with grace if no great enthusiasm.

New York's municipal welcoming tug, *Riverside,* met the *Île de France* when the liner docked on the morning of June 20. The tug was crammed with notables, including some of special significance for Amelia like Bernt Balchen, Frank Hawks, Elinor Smith, and George's son David.[2]

Elinor's presence was evidence of her good sportsmanship. She liked Amelia and admired her courage but seriously questioned her ability as a pilot. In 1929 Elinor had been a demonstration pilot for Bellanca and took Amelia up to check out a plane she wanted to buy. When Amelia took over the controls her performance was so poor that Bellanca refused to sell her the craft.

As for George, Elinor actively detested him. George seems to have recognized in this attractive, vivacious woman a threat to Amelia's image, and Elinor credited to his influence her difficulty in securing reasonable press coverage. When Amelia was planning to fly across the country to take part in the 1929 air races, George offered Elinor the considerable sum of seventy-five dollars a week if she would do the heavy cross-country flying and let it appear that Amelia was doing it all. Naturally Elinor rejected this outrageous proposition, and George turned ugly, threatening that if she did not agree he would see to it that she would "never fly professionally again."[3]

But this was in the past, and Elinor did not begrudge Amelia her moment of triumph as aircraft from the Army, Navy, and National Guard vied in putting on a show overhead. Amelia took parade, awards, and speeches in stride, denying as always that she had, in the mayor's words, "contributed greatly to the science of aeronautics." And she had praise for her husband: "I want to pay tribute to Mr. Putnam. It was much harder for him to stay behind than it was for me to go."[4]

The National Geographic Society had selected Amelia as a recipient of its prestigious gold medal, which only fifteen others—none of them women—had received since President Theodore Roosevelt gave the first to Commander Robert E. Peary in 1906. Since then, by tradition the president of the United States made the presentation. So on the evening of June 21, exactly one month after her transoceanic solo flight, Amelia and George dined at the White House by way of prelude to the ceremony.[5]

George contrasted the formality of the Hoover White House with the informality of their entertainment at King Albert's palace. "When President and Mrs. Hoover appeared, they looked solemn. Everybody looked solemn. And we all filed solemnly into a solemn dining room."

Seated at the president's right, Amelia tried to make conversation with him. George had the impression that she found the going difficult, for Hoover seemed absorbed in his worries. George felt sorry for him, "conscious that somehow a very well-intentioned man, a gentleman, was laboring against odds of inhibitions to be as agreeable as the Lord would let him."[6]

Amelia liked both the Hoovers. "I think the President is too sensitive to be a politician," she said later. "It bothers him to be blamed for the depression and unemployment which seem to be worsening." She was sure he was running for re-election only because he believed "continuity of leadership" would give him the opportunity to institute recovery measures.

She mentioned her visit with King Albert, who had expressed his gratitude for Hoover's efforts to save refugees and children in war-torn Belgium. The president brightened as he responded, "Well, Amelia, I think that was one of the most satisfying assignments I ever undertook. . . . I believe we were able to present to the world a truer picture of Uncle Sam than it had before." He seized the opportunity for a graceful compliment: "You have added immeasurably to our country's stature, too, my dear."[7]

After dinner the president, his wife, and guests went to Constitution Hall, home of the Daughters of the American Revolution, which was packed to the doors. Ten thousand people had requested seats; the hall accommodated only thirty-eight hundred. In the audience were notables from many fields, and the U.S. Marine Band was on hand to play "Hail to the Chief" when the president entered with Amelia on his arm. The ceremony began at precisely 9 P.M., carried coast to coast by the National Broadcasting Company. Gilbert Grosvenor, president of the National Geographic Society, introduced Hoover, who made what Amelia called a "mercifully short speech." It was also warmly appreciative:

> ▶   She has been modest and good-humored. [Her accomplishments] combine to place her in spirit with the great pioneering women to whom every generation of Americans has looked up with admiration for their firmness of will, their strength of character, and their cheerful spirit of comradeship in the work of the world. . . .
>
>   Her success has not been won by the selfish pursuit of a purely personal ambition, but as part of a career generously animated by a wish to help others to share in the rich opportunities of life, and by a wish also to enlarge those opportunities by expanding the powers of women as well as men. . . .
>
>   The nation is proud that an American woman should be the first woman in history to fly an airplane alone across the Atlantic Ocean.[8]

Amelia accepted the medal, which only eight pilots had won before her, with her characteristic mixture of modesty, humor, practicality, and idealism. "I think," she began, "that the appreciation of the deed is out of proportion to the deed itself." She disposed of several press rumors. She had *not* landed with only one gallon of gas left; the Irish had taxed her for one hundred gallons. And no, she had *not* killed a cow, "unless one died of fright."

She paid tribute to Balchen for his part in the venture. In the foreseeable future, she hoped, transatlantic air travel would be commonplace and regular commercial air traffic instituted. If her flight "meant something to women in aviation," she would consider it justified, "but I can't claim anything else."[9]

Amelia would be the first to admit that she was no orator, but she always made an interesting talk, sincerely delivered, and obviously she knew what she was talking about. Most of her hearers responded to her and her message.

Some time later, a mutual friend relayed to George something Mrs. Hoover said about Amelia: "I often think that if a girl was to fly across the Atlantic alone and so, in a sense, represent America before the world, how nice it is that it was such a person as Miss Earhart. She is poised, well bred, lovely to look at, and so intelligent and sincere."[10]

The last week in June was crowded with ceremonies in a number of cities and towns—once again New York City, then Chicago, Cleveland, and Harrison and Rye, New York. Both of these villages had a claim on the Putnams—their house was in Harrison and part of the grounds in Rye. As Amelia remarked, "I grow my vegetables in Rye and eat them in Harrison." Boston gave Amelia a civic reception. This time Amy and Muriel met her when she landed at the airport, but they had little time to catch up. Amelia was whisked away to head the motorcade, her mother and sister several cars behind. That evening they, and George, attended a banquet in Amelia's honor.

This event might be said to represent a crossroads in Amelia's life. Muriel later wrote: "Amelia's position at the pinnacle of aviation fame demanded that she follow one of two courses: either vanish into semi-retirement as Colonel Lindbergh chose to do, or else accept the challenge of making more pioneering flights in the as-yet-unexplored skyways. Amelia, if not actually urged by GP, certainly abetted by him, chose the latter course."[11] There is a tinge of bitterness in Muriel's words. Perhaps at some level she blamed her brother-in-law for keeping Amelia on the course that eventually led to her death. Nevertheless, the choice was Amelia's.

The Vega had returned with the Putnams aboard the *Île de France* and was taken to Teterboro Airport to be reconditioned. On June 30, Balchen flew it to Newark Airport and ordered 540 gallons of gas placed in its fuel tanks preparatory to what was supposed to be a non-stop cross-country flight. The next day, Amelia would fly George and David to Los Angeles, where her husband had to attend to business connected with his movie venture. However, they broke their flight at St. Louis for an overnight stay. Coincidentally, on July 1 the Senate approved the awarding of the Distinguished Flying Cross to Amelia.[12]

On or about July 5, Amelia sent Amy "a check for 100 berries." In her usual accompanying note, she advised that her Challis cousins, Toot and Katch, were "both at Rye holding the house down." And she wanted Amy to visit when she and George returned the following month.[13]

On July 13 Amelia flew to Newark to attend to business in New York, setting a new woman's solo record of nineteen hours, fourteen minutes, fifty-five seconds. She had hoped to best Frank Hawks's record of seventeen hours, thirty-eight minutes, sixteen seconds; however, she had to make a forced landing at Columbus. She admitted that this flight tired her even more than had her Atlantic crossing, and indeed a newspaper picture of her taken in Newark shows her looking absolutely exhausted.[14]

Writing from Rye around July 20, Amelia told Amy some presents were on the way and charged her mother to see that Muriel did not spend her birthday check on the children. She had sent the money so Muriel could have a skirt altered and buy dark gloves and a hat. "She ought to look swell in the suit if she'll get decent accessories."

She soon returned to Los Angeles, and on July 29 Vice President Charles Curtis presented her with the Distinguished Flying Cross and Congressional Citation. He opened the 1932 Summer Olympic Games on July 31. The games provided Amelia with an enjoyable break in routine, although an Associated Press reporter arranged for her to pose with such great Olympians of the past as swimmer Duke Kahanamoku and runner Paavo Nurmi and with movie star Douglas Fairbanks, who with his wife, the dainty Mary Pickford, were already friends of Amelia.

It was a good year for American women athletes. One may safely assume that Amelia took particular pleasure in the prowess of the matchless Mildred "Babe" Didrikson because, as Amelia reminded Amy, she had always been a track fan.[15]

Soon she returned to her own true love, the air. On August 24 she ate a hasty meal at the Los Angeles municipal airport, and at 4:26:54 P.M. EDT took off in her Vega for Newark, setting herself a goal of nineteen hours, fifteen minutes. Nevertheless, she made no attempt to "cut corners" and followed the standard route of commercial aircraft.

Amarillo, Texas, turned on its airport floodlights in a friendly greeting she much appreciated. Elsewhere over Texas, thunderstorms and adverse winds cut down her speed to 125 miles per hour. Then she picked up tailwinds and sped on at about 160 miles per hour by way of St. Louis, Indianapolis, and Pittsburgh.[16]

At 11:30 A.M. EDT, she touched down at Newark Municipal Airport. As on her transatlantic flight, she had taken no nourishment but tomato juice. Stepping out of the plane, she asked for a glass of water. Cameramen and spectators surged toward her, and for once her composure cracked. "Don't come near me!" she exclaimed. "You know what I feel like." A few minutes' rest, a quick telephone call to George and David in New York, and, her poise recovered, she placed herself at the disposal of the newsmen with her usual smiling courtesy. This time her press photo shows her looking fit and good-natured.

She had bested by more than five hundred miles the women's cross-country distance record, previously held by Ruth Nichols. Amelia's speed, a very respectable nineteen hours, five minutes, came nowhere near Hawks's record, but this did not trouble Amelia. She explained to reporters that she had not been trying for a speed record. "I have no desire to treat my plane roughly," she said. "It is the family carryall." Her main objective was to complete the trip without having to stop to refuel; therefore, she had flown at the engine's "most efficient speed."

Still, she was sure that with favorable winds she could have broken the record.

It had been an excellent, well-conducted effort, and pilots at Newark who watched her land were generous in their praise of "the precision and judgment with which she made the flight."

In answer to queries, Amelia said that she expected to be in Cleveland for the National Air Races. She was a member of the contest committee but would not participate in any of the events.[17]

Oddly enough, 1932 marked the beginning of the two-year downswing for women at these races. Mae Haizlip, whose husband was also a pilot, broke Ruth Nichols's world speed record. One of her sons observed that Mae's time was "all right, but Dad can go faster." That seemed to just about sum up press reaction. No handicapping was permitted that year, which virtually guaranteed no victories for women who, like Amelia, flew for "the fun of it." The male pilots made their living in the air, and most flew racing planes designed and built for speed. It was not so much a case of male versus female as professional versus amateur. This obvious circumstance did not prevent the Cleveland press from remarking nastily, "Watching the race, it was easy to tell why women do not wish to compete with men pilots on an equal basis."[18]

So far as we know, Amelia told Amy nothing about the races beyond noting in a letter headed "Labor Day"—which would have been September 6—that she had returned from the races the previous day. She outlined her schedule, which was not yet firm. She would be in Rye "except for little jaunts" until late October. Then lectures would fill November and part of December. There might be a chance for Amy to go along "part of the way" if she wanted to do so. If this did not work out, she wanted Amy to spend a week at Rye. "You ain't never seen the place."

On September 18, at Amy's request, she sent money, only half of the suggested amount. "I thought if I sent the whole you would spend it on someone else and so have nothing left for yourself by the first of next month."[19]

Toot Challis ran the house at Rye while Amelia was traveling. In mid-November she went to New England. George was going with her "to the most northern points," an area she did not particularly like, so she felt the need for "moral support," as she told Amy.[20]

Later that autumn Amelia had a pleasant, nostalgic experience when her father's alma mater, Thiel College, made her an honorary Doctor of Science, citing her in part as follows:

▶ To Thiel College has come an opportunity to honor one of the greatest women of our time—Amelia Earhart, not only because she is one of aviation's pioneers, but also because she is a woman whose high character has endowed all her attainments with unusual significance. . . . Despite her choice of a career which kept her continually in the public eye and despite the honors showered upon her, Amelia Earhart has always retained her dignity, her modesty, her preference for a simple mode of life. . . .[21]

What touched Amelia more than the honor to herself was the discovery of how well and affectionately Thiel remembered her father. She met several of Edwin's classmates and others who had known him. "Everyone remembered him as so handsome and bright," she wrote Amy. "His nickname was 'Kid.' I didn't know that slang was popular then. 'Kid Earhart' now sounds like a prize fighter."[22]

Throughout the autumn and winter of 1932–33, honors continued to come to Amelia. While none was quite in the same league as the National Geographic medal or the Distinguished Flying Cross, all were given in admiration and affection and as such were to be treasured.[23]

For some months a nationwide poll had been conducted "in an effort to ascertain whom American women consider the twelve leaders of their sex who have made the most valuable contributions to American progress in the last 100 years." The results appeared in the press on December 21. It was an interesting list, headed by Mary Baker Eddy, founder of the Christian Science Church, with Amelia ranking tenth. So as her year of glory came to a close, she could have the satisfaction of knowing that she represented something fine to her fellow American women.[24]

The election of 1932 was over, and the age of Roosevelt was about to begin. Inevitably, Mrs. Roosevelt and Amelia met and struck up a friendship. The two had much in common. Both were interested in bettering the lot of humankind, especially of women. Both were basically private people, incongruously living at the height of public visibility. Since girlhood, Eleanor Roosevelt had suffered from being the ugly duckling in a handsome family. For her part, Amelia had a really absurd inferiority complex about her appearance. When George, truthfully, tried to convince her that "often she was very lovely indeed to look at," she would scoff, "You're prejudiced!" Unfortunately, both she and Eleanor were not photogenic. Once they "compared notes on their common lot and agreed that when one was made to look like a gargoyle, there was nothing really to do but grin."[25]

Realizing that the upcoming first lady's enjoyment of flying was sincere, Amelia offered to teach her to fly. "You were very sweet to think of what I said and if I am permitted I will take advantage of your kind offer someday," she wrote Amelia late in 1932.

In strict privacy Amelia lined up an instruction plane and a secluded place to practice. One of Amelia's friends, Dr. Henry Templeton Smith, gave Eleanor the necessary physical examination, and on January 15,

1933, issued her a student pilot permit. Three days later she sent the permit to Amelia, remarking in her covering letter, "The question now comes as to whether I can induce my husband to let me take lessons. I will let you know if I am successful with him. I haven't had a chance even to talk to him about it."

When she did, the president-elect vetoed the project.[26] Eleanor had not yet earned her reputation for being constantly on the go, and Roosevelt did not often squelch his wife's enthusiasms, but one may well imagine that, quite aside from the physical risks, he quailed at the notion of Eleanor Roosevelt turned loose with her own aircraft and pilot's license.

January 27 found Amelia rushing to catch the Twentieth Century Limited to Chicago, weather having prevented her flying. She was due in Portland, Oregon, on February 1, thence down the West Coast on a tightly packed lecture tour. Back in Rye in mid-February, she informed Amy that these had been "the last of the scheduled lectures." The round had been "much more intensive" than she had planned; however, George "kept trying to squeeze in more," and Amelia went along with his wishes. The times being what they were, "I thought I might as well do as much and get as much as I could." As usual, she enclosed a check, with the characteristic caution: "Please don't give it all away if the giving means fostering dependence and lack of responsibility."[27]

On April 20, Amelia and George were overnight guests at the White House. George favorably contrasted the Roosevelt regime with that of the predecessors—"homely in its simplicity, enormously informal, a sort of combination clubhouse, workshop, and drawing room, with rollicking overtones leaning at times toward the slightly lunatic."[28]

While at the White House that day, Amelia acknowledged receipt of some pictures of Muriel's children that Amy had sent her. They were good, she thought, but her sense of style broke out when she noticed that little Amy was wearing knee garters. "Do please have Pidge let the children wear sox so that they don't look like bumpkins. And why the silly hair ribbon? I'll buy em 6 pairs of sox if she will use them."[29]

From fretting about children's socks to flying with the first lady may seem a long jump, but for Amelia it was just doing what came naturally. Upon learning that Eleanor had never flown at night, an experience Amelia loved, she arranged with Eastern Airlines to have a plane available. So, on this evening she was able to offer her hostess a treat. "Why, yes—of course I'll go," replied Eleanor. She touched her evening gown, and added, "Someone fetch me a coat—and a hat, I suppose?"

"A hat if you like," Amelia answered. "Though you won't need it."

So the two women set off, accompanied by the first lady's brother, Hall Roosevelt, and a few unavoidable newspaperwomen. Amelia piloted the transport over Washington and as far as Baltimore, her white satin formal and long white kid gloves an intriguing contrast to her customary flying togs.

From the air, at night, a city appears an enchanted fairyland, and Eleanor was delighted with her little adventure. But the night was not yet over. When their car passed through the White House gates, there near the portico stood temptation—the sporty little car that Hall Roosevelt had driven to Washington for his sister.

"Amelia, let's see how it rides!" exclaimed Eleanor.

"Let's!" agreed Amelia enthusiastically. And off they scrambled for a late night spin around the White House grounds.[30]

After that, Amelia was a welcome and fairly frequent guest at the White House, although her schedule usually permitted her to eat only breakfast there. On one never-to-be-forgotten occasion, a reporter asked, somewhat impertinently, how she liked the meals at the White House. Attempting to change the subject, Amelia replied pleasantly, "I haven't eaten enough to know."

This showed up in print the next day as "I never seem to get enough to eat there." Appalled, embarrassed, and humiliated, Amelia wired her apologies to Eleanor and followed up with a letter. It was not the first time a reporter's originality had made her writhe, and she included in her letter an account of the "Prince of Wales" incident of 1928, adding, "I can laugh at it now. I only hope some day I can laugh also at the preposterous starvation interview. . . .

"I believe you know me well enough to be sure I would never put out that kind of smart ungracious stuff it contained. . . ."

The first lady answered with a note of humorous affection. When Amelia came again, which they hoped would be soon, they would brief her on how to raid the larder. She ended, "You were such a perfect guest that I welcome you back at any time and you need not feel that you have to be out for every meal! We all feel we have not seen enough of you."

She could not resist a mischievous, handwritten postscript: "I shall give you a key to the ice box next time!"[31]

Chapter 12

On the Ground and in the Sky

O
n April 21, the day after her night flight with Eleanor Roosevelt, Amelia addressed the forty-second continental congress
of the Daughters of the American Revolution. She "drew a
gasp" from the assembly "by criticizing them sharply for
agitating for strong armaments while not doing a thing toward having
women bear arms in war," as the *New York Times* reported. She argued
that "equality with men was essential and that women should be
drafted in war time."

After their initial surprise, the Daughters gave her a good round of
applause,[1] for the speaker had brought honor to the United States and
was never afraid to speak her mind. One suspects that Amelia the
pacifist rather than Amelia the feminist had said, in effect, "You want
arms? Are you prepared to bear them?" Certainly she had too much
common sense to expect that any organization in 1933 would publicly
advocate the wartime draft of women.

In May of that year, Amy finally visited the Putnams in Rye. Those
days must have been quite a contrast to her life at Medford. George
and Amelia employed a married couple, the wife as cook-housekeeper,
the husband as chauffeur or butler, according to need. Although
Amelia seldom tried her hand at cooking, George enjoyed it and from
time to time whipped up a meal. So there was little or no occasion for
Amy to take over the kitchen.[2]

Nor were there children to baby-sit. Muriel was under the impression that Amelia would have liked to have a baby, had her lifestyle permitted. Muriel sincerely pitied her sister for her childlessness. "You
are lucky, Pidge," Amelia commented one day, watching the Morrissey

small-fry at play. She added, however, "If it just didn't take so long to *make* a baby. . . . There are so many exciting flying things to be done. Maybe, next year."[3]

We doubt that Amelia truly envied Muriel. "I envy you" was an almost standard, polite comment a childless woman made to an adoring mother, especially if said mama had little else in her life to envy.

Periodically rumors surfaced that Amelia and George were separating. Helen Hutson Weber was their houseguest, recovering from a serious illness, when she read one such bit of scuttlebutt by a New York columnist. As she absorbed this item, the sounds of scuffling and squealing reached her. She laughed quietly to see the Putnams romping like children, George pushing Amelia around in a wheelbarrow, periodically dumping her.[4]

By the end of May, Amy had returned to Medford, and Amelia wrote to her offering Muriel some pictures, "illustrations for books etc." This was a more generous proposal than its casual nature would indicate. Paintings and sketches for illustrations by some of the well-known artists who worked for the Putnam firm would have fetched a pretty penny.

Less than two weeks later, fireworks erupted over Amy's plans for the summer, which involved care of four-year-old David and three-year-old Amy. This, Amelia wrote angrily, "is out of the question and I will not permit it under any circumstances. You are not the kind of woman who has no other interest but brats and I do not see the necessity of your being a drudge and nurse maid." She made several suggestions as to where Amy might spend the summer.

In another letter, undated but from the context written in late June, Amelia again expressed worry and displeasure: "I want your solemn word that you will not try to have two infants with you. I shall be compelled to withhold the monthly check if you do any such funny bizness."[5]

This threat reveals the depth of Amelia's concern for her mother and her anger at the Morrisseys for thus, as she saw it, imposing on Amy. It never seems to have occurred to Amelia that her mother might well have been satisfied with the state of affairs. In her midsixties, severely deaf, with no income beyond what Amelia gave her, this proud daughter of Judge Otis could easily have seen herself as a burden had she not been able to help Muriel. Keeping house and tending her grandchildren allowed her to fulfill one of the most basic of human needs—the need to be needed.

Fortunately for the family stability, Amelia had flying commitments that turned her attention skyward. The National Air Races were coming up, and the only female entrants were the two neighbors from Rye—Amelia Earhart and Ruth Nichols. Neither stood a chance against such professional racers as Colonel Roscoe Turner in his Wedell Williams "special" with its Wasp engines capable of producing almost 900 horsepower, in contrast to the 450 horsepower of Amelia's Vega, especially as they had received only two weeks' notice, whereas the male competitors had been practicing for months. But a special prize of two thousand dollars had been offered for the first woman to finish. Hampered by headwinds and by the motor that was heating badly, Amelia knew she was "hopelessly out of the race"; however, she came in ahead of Ruth. Turner came in first, but a few days later was disqualified, and Jimmie Wedell was declared the winner.[6]

On the way back east, leaving Los Angeles at 11:12 P.M. EST, Amelia cut her own transcontinental record by almost two hours, in spite of having to make two stops on the way. First, the hatch on the Vega's cockpit worked loose, and Amelia had to hold it in place with her right hand for some seventy-five miles. This accident necessitated leaving her course to land at Amarillo, Texas, for repairs, which ate up about two and a half hours. She had to make a second stop, this one at Columbus, Ohio, for refueling, taking off at 4:40 P.M. in heavy rain. But the tailwinds she encountered all across the country helped overcome the delays. She arrived at Newark at 8:14 P.M., and a crowd of roughly three hundred, including George, cheered her as she landed.

Amelia apologized for "looking dirtier than usual." Her white coveralls were grease-stained, her hand was sore from wrestling with the hatch, and she was slightly queasy from gasoline fumes. She told reporters that she was "not very proud of this record" and hoped "to hand up a good one next time."[7]

Back in Rye, Amelia plunged into business. She, George, and Paul Collins were forming a small airline as a subsidiary of the Boston and Maine Railroad. They planned on five trips daily between Boston and Portland, with two daily between Boston and Bangor. She wrote Amy in mid-July that she and George might have to go to Europe on a business trip, and she was not looking forward to it.

"I hope you are getting some cool weather," she wrote. "Mayhap I'll be up that way some time next week." Amy was spending July and August in Marblehead, and if she took along either or both of Muriel's children, Amelia did not mention it in her letters.[8]

Later that month the Putnams entertained as houseguests two aviators almost as celebrated as Amelia—the British "Flying Mollisons." James Mollison and his wife, the former Amy Johnson, had flown in competition against each other for three years, then decided to fly together. Jimmie had soloed both the North and South Atlantic; on July 22 he and his wife set out together to cross from Wales to New York. Unfortunately they had to make an emergency landing in a swamp

near Bridgeport, Connecticut. The impact knocked Jimmie unconscious, and despite a badly injured arm, Amy managed to drag him
free of the plane. Amelia visited them in the hospital, and when they
were released brought them to Rye to recuperate.[9]

In August David Putnam returned from a three-month exploration
in British Guiana and Brazil. He announced that he was through with
exploring and hoped for a job with the airways company of which
Amelia was vice president. The Putnams and members of the press
were gathered in a hotel room when the talk turned to odd stories fea-
turing animals. Amelia recounted the mystery of the nibbled fruit.
"Every day for weeks the butler found two small bites taken out of
every piece of fruit on the dining-room buffet," reported the *New York
Times*. "One night members of the family disguised themselves as
pieces of furniture and watched an obese chipmunk waddle in and
taste the fruit."[10]

David and the chipmunk provided a light touch in Amelia's busy
schedule. In mid-September she brought her mother up to date. She
had "begged off" going to Europe with George and would soon start a
new lecture tour. When she did so, late in September, she took Amy
along, driving to Chicago to visit the Century of Progress Exposition.
Leaving her mother with the hospitable Shedd family, Amelia struck
out on a heavy schedule: twenty-three lectures in twenty-five days.[11]
For several engagements she stayed with the Challises in Atchison
and had "a sort of old home week," as she wrote Amy. At Lawrence College the chancellor amused her by stating that many of her family had
been students there and two of her grandfathers had been regents. "I
wondered how many he thot I had."[12]

These swings through the country were not the grind for Amelia
that they might have been for someone who enjoyed driving less. In
the 1930s driving was not the horrendous experience it can be today.
In some of the broader reaches one could drive for miles without encountering another vehicle. Many used their cars for recreation, piling
in the family with no particular destination in mind, just enjoying the
scenery, stopping for a bite to eat along the way.

Amelia loved such food and gas station stops, saving up her
adventures to relate gleefully to George and their friends. Someone always wanted to know if she really was Amelia Earhart. On one treasured occasion, an "American-Gothic kind of woman" strode up to her
outside a lunch wagon and announced uncompromisingly, "No, you're
not."

Amelia smiled. "I'm not what?"

"You're not Amelia Earhart" was the surprising reply. "My daughter
said you were. I said you looked like her in profile, but now I see you
full face, it's clear you're not her."[13]

Such cases of mistaken identity were not unusual. Once at a party a "strange little gentleman" spoke to her. "Now don't tell me! I know your face as well as I know my own. In just a minute I'll have your name."

He groped through the mists of memory. "You've been on the stage, haven't you?"

In the course of her lectures, Amelia had been on many stages, so could answer honestly, "Well, yes. . . . But most of my work—the air—"

"Of course!" he broke in, light dawning across his face. "The radio! Now I know. I was sure it would come to me. You're—you're Gracie Allen!"[14]

There were few people Amelia resembled less than the beloved little comedienne; however, one can understand these confusions. Some of her photographs could have been almost anybody. These images, ranging from downright homely to the verge of beauty, go far to explain why, after her disappearance, "sightings" of "Amelia Earhart" kept cropping up.

At times her habit of stepping on the gas drew the attention of highway policemen. Amelia neither asked favors nor tried to throw her weight about, and both parties usually parted with mutual esteem.

"So it's you," observed the officer who pulled her over on a little-frequented road in Massachusetts, Amy Mollison beside her.

Amelia allowed as how it was.

"Well, we had a little argument back there; my buddy said it wasn't you—it couldn't be—as what would you be doin' on this road—dog-gondest dullest road you ever saw in your life. But I said it was you." He noted the culprit's license and registration number, then asked for her autograph so that he could hand his partner the "ol' horse laugh."[15]

On another occasion it was about 1:30 A.M., and Amelia was alone, heading to Boston from a speaking engagement in Concord, New Hampshire, when a patrolman caught up with her.

"Oh! So it's you!" he said with weary patience, checking her license. ". . . I get *all* the big ones on this road. Once I got the President's son. *He* had a tale! . . . Last week it was the Governor. . . ."

He appeared to think things over, then invited Amelia to follow him to his home and say hello to his wife. "She'd be tickled."

Although doubting that Mrs. Policeman would be "tickled" at being routed out in the wee small hours, Amelia could recognize a quid pro quo when she saw one. But sure enough, after her initial resistance, the woman came downstairs and welcomed the unexpected guest hospitably. The three ate chocolate cake and drank milk, and Amelia continued on her way, reprieved.[16]

The end of 1933 found the Putnams living in their hotel suite in New York, having decided that with Amelia "away so much and so busy in town when at home," it would be impractical to keep the house open.[17]

Amelia no longer possessed the Vega that had carried her over the Atlantic. It was now an exhibit in the aviation section of the new Benjamin Franklin Memorial and Franklin Institute Museum in Philadelphia. Standing beneath the Vega, on December 17, the thirtieth anniversary of the Wright brothers' historic flight, Amelia made the dedicatory speech. To the audience that included Orville Wright, Amelia expressed the hope that "in the increasing ubiquity of airplanes," they would not forget "the spirit in which these planes were conceived and the beauty of flight itself, which I think is one of the most important things the Wright brothers opened to humanity."

Orville Wright's physician had forbidden him to make a speech, but the honoree smilingly acknowledged the standing ovation the audience enthusiastically gave him.[18]

As the New Year began, Amelia's eyes, like those of everyone else interested in aviation, turned toward the Pacific. On January 11, 1934, six U.S. Navy planes crossed from California to Hawaii, the first conquest of that particular stretch of sky, although not the first Pacific flight. As early as 1928 Sir Charles Kingsford-Smith and his crew reached Brisbane, Australia, after taking off from Oakland. Three years later, Clyde Pangborn and Hugh Herndon Jr. had flown nonstop from Japan to Wenatchee, Washington. No one, however, male or female, had made the crossing from Hawaii to California. Here, then, was one more new frontier to whet Amelia's appetite.[19]

But she could not just drop everything and go. Aside from the technical aspects of preparing for a long flight, Amelia had heavy commitments. In March she testified before the Senate Post Office Committee, which was contemplating turning over new airmail schedules to the Army, a policy Amelia opposed. In an interview she expressed her opinion that the government's role should be to provide navigational aids such as "radio beams, night flying beacons, emergency airports, weather reporting and broadcasting." Such assistance should not be considered subsidies any more "than is the provision of a lighthouse thought to be a subsidy to shipping."

During the spring she lectured in the Midwest and New England; then she and George spent August at Carl Dunrud's dude ranch near Cody, Wyoming. Amelia had a soft spot for Wyoming as the first government in the world to grant women the right to vote. She loved the outdoor life amid the beautiful scenery and pure, invigorating air, and thought of building a summer home nearby.[20]

That autumn, after the Putnams had returned to Rye, George came in from his usual commuter train trip, loaded down with newspapers and a briefcase, to find his wife sitting by the fireplace, clad in gold-colored lounging pajamas and reading the evening paper. At George's entrance, she looked up in a preoccupied way and announced, "I want to fly the Pacific soon."

George leaned against the doorway and countered, "You mean from San Francisco to Honolulu?"

"No; the other way; it's easier to hit a continent than an island," she replied with her usual gleam of humor.

"When do you want to do it?"

"Oh, fairly soon. But only when I'm ready—and the ship."[21]

There was no question of George's vetoing the project; it had been over two years since Amelia had produced a front-page leader headline.

Amelia's decision necessitated changes in the Putnams' lifestyle. Amelia had to go to California so that the Lockheed factory could overhaul the Vega she had purchased from Elinor Smith to replace the Atlantic veteran, now a museum exhibit. The replacement plane, built in 1931, was painted a cheerful red with gold stripes down the side.

George remained behind temporarily. On such occasions when their paths diverged, they closed their home and George moved in with his mother. Jim, the Putnams' houseman, stayed in charge at Rye, under orders to lock the doors and turn off the heater as soon as the water company had cut off the water supply and drained the pipes. This accomplished, Jim locked up but forgot the heater. The result of an almost full tank of oil heating an empty boiler was inevitable.

A motorist who happened to be passing at about 4 A.M. heard the explosion, saw flames flaring out of the Putnam home, and called the fire department. The firefighters were able to save part of the first floor and most of the second. Concerned neighbors got in touch with George, who hurried home and sadly assessed the damage. Then he telephoned the news to Amelia.

"How about the Rockwell Kent paintings?" she asked.

"All gone, I'm afraid," her husband answered.

Amelia also asked about his father's collection of books, most of which were safe, thanks to sturdy built-in bookcases. But the silver on the dining room buffet was "a shapeless mass in a pile of ashes." Most of Amelia's papers were intact, but she lost a small box in which she kept her bits of poetry.[22]

In one respect, this domestic crisis seemed like the finger of fate pointing westward. Amelia was already in California, and her health always improved in its sun and warmth. George had business interests in Hollywood and needed to touch base with Paramount Pictures. They had been associated for some time; it was George who had persuaded Paramount to produce *Wings,* a story of World War I aviators. The movie was a hit from the start and won the first Academy Award for "best picture." It starred three of Hollywood's brightest luminaries: Buddy Rogers, Richard Arlen, and Clara Bow, with a brief appearance by a tall young fellow named Gary Cooper. Stunt flying in the picture had been in the capable hands of Paul Mantz, who became Amelia's technical adviser. Mantz and his wife, Myrtle, lived not too far from the bungalow the Putnams rented, which was another point in California's favor.[23]

Mantz made his living primarily as a stunt flier for the movies. His expertise was beyond question, but opinions of him as a man were widely varied. A number of his Hollywood associates found him one-dimensional, incapable of an intelligent interest in anything but flying. At times he seemed to be playing the role of himself, the colorful stunt pilot. Novelist Irving Wallace thought him "rather empty-headed and shallow, a man of no real perceptions and sensitivity." Withal, he was quite handsome and could be charming and amusing when he chose. His work brought him into contact with bevies of the movies' glamor girls, and he frankly enjoyed their wide-eyed admiration. This annoyed his spirited, red-haired wife, who was very jealous of him. Myrtle was also a pilot, although not in his class.[24]

The Putnams had many other friends in the Hollywood area, either residents or transients, such as Will Rogers, Wiley Post, Mary Pickford, William S. Hart, and Will and Ariel Durant. Not too far away, in as-yet-undeveloped Palm Springs, lived a very special couple—industrialist Floyd Odlum and his wife, Jacqueline Cochran. Odlum, founder of Atlas Corporation, possessed wealth that made George Putnam's income look like small change. Jackie, however, had pulled herself out of poverty so abysmal as to make Edwin Earhart's early years seem idyllic. She differed from Amelia in being one of the accredited beauties of the day. Jackie had received her pilot's license in the summer of 1932 after less than three weeks' instruction and ever since had been eagerly committed to flying. "I loved Amelia with a deep, true and loyal affection," she wrote some twenty years later. "She was a great flyer and an even greater woman." Jackie was not fond of George, but Amelia and Odlum hit it off so well that she would dedicate her last book to him.[25]

To complete Amelia's satisfaction with the California scene, her mother came to visit. With her knack for inspiring devotion, Amy soon made friends who loved her for herself, not just as "Amelia's mother." The Odlums, Paul Mantz, fliers like Louise Thaden and Blanche Noyes, and various members of the Ninety-Nines, kept in touch with Amy until the end of her long life, years after Amelia vanished. She maintained a truly awesome correspondence, sometimes writing fifty letters a day.[26]

As always, Amelia kept her preflight plans as quiet as possible. A hint appeared in the press when on November 21, 1934, she received permission from the Federal Communications Commission to "install and use radio equipment on the airplane NC-965-Y." The FCC specified that this be used "only for communications with ships and coastal stations when in flight over water." No great mental powers were required to deduce that Amelia was preparing some sort of transocean venture. But George denied that his wife was "contemplating any long flight." She was in California on a lecture tour and had obtained the FCC's approval for equipment "to be used in experimental radio work."[27]

Not until nearly a month later did George announce that Amelia would take her airplane along when they sailed for Honolulu on Christmas and might fly back. This information appeared in such an exceedingly brief news item that any but the most scrupulous reader of the daily papers would have missed it.[28] The Putnams really had no choice but to make this announcement; an aircraft secured to the deck of a popular passenger vessel would be noticed, to put it mildly.

Amelia had lost her chance to be the first to fly from Hawaii to the West Coast. In November 1934 Sir Charles Kingsford-Smith and Captain F. G. Taylor had flown their famous craft, *Lady Southern Cross,* from west to east. But she would be the first woman and would make the first solo flight in that direction. This would be enough to give Amelia genuine satisfaction, and George ample material for press coverage.

Chapter 13
West to East

*T*he Putnams and Mantzes sailed for Honolulu aboard the Matson liner *Lurline*. Amy remained behind, and George remarked to Amelia that she was "an awfully good sport to stay alone in the little house." In a letter to Amy dated December 26, Amelia conceded that while she was "not fond of boats" this trip had been enjoyable. The Vega was "perched on the aft tennis deck and excited considerable interest." The motor responded obligingly at each warm-up. Amelia was enthusiastic about the aircraft's radio; it brought in stations as far away as Kingman, Arizona.

In this letter, Amelia told her mother that, along with her other Christmas presents, she had enrolled Amy in the Book-of-the-Month Club. As usual, she had a few words of instruction in case newsmen called on Amy. "If so, be pleasant, admit you're my mother if you care to, and simply say you're not discussing plans. If they ask what you think of my doing such things, say what you think." She added affectionately, "Please try to have a good time. You have had so many squashed years."[1]

While aboard *Lurline,* the four travelers received invitations by radio to be the guests of Chris Holmes, whom Amelia described to Amy as "a wealthy cultivated 'playboy' friend of Paul's." He was not present in person but made his beautiful Waikiki home available to the quartet. They loved the sunshine and the exotic meals prepared by Holmes's "incredibly efficient" servants. The estate manager wanted to arrange a number of parties, but the guests declined—Amelia must be rested in case conditions permitted a sudden takeoff.

The group made one jaunt as guests of Stanley C. Kennedy, President of Inter-Island Airways, to the Kilauea volcano on the "big island" of Hawaii. At Liliuokalani Park Amelia planted a tree, as many celebrities had done. Frequently this entailed a single ceremonial spadeful on the part of the guest; Amelia, however, dug the hole and planted her tree herself.[2]

Nevertheless, it would be a mistake to picture Amelia as the strong, invincibly healthy outdoors type. In fact, she was rather fragile, and such interludes of relaxation and undemanding pleasure as she experienced in Hawaii were important to her well-being.

Everything in Hawaii was not pleasant for Amelia and her party, however. She had not yet formally announced her plans when criticism began. On December 29, while Amelia and Mantz were preparing at Wheeler Field, the Honolulu *Star-Bulletin* claimed that Army airmen there were "uneasy," lest Amelia try to fly to California. "If Amelia intends to fly solo from Hawaii to the mainland, responsible authorities should stop her from doing it," the newspaper pontificated. "There is nothing intelligent about flying solo from Hawaii to the mainland in a single-engined land plane, which is very poor equipment for a long across-water flight. Even if she is successful, nothing beyond what is known would be proved. If she fails, the ghastly Ulm search would be repeated, probably with more enthusiasm, which in the air means greater risks and probable loss of life."

Imperturbably, George said to reporters, "Go ahead and say what you like. We will go ahead in our quiet way."[3]

The "ghastly Ulm search" referred to the twenty-seven-day hunt that the Army, Navy, and Coast Guard, as well as many fishing boats, had conducted when Captain Charles T. P. Ulm with two Australian companions disappeared off Oahu in a flight from Oakland the previous November.[4] Naturally, this tragic occurrence was still very much alive in Hawaiian memories. In view of certain later criticism, it is worth noting that Amelia Earhart was not the only flier who rated a large military rescue commitment upon disappearance.

On December 30, Amelia declared that her plans "were still undetermined." She would defer final decision until after "exhaustive tests" on her plane's equipment and "until she had studied every contingency."[5]

The U.S. Navy refused to clear the flight, claiming that the Vega's radio "lacked sufficient range for safety." Amelia's statement that she had received Kingman, Arizona, while the aircraft was aboard *Lurline* left the Navy either unbelieving or unmoved.

On January 2, Amelia made her only public appearance, speaking in the University of Hawaii's Farrington Hall on "Flying for Fun." Even as she spoke, Mantz took the Vega up to twelve thousand feet over Honolulu and made two-way voice contact with mainland stations, including Kingman. Globe Wireless Pacific coast stations as far north as Seattle heard his voice. Honolulu's radio station KGU sent George a message to that effect as he sat in the audience listening to his wife. Mantz had effectively answered the Navy, which perforce cleared the flight.[6]

This by no means ended the hassle. On January 6, Captain Frank A. Flynn of the National Aeronautical Association sponsored an open letter to Amelia, urging her to reconsider. "Fifty per cent of the planes that have started on the transpacific hop have not come through," he said. "A flight at this season of the year, when storms sweep down suddenly from the Aleutian Islands, could be especially dangerous."[7]

This at least was an honest expression of concern for Amelia's safety. The same could not be said for the next teapot tempest. The Hawaiian Sugar Planters Association had been involved in an extensive publicity campaign against the sugar control legislation pending in Congress. George had suggested that this group sponsor Amelia's project with an award of ten thousand dollars, half to be paid in advance, the balance upon successful completion of the flight. A rival business group claimed that Amelia had "sold her soul" to the sugar interests in exchange for her supposed influence in favor of a reduction in the tariff on sugar. The sponsors hastily called an emergency dinner meeting with Amelia in attendance and suggested she call off the flight in view of the adverse publicity.

Amelia set them straight: "I have no idea where the rumors of my political influence started. It is inexplicable to me that you gentlemen would accept such a stupid rumor as gospel truth without giving me a chance to deny it as, of course, I most emphatically do. My business is flying." She added, "I have spent nearly half of the sum you promised me to get my plane in condition to bring it here, but I can soon recoup that loss. I intend to fly to California within this next week, with or without your support." Shamed, the group renewed their offer, and that particular problem faded away.[8]

Amelia would have been more—or less—than human had the criticism not gotten under her skin. Occasionally George "caught a strange look in her eyes, a kind of anxiety that was not normal to her." And she wrote him a brief letter dated January 8 that she had left with him when she took off:

▶ It is difficult to write what follows, but I feel I must because of the unwarranted criticism which has been levied at me and my flight plans. As you know, the barrage of belittlement has made harder the preparations in many ways.

I make the attempt to fly from Honolulu to the mainland of my own free will. I am familiar with the hazards. However, to balance these, I believe my equipment is as good as can be obtained, and in the best of condition. . . . If I do not do a good job it will not be because the plane and motor are not excellent nor because women cannot fly. . . .[9]

In a few sentences Amelia had made several points that could spare others much criticism if she perished on this flight: (1) She had made the attempt of her own free will; (2) neither the Lockheed firm, Mantz, nor any mechanic who worked on the Vega could be faulted—in that the plane and motor were excellent and in the pink of condition; and (3) if she failed, she failed as an individual, not as a woman.

She wrote to Major Clark at Wheeler Field on January 10, thanking the Army personnel concerned for their assistance and courtesy. Then she took them off the hook:

▶ It is clearly understood that in assisting me the Army is in no way chargeable with any responsibility connected with the flight, actual or implied. You did for me only what you would do for any other responsible pilot under similar circumstances, properly pointing out the risks involved, which latter, of course, I fully recognize.

The entire responsibility for the flight I assume.

This letter she also left with George, to be delivered only in the event of her death.[10]

On the morning of January 11, Amelia digested a sheaf of weather reports, ate breakfast, and settled down for a sunbath while George and Mantz went to Wheeler. At noon, George returned to bring Amelia to the field. There in the home of Lieutenant George Sparhawk, a radio expert who had been of much help to Amelia, and his wife, she went over more weather reports, and a Navy weather expert, Lieutenant E. W. Stephens, briefed her.

The prospects did not look good, with rain coming down like a waterfall. The group ate lunch, and Amelia took an hour's nap. By 3:30 P.M. the rain let up a bit, and Stephens decided that Amelia could get off; if she did not make it that day, worse conditions were in the offing and could delay her for several days. The problem was not so much the rain clouds, which the Vega could break through easily, but the condition of the unpaved runway. Several inches of thick mud could pose a very real hazard to the heavily laden plane. When George woke Amelia, she decided that now was the time. The rain stopped at about 4 P.M., and twenty minutes later George and Amelia, she clad in a warm flying suit, drove to the hangar.[11]

Amelia took with her a thermos bottle of hot chocolate, her customary tomato juice, water, some sweet chocolate, and malted milk tablets. The plane's six passenger seats had been removed to make room for tanks to hold 520 gallons of gasoline, and new landing lights had been affixed to the wing's leading edge.

The Army had mowed the long grass to give Amelia a clear path and placed small white flags to help guide her. But conditions were still far from ideal. The runway at Wheeler was then some six thousand feet in length, laid out in the direction of the prevailing winds, which refused to prevail. The usual northeast trade winds chose this particular day to blow steadily from the south and southwest. So Amelia could expect no help from the wind in her takeoff, or from the field's surface with its deep, clinging mud.[12]

Amelia was smiling as she climbed aboard, and reporters noticed that she "appeared much more at ease" than George. "There was obviously a studied effort on the part of Miss Earhart and her husband to avoid looking at each other. They quite evidently had said farewell to each other before leaving Sparhawk's home."[13] Emotional public scenes were not Amelia's style.

Taxiing to the takeoff path, she saw her mechanic, Eddie Tissot, running along beside the Vega. She noted "that with every step he took the mud squashed up to his shoe tops, so soft was the ground." He looked gloomy, "his face as white as his coveralls." George, too, never forgot Tissot's "ashy face."

As Amelia looked in the other direction, her irrepressible sense of humor took over: "I noticed three fire engines drawn up in front of the hangars, and one ambulance. The Army to a man seemed to have those little squirt fire extinguishers, and the women present had their handkerchiefs out, obviously ready for any emergency."

The adhesive mud impeded her progress well down the runway, and then Amelia had her first stroke of luck of the day. The Vega hit a bump on the surface and bounced into the air. Amelia "pushed the throttle ahead to the farthest notch" and gave the aircraft full power. After a moment of hesitation, the plane soared safely skyward.[14]

George's heart had been in his throat during this scary takeoff. He was perspiring as the Vega took the air, and he exclaimed, "I would rather have a baby!"

This homely expression, meant only to convey that he would rather endure almost anything than go through another such experience of fear, worry, and strain, was misinterpreted in certain quarters. Some editors, deficient alike in understanding and humor, believed that George meant he would rather Amelia had a baby than make the Honolulu-mainland flight. Amelia later told reporters that George "has been writing letters ever since reiterating what he really did say and that he is not a frustrated husband."[15]

After the drama of takeoff, the flight was uneventful, probably the most enjoyable of all Amelia's long hops. She kept tuned to KGU and heard the announcement, "We are interrupting our musical program with an important news flash. Amelia Earhart has just taken off from Honolulu on an attempted flight to Oakland." A little later the announcer added, "Mr. Putnam will try to communicate with his wife." Suddenly there was George's voice, sounding as if he were right in the plane: "A.E., the noise of your motor interferes with your broadcast. Will you please try to speak a little louder so we can hear you." Not a sentimental message, but to Amelia, "out there over the Pacific," the sound was thrilling.[16]

George was having what he later described as "rather a weird night." Holmes's manager had been frustrated by the Putnams' refusal to permit parties in their honor. Now, with Amelia on her way and George and the Mantzes sailing on the *Lurline* the next day, his sense of Hawaiian hospitality could no longer be denied. He insisted upon a lavish wingding, to which those of the Army and Navy who had been most helpful, "with their ladies," were invited. George remembered "a miraculous Hawaiian orchestra and two sets of exotic hula dancers." Several times he slipped away to the office of the Honolulu *Advertiser* to check on incoming dispatches and radio contacts. There he heard Amelia's voice frequently.[17]

Her messages were brief and workmanlike. At 7:17 P.M. she said, "All is well. Ceiling 5,000 feet." About half an hour later, she reported temperature in the plane as forty-five degrees. There was considerable static, and the Navy radiomen asked her to change wavelengths. This she did, reporting at 10:28 P.M., "Shifting transmitter frequency from 3105 kilocycles to 6210 kilocycles," adding, "Perhaps other stations may hear more easily on this band. All well." Signals were faint, however, and the radiomen advised her to switch back to the former frequency. For some reason—perhaps she did not receive the request— Amelia continued to use the 6210 frequency, to the annoyance of the log keeper who grew downright querulous. At 11:20 P.M. the record read in part, "Miss Earhart persisting in new frequency and sending out '1 2 3 4' signals. Disregarding admonitions to return to original frequency." As she moved farther away, her signals became fainter.[18]

Amelia remembered saying into her hand microphone, "I am getting tired of this fog." All that was picked up was "I'm getting tired. . . ." So, Amelia wrote later, "a nurse and a physician were dispatched to the airport at Oakland to revive the exhausted flyer when and if she arrived. Of course I wasn't tired at all."

Of all those concerned with Amelia's flight, she was probably the least perturbed. She experienced no such mechanical problems as had plagued her in crossing the Atlantic, and apart from the routine tasks of piloting and navigation she was free to drink in the beauty of "a night of stars. . . . I have never seen so many or such large ones."

Dawn was an experience both awe-inspiring and disconcerting, for the sun rose somewhat to the right of where she expected to see it. But shortly thereafter she spotted the Dollar Liner *President Pierce* and followed its wake. Having no direct communication with the ship, she radioed San Francisco for its position. The answer placed her three hundred miles off the California coast, "exactly on my course."

To Amelia the last hour of any flight was the hardest. "If there are any clouds about to make shadows one is likely to see much imaginary land." At about seventy-five miles off California she reported that "everything was okeh and that she was enjoying the broadcast of the Metropolitan Opera from New York."[19]

Unsure of where Amelia would land, crowds had gathered at various coastal cities to greet the first person—not just the first woman—to fly solo from Hawaii to the West Coast, for this was what made this particular flight special. In crossing the Atlantic, she had followed Lindbergh; this time she was the trailblazer. At Oakland Airport a good ten thousand had been waiting for several hours, yet when she came in she surprised them. They had been craning their necks looking for a lone aircraft flying high and obviously seeking a place to land. But Amelia did not even circle the field; she brought the Vega in straight as an arrow at a scant two hundred feet, landing at 1:31 P.M. Pacific time. The crowd set up a roar, broke through the police lines, and could be halted only when dangerously near the still-whirling propeller. From the road circling the airport, a chorus of automobile horns honked happily.[20]

This was what none of the critics and carpers could spoil or even understand—the love of the American people for Amelia Earhart. She was no longer in her first youth, had never been a real beauty, and there were other women pilots more technically proficient than she. But these things did not matter—she was their Amelia, outspoken and humorous, brave and friendly, and every inch a lady.

Surprised that so many "were waiting to see a bedraggled pilot climb out of an airplane," as she put it, Amelia hastily ran a comb through her hair and left the Vega. She clasped the enormous bunch of roses someone thrust into her arms and finally admitted she was tired. Soon, airport attendants pushed the Vega into a hangar and closed the doors between Amelia and her multitude of admirers.

Within two hours she had eaten a light meal—chicken broth, muffins, and her favorite buttermilk. Saying "I want sleep more than anything else," she was escorted to a hotel where soon she settled into a bed, and with her gift for instant relaxation fell deep into slumber, a guard placed outside her door.

Reporters sought out her mother, who took it all in stride. "I knew she would do it. There was nothing to be excited about," said Amy placidly. "Of course, I'm glad Amelia made it. But not because it is a record. Or not because Amelia is famous. No. But because Amelia and I like trying things. We like to see what a person can do. . . . She is a good child, unspoiled. . . ."[21]

At 9:45 A.M. Hawaii time George was in the United Press office after a sleepless night. At that time Amelia's call letters KHABQ merely indicated that she was on course and expected to land soon. As George and the Mantzes were to sail at noon, this seemed a good time to get a shave. He was in the barber's chair, face coated with lather, when he received the flash that his wife had landed safely. He sent off a characteristic wire: "Swell job. Hope it doesn't become a habit. Love."[22]

Chapter 14
Mexican Venture

*A*melia slipped out of Oakland with little fanfare. The Vega had been refueled and tuned up during the night, and Amelia reached the airport shortly after 10 A.M. on January 13, ready to go. Once more, however, mud gave her problems. The plane "sank to the hubcaps" and refused to budge until a tractor came to the rescue. At 1:21 P.M. Amelia soared aloft. No one knew exactly what her immediate plans might be, but all agreed that she would be in Los Angeles to greet her husband, who was due to reach there on the seventeenth.[1]

About three hours after takeoff, Amelia touched down at Burbank's Union Air Terminal. Somewhat to her surprise, two thousand people had gathered to welcome her. She spent about an hour at the airport, obligingly posing for photographers and consulting weather observers. To reporters she revealed that her plans upon leaving Honolulu had ranged far beyond just reaching the mainland: "I intended to fly directly to Washington with one stop, either at Oakland or at Salt Lake City. In this manner I intended to demonstrate how easy and little fatiguing such a trip would be by air, and to link the Hawaiian capital with the national capital.

"Naturally I am disappointed that I was able to accomplish only one half that which I intended to accomplish."

She still hoped to continue on to Washington, but weather conditions were highly unfavorable. So friends drove her to North Hollywood to stay with Amy. There the two women were almost inundated with telephoned and telegrammed congratulations, sacks of mail, and lecture invitations.[2]

Eleanor Roosevelt called Amelia's exploit "just grand" and stated that it had brought nearer the time when one could say, "It's nothing to go to Honolulu. I can do it in a day." The president refused a suggestion that he broadcast congratulations, on the grounds that this would set a precedent, but he prepared a cordial message to be read at a dinner in Amelia's honor scheduled for Saturday, January 19.[3]

On Thursday the seventeenth, Amelia boarded the quarantine boat to meet George aboard *Lurline*. Then on Saturday the Putnams and Mantzes flew to Oakland for the dinner. Perhaps to be rested for the upcoming ceremonies, Amelia ceded the controls to Mantz. As the Vega approached Oakland, eleven Navy planes escorted it to a landing. Former President Hoover and California's Governor Frank F. Merriam were among the speakers, Roosevelt's message arrived via wire-photo service, and Amelia received a bracelet of California gold nuggets "bearing the likeness of a small airplane set with a diamond. . . ."[4]

Within a few days, Amelia was flying the Vega east, with George as a passenger. "Headwinds and approaching darkness" necessitated an overnight stay in Cleveland on January 27. During its storage, the Vega developed cylinder condensation, and the takeoff the next morning was delayed while mechanics removed and dried the eighteen spark plugs. Then on to Newark, where George at first refused to talk, claiming his jaw was stiff from the cold. Laughing, Amelia pointed out that the temperature in Newark was colder than that above. "In fact," she added, "I had to circle the field once because as we neared the ground the extreme cold congealed the oil on the stabilizer worm so that I could not set it for landing." After seeing the plane safely in the Standard Oil Company hangar for checkup, the Putnams left for Rye.[5]

Amelia did not have long to rest. January 31 found her a breakfast guest at the White House, and there she received the president's congratulations in person. Immediately after breakfast she went back to New York.[6]

In about a month she returned to Washington by train on the morning of March 1. Again she stayed at the White House to attend a luncheon for fifty guests, followed by a musical program in the East Room. That evening she gave "a vivid account" of her Pacific flight to the National Geographic Society. She also "discussed as a certainty rather than a possibility" air passenger service between the West Coast and Hawaii in the near future.[7]

She wrote to Amy from the White House on March 4 and apologized for not having written sooner. Upon arrival in New York she had to face "the most strenuous lecture engagement ever undertaken." Her few days in Washington were something in the nature of a breather.

She planned to head west around the middle of the month and had a speaking engagement in Los Angeles lined up for March 30. "GP has left Paramount," she added, "and is in a state trying to decide what alley he will run down."

Amelia enclosed a check for Amy's birthday and, as usual, had a few words of advice: "Keep your ties and clothes clean." If she ran short of money, Amelia would pay the bills.

"Paul Mantz will stand by in an emergency. I hope you had him check the car." Amy's auto had recently broken down.[8]

Mantz was having problems quite unconnected with either Amy's car or Amelia's Vega. His marriage to Myrtle was already fraying when they returned from Hawaii, and on the voyage back to California he had gotten drunk. On March 24 the marriage came apart, not with a whimper but with a bang. He was propped up in bed reading a magazine when Myrtle popped up at the window, brandishing a .32-caliber Smith & Wesson pistol, remarking, "Look what I've got!"

Mantz broke out in a cold sweat but kept his eyes fixed on his magazine. There was a good chance Myrtle might miss; if not, the blankets would provide some small protection. Later he admitted, "The tension on my part for those few minutes was terrible." Sure enough, Myrtle did fire and miss. Mantz leaped out of bed, rushed outside, snatched the pistol from Myrtle's hand, and slapped her face. Not unnaturally, Mantz moved out and that ended the marriage.[9]

Meanwhile, Amelia was deep into preparations for another major venture. President Lázaro Cárdenas had invited Amelia to make a goodwill flight to Mexico, where she would receive a medal from the Mexico Society of Geography and be made a member thereof. On March 16 she accepted the invitation. She was enthusiastic about this opportunity and, as always, prepared for it carefully. Equally as usual, she kept her own counsel until almost ready to take off.[10]

She confided in Wiley Post, who asked what route she planned to take on the return trip from Mexico City to New York. The projected route cut across the Gulf of Mexico. Post protested, "That's about 700 miles. Almost half an Atlantic. How much time do you lose if you go around by the shore?" Upon Amelia's admission that this would cost her at most a little over an hour, he cautioned against the direct route: "Amelia, don't do it. It's too dangerous."

"I couldn't believe my ears," Amelia wrote later. "Did Wiley Post, the man who had braved every sort of hazard in his stratosphere flying, really regard a simple little flight from Mexico City to New York across the Gulf as too hazardous? If so, I could scarcely wait to be on my way."[11]

To help finance the project, the Mexican government issued a commemorative stamp, and George sold 780 autographed covers. Some philatelists expressed doubt about this issue, but George, who preceded Amelia to Mexico City, guaranteed authenticity.

On April 18, Amelia informed the press that she had completed plans for two nonstop flights—to and from Mexico City—and the next day, at 9:15 P.M., she was off from Burbank, the autographed covers on board the Vega, along with 544 gallons of gasoline, a spare parachute, and a barograph. She denied any hope of bettering the current nonstop record of eight hours, nine minutes, set by Leland Andrews. "My plane is not equipped for such a record breaking attempt," she said realistically.[12]

She flew down Baja and the Gulf of California, enjoying the moonlight, and at Mazatlán turned east toward the Mexican capital. She was close to her destination when, as she wrote, "I suddenly realized there was a railroad beneath me which had no business being where it was if I were where I ought to be." As she consulted her maps to reconcile the discrepancy, a tiny insect flew into one eye. This was not only "extremely painful," it "played havoc" with her sight, for the other eye "went on strike in sympathy with its ailing mate." Unable to read her maps and "having the feeling of being lost anyway," she decided to land and try to find out where she was.

The Vega jarred to a halt in a pasture, actually the dry bed of a lake. Amelia noted "the stolidity of some Mexican cows," which refused to move. Cowboys and villagers sprang up as if out of the ground. To Amelia's surprise, they recognized her. They were very polite and eager to help, but as they spoke no English and Amelia no Spanish, they could communicate only by signs. Into this unpromising situation stepped an intelligent young boy, who pointed to a spot on the map—the village of Nopala, in Hidalgo. She was only about fifty miles from Mexico City. She took off without difficulty and within half an hour had reached her goal, very disappointed that she had failed to make it nonstop.

Foreign Minister Emilio Portes Gil and George were awaiting her at Balbueno Airport, as were members of the cabinet and of the diplomatic corps. Although some spectators had drifted away when word came of her forced stop at Nopala, enough remained to make this the largest crowd the airport had seen since Lindbergh landed there in 1927. Applauding wildly, they broke through the guard line of soldiers and rushed toward the plane. The foreign minister presented Amelia with a bouquet on behalf of President Cárdenas.[13]

For the next few days Mexico's upper crust outdid itself in honoring Amelia. In a government-sponsored broadcast on April 21, she said, "I am deeply touched for this opportunity offered to me to express my gratitude to the Mexican people and its government for their splendid hospitality."

The next day the Foreign Ministry declared Amelia and George "official guests of Mexico," and that evening they attended a garden party given by President Cárdenas. As always, reporters clustered around. To them Amelia explained that while she hoped to fly nonstop "either to Los Angeles or to New York," this might not be feasible because the thin air of Mexico City's high altitude made takeoff difficult for a heavily loaded aircraft.

George, too, was agreeable with the fourth estate, saying he had nearly resigned himself to waiting for Amelia while she set new records. "Most men wait for their wives at some time or other," he said genially. "Some wait for them to get home from bridge parties, others to get dressed for the theatre or to go out at night.

"As for me, I regard it as very much worth while to wait while Miss Earhart is accomplishing something which she really wants to do and which represents a real achievement."[14]

Cárdenas received the Putnams at the National Palace on April 23. A little later in the day Amelia and George were luncheon guests of famed muralist Diego Rivera and his wife.

City Council fêted Amelia on April 26. Mayor Aaron Saenz presented her with a gold medal and a scroll. "Mexico is honored by your visit and wishes further success to your already brilliant career," he said. "This function is no mere courtesy, but in profound admiration for what you have done for humanity by bringing peoples closer together."

As she had in Paris, Amelia found exactly the right words to gratify her hosts: "You are trying to make Mexico City more beautiful. A world record flight would be easy compared to that, for this capital could not be made more wonderful."

Amelia had one disappointment in Mexico City. She wanted to meet with working women to discuss with them what degree of independence they enjoyed and their opportunities to support themselves. This project did not work out.[15]

She hoped to begin her nonstop flight to New York promptly, but weather conditions were consistently unfavorable. Meanwhile, at the suggestion of Colonel Roberto Fierro, chief of Mexican military aviation, solders were leveling an additional two miles of runway to facilitate her takeoff. On May 2 she checked on progress. Fueling the Vega had almost been completed, and she was pleased with the new runway. But reports showed cloudiness all the way to the gulf and "rain and thunderstorms over Virginia."

"Nature does as thorough a job as man," Amelia commented resignedly as she prepared to drive back to her hotel. She still hoped conditions would be better during the night. George would return to the airport around midnight to recheck weather reports. If they proved satisfactory, he would awaken Amelia for an early start.

Conditions aloft remained unfavorable, however, and on May 4 George flew to New York to be ready to greet his wife upon her arrival, whenever that might be. During a stopover at Dallas, he indicated that he and Amelia were "planning a few months of domesticity": The house at Rye had been rebuilt, and their presence would be necessary to add "home touches."[16]

Not until May 8 did everything come together. Early that morning Amelia arrived at the airport where "a small crowd waited in a biting wind" to see her off. Among them were officials of the Foreign Affairs Ministry and General Samuel Rohas, in command of the First Air Regiment. In spite of Amelia's brush-off of Wiley Post's warning, she knew that her current undertaking was no milk run. Only one other nonstop flight between New York and Mexico City had been attempted, and it had ended in disaster. Not as sensible as Amelia, Captain Emilio Carranza of Mexico ignored warnings of bad weather and took off from Roosevelt Field on July 12, 1931. He made it no farther than the New Jersey pine barrens, where he crashed and perished in a violent storm. A memorial to him was erected in the pines.

"This is the most hazardous takeoff of my experience," Amelia said frankly, just before entering the Vega. "I shall probably have to taxi at least a mile and a half. I hope to arrive in New York but there is a possibility that I may run out of gas. I shall likely have favorable winds for half the journey and head winds for the other half." She added, "I do not expect to add any scientific data to aviation records on this flight. The trip should require about fifteen or sixteen hours."

She took along her usual light lunch: a chicken sandwich, a hard-boiled egg, and tomato juice. In reply to a later inquiry, she said, "No, I did not carry any good-luck charms or tokens. I prefer good mechanical work to rabbits' feet, and the Mexicans are very good mechanics."[17]

By departure time, flying conditions were ideal. Nevertheless, her takeoff at 6:10 A.M. required nearly every foot of the extended runway and all of Amelia's skill. Her route followed almost a straight line across the Gulf of Mexico from Tampico to New Orleans, a jog over to Mobile, then over Atlanta and Washington to Metropolitan Airport at Newark. "All in all, the flight was marked by a delightful precision," she wrote. "Everything worked as it should."

Except for about one hour over the Gulf when she flew sandwiched between cloud layers, "the weather was about as good as it could be." She kept in radio contact with airports and weather stations along her route. At many fields spectators gathered to catch a fleeting glimpse of her aircraft as it passed overhead and to hear how the flight was progressing.

A large crowd awaited her at Washington's Hoover Airport. She flew over at 9:05 P.M., having bettered Lindbergh's nonstop time between Mexico City and Washington by almost fourteen hours. This figure attested to the progress of aviation technology from the *Spirit of St. Louis* to the Vega. Among those at Hoover Airport was Eugene Vidal, who radioed her, "You've done a splendid job, so come down."

This rather peremptory message had no effect on Amelia's plans. "Thanks for the invitation," she replied. "I am going on through."[18]

Go on through she did. As she approached, Metropolitan Airport turned on its floodlights and Amelia "made a great half circle" and "came down to a perfect three-point landing." Watching her performance, Paul Collins, who had racked up over a million miles in the air, paid her the ultimate compliment: "That's a *flier!*" And Doc Kimball added, "Such people are good for all of us."

She touched down exactly fourteen hours, eighteen minutes, and thirty seconds after takeoff. Immediately the crowd of more than three thousand surged through police lines, running toward the aircraft. Somehow police radio cars nudged through the cheering spectators. The police formed another cordon, only to have it, too, break under pressure of the good-natured but determined crowd. Smiling, Amelia dropped from cockpit to ground and perforce stood there for several minutes.[19]

Later Amelia described vividly what happened next:

▶ In due course I was rescued from my plane by husky policemen, one of whom in the ensuing melee took possession of my right arm and another of my left leg. Their plan was to get me to the shelter of a near-by police car, but with the best of intentions their execution lacked coordination. For the arm-holder started to go one way while he who clasped my leg set out in the opposite direction. The result provided the victim with a fleeting taste of the tortures of the rack.[20]

They soon sorted themselves out, and Amelia walked between them toward the New Jersey National Guard hangar, which had been earmarked for her use. Partway there, George came toward them, and Amelia greeted him warmly. He was upset with the police for not controlling the crowd, but Amelia only laughed.[21]

She could sympathize with Lindbergh's distaste for the more exuberant manifestations of hero worship but, ever sensible, could accept the fact that if one lived publicly, one gathered a public. Her public, if a trifle overenthusiastic at times, was affectionate and admiring; her part was to be friendly, accepting, and gracious.

Chapter 15
Work and Honors

When George told reporters that he and Amelia planned "a few months of domesticity" after the Mexican venture, he demonstrated a most peculiar idea of domesticity. He had lined up for his wife a schedule of lectures that precluded home life except for very brief layovers. By George's own count, Amelia spoke "136 times in 1935 before audiences totaling 80,000."[1] On May 19, she wrote to Amy giving her projected schedule for the rest of the month: Chicago on the twenty-third; Washington (undated); on the twenty-sixth Atlanta, where she would receive an honorary degree at Oglethorpe University; two days later, back to New York for a "Mexican Dinner"; then the next two days at Indianapolis; and winding up the month at Muncie, Indiana.

Then she would be home for a few days before flying to Atchison for a Kansas editors' convention on June 7. June 10 would find her in Tulsa, "and then points west." She was not sure when George could follow; he was writing a book and tied up in "picture negotiations." They had rented the house for a year.[2]

Meanwhile, on May 10, Mayor Fiorello H. La Guardia presented Amelia with New York City's Distinguished Service Certificate. She wore a blue suit and matching blue hat, which she confided to the "Little Flower" was the only outfit she had available "because she had been flying so much."[3]

In Chicago, on May 23, Amelia spoke at a luncheon in connection with a conference of women's club officers. To the audience of two thousand, she described her Mexico City–New York flight. It was on this occasion that Giuseppe Castruccio, Italian consul general, presented

141

Amelia with the "Balbo medal of the Italian government." Later the Italian Embassy in Washington declared that there was no such medal, and, as mentioned before, Amelia promptly returned it to Castruccio.[4]

On May 26, Amelia received a doctorate of public service from Oglethorpe. She was one of twelve women on whom the university, "founded primarily for the education of men," bestowed degrees in various fields. Amelia accepted hers with a typical touch: If the degree was presented "because of what I have done in aviation, then my plane should share it with me."

That evening, as she stood at her hotel window watching twilight fall, she was in a different mood. With her was Alice Denton Jennings of the Atlanta *Journal*. Something impelled her to ask Amelia suddenly, "What is your idea of God?"

The answer came so promptly, with no groping for words, that it was obvious Amelia had given the subject much thought, although she seldom spoke of religious matters: "I think of God as a symbol for good—thinking good, identifying good in everybody and everything. This God I think of is not an abstraction, but a vitalizing, universal force, eternally present, and at all times available."[5]

The next day she was back in New York for the dinner the Mexican government gave in her honor at the Hotel St. Moritz. A distinguished party of forty "leaders in aviation, literature and journalism" assembled, including explorers Sir Hubert Wilkins and Roy Chapman Andrews, novelist Fannie Hurst, journalist Arthur Brisbane, and Juan de Dios Bojorquez, Mexican minister of the interior. All the speakers praised Amelia for having brought New York City within fifteen hours of Mexico City. Amelia claimed in reply "that that time would be cut in half very shortly."[6]

Among the guests at this dinner had been Edward C. Elliott, president of Purdue University. Shortly thereafter, he met with Amelia and George at luncheon. He offered Amelia the opportunity to come to predominantly male Purdue as a visiting faculty member, primarily to counsel the some eight hundred women students. Amelia accepted, and on June 2 Purdue announced that, beginning in September, she would be a "consultant in the department for the study of careers for women" and also would "serve as technical adviser to the Department of Aeronautics."

This modest announcement was overshadowed because, on the same day, Amelia made her first parachute jump. This was not a lifesaving venture: She was testing a device, "controlled and foolproof," designed to train fliers in the use of the parachute. The test took place at Lahaway, near Prospertown, New Jersey. Among others present were Eugene Vidal, who also tested the apparatus; the head of the Parachute School at Lakehurst Naval Air Station; and the parachute instructors from that installation.[7]

As Amelia had written to Amy, she was due in her home town of Atchison on June 7. Naturally, Atchison went all out to honor its most famous daughter. In a mile-long parade reminiscent of "old corn carnival processions," Amelia "rode in a flower-decked airplane float which the city firemen built." That evening the Kansas Editorial Association fêted her at dinner. Then came another parade, units of the Kansas National Guard escorting her to Memorial Hall, where, "after her introduction by Governor Alf M. Landon, she told of her exploits in the air." In between these events, she was able to snatch a visit with her Challis cousins.[8]

In view of the murderous schedule Amelia had been following so far in 1935, it is not surprising to find her writing to Amy from Cedars of Lebanon Hospital in Los Angeles on June 25. "The sinus is kicking up and I am tired of being beaten up with washings out so Dr. Goldstein is going to work on me tomorrow."

She had lectured the previous night in Pasadena, and sent Amy her fee of two hundred fifty dollars with instructions to use it "for 3 weeks near at hand for Pidge and the children and you." She continued in the motherly tone she so often used toward Amy. If the children needed clothing, Amy was to send her the bill. "You need some white shoes and a simple white dress, I know. Get some low heeled shoes for beach wear." She added a rather forlorn little PS: "Sorry you ain't here."[9]

The next day Amelia had her operation. Dr. Joseph Goldstein told the press that it was "minor and unimportant," and the patient would "leave the hospital in a day or two."[10] Nevertheless it was a painful nuisance to Amelia. She left Cedars of Lebanon as soon as she was able and went to a friend's. She wrote to her mother on July 5: "There is a backache I had which I thot was a strained muscle turned into pleurisy. I am still in bed with my side strapped. GP arrived yesterday, which helps. I am getting on now and can get up as soon as 3 days pass in which I run no temperature. The nose is healing O.K. though I am warned I'll have a headache for another week!"

Far more of her letter was devoted to fussing over Amy in her mother-cat-with-one-kitten fashion. She wanted her mother and sister to have a good, carefree vacation: "I should rather you take a place for a shorter time and have a real rest, not a cheap hole where there are things to put up with. *For instance, I do not want you and Pidge to do house work. In fact I forbid that.*"

And they were to buy "a few simple decent clothes. . . . Not awful cheapies, so people who don't look below the surface won't have anything to converse about." She wanted Amy to find the vacation spot. "Get listings of good places. . . . *Don't let Pidge just bungle around.*" Her PS combined anxiety and playfulness: "What do you mean your throat [is] swollen? What sense is there in neglecting health? You know I want you to be treated whenever necessary. *See a doctor and write me.* You may be a menace to the children besides yourself. I never heard of such stuff. !!!!!!"[11]

George arrived and after a spell of "letting off steam . . . how he could not leave the east, etc. etc.," surprised Amelia by asking her "to drive him around the Toluca Lake district." There at the end of Valley Spring Lane they found a little house for sale, well located between a golf course and a large vacant lot. The next day they offered for it. Shortly thereafter, George had to fly east. Precisely two minutes to takeoff, the real estate agent rushed up with the acceptance.

Amelia wrote an account of this transaction to Amy on July 28, advising, "I am going into business with Paul Mantz in United Air Service. My ship is still undergoing repairs, that is repainting and reupholstering and when it is finished I shall put it in with his fleet for charter. We are going to have a school and plan all kinds of things. GP is as excited as we are."

This and other plans came to naught. As she wrote Amy, her fall schedule was "a Tartar." She was to speak at Chatauqua on August 9, be in the New York area until the fifteenth, speak at Lakeside, Ohio, on the seventeenth, and then go back to California.[12]

On August 6 she "strode into a Senate committee hearing . . . crushed her brown felt hat on a table and expressed approval of further Federal regulation of aviation with reservations."[13]

A few days later she was back in California, generally at Burbank working with Mantz and discussing Wiley Post's projected flight with Will Rogers, to follow the Arctic Circle route.

Five days after Amelia's Senate appearance, she and George visited the Rogerses at their Santa Monica ranch. Also present were Will and Ariel Durant, the Fred Stones, and Wiley Post. It was the last get-together for this congenial little group. Post's plane, a modified Lockheed Sirius, crashed near Point Barrow, Alaska, on August 15, killing both men.

Amelia was never one to make a parade of her deepest emotions, but she mourned her friends, as indeed did most of the United States. Post was a prime public favorite, and Rogers a unique national treasure. In addition to her personal grief, Amelia keenly felt the loss to aviation, for she believed that Rogers had done more for civil aviation than anyone except Lindbergh.[14] He was enormously popular. His readiness to fly and his championship of aviation won many converts.

Perhaps it was an unconscious recoil from this sorrow that Amelia and Mantz decided to enter the Bendix Trophy race from Burbank to Cleveland, to take place on August 30. Each owned a Vega; they tossed a coin to see which aircraft to enter, and Amelia's veteran plane won. It had a top speed of 195 miles per hour, and they knew they did not stand a chance of winning against such speed kings as Colonel Roscoe

Turner and Benjamin O. Howard, who flew aircraft built for racing and capable of over 300 miles per hour. The already powerful Hornet engine of Turner's Wedell-Williams had been upped to nearly a thousand horsepower. Howard's high wing monoplane, *Mr. Mulligan,* had a Wasp engine reportedly able to reach 310 miles per hour.

Before the flight, Mantz gave Amelia a folded piece of paper, asking her not to look at it before they landed at Cleveland. They took off at 12:34 A.M., Amelia at the controls. Paul sat in the cabin, playing gin rummy with Al Menasco, an engine builder and friend of Mantz's. Amelia flashed across the finish line with only minutes to spare before the deadline. Just as they figured, she had placed fifth. "Old Bessie the fire horse came through," she wrote Amy.

After bringing the Vega to a halt, Amelia opened Mantz's note. He had listed all the entrants and how he expected them to finish. He had called the shots exactly: Turner and Howard would place first and second, a toss-up either way. (Howard won by a margin of 23.5 seconds.) As Mantz further predicted, Russell Thaw came in third and Roy Hunt fourth.

So far so good—an on-the-nose prognostication by a man who knew fliers and aircraft. What moved Mantz's listing into the realm of the uncanny was the funeral wreath he had sketched beside the name of Cecil A. Allen. Allen died when his plane crashed a few minutes after takeoff.[15]

Mantz probably knew that Allen's Gee Bee aircraft had been made from parts of similar planes. In addition, he had to take off in heavy fog that rolled in after the others had departed in clear weather. It was a recipe for disaster.

Last to take off was Jacqueline Cochran, flying her first Bendix. She dropped out at Kingman, Arizona. Later she told reporters, "I just got tired and quit." Actually she had experienced the same blinding fog, as well as mechanical problems, and she was heading into a violent thunderstorm when she decided to call it a day.[16] But Jackie scorned alibis herself—a refreshing contrast to George, whose press releases blamed Amelia's setbacks on anything except pilot error.

For most of November Amelia was at Purdue. She was so happy and so successful with the girls, who adored her, that here, perhaps, is a glimpse of what she might have done for many productive years had fate willed it so. At Purdue she found that "miraculously, there exists a real comprehension of the quaint viewpoint" she espoused, such courses as mechanical training and engineering being readily available to women students.

She realized that a smattering of such knowledge would even benefit those who had no hopes or plans beyond marriage. "Many a stay-at-home girl would welcome practical training in what to do when the doorbell fails to function, the plumbing clogs, the gas-range leaks, the fuse goes out, the windmill pump goes haywire. . . ."

She sent around a questionnaire to give her an idea what these young women wanted to do after college. Results showed that ninety-two percent of them planned to earn their own livings. Her advice was sound if unorthodox: Try one job, work hard at it, and if what looks more appealing turns up, don't hesitate to change. "It may turn out to be fun. And to me fun is the indispensable part of work."[17]

This pleasant interlude was over by the end of November, and Amelia took to the road once more, speaking on the twenty-sixth at Frankfurt, Indiana; at Zanesville, Ohio, the next day; and then on to Buffalo on the twenty-eighth for a lecture and a few days' time out with George. She needed the break, for her December schedule was a killer. Up to the twentieth, she frequently had two or even three engagements in one day, some of them in different cities.

Somehow she squeezed out a weekend to visit the Morrisseys, where Amy was again living. Muriel's marriage was still rocky, although she had worked out a life for herself centering around her children, her church, and her teaching work. Sometimes she toyed with the idea of divorcing Albert but never could bring herself to start proceedings. While divorce was becoming socially acceptable, it was still a rather messy business of charges and countercharges. And Muriel had nothing concrete to present to a divorce court. Albert didn't beat her or abuse the children; there was no "other woman" or women; he didn't even smoke or drink. In fact, there is no direct evidence of just what the trouble was. Reading between the lines, it seems most likely that Albert simply didn't care, and for affectionate, domestic Muriel that may well have been the ultimate cruelty.

If she moved out, however, she might be charged with desertion, in which case she would have no right to alimony or child support. In a way, Muriel was the victim of her own pride. She had tried so hard to put a good face on things that Medford had no idea all was not well in the Morrissey household. Albert, too, showed his best side in public, and as a result he was considered a fine family man and all-around good fellow. When push came to shove, Muriel could not bear to destroy the image. And she had her son and daughter, who so made up for everything that she actually could pity Amelia.[18]

Amelia loved her mother and sister, but one may well imagine that she drove away from the Morrissey home with relief and possibly counting her blessings. George Putnam might not be every woman's cup of tea; he might be pushy, he might bask too openly in his wife's reflected glory, and he might book her for lecture schedules guaranteed to exhaust an Olympic marathon runner. But the Putnams had a civilized life together, a life of shared interests and mutual friends.

Amelia's sense of responsibility toward her own family was endless. Writing from Syracuse, on December 17, following her visit to Medford, she sent Amy "a small check for your personal gifties" and charged her not to send all of it to the Balis relations. "You know I contribute every month to their upkeep." She had left money "with Pidge for the brats."

She added that she was "in the process of paying off about $3000 on Dad's hilltop." This turned out to be somewhat complicated, as she explained to Amy later; "while the land once was clear there was so much assessed against it, including taxes etc etc that it really amounted to rebuying it to get a clear title."[19]

That hectic month Carrie Chapman Catt, the veteran suffrage leader, selected Amelia as one of the ten outstanding American women. Eleanor Roosevelt headed the list, which included, among others, Secretary of Labor Frances Perkins and Anne Morrow Lindbergh. No doubt this accolade added to Amelia's drawing power at such events as a dinner held in her honor at the Lotos Club in New York City on December 22, which drew an attendance of more than 250.

To Amelia's indignation, one of the speakers launched an assault on the Roosevelt administration, claiming that unless American women united to save business, the government would collapse into communism or fascism. At the time Amelia made no reply, confining herself to her prepared talk on aviation. But the next day she expressed her displeasure publicly: "I was unaware that politics was to be interjected." She inserted a little political needle of her own in her protest: "I feel that some of the evils cited by Mrs. [Preston] David are but products of the type of government she advocates." Amelia ended graciously, "I am sure that my host did not intend placing me in the position of identifying myself with a partisan meeting."[20]

Thus ironically 1935 ended as it had begun, with Amelia, who had worked so hard for the nonpolitical causes of civil aviation and education for women, inadvertently brought into a minor political hassle.

Chapter 16

The Flying Laboratory

*T*he year 1936 began with three weeks of engagements in the South. From Knoxville on January 18 Amelia sent Amy a check, with the apology, "I am sorry to be late but I have been leading a terrific life." She and George would be getting together soon at Bowling Green, Kentucky. "I am not sure whether it will be more or less strenuous with him."

Later in the month Amelia went to Nashville to pick up Blanche Noyes, who had been working as an actress with the Orpheum Players. Blanche's husband, Dewey, had recently died, and she wanted to resume her flying career in California. So Amelia drove her out by way of Texas, Oklahoma, and Arizona, stopping to fulfill a few of Amelia's commitments en route. They reached their destination early in February.[1]

Meanwhile, an annoying situation had developed. Myrtle Mantz was suing Paul for divorce and had named two correspondents: Theresa Minor and Amelia Earhart. On the stand Mantz indignantly denied any but a business relationship with Amelia. He was having financial problems. Fewer movies called for the serial stunts in which he specialized, his mother was bedridden in Redwood City, and bills were mounting. The last thing he needed was a scandal that could jeopardize his profitable relationship with the Putnams. His position as Amelia Earhart's technical adviser gave him priceless publicity as well as unrivaled professional cachet—not to mention his hundred-dollar-a-day salary.[2] This was an immense sum for 1936, when a hundred dollars a month was not bad pay.

For years, with the avidity of Hollywood columnists, various writers tried to link Amelia romantically with a number of men whose orbit touched hers. High on the list was Paul Mantz. Granted that romantic love is the least predictable, most irrational of all human emotions, still it is most difficult to imagine Amelia seriously considering joining her lot with that of Paul, who seldom if ever had a thought beyond aircraft. Amelia was a well-educated woman, acquainted with the world of ideas, books, music—a world that Paul scarcely knew existed.

In any case, Paul was not in the least in love with Amelia. He was devoted to Terry Minor, his future wife. Terry was the widow of racing pilot Roy Minor and had a son and daughter. She and Paul met at the 1935 Cleveland air races, some six months after his separation from Myrtle. They seemed to feel a sense of predestined togetherness: They shared the same background, the same circle of friends, the same interests. And as Terry was not a pilot, there was no cause for professional envy or jealousy. Paul and Terry were very discreet, for she did not want to be in the position of dating a married man. But somehow Myrtle must have gotten wind of—or guessed at—their attachment.[3]

Amelia did not mention the Mantz case when she wrote Amy on February 25 from Fort Worth on her way to lecture at San Antonio, Birmingham, St. Petersburg, and Miami. She was traveling by commercial air, leaving her "ship and auto and husband in Los Angeles." She and George had almost finished alteration plans for the North Hollywood house and hoped to begin work on it in May. "In the meantime have Pidge send me the bill for glasses etc."

George wrote to Amy on March 5, telling her not to worry about the Mantz divorce "mess." He thought that some lawyer had dragged in Amelia's name to harvest cheap publicity. In a letter to her mother on March 23, Amelia mentioned the subject with a sort of bored contempt:

▶ Poor old Myrtle Mantz had to get nasty in the trial. The only two women she had not driven away from Paul paid for their loyalty by being dragged into a divorce suit. The silly accusations fell of their own weight and I cannot but feel she will eventually do something so disgraceful that the world will know what she is. Because, of course, after her self inflicted publicity she will be watched. I really have been fortunate, for any one who has a name in the paper is a target for all sorts of things.[4]

If Myrtle had hoped to break up the professional partnership between Paul and Amelia, she did not succeed. Never had Amelia needed Paul's expertise more, for a cherished dream was reaching fruition. After her Honolulu-Oakland flight, she "thought of a hundred things" she could do with a new and better aircraft. "Not only did I want to make a longer flight than any I had attempted before, but I wanted to test some human reactions to flying."[5]

In the summer of 1935, President Elliott of Purdue had asked George what most interested his wife "beyond immediate academic matters." George was not the man to drop the ball after such a kickoff. Amelia, he said promptly, wanted "a bigger and better airplane. Not only to go to far places further and faster and more safely but essentially for pioneering in aviation education and technical experimentation."[6]

Elliott looked with favor upon this suggestion and set about turning the necessary academic and financial wheels, all of which took time. Not until April 19, 1936, did Purdue announce the establishment of the Amelia Earhart Fund for Aeronautical Research, amounting to more than fifty thousand dollars. The plane in which Amelia would "hop here and there around the world" was under construction at the Lockheed factory in Burbank.[7]

The type of aircraft selected was a Lockheed-10, known as the Electra. These twin-engine monoplanes were designed as medium-sized ten-passenger transports, primarily intended as feeders between major airports and smaller fields lacking long-range flight capacity. This was Lockheed's first all-metal plane. It had retractable landing gear that increased speed and radius but, of course, imposed an added responsibility on the pilot or copilot at takeoff and landing. The Electra's wingspread was fifty-five feet, her length slightly less. An observer would immediately note the tail with its twin vertical fins.

Originally the Electra had four fuel tanks in its wing roots—located between the engine and the fuselage—consisting of two main tanks with a capacity of 81 gallons each and two auxiliary or emergency tanks, each holding 44 gallons. The total fuel capacity of 250 gallons and a cruising radius of 750 to 1,000 miles was, of course, far below what Amelia would need for long-distance flights. So the ten passenger seats were removed, fuel tanks substituted, and the fuselage strengthened to support the weight, a measure that included removing all the windows and covering the holes, except for the window in the cabin door and the one directly opposite.

The six new tanks had a capacity as follows: One held 81 gallons, three held 153 gallons each, and two held 132 gallons each. In addition, two 102-gallon tanks replaced the original 44-gallon containers. The two 81-gallon tanks remained in place. Two 16-gallon tanks on the wing stubs held reserve lubricating oil. These "were not connected to the fuel-supply piping." Thus Amelia's Electra, No. 14 R 16020, had a total tankage of 1,200 gallons, with fuel capacity of 1,170 gallons—not 1,150 or 1,151, as widely reported later.[8]

Other changes, mostly made at Mantz's suggestion, included a "Clipper-type" hatch in the navigating compartment to facilitate celestial observations; a latch on the cabin door to hold it open some four inches to allow for operating the drift-sight; and a catwalk over the cabin tanks for access between the navigating compartment and cockpit.

Jean L. Backer, who compiled *Letters from Amelia,* noted that Purdue's project "raised some eyebrows as to just what scientific use the plane would be put in the skies over Indiana, and after her disappearance many were certain the whole thing was a plot hatched by the intelligence services with University cooperation."[9] Actually, there was no question of the Electra being confined to Indiana's skies. From the first, the press made clear that this was a transport plane capable of and intended for long-distance flights.

Paul worked over the plane tirelessly to make it the best and safest of its kind possible in the state of the art then. He insisted upon the Sperry robot pilot, telling George that it would eliminate fifty percent of Amelia's fatigue. He ensured that the instrument panel held duplicates of every important gauge. He had the Wasp engines' mixture controls changed from automatic to manual "to stretch out the gasoline supply for long hops."

To increase the Electra's range, he called in Clarence M. Belinn, superintendent of engineering for National Airways, Inc., located at Boston Municipal Airport. He was an acknowledged expert on "gasoline-tank crossfeed" problems. Mantz considered him uniquely qualified to provide Amelia with "an auxiliary tank system that would be easy and foolproof to operate." Belinn installed a system controlled by a master valve in the cockpit floor. Three tanks were in each wing root, with six more placed between cockpit and navigation room for a total of 1,202 gallons. This Belinn considered sufficient for distances of between twenty-five hundred and three thousand miles, "depending on winds and how she flew."[10]

Meanwhile, Amelia continued her schedule of lectures. From De Kalb, Illinois, she wrote Amy on April 1, mysteriously promising "a grand surprise" for her mother, assuring her that it had nothing to do with her, Amelia. She added, "the rumor about the world flight in June is applesauce. Confidentially I shall have a new airyplane to play with then I hope, but as I'm busy lecturing until May or thereabout, I shall not hop off in June. It would take months to prepare such a trip— maybe a year." Significantly, Amelia did not promise never to "hop off" on a world flight.

Toward the end of April a severe cold confined Amelia to bed, but a request to testify before a Senate committee necessitated her hurrying to Washington.[11] On May 1 she appeared before the Senate Air Safety Committee on behalf of pilots and the inventors of navigation aids. Public opinion had been questioning the integrity of airmen, and Amelia testified firmly, "I know of no group more loyal, more interested, than the men who run our far-flung airways. I think I have flown on every airway in this country as a passenger or a pilot and have found no better service than that given in the air, and our facilities are superior to any other country."

She added that air navigation aids, like highway signs, were "a means for increasing performance in the highest speed brackets." But she made it clear that the future of aviation did not depend upon congressional provision of such assistance, "that if all aids were abandoned tomorrow, airplanes would still fly."[12]

By May 9 Amelia could no longer contain her "grand surprise" for Amy. "You are going abroad this summer!!!!!!!" she wrote her mother. Amy's niece, Nancy Balis, a student at Bryn Mawr College, would go along "as companion and hand maiden." Amelia had booked passage for the two on the Red Star Line's *Westernland,* to sail on June 13 and return August 3. The *Westernland* was not "a *socially* interesting ship," but its passengers probably would be teachers, students, and the like who would be "more humanly interesting."

Later that month, some time after the twenty-second, Amelia wrote again: "Pidge says you are beautiful with your new perm. . . . I am paying for a washer 'ooman for Pidge, so lay off that from now on." After Amy returned, Amelia wanted her in the new house in California, where she and George expected to "spend more and more time."[13]

These two brief notes reveal Amelia at her most likable—full of joy at arranging a treat for her mother. At around the same time, she sent Amy a long, undated, and unsigned memorandum that illustrated another phase—Amelia the organizer. In the midst of her heavy schedule, she prepared a list of "suggestions and comments" as meticulous as the checklist for a major flight. The tone, however, was that of an anxious mother preparing her little girl for her first summer camp.

She began by suggesting what suitcase to take and what to put in it. "Keep shirts laundered, ties pressed and shoes shined." If reporters discovered who she was, Amy was to be cheerful with them and smile when photographed. "Don't express international opinions. . . . You approve of my flying; you don't know my plans for the future." Amy was to praise English things in England, French things in France, and "never tell of mishaps, lost baggage, cold mutton chops, runs in your hose, etc."

Next Amelia listed Amy's clothes for the voyage in "order of dressiness" and instructed her to stay in bed the first day out. "Keep manicured and have hair done every 10 days. . . . If raining don't wear kid gloves. They'll spot and be ruined." She had given Amy "very decent stockings," and Amy must not wear the very sheer ones for everyday. "Do not yank *any* hose on from the *top.*"

Then Amelia listed Amy's evening dresses and advised her to save the best one for the ship's "festive night." She added, "Don't be reactionary with Nancy. Let her be radical. Youth which isn't is pretty poor and all her family are sticks.

"Last, have a good time."[14]

This was Amy's first trip abroad, but she was neither half-witted nor ill-bred. She certainly did not need to be told to polish her shoes and shampoo her hair or to be briefed on how to put on her stockings. One wonders if Amy reacted with irritation or indulgent amusement.

Tucked into this list of instructions was a paragraph so remarkable that it demands special attention:

▶ Please don't down the Roosevelt administration. It's all right to be reactionary inside but it is out of step with the times to sound off about the chosen people who have inherited or grabbed the earth. You must think of me when you converse and I believe the experiments carried on today point the way to a new social order when governments will be the voice of the proletariat far more than democracy ever can be.[15]

Amelia referred to Roosevelt's New Deal experiments. Possibly, like many of her contemporaries, she expected the New Deal to evolve into a form of benevolent socialism. Indeed, that year she abandoned her previous nonpolitical stance and would actively campaign for Roosevelt. The statement she gave when announcing her decision clarifies her position: "I am aligned with President Roosevelt because of his social conscience. Throughout his term of office he has fought against odds to reduce human misery. He has realized that obsolescence can affect parts of the machinery of government just as it does the machinery of industry."[16]

Various incidents in Amelia's life demonstrated that she, too, had a "social conscience," and her settlement work in Boston had given her a closer look than most women of her class ever had into slum conditions. No doubt that experience made an indelible impression on her mind.

In May of 1936, however, Amelia was taken up primarily with her own business. Rumors were flying that she planned a round-the-world flight. This was the case, but she always preferred to work in secret until her plans and preparations were complete and the project ready to roll. Therefore, she laughed off the report on May 22, when she and George stopped off at Salt Lake City to meet Paul Mantz: "Somebody invented that. My new plane is only 80 per cent finished, so I don't know what it will do." She added that the plane's purpose was research in connection with the foundation at Purdue. "Today's planes are good for experienced pilots," she said, smiling, "but what we need is a craft papas and mamas can handle with safety."

The Putnams and Mantz went on to Los Angeles together.[17] There Paul put Amelia through an intensive course of instrument flying instruction, using the Link trainer in his hangar at Burbank.[18] On June 6 she piloted a party of four through a five-hundred-foot-thick blanket of fog to test a compound designed to clear away fog. Its inventor, C. R. Pleasants of San Francisco, released it from the aircraft.

"The effect really was remarkable," said George. "Holes appeared below us through which we could see the ground." He thought that the compound might well "prove of extraordinary value to aviation."[19]

Eight days later Amelia addressed the national convention of the Women's Christian Temperance Union at Tulsa. She broke off her narrative of her Atlantic solo to remark, "Incidentally, I would be afraid to use any kind of stimulant either during or before an important flight." She added that the commercial airlines forbade a pilot to drink for twenty-four hours before a scheduled flight. The delegates cheered Amelia with enthusiasm.[20]

Paul flew Amelia's Vega to Tulsa; he was to "pick up another plane at Houston." George had to stay in New York, where he and Amelia had gone after the fog-dispelling experiment, so Amelia asked a woman pilot friend to come to California for a visit. They had two enjoyable weeks of flying and horseback riding, and then sorrow struck. George's mother, Fannie, had been "getting weaker but not alarmingly so" until the last days of June. Amelia wired George "to stand by, but the end came" before he could reach California. Amelia wrote the news to Amy, then in London. She ended her letter on a more cheerful note: "Our house is coming along *slowly*. I am afraid you'll have to live in a tent for a while under a cactus. . . . have a good time and dance with the Prince of Wales."[21]

Amy didn't dance with the Prince of Wales, but she certainly had a good time. Amelia arranged the trip so that, in addition to seeing the usual tourist sights of England, France, Belgium, and Holland, Amy and Nancy made some special side trips. Remembering how Amy loved the world of Scott and Dickens, Amelia scheduled them through the Lake Country, Devon, and Cornwall. The press paid no attention to them, for they traveled as "Miss Balis and her aunt."[22] In the last full year of her life, Amelia had the happiness of making a lifelong dream of her mother's come true.

Chapter 17

Plans and Warnings

O n July 21, 1936, Lockheed test pilot Elmer C. McLeod, with Amelia as copilot, took the new Electra up for "its first official flight." It was a moment of sheer delight for Amelia, and as she posed for newspaper photographers she looked two decades younger than the thirty-nine she would be on July 24. Years on the "mashed potato circuit" had not blurred her slim figure, tamed her blond mop, or suppressed her engaging grin. "We've improved the mechanical features of aviation marvelously," she told reporters, "but the observation of the human factor in flight has been neglected." Amelia wanted "to conduct a sort of clinical survey to determine the effects, upon varying individuals, of speed, altitude, pressure, fatigue, mechanical aids and other conditions of flying."[1]

She applied to the Department of Commerce in Los Angeles for a restricted license. "Long distance flights and research" was the aircraft's designated use. For the next month or so, she "wore a groove between San Francisco and Southern California" every few days to observe progress on last-minute adjustments. "It's simply elegant," she said to the interested mechanics who clustered around. She was too busy to take time to greet her mother and Nancy Balis when they returned from Europe, so George went in her stead.[2]

At the end of August, she, Paul, and her mechanic, Bo McKneely, flew the Electra to New York. Their first stop was Kansas City, where they remained overnight. To the inevitable reporters she stressed that she was not trying to set any records, just to "find out what the plane could do" and then decide whether to enter the transcontinental Bendix air races on September 4. Amelia had no illusions that she could win. "After all, this is a transport plane, not a racing machine," she told newsmen at New York.[3]

Bendix offered a special prize of twenty-five hundred dollars to the first woman to cross the finish line, regardless of how far behind the winners. This annoyed the female pilots, for it implied that none of them could possibly win. In 1936, however, Amelia's friend Louise Thaden, with Blanche Noyes as copilot, won the race, to their own great astonishment. They had run into a storm at St. Louis and approached Los Angeles at about 230 miles per hour. They landed at Los Angeles Airport convinced that they were among the latecomers. Laura Ingalls, flying alone, placed second. Die-hard antifeminists could console themselves that the top two favorites did not finish. Roscoe Turner crashed his plane en route to the race, and Benny Howard was well in the lead when his aircraft lost a propeller. As a result of the ensuing crack-up, Howard lost a leg.[4]

Already Amelia's projected transworld flight was being spoken of as a settled fact. On September 3, Colonel J. M. Johnson, assistant secretary of the Department of Commerce, stated that Amelia planned such a project. He admitted that she had "a very well-thought-out program," but made it plain that he disapproved of such attempts because "stunt planes were overloaded with fuel." Licenses were issued on the basis of airworthiness, but did not consider "whether they are beneficial in the long run." He added, "There's no advantage in going across the ocean if you only take fuel."

He pointed out that American, British, French, and German pilots were ready to begin experimental transatlantic flights that would carry mail and passengers on two routes: the northern from New York to England via Nova Scotia and Ireland, the southern via Bermuda, the Azores, and intermediate refueling stops. Pan American Airways was scheduled to carry passengers and mail across the Pacific, "two commerce inspectors having just returned from an investigation of that possibility."[5]

Johnson had a point. The conquest of the air was following the normal path of exploration: first the discoverers, then the explorers, then the adventurers, and now the settlers were coming. The Wild West days of aviation were over. Nevertheless, certain unconquered pockets remained. One of these was a round-the-world flight the long way, as close to the equator as possible. It might serve no useful purpose but, like Mount Everest, it was *there*—a challenge to be met.

Another record fell when on September 5 Beryl Markham flew the Atlantic solo from east to west. She left Abingdon Airport, London, headed for New York, but, like Amelia, had to settle for an emergency landing, coming down on Breton Island between Nova Scotia and Newfoundland. American women fliers were generous in their praise. "I am delighted that another woman pilot has done a solo across the ocean," said Amelia. She laughed when a reporter asked if she might try to cross the Atlantic east to west. "I don't know—you know, I've seen that ocean twice, and it doesn't get any prettier."[6]

Meanwhile, Amelia was arranging for her flight with her usual efficiency, believing that preparation was "rightly two-thirds of any venture." Not until November was the flight itinerary finalized. At one time the schedule called for a refueling stop at Midway en route to either Tokyo or Manila; however, Midway had no adequate facilities for land planes, although it could accommodate seaplanes with ease. Early in October George sounded out the Navy as to whether aerial refueling over Midway would be possible. If so, would the Navy be willing to cooperate? This involved a tanker aircraft hovering over the receiving plane and inserting a pipe or hose into the latter's gas intake. The first successful air refueling of any consequence was done by the Army Air Corps' Captain Ira Eaker in 1929; however, in 1936 the technique was still in its infancy.

The Navy responded cautiously. While refueling over Midway "was technically possible, it involved considerations of policy and precedent and would have to be studied from those angles." One officer in the Bureau of Aeronautics, Captain (later Vice Admiral) A. D. Bernhard, wanted no part of the project. He wrote in pencil on a routing slip dated October 23, "I believe we are sticking our necks out on this. It will set an inconvenient precedent, do the Navy no good, probably excite the Japs, and if the flight fails Navy will be criticized for sponsoring it. If flight is successful, nothing new will be learned. I recommend reconsideration."[7]

On October 15, at the direction of the State Department, George wrote to the Bureau of Air Commerce giving certain data about the proposed flight, including approximate itinerary, with a tentative date of "late February or March 1937." The plane would carry no firearms or movie cameras. "Two small hand cameras probably will be carried." He closed by advising that the project was "part of the program of aeronautical activities being conducted under the auspices of Purdue University, Lafayette, Indiana."[8]

The next day, October 16, George wrote directly to the secretary of the Navy to solicit the Navy's cooperation in the Pacific Ocean leg of the flight. He explained: "Our desire is to avoid the hazards of the takeoff at Honolulu with full load. The full cargo of gas involves a considerable overloading. Further to stretch out the gas-mileage to the maximum means very slow speed, which obviously adds to hazard by increasing the time over water, and likewise places a harder burden on the engines." So he requested "an aerial refueling operation" at Midway of five hundred, possibly four hundred, gallons, which should supply "ample margin for the remaining 2,800 miles to Tokyo, or possibly a route via Guam to Manila." He asked that "the entire project be held in strict confidence."[9]

As Mantz's biographer pointed out, "Nowhere in his letter did GP suggest how he expected Amelia to stay awake on such a grueling non-stop overwater flight of nearly 4000 miles, Honolulu to Tokyo." It was an example of what Paul considered the "coldly impersonal drive" with which George promoted his wife's flights, which bothered Paul considerably.[10]

But there is no evidence that Amelia protested this arrangement. On the contrary, when by November 10 the Navy had not responded, she wrote directly to President Roosevelt. She outlined her plans, explained the problem as being "primarily a matter of policy and precedent," and asked the president's help in securing Navy cooperation. She thought that "a project such as this (even involving a mere woman!) may appeal to Navy personnel." She assured him that the proposed flight had "no commercial implications" and added a typical touch: "Like previous flights, I am undertaking this one solely because I want to, and because I feel that women now and then have to do things to show what women can do."

Evidently Roosevelt was sympathetic, because he jotted on this letter a handwritten note: "Do what you can and contact Putnam."[11]

Nine days later, the Navy agreed to refuel the Electra over Midway and to rehearse the maneuver in California; however, a new factor had entered the equation—Howland Island. First sighted by an American skipper on December 1, 1838, Howland had been lost and rediscovered periodically and attracted very little attention until the 1930s, when such isolated spots as Howland and its neighbor Baker came under consideration as potential refueling stops for transpacific flights. Howland was a mere speck in the vastness of the Pacific, rising no more than twenty feet above the sea, in size roughly two miles long—north and south—and a half-mile wide—east and west.[12]

A Honolulu-to-Howland leg made sense from Amelia's standpoint. Her object was to circumnavigate the globe as close as possible to the equator, and a stopover at Tokyo or even Manila would take her far off the objective, whereas Howland was only a few miles from the equator, some eighteen hundred or so miles southwest of Honolulu.

Just when all seemed settled, a bureaucratic hitch at the Department of the Interior, which had jurisdiction over Howland, necessitated another appeal to Roosevelt. This time Amelia sent him a telegram dated January 8, 1937. She explained that since her letter of November 10, the "difficult and costly" refueling maneuver was no longer necessary; "instead I hope to land on tiny Howland Island where the government is about to establish an emergency field." All concerned had been helpful, and a construction party was due to sail shortly. But now,

she continued with obvious exasperation, a Works Progress Administration (WPA) appropriation of three thousand dollars, which would
cover "all costs other than those paid by me for this mid Pacific pioneer
landing field," a facility that would be "permanently useful and valuable," was being held up. The requisition was on the desk of an official
in the Bureau of the Budget and would require executive approval to
move it. Could the president "expedite an immediate action?" She
ended engagingly, "Please forgive troublesome female flyer for whom
this Howland Island project is key to world flight attempt."

She did not appeal in vain. On January 11, an assistant secretary to
the President advised Amelia that Roosevelt had allocated funds to
WPA "to enable the Bureau of Commerce to carry out the construction
of such a field." The "necessary equipment and labor" would leave for
Howland by a Coast Guard vessel scheduled to leave Honolulu on
Tuesday, January 12, 1937.[13]

In view of subsequent events, Amelia's comments about this first
stage of her projected flight are particularly interesting. She had made
her previous landfalls by dead reckoning. "But then I was aiming at
continents, not small spots of land in the mightiest of oceans," she explained. "Hawaii, 2400 miles from California, would be hard to find by
this method alone. Howland Island—dimensions less than a mile by
two miles—1800 miles further on, would be a fantastically tiny target."

Amelia acknowledged that it "did not seem good sense" to tackle this
project without a navigator. She chose Captain Harry Manning, who
had skippered the liner *President Roosevelt* when Amelia returned
from the *Friendship* flight in 1928. During the voyage they had discussed navigation and agreed that some day they might join forces on
a flight. "Now, eight years later, he still wanted to ship on such an serial voyage and I still wanted him to." So he took a six-months' leave
of absence from his liner. Among his qualifications was a knowledge of
Morse code; he could receive at some fifteen words per minute.[14] While
this was admittedly slow, it was fifteen more than Amelia could do.

The logistical and diplomatic arrangements for such a flight were
staggering. The route would touch upon or overfly many countries and
require fuel stocks at various points. Just assembling the necessary
charts and maps took many weeks. Once these were in hand, Commander Clarence S. Williams, formerly of the U.S. Navy, who had
helped Amelia plot other flights, charted the round-the-world course.
Amelia almost crooned over the finished products: "In final form flight
charts are really lovely things. On them are drawn the compass
courses with their periodic changes, distances, airports and the like As
supplementary data accumulates the marginal notes assume encyclo-
pedic proportions. They concern details about airports, service facilities, prevailing winds, characteristics of local weather ad terrain, critical altitudes, emergency landing possibilities, and the like."[15]

Years later, when researching Amelia's last flight, Captain Laurence F. Safford, USN, examined Williams's flight charts, known as strip maps. He found them anything but "lovely," in fact, "almost devoid of information of value to a navigator. Special maps may have been necessary for the flights across Africa, but for the ocean flights AE would have been much better off if she had carried the regular ocean charts prepared by professional cartographers and used by mariners the world over." In his strip maps, "Williams omitted details of terrain and other essential information which were more important for aerial navigation than for surface navigation."[16]

A major contributor toward the flight was the Putnams' old friend, Jacques de Sibour. A pilot himself, as was his wife, Violette, he was familiar with flying conditions in "much of the most difficult territory involved." In addition, being associated with Standard Oil Company of New Jersey and its affiliates, he was invaluable in planning for fuel supplies to be available at designated locations. Bob Oertel performed a similar service for the South American legs of the flight.[17]

George worked hard on these behind-the-scenes arrangements. As early as June 1936, he wrote to Eleanor Roosevelt, asking her to help him get in touch with the appropriate individual in the State Department. He ended, "Do please emphasize that the project is for the present confidential. As you know, A. E. likes to avoid advance discussion of flights—their realization depends upon so many factors."

George spent an entire month in Washington, visiting the various embassies to secure passport visas necessary to take off and land, as well as permission to overfly. From Standard Oil he arranged the purchase of fuel, from Pratt & Whitney such spare parts as might be needed. Sibour not only helped in designating suitable refueling stops but also sent to them men experienced in handling such equipment and arranged for it to be ready when Amelia would need it.[18]

While all this was going on, Amelia had kept up her usual routine of lectures and campaigned for Roosevelt's reelection. Here was another area in which she might have done very well had she chosen to try. She had the name recognition and charisma to have made her a campaign manager's dream candidate. She had one handicap as a political speaker: Her pleasant, low voice, one of her chief charms, did not carry well in the open air.[19]

At this busy time, Muriel's married life took another downswing. Amelia wrote to Amy from New York around September 28 that she and George would be visiting Medford shortly to talk with Muriel and Albert. The immediate problem was financial; George and Amelia came to the rescue. Muriel's relief must have been considerably tempered when the Putnams told her they were earmarking quarters for Amy in their California home—a room that George considered "just about the swellest in the whole house," plus its own bathroom, a "roman dream of elegance." Muriel would have been the first to concede that her mother deserved the best but must have wondered how she could keep the Morrissey boat on an even keel without Amy's helping hands.[20]

George and Amelia had a pleasant break when they were weekend guests in Annapolis of the Naval Academy superintendent. Amelia addressed the midshipmen on November 6 and, with the admiral and his wife, the Putnams attended the Army-Navy football game. Ten days later, back on the lecture circuit, she sent a telegram to a meeting of the National Women's Party. It read in part: "Today women still stand victims of restrictive class legislation and of conflicting interpretation of statute. To clear the situation their rights must be made theirs by definition—that is, by constitutional guarantee."[21]

An incident just before Christmas hinted at another aspect of Amelia's inquiring mind. A Western Air Express plane, carrying seven persons, had disappeared over Utah on its way to Los Angeles. An extensive land and air search failed to find any trace of the missing aircraft. A newspaper story datelined Salt Lake City, December 21, 1936, contained this paragraph:

> ▶ Amelia Earhart came here today to follow up a "hunch" concerning the missing Western Air liner. She flew her monoplane along the eastern shore of Great Salt Lake for an hour, then returned with the same report that has come regularly from nearly a score of searching fliers:
> "No trace sighted."[22]

No "hunch" had sent Amelia on this search, and she spent considerably more than an hour on the job. She was there in consequence of an experiment in extrasensory perception with Jacqueline Cochran.

The friendship of the Putnams and Odlums had become very close, marred only by Jackie's reservations about George, who, perhaps misled by her very feminine beauty, made the mistake of patronizing her. "Well, little girl, what's your ambition in flying?" he asked her one day.

The phrase "little girl" was asking for trouble. "To put your wife in the shade, sir," Jackie replied sweetly.

In fact, Jackie never felt competitive toward Amelia. For one thing, their primary areas were different, requiring different techniques. Amelia specialized in long-distance flights, with speed a secondary consideration; Jackie was after speed records. She admitted that she could be a "positively fearsome" competitor in her own field, "but Amelia was different. She was such a gentle lady."

Floyd Odlum made a hobby of psychic phenomena and took a serious interest in the experiments being carried out at Duke University by J. B. Rhine. Some tests proved that Jackie had unusual gifts in that area.

Only a few of her friends, including Amelia, knew of this side of Jackie's life. She believed ESP worked for the same reason she believed her aircraft would fly—personal experience.

There is no evidence that Amelia had any extrasensory talents, but she was interested in Jackie's experiments. So when word came to the Odlum ranch that an airliner had disappeared over Utah, Amelia, who was visiting the Odlums, suggested that Jackie try to locate it. For two hours the two friends sat quietly while impressions poured through Jackie's receptive mind. She named mountains and mentally followed roads and transmission lines. Neither Jackie nor Amelia was familiar with this area, so the latter telephoned Paul Mantz. Would he verify the details on an air map and call back? His return call confirmed Jackie in every particular.

Amelia was too excited to wait for daybreak; she drove to Los Angeles through the night and took off for Salt Lake City at dawn. She verified Jackie's landmarks and, thus encouraged, searched for three days before giving up. She and Jackie felt rather foolish. But the next spring, when the snows melted, the plane was found within two miles of the spot Jackie had pinpointed.[23]

George and Amelia stayed with the Odlums over the New Year, 1937, holiday. Jackie "had plenty of 'hunches' about that flight and none of them was on the optimistic side." She had no doubt of Amelia's ability but entertained serious questions about Manning. He was "an exceedingly fine man," but she did not believe he could handle "high-speed navigation in a plane." She issued Amelia a challenge: "Take him out to sea for a distance from Los Angeles and fly in circles for a while. Disorient the man and then ask him to pick the course back to L.A."

Amelia did so, and the results justified Jackie's pessimism. Manning hit the shore roughly half-way between Los Angeles and San Francisco—a good two hundred miles off course.[24]

Another who questioned the wisdom of Amelia's latest project was Louise Thaden. One day that January Louise cornered Amelia in her office in Paul Mantz's hangar and scolded her with all the frankness of a concerned friend: "Look here, you've gone crazy on me," she said bluntly. "Why stick your neck out a mile in this round-the-world flight? You don't need to do anything any more. You're tops now and if you never do anything else you always will be. It seems to me you've got everything to lose and nothing to gain."

"You're a fine one to be talking to me like that," Amelia answered quizzically. "Aren't you the gal who flew in last year's Bendix with a gas tank draped around your neck?"

Then her mood changed, and she continued in a serious voice, "I've wanted to do this flight for a long time. . . . I've worked hard and I deserve one fling during my lifetime. If I should bop off, it will be doing the thing I've always wanted most to do. Being a fatalist yourself you know. The Man with the little black book has a date marked down for all of us—when our work here is finished."[25]

Flight Into Mystery

With famous aviator Wiley Post in Cleveland, March 1935. Post and Will Rogers died in a crash in Alaska during an attempt to fly around the Arctic Cricle.

Emerging from her plane on arrival in Oakland after her January 1935 flight from Honolulu. Amelia was the first person ever to make this solo trip.

Reporters interview Amelia with her husband at her side in front of an enthusiastic crowd at Newark Airport.

Greeted by a Mexican official at Newark Airport after her successful flight from Mexico City in May 1935.

Standing beside her Vega at March Field, California, 1936. This plane was replaced by the "Flying Laboratory," the Lockheed Electra 10E, later in the year.

With Edward C. Elliot, the president of Purdue University, holding a model of her "Flying Laboratory," then under construction.

Watching mechanics repair her Electra in Burbank, California, after her 1937 crash in Honolulu.

Amelia and her husband study the route she plans to take on her around-the-world flight in 1937.

Preparing two distress signals before her attempt to fly around the world.

Amelia prior to her final flight. From left are: George Putnam, Amelia, Harry Manning, and Bo McKneely, a mechanic at Union Air Terminal in Los Angeles. Manning, originally scheduled to be Amelia's navigator, had to return to his ship after the trip was delayed.

Amelia and navigator Fred Noonan in San Juan, Puerto Rico, where they finished a leg of their flight.

The pilot with her navigator and Vicomte Jacques de Sibour, who had helped to arrange the flight, in Karachi.

Amelia, a well-rounded person, enjoyed tending the garden at her Rye, New York, home.

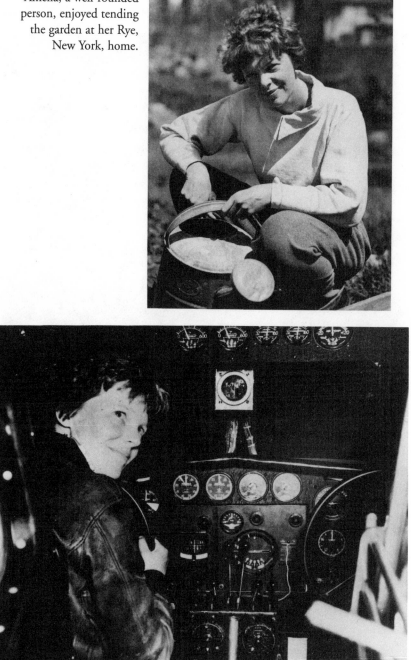

Amelia in the place she loved best, the cockpit of her plane.

Chapter 18
False Start

*T*oward the end of January, when Amelia was almost ready to announce her plans, discord again raised its head in the Morrissey household and demanded Amelia's attention. She wrote Muriel, "You have taken entirely too much on the chin for your own good or that of any man who holds the purse strings." She could understand her sister's position: "One hesitates to bring on a quarrel when it can be avoided by giving in." This, however, could cause damage: "Given a little power over another, little natures swell to hideous proportions."

If Muriel planned on leaving Albert, she would need a legal separation to ensure a monthly income. Amelia urged her sister to consult a good lawyer and, in the meantime, not to sign anything or move out of the house. She ended, "You had better plan to come out here for the summer. Or before, if you have to. . . . Then Albert *might* miss you and the children if you came. It's worth trying."[1]

However distressed Amelia might be over her sister's unhappiness, she had to concentrate on her own affairs. Sometime before her flight, George asked her "if she could not give up this project. Life held so much else." He remembered her reply word for word: "Please don't be concerned. It just seems that I must try this flight. I've weighed it all carefully. With it behind me life will be fuller and richer. I can be content. Afterward it will be fun to grow old."[2]

Runway construction at Howland began on January 30, 1937, under the supervision of Robert Campbell of the Airways Division, Department of Commerce. He was experienced in this type of work, but it moved slowly because "the equipment was antiquated and in poor condition." Campbell kept W. T. Miller, also of the Airways Division office in Washington, informed of progress—or lack of it. Miller had been in charge of the investigation the previous year of Howland, Baker, and Jervis islands as potential commercial refueling stations.[3]

By early February Amelia was ready to announce her plans. She had passed her deadline for worry—"three months before a flight. Decide then whether or not the goal is worth the risks involved. If it is, stop worrying. To worry is to add another hazard. It retards reaction, makes one unfit." At this point she grinned and added, "Hamlet would have been a bad aviator."[4]

Despite the result of her test of Manning's aerial navigation skills, Amelia retained him, and he was with her when she held a press conference in the Hotel Barclay in New York on February 11. Amelia looked "wholly calm and very fit" as reporters, photographers, and newsreel cameramen clustered around her. Using a globe, she pointed out her proposed flight path. She explained that she had selected the east-to-west route "after some deliberation." South of the equator, easterly winds prevailed, and "on a great part of the trip" she would take advantage of them. Her aircraft's "limited range" was another reason for choosing this route.[5]

After her formal briefing ended, reporters asked questions. She could not resist a little gentle swordplay, saying with a chuckle, "You know, I feel you men have pushed me into this. You're the ones who've kept saying and saying that I was going to fly around the world until you've compelled me to think seriously about doing it."

Carl Allen of the New York *Herald Tribune,* a long-time acquaintance, took up the challenge. "Oh, come now!" he protested, smiling. "Nobody has pushed you into it. You know you've been wanting to do it all the time."

"Yes, I suppose you're right," she acknowledged cheerfully. "I didn't get away with that, did I?"

Other newsmen asked the predictable question: "What are you going for?" This time she answered that she just wanted to fly around the world at the equator. Captain Manning would accompany her part of the way: "I don't believe the pilot on such a flight can navigate too."

She had no idea how long the journey would take, for it was without precedent. "I'm simply going to fly as and when I can, race nothing and nobody." Eventually round-the-world flight would be routine. In the meantime, every flight was "potentially important. It may yield valuable knowledge."[6]

And when she returned? "My lovely home in North Hollywood—California sunshine—books—friends—leisurely travel—many things!"[7]

Later Amelia clarified her reasoning:

▶ "*Why* are you attempting this around the world flight?" Such was one of the most pertinent queries, whose answer may as well be recorded here.

"Because I want to." That was as near a complete reply as I could devise. Here was shining adventure, beckoning with new experiences, added knowledge of flying, of peoples—of myself. . . .

Then, too, there was my belief that now and then women should do for themselves what men have already done—and occasionally what men have not done — thereby establishing themselves as persons, and perhaps encouraging other women toward greater independence of thought and action. . . .[8]

On February 13, 1937, newspapers announced that Amelia would carry "10,000 special covers for stamp collectors," to be postmarked at various points, including "the Howland Island cachet, the first to be used from this Pacific islet." Gimbel Brothers in New York were the exclusive agents for these covers. This was one of George's financial coups, which brought in more than twenty-five thousand dollars, a most welcome addition to the flight fund.[9]

Two days later, the secretary of the Navy issued his orders covering the Navy's part in Amelia's flight. He instructed that a seaplane tender be sent from Pearl Harbor to "take station about midway between Honolulu and Howland, returning Pearl Harbor after Earhart landing at Howland." Lieutenant Arnold E. True and two aviation mechanics would go to Howland by Coast Guard cutter "for aerological forecast and service to plane." The governor of Samoa would be responsible for collecting "useful weather information" and transmitting it to True. The USS *Ontario* would "take station about midway between Howland and British New Guinea for plane guard and weather reports." Miller of the Commerce Department would be in Oakland about February 25 and would coordinate the plans for the flight.[10] This was excellent cooperation on the part of the Navy and lent an air of finality to the project.

George and Amelia dropped by New York City Hall on February 17 to say good-bye to Mayor La Guardia, who wished Amelia "the best of luck," adding, "I just don't know why you didn't make your start from New York, but we will have to make up for that when you come back."

Amelia explained amiably that she would need the latest weather reports for the long hop across the Pacific, hence could not start from New York. But she promised "that on her return, as soon as she got her face washed, she would come into New York." The mayor in turn "promised her a real official reception" when she did so.[11]

The next day she, George, and Manning left New York for Cleveland on the first leg of a leisurely flight to the West Coast. Aloft, Amelia made her first tests of her new radio aids, successfully contacting the control tower at Newark Airport. They reached Burbank on February

21, and Amelia announced that she planned on starting her flight not later than March 15: "This is about the latest I can hope for the best flying weather."[12]

Work at Howland had slowed to the point where, on March 6, Miller had to radio Pearl Harbor to delay the sailing of the tug *Ontario,* the minesweeper *Whippoorwill,* and the Coast Guard cutter *Shoshone* until advised "to allow for the completion of runway construction on Howland."[13] This was cutting it very fine.

Meanwhile, Amelia devoted her attention to last-minute tests and preparations. Paul Mantz had temporarily abandoned the movies so that he could work on the Electra without distractions. By March 9 Amelia and Manning had stacked their food and maps on a table in Mantz's hangar. Having "declined all invitations to receptions or social functions along the route," Amelia would need only a few changes of slacks, blouses, boots, and underwear. To the press Manning praised Amelia as a pilot and as a "very unusual person," adding, "She won't have any real need for a navigator after the Pacific crossing."[14]

Shoshone, the designated guard at Howland, departed Honolulu for that destination on March 10. In addition to her crew, she carried the following:

▶ Richard B. Black, Field Representative, Department of the Interior
Captain H. A. Meyer, Nineteenth Infantry, Adviser and Liaison Officer
Lieutenant Arnold E. True, USN, Aerographer
First Lieutenant Daniel A. Cooper, Air Corps, USA
Arundel M. Keane, Associated Press
V. M. Culver, United Press
Six Army enlisted men
Five Navy enlisted men
Three Hawaiian boys as replacement colonists
Lieutenant Commander Frank T. Kenner, USCG, on temporary duty
Assistant Surgeon David J. Zaugg, Public Health Service

Shoshone also had a cargo of food, water, gasoline, and miscellaneous equipment for the islands it would visit following the stint at Howland. Likewise aboard were fifty-one drums of aviation gasoline for Amelia's plane. The ship reached Howland on March 15. Two days before landing, Black wired the director of territories in Washington: "Will arrive Howland about nine Monday morning Stop Runways ready now Stop Will radio upon arrival."

This was incorrect, as Black could have determined had he held up his report until he could see for himself. The north-south and the northeast-southwest runways were completed, "but the all-important west-east runway, heading into the prevailing winds and which was too short for a safe take-off to begin with, lacked 500 feet of completion." It was not finished until late June and might well not have been done then had not Lieutenant Cooper pushed the project.[15]

On March 13, the same day as Black's wire, Amelia announced her plans to leave the next day at about 5 P.M., but a low-pressure area moving toward the coast promised poor flying conditions between Oakland and Honolulu.

To the press, Amelia spoke enthusiastically about her project: "It's going to be interesting, really. You see, it's hard to get any accurate value on a flight of this kind. But we do know that commercial airlines never are established until several such experimental flights have been made. Each one adds its little contribution of knowledge about weather and flying conditions, and those pieces of knowledge fit together to make the total which must be had before air routes are safe." She remarked that people often asked her how her husband felt about her flights. "Well, he knew what I was when he married me," she said, smiling. "All the same, I know I'm lucky to have him, for I never could do it without his help. He takes care of everything."

The Oakland *Tribune* reported that Captain Frederick J. Noonan would act as Amelia's navigator as far as Howland. Manning would continue with her to Darwin, Australia, after which she would proceed alone. But on March 13 George stated that it had not been "finally decided" whether Noonan would accompany Amelia and Manning on the first leg of the flight.[16]

This statement was patently false. No way would Amelia be planning to take off within days without knowing exactly who was going with her and why. Moreover, Noonan, whom Amelia called "tops among aerial navigators," would not have signed up on such an iffy basis. In fact, he had just accompanied Amelia, Manning, and Paul on a two-hour test flight.

Manning would need experienced help on the critical Honolulu-to-Howland stage. From the technical standpoint, Amelia could have done no better than Fred. He had gone to sea at the age of seventeen aboard a British square-rigger. During World War I he had served as an officer on a Royal Navy munitions ship. After the armistice, he switched to aviation and became both a pilot and a navigator for Pan American Airways. He rose to become inspector of Pan Am's airports and had mapped the company's transpacific routes. Unhappily, Fred was an alcoholic, rumored to have "a two-bottles-a-day habit." Associates claimed that they never saw him unable to perform his duties because of drink; however, it was rumored also that Pan Am had considered him "a bad risk" and let him go. Later it appeared that he had resigned, believing that he had gone as far up the corporate ladder as he could. He claimed to have his alcoholism under control, and Amelia apparently decided that his professional skill justified taking a chance on him.[17]

Perhaps George's statement to the press was meant as a signal to Fred: Any last-minute slip off the straight and narrow, and he would be out. As in the case of Bill Stultz, Amelia's writings make no mention of Fred's problem. But it is a strange coincidence that on both her first and last transocean flights she should have been willing to entrust her safety to men who suffered from the same disease that had spoiled her childhood happiness.

A storm forced postponement of the takeoff on March 14, and the weather also made the Pan Am Hawaii Clipper turn back a few hours out of Alameda. George could give the press no definite departure date. He confirmed that Noonan would be "relief navigator" as far as Howland. Manning would go on with Amelia to Darwin. He also announced that Paul Mantz would serve as relief pilot on the Oakland-Honolulu leg.[18]

Mantz's presence was something of an afterthought. He was satisfied with the Electra but thought Amelia's piloting technique could profit by a little smoothing. He had suggested that they fly Los Angeles to New York, then back to Oakland; however, Amelia considered this both a waste of time and unnecessary hours on the engines. But she was glad when Paul suggested that he "hitch-hike to Honolulu." He could act as relief pilot and make a final check on the aircraft before she proceeded on to Howland. She was amused to find that Paul had another motive: "Parenthetically, it was only after I had agreed to take him that I awoke to the fact that I was unwittingly playing the role of understudy for Cupid. For Paul confessed that the big reason he wanted to go to Honolulu just then wasn't solely his professional devotion to my project, but the fact that his fiancee, Mrs. Theresa Miner, was already at sea . . . Hawaii-bound. . . ."[19]

Pan Am's "pioneering hop" to New Zealand by way of Honolulu, Kingman Reef, and Samoa was scheduled to leave that same afternoon, March 17, as was the Hawaii Clipper, "on a regular run"—Honolulu-Midway-Wake-Guam-Manila-Hong Kong. She carried seven passengers, "one of them a woman," and an eight-man crew. It is rather quaint to read that "three planes in the air at the same time" would tax Pacific communications facilities. Nevertheless, the symbolism was clear: The pioneering past and the commercial present would fly within hours of each other as far as Honolulu; then their paths would diverge.

Finally the sun broke through the clouds, and at 3:06 P.M. the Hawaii Clipper headed out, followed by the New Zealand–bound flight at 4:19 P.M.[20] Immediately the Electra was brought out of the Navy hangar that had housed it, Paul checked the engines, and Amelia said "a brief good-bye" to George and took the pilot's seat. She wore "brown slacks and a soft shirt and a bright scarf." In honor of St. Patrick's Day, Fred sported a shamrock in his lapel.

With Amelia at the flight controls, Paul moved the throttles forward and warned Amelia, "Never jockey the throttles. Hold her straight with the rudder and push everything to the firewall, smoothly!"

Amelia took over at eight thousand feet and piloted the plane for fifty minutes of every hour while Paul kept the log. At 5:40 P.M. Pacific Coast Time, they overtook the Pan Am Clipper piloted by Captain Edwin C. Musick. Amelia dipped the Electra's wings in greeting and snapped a picture. This was the first time she had ever seen another plane at sea.

Paul was pleased with the skill Amelia was demonstrating and with Noonan's quiet professionalism. He was annoyed with Manning, who kept popping into the cockpit "to work the radio over Amelia's head, and to shoot a string of star sights through the upper hatch."[21]

Intraplane communications were primitive, to say the least: "Communications between our pilot's cockpit and the navigators in their cubbyhole was carried on by means of a cut-down bamboo fishpole, with an office clip at the end to hold the cards upon which messages were written."

This was the first time since 1928 that Amelia was not alone on a transocean trip, but all concerned were too busy to talk or, for that matter, to eat, taking mostly coffee or hot chocolate from thermos bottles.

Amelia's log was a mixture of the practical and poetic, reaffirming her joy in the beauty of flight: ". . . golden edged clouds ahead, then the golden nothingness of sunset beyond. . . . The aft cabin is lighted with a weird green blue light. Our instruments show pink. The sky rose yellow. . . . Night has come. The sea is lovely. Venus is setting ahead to the right. The moon is a life-saver. It gives us a horizon to fly by. . . . We are now using the Sperry to save our eyes as there is practically no horizon."[22]

A few hundred miles out of Hawaii, Paul told Amelia to keep the Makapu beacon "ten degrees on the starboard bow." This, Amelia explained, meant "that I should tune by Bendix radio direction finder to indicate the location of the beacon, and then head the plane as he directed."

This was the first time Amelia had used this new navigation aid; she performed skillfully, allowing for "a wind drift correction Noonan had figured out." The device worked perfectly until some hundred miles out of Honolulu when, in Amelia's words, "The generator just went out. Harry has held the key down so long it grew tired." More technically, Manning was depressing the key so that Makapu Point could get a fix on the Electra. The failure did not matter at this stage because the plane's "DF [direction finding] compass was working properly."[23]

At 5:40 A.M. they sighted Diamond Head "exactly where she and Fred expected it," according to Amelia. "Making the landfall that morning was even pleasanter than my first view of California's shore line two years ago. After all, it would require ingenuity to miss a continent, which I was aiming for then. Hawaii, however, is something else again and we all knew how easily it could be passed by."

As they approached Wheeler Field, Amelia asked Paul to land the plane. "She was very fatigued and kind of exuberant," he said later. The exuberance one can understand, but there seems little reason why, with a relief pilot and two navigators, Amelia should have appeared so "groggy" that Paul worried over her stamina.[24] Perhaps the very fact that she had a crew may have been a distraction as well as a heavy psychological burden. This time she was responsible not only for her own life but also for three others.

When Amelia climbed out of the Electra to receive "flower leis from a reception committee of army officers," she admitted that she was "terribly tired" and that the flight had seemed longer than her Honolulu-Oakland flight of 1935. Rather to her amusement, the Electra's time of fifteen hours and forty-seven minutes had set a new record. She found this "an interesting commentary on the progress of flying equipment" because, far from trying to establish a speed record, they had been going "about as slowly as possible."

A few minutes after landing, Amelia was on her way to the home of Lieutenant Colonel and Mrs. John McDonnel for "the so-fresh scrambled eggs miraculously awaiting us."[25] She had hoped to take off for Howland after a rest of only "eight hours or so," but the weather turned bad. They stayed with Christian and Mona Holmes, who had placed their home at her disposal for the west-to-east flight. The Holmes had arranged a real Hawaiian luau with hula dancers, but Amelia made her excuses and retired to her room to rest. Terry Miner, who had awaited Paul in Honolulu, did not know quite what to make of Amelia: "Amelia was not very social. She was awfully nice, but rather hard to know." On this occasion, she was just plain tired. By the next day, a long sleep, a sun bath on the lanai, meals that "appeared wherever and whenever she awoke," plus "fabulous" quantities of pineapple juice, had dispelled her fatigue.[26]

Paul was at work early. Dissatisfied with Wheeler as a takeoff point, he flew the Electra to Pearl Harbor, where the Army's Luke Field (later Ford Island Naval Air Station) had a three-thousand-foot concrete runway. There he found that water and sediment had contaminated the commercial gasoline brought there by tank truck. Fortunately he was able to buy 590 gallons of high-test military aviation fuel from the Hawaiian Air Depot.

Meanwhile, Wilbur Thomas, a motor expert and Pratt & Whitney's representative in Hawaii, was looking over the Electra's engines. "I told him he was one of the very few men in the world I would let touch them before the time rolled around for their regular overhaul," wrote Amelia. She believed that undue tinkering with "beautiful motors" could be harmful.

It was fortunate that she gave Thomas his head, for he discovered a dismaying circumstance: Amelia had landed with the propeller bearings almost dry. He decided that "improper lubricant at Oakland . . . caused the dangerous situation." Thomas also stated that if Amelia had taken off as originally planned, it might have forced her down at sea.[27] Thus, despite all the expert care and attention the Electra had received, a major discrepancy somehow had slipped by.

A small group of civilians and military men, including Brigadier General Barton K. Yount, commanding the Army Air Forces in Hawaii, gathered to see Amelia off in the early morning of March 20. The plane carried nine hundred gallons of gasoline, by no means an overload, but enough to permit return to Hawaii after eight hours aloft if necessary. The weather reports were not entirely favorable.

At 7:35 A.M. mechanics pulled away the chocks, and the Electra sped down the runway so smoothly that Amelia "thought the take-off was actually over. . . . There was not the slightest indication of anything unusual." Then spectators saw a wing dip; the plane slewed to Amelia's right. In a flash, she reduced power to the right engine and for a moment thought she had corrected the situation. "But, alas, the load was so heavy, once it started an arc there was nothing to do but let the plane ground loop as easily as possible." The right landing gear dropped free and "gasoline sprayed from the drainwell." Thanks to Amelia's promptly cutting the ignition, there was no fire. "I've seen and participated in many crashes," said Yount, "but I never saw anybody come out of one so coolly as she."[28]

Sparks flew, however, and that was enough to start a brief disaster rumor. George was waiting at the airport office in Oakland with newsmen, Bill Miller, and two Coast Guard radiomen with a portable set. The radio had just announced that takeoff was imminent when the phone rang and George answered. "Putnam?" asked the caller, a press association representative. Upon George's "Yes," the newsman continued, "Have you heard? They crashed . . . the ship's in flames. . . ." That was all George could take. He handed the receiver to Miller and walked unsteadily outside. Almost immediately, his friends raced after him shouting, "No fire. . . . No fire at all. False report! No one hurt!"

George's hand was still shaking when he wrote out a telegram for Amelia: "So long as you and the boys are okay, the rest doesn't matter. It's just one of those things. Whether you want to call it a day or keep going later is equally jake with me."

George knew that there was little likelihood of Amelia's wanting "to call it a day," and she, who deeply appreciated this gallant message, knew that if their positions were reversed, George would want to continue.[29]

Exactly what caused the accident is still a mystery. Those nearby saw Amelia stick her head out of the cockpit and say, "Something went wrong. It seems as if I hit a wet spot. The ship began to go off the course and I could not stop it." Various Army aviators agreed that the wet runway was partially responsible. Light rain had fallen all night. Yount, however, insisted that the runway was in good shape; he blamed a blowout. And indeed investigation showed that the right tire had burst. Others thought the gasoline "washing back and forth in the tanks set the plane to swaying."[30]

"I don't know what happened, Paul," Amelia, her face white, said to Mantz, one of the first on the scene.

He flung a comforting arm around her shoulders. "That's all right, Amelia. As long as nobody was hurt. You just didn't listen to Papa, did you?"

Amelia managed a faint smile and headshake, but was not convinced, as was Paul, that she had "jockeyed her throttles." She carefully studied the tracks on the runway and in consequence also doubted the blown tire theory. "Possibly the landing gear's right shock absorber, as it lengthened, may have given way." Amelia may have been right, because ten weeks later the landing gear did fail; however, the Electra was on the ground at the time, so came to no harm.[31]

Here, then, hard on the heels of the propeller bearings incident, came this accident. One cannot help wondering whether the Electra was not what an old-time sailor would have called "a jinx ship." Nevertheless, the project would go on. Amelia, Fred, and Manning were not even scratched; the plane was repairable. They would just have to return to California and start all over again.[32]

Chapter 19

Entr'acte

*T*here can be no doubt that Amelia was in a state of emotional turmoil as she walked away from her damaged aircraft. The postponement of a project so carefully and happily planned, the humiliation of cracking up amid a flood of publicity, the sense of having let down her colleagues at Purdue, the realization of the appalling increase in expense—Amelia never wrote of such emotions, but one must credit her with the sensations any intelligent, sensitive human being would experience under similar circumstances.

In addition, there was a special personal grief, for the Electra had been, in effect, Amelia's pet. Amy would later observe that she and Amelia "considered the plane she used as if it were a living creature. It was like a favorite pony. We said goodnight to it and petted its nose and almost fed it apples. The last plane . . . was the one we were especially attached to. . . ."[1]

But Amelia wasted no time in repining. After checking the damage, she returned to the Holmes residence and telephoned for reservations on the *Malolo,* due to sail at noon the same day.[2] Her courtesy failed no more than did her courage. Before boarding, she telephoned George with a message for Richard B. Black, Interior Department representative at Howland, to tell him "how sorry she is to break that engagement for tonight, to which she had looked forward.

"She is sorrier for the trouble she has given you and the Coast Guard officers and personnel with you.

"She is going to try again, and next time hopes to be less of a nuisance."[3]

In her own account of the abortive initial attempt, among those Amelia thanked were "Richard B. Black, and all of the personnel of the *Itasca,* with their fruitless waiting at Howland."[4] Actually, the Coast Guard cutter at Howland at this time was *Shoshone. Itasca* was positioned there for the second try. In view of future events, the mistake is pathetic and somewhat eerie—as if Amelia were apologizing in advance for causing trouble for *Itasca's* officers and crew.

Paul Mantz also had a message for George, a cable report of the Electra's condition: "Starboard panel damaged, starboard fin damaged. Starboard and port landing gear damaged. No wrinkles in center section or fuselage. Right starboard motor mount bent up. All four propeller blades bent. No noticeable damage to engine. Port wing panel untouched. Skin slightly damaged."[5]

The Army Air Corps agreed to dismantle and crate the Electra for shipment to the Lockheed factory. On March 27 it was on its way via the liner *Lurline.*[6]

Amelia, Paul, Manning, and Fred appeared at the *Malolo's* pier about half an hour before sailing time. Amelia still wore her flying outfit of slacks and leather jacket, and a dismal drizzle soaked her hair and leis. To reporters she "looked exhausted," but this she denied.

"Of course I am coming back," she said. "But my plans just now are too indefinite to know when." She had left the postal covers in Hawaii pending a firming up of her plans. She added, "This accident means postponement only. It is my full intention to go ahead with the adventure as soon as possible."[7]

The *Malolo* docked on March 25 at San Pedro, where George and the inevitable reporters awaited Amelia and her party. "I still believe my ship is one of the very best airplanes in existence," she told the newsmen. "We were overloaded at Honolulu, but I think I will be able to resume the flight without further mishap. I am very grateful that we escaped injury." She added that she might have to change her route because "a month's delay at this time of year will result in unfavorable atmospheric conditions in the South Seas."[8]

The first order of business for Amelia was to unwind. The very day she landed, she telephoned Jackie Cochran, asking to come to the ranch. The Odlums would always put up Amelia, even if Jackie had to vacate her own bed. At Indio Amelia could find rest in the desert sun and air, congenial companionship, and an inflexible rule of the house—"no personal questions designed to put people on the spot."

On this occasion the only other guests were speed king Benny Howard and his pilot wife. Amelia sat on the floor near the fireplace and gave the party a detailed account of her latest flight and its unexpected ending. Total silence greeted her, and she inquired teasingly,

"Isn't anyone going to ask me the big question? Don't you want to know whether or not I'm going to try it again?"

The silence persisted; no one felt like risking Jackie's wrath by asking questions. Finally she said, "Come on, Amelia. You know the rules of the house." So no one asked the "big question," but they continued to discuss Amelia's plans. Jackie still had plenty of what a later generation would call "bad vibes" about the round-the-world flight, but her worries "poured out that night in Indio."

Perhaps some of her uneasiness rubbed off on Amelia. One day shortly thereafter, she and Floyd Odlum went for a drive in an old car, and it got stuck in the desert. As they awaited rescue, she abruptly asked, "Do you think I should do it?"

"Do what?" inquired Floyd.

"Fly around the world?" Her tone made it a question.

He avoided a direct reply: "Amelia, if you are doing this to keep your place at the top among women in aviation, you're wasting your time and taking a big risk for nothing. No one can topple you from your pinnacle. But if you are doing it for the adventure and because you simply want to do it, then no one else ought to advise you. No one else should make that kind of decision for another."[9]

Right there, if she had not done so before, Amelia should have taken a good, hard second look at the project. The very fact that she had asked for advice meant that she was not perfectly sure of what she should do. The Atlantic solo had been a psychological necessity for Amelia; she never could have been content until she had exorcised the ghost of the *Friendship*. The Honolulu-to-Oakland flight had established a legitimate record, making Amelia the first person—not just the first woman—to make this solo crossing. But there was no compelling reason for this around-the-world project. As first Louise Thaden and now Floyd Odlum said, her place in aviation history was unassailable—and coming from the husband of Jacqueline Cochran that assessment meant much. Any scientific experiments Amelia might make en route would be largely worthless, because the conditions most likely would never be duplicated. Here was the perfect opportunity to bow out gracefully, if only for financial reasons.

Expenses would be a real headache this time around. For the original flight plan, everything had been under control dollar-wise. The special Earhart covers alone would have met maintenance expenses; lecture fees and payments from news and photo services would cover the rest. But the accident in Hawaii had added a good fifty thousand dollars to the budget—a formidable sum to raise in 1937 with the country still in the Depression. The plane had to be repaired painstakingly, with "some actual redesigning." That alone cost about twenty-five thousand dollars. An equal sum was required to cover the cost of such expenses as fuel and the services of mechanics along the route.

Amelia hated to ask her friends for help; however, she and George could not handle the entire sum alone. The Odlums "advanced a substantial sum." Presidential adviser Bernard Baruch sent twenty-five hundred dollars "because," he wired, "I like your everlasting guts!" Admiral Byrd sent fifteen hundred dollars and reminded Amelia that she had given him that sum at the cost of considerable embarrassment to herself. Possibly the gift that Amelia most appreciated came from the Lockheed mechanics, who worked on her plane an entire Sunday and refused to accept any pay.[10]

In April Amelia went to New York on business. George had negotiated another issue of the letter covers, with the addition of a red box with the words "2ND TAKE OFF." These were as popular as the first issue and may well have accounted for the fact that Amelia's first appearance in New York since her crash was at the Gimbels Stamp Club. Five hundred members gathered on April 24 to hear her avow her purpose to try the flight again "sometime around the middle of May." The flight, she said, would follow the same route as before. Repairs to the Electra had been nearly completed, but the exact takeoff date would depend on "weather and flying conditions." Manning had to return to his ship, and Noonan would take over.[11]

Manning's departure left a void that no one concerned seemed to take very seriously, but which could have contributed to the final tragedy—he had been the only crew member skilled in Morse code.

It seems incredible that neither Amelia nor Fred had ever learned Morse, which would have extended their radio range appreciably. While nothing was too much trouble or too costly to put the Electra in tip-top condition, they neglected this rudimentary safety measure that would have cost them merely a few hours of their time.

While in the East, Amelia went to Medford to see the Morrisseys and to take Amy back to California. There Amelia reiterated her advice to Muriel—not to leave until she had arranged "a satisfactory property and support agreement." Then she could bring the children to California and look for a teaching job near Amelia.

Amy and Amelia left for California believing that summer would see the three united. Muriel, however, decided that her personal happiness should not outweigh her children's need for a two-parent home. Amy fretted and Amelia was irritated; both women had expended large amounts of thought and emotional strength—and, in Amelia's case, money—in trying to make Muriel happy. Now she had thrown it all away.[12]

Still, it was Muriel's choice to make. Such a sacrifice on the part of an unhappily married woman was far from rare in those days; indeed, it was almost expected. And probably Muriel was not all that miserable. She adored her children, found pleasure and fulfillment in teaching, and had the satisfaction of having done what she considered the right thing.

Amy settled happily into the Putnam home. She loved her corner room with the view of the Hollywood hills. On a little walnut table from the Otis home in Atchison, Amelia had placed an illuminated globe, so that Amy would be able to follow her daughter around the world. She had no household duties; the Putnams employed a Filipino houseman named Fred, while Amelia's secretary, Margot De Carie, handled correspondence, household accounts, and any other task she could take on. On the cook's day off, George usually took over the kitchen, so Amy had little to do beyond bake an occasional chocolate cake, while Amelia scooped up the icing clinging to the bowl, licking it off her finger with all the relish of her childhood.[13]

Much more was involved in preparing for the flight than repairing the Electra and raising funds. The entire route had to be reevaluated in the light of setting back the takeoff three months. Amelia and Fred restudied weather maps and consulted with meteorologists. Amelia wrote:

▶ The upshot of those consultations was that I decided to reverse the direction originally chosen for the flight. . . .
A compelling factor in our decision was the probable imminence in the Caribbean and African areas of much less favorable weather later than early June. So it seemed sensible to get this part of the journey over as promptly as possible.

Arrangements with the Coast Guard and Navy for the Pacific portion had to be worked out again, and permission secured once more from a somewhat reluctant Bureau of Aeronautics. "Its policy was to discourage extracurricular undertakings of the kind, the common or garden term for which sometimes is 'stunt flights.' But having granted me permission once, the ships, personnel and flight plan being the same, it would have been difficult to withdraw it."

Even more troublesome were the reams of paperwork from the State Department. We can do no better than let Amelia speak for herself:

▶ Then there was the matter of "permissions." We had already accumulated, with the kindly co-operation of the State Department, an impressive collection of credentials. They were multitudinous and varied. In addition to routine passports and visas, in much of the territory it was necessary to secure special authority to land a plane. Here and there were forbidden regions over which one might not fly. In and over other territories no firearms or motion picture cameras were permitted. Medical credentials were necessary; pilot and navigator were swollen with a full personal cargo of vaccines and inoculations. A couple of countries required testimonial of character and a negative police record. These I contrived.[14]

During this busy period, her fan letters gave Amelia some light moments. A "staggering number" of youngsters wanted to go with her around the world—"bless their hearts." She chuckled over one letter from a little girl who had adopted "Amelia" as her middle name. "I would have named my duck Amelia but since it is a he duck I can't."[15]

On May 3, when Amelia arrived in Los Angeles from New York, she stated that she hoped to set off before June 1. "I can't set an exact starting time, of course. It all depends on the weather.

"My route will follow the original charter course save for a few minor changes, owing to the weather conditions along the way."

The newspaper article added that she would probably take Noonan along for the "Pacific portion" of the flight, then proceed alone from Port Darwin.[16]

This was in accordance with the original plan whereby the navigator—then Manning—would drop off after the Pacific was behind them. But this arrangement was manifestly absurd because the route would cover miles and miles of wild territory, some of it quite as dangerous as the ocean itself. With the view to publicity, George wanted Amelia to make at least part of the flight solo. But Amelia insisted upon a navigator the whole way.[17] George was not a pilot, and his wife was not the complaining type, so he may not have realized the impossible position he was putting her in.

On May 7, Admiral William D. Leahy, chief of naval operations, assured George that the Navy would be "glad to cooperate with Miss Earhart's flight in a similar manner as before." This time Lieutenant True would remain at the Fleet Air Base, Pearl Harbor, where he believed better aerological services were available. Indeed, True's report of April 6, 1937, covering the weather reporting for the aborted March flight to Howland, made clear that this vital function left much to be desired as arranged at that time.[18]

George replied to Admiral Leahy promptly. On May 8 he confided "the exact situation." As usual, he stressed confidentiality.

▶ The delay from the chosen mid-March date has resulted in changed weather conditions on several stretches of the proposed route. In a couple of instances these are drastic. Specifically, the weather probabilities in the stretch from Natal north are increasingly bad as June advances. The same is true of the Dakar-Aden-Karachi route. Obviously it is therefore desirable to get to Natal and across the South Atlantic as promptly as possible.

So Miss Earhart has decided to reverse the route and to proceed from west to east. . . .

For this reason George could not yet give Leahy a firm ETA for Howland, but would try to do so "about a fortnight in advance."[19]

At the time, no doubt this reversal of route seemed logical, but it is highly questionable in retrospect. The change meant that the Howland-Honolulu leg—the longest, most difficult, and potentially most dangerous segment of the route—would come at the end of the circuit, when Amelia and Fred could not help but be tired. Moreover, instead of tailwinds easing the Electra along, the prevailing headwinds would be pushing against her. If the new conditions presented a real problem, it might have been wiser to postpone the project for a year, then proceed as originally planned.

During these last days of preparation, Amelia made another visit to the Odlum ranch. She and Jackie pored over maps and, according to Jackie, it was then that Amelia finally decided on the new flight pattern. Full of foreboding, Jackie gave Amelia several emergency items: a large, colorful kite, fishhooks and lines, "and one of those all-purpose, super-duper knives with a blade for every conceivable purpose."

The two women decided that Jackie's ESP talent was sufficiently powerful that she might be able to pinpoint Amelia's location should she be forced down. It was certainly worth a try. Meanwhile, Jackie would practice.[20]

On May 18 the reconstructed Electra was ready for pickup, and Amelia jubilantly wired President Elliot at Purdue, "Our second attempt is assured. We are solvent. Future is mortgaged, but what else are futures for?"[21]

Most of the work had been to put the aircraft back into its original condition, but some changes were made, such as installing dump valves on the fuel system. One improvement begging to be made remained undone: No simple "intercom" was installed between pilot and navigator. Incredibly, Amelia and Noonan still planned to circumnavigate the globe with no better means of intraplane communication than the bamboo fishpole and clip.

Most of the navigational equipment on the Electra (plane number NR 16020) were, in Safford's words, "the best available in 1937 and entirely adequate for their intended purpose." He doubted, however, that the Bendix direction finder was foolproof. "In the hands of an expert who appreciated its good points and its limitations, AE's D/F was a good piece of apparatus. In the hands of amateurs like Amelia and Fred Noonan it was a booby trap. . . ."[22]

Shortly after Amelia had received the plane, Jackie, driving Floyd to Palm Springs, received a quick but strong impression that one of the Electra's engines had caught fire. She assured Floyd that it wasn't serious; "a crew was dousing it that very moment." Confirmation came by radio that night and by newspaper the next day.[23]

On May 22 newspapers reported that fire had broken out in one of the Electra's engines "a moment after" Amelia had landed in Tucson on what was announced as a test flight. George, Fred, and Bo McKneely, Amelia's mechanic, were aboard.[24] Amelia's account is more colorful: "After landing and checking in, when I started my motors again to taxi to the filling pit the left one back-fired and burst into flames. For a few seconds it was nip-and-tuck whether the fire would get away from us. There weren't adequate extinguishers ready on the ground but fortunately the Lux apparatus built into the engine killed the fire. The damage was trivial. .'. ."[25]

"Trivial" the actual damage may have been, but the fact that fire broke out in a plane just out of the factory after major overhaul was no small matter. Had Paul Mantz been aboard, undoubtedly he would have insisted upon either returning to Burbank or at least staying at Tucson long enough for a thorough checkup. Whatever Bo McKneely may have said or thought, he did not have the clout to call a halt at this time.

As for the newly married Fred, he was eager to get on with the rest of his life. He wanted to open a school for air navigators as soon as he returned from Amelia's flight. For some reason, George forbade him to use Amelia's name or his role as her navigator in advertising his projected school—a futile prohibition because the press had been full of references to Fred Noonan as Amelia's navigator. This may be why Amelia overrode George and gave Fred the green light.[26]

Later Amelia wrote quizzically, "As to Noonan, I came to realize that there was a humanitarian aspect to the flight. Shortly before the Oakland takeoff Fred was in a serious automobile accident. Soon after our return to California he survived another highway smash-up. So he and Mrs. Noonan were eager for him to take to the air for safety!"[27]

Had Amelia been of the seafaring persuasion, she could have been forgiven if, at this stage, she decided Fred was a Jonah and jettisoned him. But she had faith in him and had too much of a sense of humor to be superstitious. In any case, it would have taken more than a minor fire to turn her back, for this particular flight was not, in fact, a test run; it was the first leg of Amelia's around-the-world flight.

Chapter 20
Miami Takeoff

*P*aul Mantz was in St. Louis, participating in an aerobatic competition, when Amelia slipped out of Oakland on May 21, 1937. He learned of her departure over the radio, and to say the news upset him would be a vast understatement. He was furious, dismayed, and frightened. He considered that Amelia "had been pushing too hard, trying to meet the tight schedules set up by her promoter-husband." The "money-making schemes" and public appearances had left her "little time to devote to her flight preparations. She'd left it all up to Paul."

In his opinion, Amelia was by no means ready to begin her big flight. He had planned to check the Electra's radio a final time, test the fuel consumption, and give Amelia "a list of optimum power settings for each leg" of the flight. Without these last-minute preparations, Paul believed that Amelia would be "flying by guesswork."

She always tried to get off on her trips as unobtrusively as possible, but this secretive departure was carrying discretion to absurd lengths. Paul was not an importunate newsman; he was Amelia's technical adviser who had worked closely with her for years. She was ill-advised and thoughtless not to have taken him into her confidence, and it was unprofessional and foolhardy to depart without Paul's assurance that everything that could be done had been done. He greatly feared that "all his careful planning was a waste of time, because of her sneak departure."[1]

Meanwhile, on May 22, Amelia, George, and Bo took off from Tucson in a heavy sandstorm. Amelia skillfully guided the Electra over it, and they reached New Orleans that night. The next morning, a Sunday, they set out for Florida, crossing the northeasterly corner of the Gulf of Mexico. It was Bo's first long overwater flight, and Amelia noted, "I am not sure he was very enthusiastic about it." Late that afternoon they reached Miami, to begin Amelia's final week of preflight preparations, "with the generous aid of Pan American personnel."[2]

Amelia told reporters that "her present series of short hops" were designed to tune up the Electra. She added that she would stay in Miami two or three days and had not yet decided on her next stop.[3]

She had contracted to write the story of her adventure and planned on giving a detailed account of these last-minute preparations, which she found "really colorful," and she believed she could make the story interesting "even for non-flyers."[4] Here was another decision, most likely George's, that in retrospect was questionable. Amelia was not the type to make a commitment and not give it her best. She enjoyed writing, and one would have been sorry to miss her own account of this last flight, but it represented a heavy expenditure of time, thought, and creativity. She would have been better advised to have devoted all that energy to familiarizing herself with her equipment, especially communications, and fine-tuning the flight plan, or else have spent the time in rest and undemanding relaxation, so necessary to keeping in the best possible physical condition.

In Miami, preparing for takeoff, Amelia was much too busy to write a detailed account. She planned to pick up the thread of the narrative later, but never found the opportunity to do so.[5] Fortunately, the Putnams' friend, C. B. Allen of the *New York Herald Tribune,* was covering the story. He left a perceptive and affectionate account of Amelia's days at Miami. He noted that the Pan Am men earmarked to work with her were less than thrilled with the assignment. Evidently they expected an engine-ignorant prima donna who would either take over at the last minute in a blaze of flashbulbs or else breathe down their necks, offering useless suggestions. Instead, they met a likable woman who knew her plane, knew what had to be done, and let the mechanics do it without interference. When she could help, she did, and if anyone pointed out a smear of grease on her clothes or in her hair, she merely chuckled and kept on with the task at hand. Soon, as Allen put it, "there was an almost audible clatter of chips falling off skeptical masculine shoulders."

Photographers and autograph seekers haunted the airport. Amelia escaped them when she could; when she could not, she was pleasant and cooperative. Allen admired her for never revealing whatever exasperation she might have been feeling on these occasions, and for never stooping to the expedient of "turning on the charm."

When lunchtime rolled around and she was too busy to leave the area, she ate at the far-from-fashionable restaurant across the highway from the airport. The ambiance was strictly "greasy spoon," but the food was good, and the restaurant served her favorite beverage, buttermilk.

She would have enjoyed an occasional swim and sun bath, but time did not permit. Of course, she had plenty of Florida heat, working in her metal aircraft that the sun had turned into an oven, but, she protested, "I want to soak up a little sunshine, not be fried by it."[6]

She found time for one of her undated, unsigned notes to Amy: "*Very confidentially* I may hop off in a few days. I am going to try to beat the newspapers. So you don't know nothin!" She enclosed "some doe"; Amy would "probably need a cool dress or two."[7]

While Amelia was thus busily and happily preparing for her adventure, Paul paced his hotel room in St. Louis. His worry centered on the Electra's radio equipment. True, it was the best available in 1937, and modified to operate on the 500-kilocycle international emergency wave length as well as on the standard 3105 and 6210 kilocycles. Voice communication presented no problems, but the set was deficient as a navigation aid; it did not generate enough power to serve as a "fix" for direction finders on land or for ships at sea. Paul had checked this out with the manufacturer, Western Electric. Their reply: "To obtain satisfactory results on 500 kilocycles, a trailing wire of at least 250 feet long should be used."

The trailing antenna had been duly installed, but Amelia complained of the trouble of reeling it in and out. Full of misgiving, Paul wrote an airmail letter to George, asking if everything was all right. George's reply was a real stunner. He wrote that Amelia and Fred had left Miami on June 1. He continued:

▶ Talked with Amelia on the telephone at San Juan from Miami. She says that at last they got the Sperry [autopilot] really working perfectly. Between ourselves, the radio gave unending trouble. As I understand it, it was finally decided by the technicians that the longer aerials were improper. One part of them just canceled out the other, so they shortened the aerials and apparently got the thing pretty well licked. . . .[8]

Or, as Safford wrote more graphically, ". . . some nit-wit radio technicians at Miami Airport told AE that her trailing-antenna was no good so she impulsively removed it." He attributed Amelia's action to "ignorance compounded by bad advice." For the bulk of the flight, loss of the trailing antenna would not be too dangerous, but it meant that the Electra would be out of touch with the surface for several hours of the long south-central Pacific stretch.[9]

Allen's dispatch to the *New York Herald Tribune* datelined May 30 gives some background about this unfortunate incident:

▶ Miss Earhart tried in vain to communicate with a local broadcasting station which was listening in for her calls on 6,210 and 3,105 kilocycles or
with the Bureau of Air Commerce airways station at the city's flying field
which normally operates on these aircraft communications bands. Her
failure to "raise" either station was ascribed by Pan American radio technicians to a new antenna recently installed on the "flying laboratory,"
which they believe to be of improper length to give her transmitter its
maximum efficiency and range. They set to work this afternoon experi-
menting with antennae of various lengths and hope to have this problem
solved in time for another test flight tomorrow.[10]

In brief, it appears that in trying to improve the 3,105 and 6,210 frequencies, they had canceled the 500 emergency channel. According to
Muriel, Amelia believed that the presence of the Coast Guard cutter
Itasca, with its powerful equipment, constituted "sufficient coverage."[11] If this optimistic guess proved incorrect, only Fred's skill as a
navigator would enable the Electra to reach Howland Island.

Amelia was plagued by no such all-too-real worries as Paul's or such
nebulous fears as Jackie Cochran's. Nevertheless, she believed this
would be her last long venture. "I have a feeling that there is just
about one more good flight left in my system, and I hope this trip is it,"
she told a few friends, including Carl Allen. "Anyway, when I have finished this job I mean to give up long distance 'stunt' flying."

This did not mean that she was retiring from aviation, she
explained. She planned to continue flying, and especially looked forward to "an extensive flight research program" at Purdue.

Allen wanted to print this "darned good news story" right away, but
Amelia asked him to sit on it. She was opposed to advance announce-
ments unless "absolutely necessary"; too many things could happen to
change one's plans. "If you use the story at all, wait until the round-
the-world flight is over, or nearly over; I think it would be absurd to
make such an announcement now, especially if I should be forced to
give up my present program or to postpone it, for any reason, when I
had just started."

She said that several reasons prompted her decision: George's urg-
ings that she give up dangerous projects and her own belief that she
had done her share and should step aside. Laughter lit up her eyes as
she added, "I'm getting old and want to make way for the younger generation before I'm feeble, too."[12]

George was sure that he could have stopped the present venture, but knew that to abandon it would cause Amelia "spiritual unhappiness."[13]

In a story datelined May 31, the *New York Times* announced that
mechanics had completed work on the Electra. Amelia planned to
leave for San Juan at dawn the next day, "with Fred J. Noonan beside

her charting the course he has flown hundreds of times for a commercial airline."[14]

It was believed that the adjustments made on the thirtieth to the radio transmitter and to the Sperry gyroscope "would result in the satisfactory performance of both." But Amelia declared that if this did not prove to be the case, takeoff would become "just another test flight" and she would return within the hour.

Arrangements had been made for Pan Am's meteorologists to send her weather reports every hour on the hour from Miami's radio station WQAM. This would continue until the Electra moved out of WQAM's range. Allen explained to his readers that this relay was necessary "because all of Pan-American's radio transmission is of the telegraphic or code variety and neither Miss Earhart nor Captain Noonan can receive this sufficiently well to warrant anything but radio telephone communication." For her part Amelia would send brief messages giving position and flight conditions fifteen minutes before and fifteen minutes after the hour. Her call letters were KHAQQ, operating by day on 6,210 KC and at night on 3,105.[15]

The morning of the thirty-first passed pleasantly as Amelia, George, and Fred visited Pan Am's terminal and base at Dinner Key, where they toured the facility, picked up "a few spare parts" for various instruments, and thanked the company's mechanics and officials for their assistance and cooperation.

This was something of a homecoming for Fred, who had spent years with the airline. Some of his old cronies were ready to commiserate with him for being stuck with a woman pilot, but in short order decided that their sympathy was wasted. Amelia's expertise was obvious from her intelligent appreciation of every aspect of the huge facility.[16]

George and Amelia had lunch at the home of an old friend, Harvey Firestone, the automobile tire manufacturer. Amelia spent most of the afternoon napping, to be "thoroughly rested and in the pink of condition" for the early morning takeoff. At the airport, mechanics put eight hundred gallons of gas aboard the Electra.[17]

Amelia had dashed off what may be her last note to Amy: "Hope to take off tomorrow A.M. to San Juan, Puerto Rico. Here is three hundred bucks for Margot to put in the household fund."[18] Margot de Carie was Amelia's Girl Friday.

George and Amelia spent their last minutes together sitting on the concrete apron "watching the rising sun brush back the silver gray of dawn," while Bo "resoldered a broken thermocouple lead which supplied the cylinder head temperatures of the left engine." Husband and wife had little to say to one another but, George would write later, ". . . the feel of her hands in mine told more than the words we did not speak could have told."

Bo's "okeh" announced that the trouble had been fixed, and George briefly watched Amelia as she moved toward the plane. To him "she seemed very small and slim and feminine. . . ." He followed her to the Electra and, when she and Fred had taken their places inside, he leaned in to say good-bye.

Despite the early hour, a crowd had assembled to see Amelia off. In a quick last look through the window she spotted David Putnam's "Viking blond head," and waved to him. Then she started the motors. They had been well warmed up, so after a moment of enjoying "their full-throated smooth song" she signaled for the wheel chocks to be removed and taxied to the end of the southeast runway. She and Fred were off, as she wrote with typical humor, "bound for California by about the longest route we could contrive." George and David hurried to the roof of the Administration Building, where they watched until the Electra was out of sight.[19]

Back in the element she loved, Amelia put the Electra into a slow climb, then headed for Puerto Rico, savoring the beauty of the line where the deep blue of the Gulf Stream "met the aquamarine of the shoal waters off coast." Shortly after 6 A.M., she tuned in to WQAM for its hourly summary of weather conditions. The first broadcast was held up because the Miami radio was sending out a vivid description of her takeoff, evidently a transcript of the actual event being rerun for the benefit of breakfasting Miamians. It amused her to listen to the announcer turning a "very normal departure" into a "breathlessly exciting" event.

The beauty of the sea below was in sharp contrast to the North Atlantic and the Pacific. She noted in her log, "A friendly course. Hardly out of sight of one island but another pancakes on the horizon. . . ." But there were many not-so-friendly rocks and reefs barely visible above water. "So few lighthouses in this mess—one pities the poor mariner."

About midmorning Fred estimated arrival time at San Juan as 1:10 P.M. He had been only one minute off his predicted arrival at Tampa, so Amelia had come to have "implicit faith" in his "powers of divination." Indeed, she wrote, "What with such expert navigational help and the assistance of the Sperry gyro-pilot, I began to feel that my long-range flying was becoming pretty sissy. The ease and casualness were further accentuated by the marvelous help given by radio."

Around noon Fred told Amelia they were too far south, and she adjusted the course accordingly. Shortly thereafter they sighted Puerto Rico,[20] and landed at San Juan's Pan American airport at 2:30 P.M. About two hundred people, mostly women and children, cheered as Amelia left the plane. She looked fresh and not at all tired. She spotted and waved to fellow flier Clara Livingston. Amelia and Fred told reporters that the flight was "slow, almost lazy and eventless." They planned to leave the next morning, either for Paramaribo or "some Venezuelan port."[21]

As usual when flying, Amelia had neglected to eat, so she was more than ready for the luncheon provided the two fliers by Mrs. Thomas Rodebaugh, wife of the Pan Am manager. Acting governor Menendez Ramos offered to put them up, but Amelia had arranged to stay with Clara Livingston. The Electra taken care of, Livingston drove with Fred and Amelia to her sixteen-hundred-acre plantation twenty miles out of San Juan.

Whenever possible, Amelia preferred to stay with a fellow flier such as Livingston, who understood that on the halts between steps of a major flight the pilot needed "quiet and sleep," not socializing with even the most congenial people, "for meeting and talking to them adds immeasurably to the fatigue factors, nervous and physical." So Clara understandingly omitted all "social trimmings." The three spent the early evening listening to "the surge of the sea at the very front door, background for the soothing song of frogs and night insects."

Shortly before they retired at 8 P.M., George telephoned from the *Herald* office in Miami. The brief account of the Miami-to–San Juan journey that Amelia had left with the cable office for forwarding to newspapers had failed to arrive. Amelia "never did discover whether the local operator just didn't think it was worth bothering with. At that, he was probably correct. It's hard to turn correspondent after one has been a pilot all day." She suspected, however, that George "just wanted to say 'Good night.' That was pleasant."[22]

In San Juan, Amelia had the odd sensation one sometimes experiences when traveling—a familiarity, even a sense of homecoming, in a totally strange place. "As to San Juan, I had a curious feeling I had been there before," which she had not. She regretted that time did not permit visiting the "lovely white Caribbean cities . . . nestling among green hills." She promised herself that "next time" she would refly her course, "really seeing the lands I've only skimmed over now . . . and visiting their people in a decently leisurely and civilized manner."[23]

Chapter 21

South America and South Atlantic

melia rose at 3:45 A.M. on June 2 for a planned takeoff at dawn; however, the Electra did not lift off until nearly 7:00. Part of the airfield was under construction, so the available runway was short, "making a heavy fuel load a bit difficult." This fact contributed to Amelia's decision to make the day's objective Caripito, Venezuela, instead of Paramaribo, Dutch Guiana.[1]

For the first part of this leg, all that the Electra's crew could see were the sea and little fluffy clouds "like white scrambled eggs." Amelia's first glimpse of South America was the Venezuelan coast, then mountains, plains, and jungle. She reflected that the last was "about the least desirable of landing places." She had heard of pilots crashing into or even on treetops and walking away from the site. But she believed the story would be different in a real jungle.

They followed a muddy river through a mountain pass. A few miles from the coast they sighted Caripito, with its "squat oil tanks on the outskirts." This little town sported an excellent airfield under the joint management of Pan Am and Standard Oil. There the Electra landed at 10:18 A.M. The president and the secretary-general of the state of Monagas, with their wives, welcomed the travelers.[2]

While the Electra was being refueled, Henry E. Liman, Standard Oil's general manager in Venezuela, bore Amelia and Fred off to his home to stay the night and he regaled them with an "elaborate and delicious meal," including steak and fruitcake. At Amelia's place was a corsage of such orchids as at home she could have worn only on special occasions. Here in Venezuela they grew wild.

Puerto Rico and Venezuela provided Amelia with her first experience of lands inhabited almost exclusively by brown-eyed people. She began to play a little game with herself—a version of the child's game of "Beaver!"—the object of which was to spot a man with a beard. Amelia looked for blue eyes.[3]

Rain clouds threatened as she and Fred left Caripito early the next morning, and Amelia "played hide-and-seek with showers" for much of the way. She decided they had better "forgo the scenery, such as it was," and lift over the rain. Climbing through the clouds into the realm of the sun, she reflected, "Now and again that sun illumines mystic caves and rearing fortresses or shows giant cloud creatures mocking with lumpy paws the tiny man-made bird among them."

The Electra was quite far out at sea when it passed Georgetown, British Guiana, and the delta of the River Nickerie separating the two Guianas. Mostly, however, the plane flew overland, a circumstance Fred found especially interesting. "Instead of following the coastline as Pan American seaplanes do, and I have always done before," he wrote home, "we cut straight across dense virgin jungle. It was so thick that for hundreds of miles all we could see was solid tree-tops broken by an occasional large river."

Strong headwinds and rainsqualls forced Amelia to fly low, which cut down on speed, because "to open the throttles wide when near the ground" did the engines no good, and she had too much respect for them to "knowingly mistreat" them. She was in no hurry; all she asked of the Electra and the elements was to let her come reasonably close to her schedule.[4]

A few tiny clearings began to break the jungle, and the River Suriname came into view, alerting Amelia and Fred that they were nearing their goal—Paramaribo—located twelve miles from the river's mouth. The Zandery Airport was twenty-five miles farther inland. In accordance with instructions, they followed a narrow-gauge railroad track. Still, nothing but small rice fields and huts hugging the railroad interrupted the jungle. Amelia tried uneasily to gauge the wind direction from such omens as clothes hanging on lines, fearing that in such surroundings the airport could be "only a meager clearing."

She was delighted to find, instead, a beautiful natural landing field where nothing had been neglected to aid the fliers. Amelia noted an orange wind sock, instantly augmented by a bonfire, to give her the wind direction. White cloth strips outlined the best landing area, and a man waving a white flag stood by to guide the Electra to a stop. Officials of the Dutch Army, as well as James Lawton, the American consul at Paramaribo, were waiting to welcome the "hot and famished" fliers with orange juice, coffee, and sandwiches. Soldiers pumped gasoline into the Electra and stood by to guard the plane, which had to be staked down because the field had no hangar.

Satisfied that her faithful steed had been fed, groomed, and cared for, Amelia and the others embarked for Paramaribo aboard what the *New York Times* called a trolley and Amelia more tactfully called "the railroad." This conveyance provided a picturesque hour-long journey, with chickens, goats, and dogs scrambling off the track, and women with baskets of fruit poised proudly on their heads who came up to the car at every stop.

Amelia was intrigued by the incongruity of Paramaribo—to all intents and purposes a Dutch city plunked down in the South American jungle "with the inherent virtues of Holland written in its broad tree-planted streets and its general spick-and-spanness." Especially interesting to Amelia were the bush blacks who inhabited the nearby jungle. In the bad old days, Suriname had been active in the slave trade, and these people were descendants of the fortunate few who had escaped to the jungle and made a free life for themselves. Now they came to Paramaribo's market to sell such exotic products as soft-shell turtle eggs, breadfruit, and "string beans eighteen inches long."[5]

In the Palace Hotel, where Fred had stayed often in the past, he met Carl Doake, who had been his radio operator in Haiti in 1930. Indeed, the South American portion of the flight was, as Amelia wrote, "a sort of old-home week for Fred," who knew the coastal areas and many people involved in Pan Am's operations. New to him were the inland airports and the experience of overflying the South American lands.

Gradually Fred confided to Amelia bits and pieces about his adventurous early life. He had left home at the age of fifteen to go to sea. In the next twenty or so years, he had rounded Cape Horn seven times, three of them aboard a windjammer. When World War I broke out, he shipped on a munitions carrier plying between England and New York. Later, in the Royal Navy, he had three ships torpedoed under him. Somewhere along the line he picked up the status of master mariner, unlimited, and a first-class pilot's license for the Mississippi River.

His years at sea had given him a wide perspective. Once when he and Amelia were discussing the delays inherent in such flights as theirs, Fred remarked, "It's all a matter of comparison. We're impatient about a day's delay. That's because that lost day's flying might see us across a continent or an ocean. But a swell way to learn patience is to try a tour of sailing-ship voyaging. . . . After nearly half a year on one vessel on one trip, you become pretty philosophical about the calendar!" Reflecting upon this, Amelia "decided to stick to airplanes."[6]

They were slightly behind schedule. Amelia had hoped to be at Natal, Brazil, on June 4, but had to settle for Fortaleza, capital of

Ceará Province. Taking off from Paramaribo at 5:10 A.M., she was grateful for the perfect weather that allowed a nonstop flight. This was all the more satisfying as the only intermediate field on the 1,330-mile hop was a small facility at Pará.

On this leg, Amelia passed another milestone: crossing the equator for the first time. Fred planned to enact the traditional role of King Neptune and initiate the novice, but both were so busy at the exact moment that Fred forgot to douse Amelia with the thermos bottle of cold water he had stowed away for that purpose.

They reached Fortaleza at 4:30 P.M. local time. Amelia was surprised by both the semidesert climate and the fine airport. Pan Am placed all its facilities at their disposal, so she and Fred decided to stay for a day and make their final preparations to fly the South Atlantic there rather than at Natal, as planned.

Amelia wanted her aircraft to have a good going-over. "During yesterday's flight, I noticed the control apparatus was not working entirely satisfactory," she told the press, "and the rudder was somewhat variable." However, beyond "one small leak where a gauge let flow a few drops of gasoline," the Electra needed no repairs. But it did need a change of oil, a grease job, and a thorough scrubbing of the body.

The crew required maintenance quiet as much as the plane. Amelia had packed what for her was a sizeable wardrobe—"five shirts, two pairs of slacks, a change of shoes, a light working overall and a trick weightless raincoat plus the minimum of toilet articles." She was down to her last shirt and had given up on her slacks and shoes, so she welcomed the opportunity to have her clothes laundered.

She and Fred each had several sun helmets. They had started with one apiece, but neither liked wearing a hat, so whenever they emerged from the plane or hotel bareheaded, horrified tropics-wise individuals "slapped protective headgear on our unworldly pates."

From the Excelsior Hotel in Fortaleza, Amelia wrote to George, relating the brief contretemps that had arisen: The hotel management had assigned Amelia and Fred to the same room. "They were a bit surprised when we both countermanded the arrangements!" She added, "For a female to be traveling as I do evidently is a matter of puzzlement to her sheltered sisters hereabout, not to mention the males. I'm stared at in the streets. I feel they think, 'Oh, well, she's American and they're all crazy.'"[7]

Amelia did a bit of staring herself the next day when she stole some time to shop and look around. Her purchases included sponge rubber for the cockpit hatch, and the storekeeper refused to let her pay for it. Like any tourist, she marveled at the skill of the fishermen who went miles out to sea in a *jaganda*—a sort of log raft with a triangular sail—and at the women balancing loads on their heads.

Meanwhile, Fred bought coveralls made from scratch. He entered a tailor shop at 11 A.M., was measured, and the cloth was cut. As soon as one piece was ready, one of the ten or more women at the sewing machines grabbed it. By afternoon he was wearing the garment.

He and Amelia had plenty to do. While mechanics worked on the Electra, pilot and navigator "cleaned house," repacking spares, mailing home the maps used thus far, and washing the engine and propeller covers. These were of Amelia's own design and had been made for her at Burbank—"close-fitting union suits to protect engines and propellers from sand and dust."[8]

Cows crunching the thick grass at the airport took a dim view of the racket when the Electra began warming up. Unlike the Irish cattle at Londonderry that had panicked at Amelia's approach, these proud bovines merely turned their backs and walked away contemptuously.

Although rains had poured down the previous night, the field was well drained, and Amelia had no difficulty in taking off at 4:50 A.M. for the roughly two-hour hop to Natal. Clouds and squalls "chased each other across the sky" but were not heavy enough to impede progress. The Electra had just landed at Natal when the rain caught up with them, "a muddy tropic deluge which blotted out vision fifty feet away."

Amelia had planned this early arrival in case they were able to start their transatlantic hop that evening. On arrival she wisely consulted with those who knew the South Atlantic skies best, the French airmen who had been flying this route twice a week for several years, "carrying mail but no passengers." She talked with the crew of the next scheduled flight; they told her they preferred an early morning takeoff, because the worst weather usually occurred "during the first 800 miles."

Accordingly, Amelia decided to postpone departure until early morning. Immediately she began to examine the Electra and to supervise the oiling. She studied weather charts provided by the French, who had two ships stationed in the South Atlantic to supply weather data. She was particularly interested in the area between Fernando de Noronha Island and the São Paulo inlets, an area usually full of fog and rain.

The food at lunch was surprisingly homelike to Amelia and Fred: corn on the cob and apple pie à la mode. Wherever they went, hospitality in the form of meals and packets of sandwiches and cake had been unstinting. If this kept up, Amelia half-seriously worried that she and Fred would have trouble fighting off pounds, although both were thin by nature. This was not vanity; Amelia explained, "the measuring stick of avoirdupois aloft is gasoline. Six added pounds offset one precious gallon of fuel." And gasoline was very much on her mind. The Electra would take aboard 850 gallons of it plus 8 of oil for the long overwater flight.

As she wrote her account for the press, from her window she could see two children at play in the sand and experienced a rather wistful wish that she could join them in their game, or at least sunbathe with them.[9] But her schedule allowed only time for necessary sleep before she must rise shortly after midnight. When she and Fred reached the takeoff area, they discovered that they could not use the long, lighted runway, because "a perverse wind blew exactly across it." They would have to resort to the secondary one, unlighted and with a grass surface. The two fliers had trouble even locating it in the darkness, so, armed with flashlights, they walked the full length to familiarize themselves with the terrain before entrusting the Electra to it.

A light rain was falling, frustrating a press photographer whose old-style flash pan refused to ignite, to Amelia's amusement. Fred boarded first, then Amelia joined him and waved to the group that had gathered. She made what newspapers called "a perfect take-off."

Amelia began her account of the crossing by noting that it was "uneventful." She added thoughtfully, "Such uneventfulness, I suppose, is a part of expeditioning which comes off successfully. If all goes well, there is not much to report. If all doesn't, there are 'incidents'."[10]

The truth of this observation was amply demonstrated by the newspaper coverage of the successful stages of this final journey. One must be struck by the paucity of the accounts in most of the U.S. press, except for the papers carrying Amelia's step-by-step narrative. The stories were brief, the bare bones of fact, often buried in the back pages. This same press had reported her early exploits in the blackest of headlines and the most detailed of stories. In a way, this about-face was a tribute to Amelia and her fellow aviation pioneers, who in a few short years had changed the press's "Gee whiz!" to "Ho hum." Safe completion of a flight was no longer news.

This particular flight was not devoid of incident. Shortly after take-off, Amelia felt quite ill from gasoline fumes. As she noted in her log, "In refueling at Natal boys spilled so much gas it was funny. I am charged with 165 gals. in a 149 gal. tank."

Headwinds of about twenty miles per hour prevailed during the first part of the journey. Amelia made no attempt to make up speed by opening the engines. "With plenty of work ahead, I wanted to treat them as gently as could be."

Once they passed an Air France mail plane but could not communicate because its radio equipment was telegraphic and the Electra's was voice telephone. As was her custom, Amelia broadcast her position each half hour. "Whether it was heard at all, or understood if heard, perhaps I shall never know." At least one was picked up some four hours after takeoff: "Everything is going fine."

Probably the most notable event of the flight was the dense rainstorm they encountered about halfway across. "Tons of water descended," crashing against the Electra so heavily that Amelia could almost feel it. It looked brown against the cockpit windows, "a soiled emulsion mixed with the oil spattering from the propellers." She was thankful for her dry cockpit—"boys at Lockheed did a good job. . . . Glad I got that new rubber lining at Fortaleza."

Both engines began "bumping" but soon started up again. "Only too much oil I think." Nothing but static came over the radio. "Have never seen such rain. Props a blur in it." Undisturbed, Fred dozed. Amelia noted, "I never seem to get sleepy flying. Often been tired but seldom sleepy."

With a few hundred miles to go, Amelia noted cryptically, "Fred goes back to catch a bug." Thus flippantly did Amelia refer to a serious scientific project. Fred C. Meier of the Department of Agriculture had given Amelia a "sky hook" to collect samples from the air. These would be placed in aluminum cylinders for future examination in laboratories. Meier wrote to Amelia in explanation: "This phase of research was originally opened by Louis Pasteur in classical experiments recorded in 1860 which have since been followed by medical men and botanists of many countries. The results of our new upper air studies bring to light fundamental principles of the spread of microscopic-organisms by winds. These principles lead to many practical applications, perhaps the most important of which are improved measures of control of diseases of plants and animals."

The "sky hook" was simple, "a metal rod about the length and size of a broomstick in whose end the cylinder is inserted." The collector extended it into the slipstream, turning the cylinder to expose the slide. As neither Amelia nor Fred would have the time to hold the gadget outside for the necessary half hour or so, brackets had been installed on the Electra's side. These microorganisms were the "bugs" Fred had been catching. By the time they crossed the South Atlantic, they had more than a dozen cylinders ready.

On one of their test exposures, Fred happened to cough on a slide. "That's ruined," he said. "The collection of germs on that slide would look like a menagerie under a microscope."

Amelia was happy to conduct these experiments, which helped justify the plane's nickname of Flying Laboratory. But she had an irrepressible sense of humor and insisted upon including the contaminated slide in their collection. "I thought it would give the laboratory workers something unique to ponder when they came upon its contents among the more innocent bacteria of the equatorial upper air. Heaven knows what cosmic conclusions Fred's contribution might help them reach!"[11]

Chapter 22
Across Africa

*A*fter a transatlantic flight lasting thirteen hours, twelve
minutes, Amelia and Fred reached Africa. They had
planned to land at Dakar, but instead touched down at St.
Louis, 163 miles north of target. "The fault was mine,"
wrote Amelia. Thick haze had prevented a position sighting. "My navigator indicated that we should turn south. Had we done so, a half
hour would have brought us to Dakar. But a 'left turn' seemed to me in
order and after fifty miles of flying along the coast we found ourselves
at St. Louis, Senegal." Once there, it appeared better to stay rather
than brave the impending tropical night.

Thus, as a good commander should, Amelia accepted responsibility
for the unscheduled change of route. It is most unlikely, however, that
she would have overridden the navigator, in whom she had so much
confidence, on a mere whim. St. Louis was not on her strip map, but it
is possible, even probable, that the Air France pilots with whom she
talked at Natal had told her of the fine airport there; perhaps her
childhood fascination with maps of Africa played a part. In any case,
the decision was fortunate. Had she turned the Electra south and
missed Dakar Airport—likewise, not on her strip map—in the haze,
they might well, in Safford's words, "have run out of gas before getting
beyond the deltas and marshes along the coast." These, too, did not appear on the flight chart.

The two fliers arrived in St. Louis in time to share "a hearty dinner
with French airmail pilots" and to receive the French Air Ministry's assurance that all facilities would be extended to Amelia across Africa.

She decided to wait until morning to decide where to take off on the next segment of her project.[1]

Amelia had a keen sense of smell that could be very useful, enabling her to detect hot oil or rubber in time to correct the problem. To her, Africa had its own scent, "a sort of strong human tang of people." The sights were equally fascinating—rather barren scenery of "brown plains, bare hills, parched vegetation and drab dwellings." Against this background was "a riot of human color. An amusing, friendly riot of bright raiment adorning good-natured ebony people." Primitive huts stood near the St. Louis airport, and their inhabitants aroused her social consciousness as well as her insatiable interest: "Tall black figures endowed with a certain innate dignity went about their own affairs without much concern for their neighbor airplanes. Seeing the majesty of these natives I asked myself what many must have asked before: What have we in the United States done to these proud people, so handsome and intelligent in the setting of their own country?"[2]

Beyond memories of a culture new to them, Amelia and Fred took along only one souvenir of St. Louis, a bag of freshly roasted peanuts. These they munched as they flew from St. Louis to Dakar, where the Air France field was, in the words of the *New York Herald Tribune*, "more favorable for a take-off heavily laden with gasoline."

There Amelia decided to remain for at least another day. Two hours out of Natal the Electra's fuel meter had given out. Now at Dakar, the "very efficient chief mechanic" located the trouble—"a piece of the shaft was broken." Amelia appreciated the difficulties in working "from a blueprint printed in English, which he did not understand, in an aeroplane he did not know." She took advantage of the delay to schedule a forty-hour engine check.

Amelia and Fred now faced what could be one of the most dangerous legs of the journey, the twenty-two hundred miles "over the wildest part of the dark continent" to Fort-Lamy, a French Foreign Legion station a little to the south of Lake Chad. They planned to break the flight midway at Niamey in French West Africa. But, as always, much would depend upon the weather, which did not look promising. Meanwhile, Amelia carefully inspected the Electra.

The two fliers were the guests of Governor General Marcel de Coppet. There they enjoyed "a quiet dinner" and a reception at the Aero Club, for which Amelia could not dress up. She explained to the pilots she met that afternoon that she "had only slacks and shirts in which to greet generals, pilots, kings and beggars."

She regretted that she could not hold an in-depth conversation with the gracious and obviously cultured de Coppet, but his English and her French were not equal to the challenge. However, with a few words in common, sign language, and much goodwill they contrived to understand "what was what without serious trouble."

That night Amelia wrote to George, asking him "to tell Jacques de Sibour how especially helpful everyone has been, and how well the arrangements made by Standard Oil had worked out everywhere."[3] George wrote of Amelia's last letters,

▶ Usually these messages were scratched in pencil on pages of her logbooks, torn out and folded haphazard into any envelope that came to hand. Mostly they were written at the end of long days as she turned in dog-tired, with a dawn take-off only a few hours before her. Much of them concerned chores I should do about the flight—little courtesies like writing, on her behalf, to those who had been hospitable to her. They showed her proceeding with placid thoughtfulness.

George was especially touched by "the frank affection and sometimes wistful loneliness of those letters."[4]

The Dakar stop was an important milestone on Amelia's journey. So far she and Fred had followed established air routes. When the fliers left the hospitable French airport, they would move into areas where aircraft flew frequently but not on schedule. The weather reports were ominous: Extreme heat in the interior threatened "tornadoes to the south and sandstorms on the north." Somehow Amelia "must try to squeeze between." This meant that to a large extent their course must be improvised.

Nevertheless, Amelia looked forward with eager, somewhat nostalgic interest to crossing central Africa. When she and Muriel were children, they had loved geography and pored happily over any map that came their way, plotting imaginary journeys. Africa especially fascinated them. "The very word meant mystery." Such place names as Senegal, Timbuktu, El Fasher, and Khartoum were sheer magic.

On the advice of Colonel Tabera of the French Air Force, Amelia decided to alter her course slightly to the north, heading for Gao instead of Niamey. The Electra took off shortly before 6 A.M.[5]

Takeoff was smooth despite a heavy fuel load. Amelia circled Quakam Airport once by way of farewell, then headed eastward toward a clear horizon. "Loafing along at a trifle under 150 miles an hour," more than once Amelia thought of her childhood self dreaming of the places now unfolding beneath her aircraft. About a third of the way to Gao, she flew over the Senegal River. Four hundred miles farther, the Electra reached the hilly country near the upper Niger River. Seven hours and fifty-five minutes had passed when Amelia touched down at Gao for "a perfect landing."

She knew that Gao had a rich history, with ruins remaining of a truncated pyramid and of a great mosque almost as old as Islam. It was still a place of some importance as "the terminus of the transSaharan motor traffic from the north," connecting with the Niger, navigable for more than a thousand miles south of Gao. But the fliers had no time to sightsee. As Amelia wrote briskly, "We wanted the keys of no city so long as the hangar doors were open and the ground crew ready." She added gratefully, "Always they were and it was." The usual fifty-gallon drums of gasoline, with Amelia's name printed on them, were always ready for "the thirsty Electra"—a tribute to the pre-flight planning.[6]

As usual, to avoid the afternoon heat, the fliers rose before dawn, to take off at 6:15 GMT, but not before their hosts had provided them with a spectacular breakfast of mushroom omelette and fine French hot chocolate.

The newspaper coverage gives no hint of the potential dangers of this and the next legs of the journey, which, in Amelia's words, "crossed stretches of country barren beyond words, a no-man's land of eternal want." The terrain reminded her of the southwestern portion of the United States, only here the "bad lands" were broken by "no aviation luxuries like radio beams and lights." Although they had the best maps available, they found them "far from satisfactory."

In a letter to his wife, Fred expressed his dissatisfaction in terms much harsher than Amelia's mild "far from satisfactory." He found the desert laps of their journey more difficult from the navigational point of view than the overwater legs so far encountered. "That was because the maps of the country are very inaccurate and consequently extremely misleading. In fact, at points no dependence at all could be placed on them." He considered it fortunate that so far he didn't think they had "wandered off the course for half an hour, although there were times when I wouldn't have bet a nickel on the accuracy of our assumed position." And they were flying over country totally new to them, so no familiar landmarks could give them a fix. Despite the difficulties, Amelia reached Fort-Lamy, in French Equatorial Africa, safely after six hours forty minutes aloft.[7]

Fort-Lamy lay near Lake Chad, a body of water that intrigued Amelia because it was impossible to tell where land ended and lake began. "Indeterminate swampy regions" extended for miles, and indeed much of the region had once been part of the lake bed. She flew too high and was too busy with her "hundred and one gadgets" to see any of the wild animals in which the region abounded. She took the disappointment philosophically: "A landing field located where one expects to find it is quite as exciting a sight as any herd of giant tuskers."

Fort-Lamy's airport was right where it should have been, and once more Amelia caught a glimpse of a culture so different from her own. There was nothing blasé about Amelia. Everything new that crossed her path was a subject of friendly interest. She especially noted that in this region the women did all the work. "Killing time appears to be the chief occupation of the males."

Amelia perforce did some time-killing of her own at Fort-Lamy. The Electra developed "a small leak in the shock absorber of the landing gear." She wrote sympathetically, "To pump it up again taxed the manpower resources of the little station almost to capacity. There are more pleasant diversions than half-pumping at a temperature well over one hundred degrees." This meant that takeoff on June 12 would be delayed until 1:30 P.M., and the fliers could expect no mercy from the heat. Amelia wrote that neither she nor Fred "particularly minded the occasional broiling." Many times the plane's metal exterior was too hot to touch, and the inside so ovenlike the fliers did not record the temperature; they would rather not know. So Amelia's concern was less for comfort than for safety. Very hot air "is thin and lacks lifting power." Landing on equatorial fields called for higher than normal speed. Moreover, after a day of intense heat, the air could be rough.[8]

Because of the delay, Amelia decided to end the day's flight at El Fasher in French Equatorial Africa instead of going on to Khartoum in Anglo-Egyptian Sudan as scheduled. The three-hour flight was not pleasant. As anticipated, the Electra bumped uncomfortably in the overheated air, and the region below was "particularly desolate."

Amelia had been warned to watch out for the "eight foot thorn hedge" circling the airport at El Fasher, intended to keep animals off the field. She experienced no problem and remarked, as she climbed out of the Electra, "It was bumpy but otherwise uneventful." Governor and Mrs. P. Ingallson of Darfur Province awaited the fliers and whisked them to their home, which had been the palace of a sultan.

Before they could do so, however, Amelia, Fred, and the Electra had to wait for a ritual they had undergone at every African stop—debugging. In expressing her appreciation of the boundless hospitality she and Fred had received, Amelia wrote,

▶ Even the unavoidable disinfecting on landing seemed to irk those who conducted it far more than the disinfectees. It would be impossible for flit guns to be handled with greater grace and discretion than were those directed on us. Everything within the place was squirted with germ-destroying vapor. Our personal luggage being infinitesimal and our cargo nil, the operation did not offer much of a problem—there just wasn't sustenance for self-respecting bacteria.[9]

The next morning the fliers were back on their early departure schedule, taking off at 4:15 for Khartoum. For the first half of the five-hundred-mile leg, the Electra flew over Dabbat el Asala, a desolate stretch which Amelia described as "utterly flat, arid, uninhabited, and lacks landmarks altogether." Her maps of the region had obviously been prepared for land travelers. Such notations as "Swamp in rain, salt pan" and "Standing water until Nov." were singularly useless as flight guides, although they might well come in handy in case of a forced landing.

Khartoum, forever haunted by memories of General Gordon, the Mahdi, and Lord Kitchener, was the largest city the fliers had seen since leaving Fortaleza, and the sound of English fell gratefully on their ears. So it was with genuine regret that they paid the three pounds, twenty-two shillings landing fee, refueled, and took off for Massawa in Eritrea. Amelia found this leg as interesting as any so far. For many miles stretched desert, broken only by scattered caravan trails and occasional small tent camps. Then gradually the desert merged into "sandy foothills," which in turn yielded to mountains. There the fliers saw almost the first green vegetation of their African journey. Passing over the Khor Baruka, a "considerable river, which drains the highland region northwest into the Red Sea," hot air seized the Electra and shook it roughly.[10]

As the mountains peaked only thirty miles from the Red Sea, approach was a snakelike spiral. Nearing Massawa, they saw "great gleaming heaps" that Amelia took for sand dunes. They proved to be enormous piles of salt that the sun obligingly produced for export, drawing off innumerable gallons of seawater daily from the evaporating pans.

They could also spot their next obstacle, the Red Sea, which belied its name by being blue. The Blue and White Niles had been equally deceitful, both being green. In the distance Amelia sighted "a shimmering land of mirages that was Arabia."

The Massawa airport was quite large, with big hangars. There Amelia had a language problem. She spoke no word of Italian, and some time passed before anyone who spoke English could be located. But an aircraft in need of an oil change and an engine checkup apparently spoke a universal language. Soon mechanics were at work on the Electra.

Massawa had a well-deserved reputation as one of the hottest cities on earth. That evening the temperature stood at a mere hundred degrees, and the night was quite comfortable. So were the quarters the Italian Army provided. "The neat apartment houses were as clean as could be, each room with a bed, chair, table and portable closet, electric lights, a fan, and a little ice-box . . . were luxuries that would delight any housekeeper."

Amelia had hoped that her old acquaintance Air Marshal Balbo might be in the neighborhood. She entertained vivid memories of his driving her in his racing car from Rome to Ostia "to show the woman pilot something about speed on the ground." However, that colorful individual was elsewhere; Amelia's host was Colonel De Silvestro Luigi.

As usual, Amelia had forgotten to eat all that day, and it had been a long, grueling one. So she was "famished" when an English-speaking officer asked, "Are you hungry?"

Amelia answered instinctively with an idiom from childhood: "As hollow as a bamboo horse!" She noted, "It took ingenuity to translate into appropriate Italian that implausible simile. . . ."[11]

Following the Electra's departure from Massawa, a little flutter of anxiety about Amelia's safety ruffled the press. Later she learned that upon takeoff from Massawa her destination had mistakenly been reported as Karachi. Actually, on June 14 she and Fred had moved down the coast of Eritrea to Assab. This sweltering town had several advantages as a launching spot for the flight along the Arabian coast to Karachi, a distance as long as crossing the Atlantic. Amelia explained "Assab was nearer our objective than Massawa, offered better take-off facilities, and as well we had a greater supply of 87 Octane gasoline spotted there."

Unaware of this development, Italian authorities at Eritrea's capital, Asmara, worried when they did not hear of her safe landing in India and hopefully charged up her silence to "poor communication facilities."

At Assab once more Amelia and Fred enjoyed warm hospitality, this time in the form of "the pleasantest possible, though abbreviated" visit with Lieutenant Colonel Rinaldo Neri and a group of officers and fliers.[12] For their part, surely the appearance, however brief, of this pleasant, amusing, and, incidentally, famous woman with her good companion on her gallant adventure was a most welcome break in routine at such lonely outposts as Fort-Lamy and Assab.

Chapter 23
India and the Monsoons

*W*hile Amelia was happily winging over Africa, George had to contend with an annoying development. Someone, somewhere, started a malicious rumor that, upon completion of the flight, Amelia would divorce her husband to marry Paul Mantz. Walter Winchell, gossipmonger to the nation, had his own version. He assured his palpitating public that Amelia was indeed going to jettison George, but not for Mantz—she would wed "an aviation inventor."

The whispers did not worry George, who knew they had no foundation. Nevertheless, so widespread were these tales that he decided to inform Paul, just in case they had not already reached his ears. "At least twenty people have told me the story today in varying forms," he wrote Paul.

Mantz and his fiancée, Terry Minor, greeted this intelligence with laughter. They were very much in love, busily engaged in building a house, and awaited only Amelia's return to be married. When it became evident that Amelia would not come home, they were married on August 19, 1937.[1]

One of the odd aspects of the Earhart story is the general disinclination to accept Amelia's marriage to George. Possibly it outraged a certain sense of romantic fitness. Surely the proper mate for Amelia Earhart was a dashing fellow flier or at least someone important in the field of aviation—not a bookish entrepreneur!

Either unaware of or unconcerned about her reputed divorce, Amelia began the Assab-to-Karachi leg of her journey. This involved skirting Arabia, whose authorities did not encourage foreign flights over that territory. Indeed, at one time it appeared that Amelia might have to reach Karachi by way of Cairo, Baghdad, and Persia, "the normal Europe-Australian air route." This detour would have added about two thousand miles to her course and carried it far north of her objective—to circle the world as near the equator as possible.

Finally, a compromise was arranged: Amelia could fly from Eritrea to Karachi, provided she did not overfly Arabian soil, but followed the edge of the sea offshore. The British granted permission to land at Aden and, if necessary, at Gwadar in Baluchistan. Learning that "unfavorable winds" at Aden might hamper takeoff of a heavily laden plane, Amelia decided to load up on fuel at Assab, overfly Aden, and land at Gwadar or Karachi, circumstances permitting.

The sun had not arisen when the Electra left Assab, cut across "a deep indentation on the Eritrean coast," thence over Bab-el-Mandeb, the southern access to the Red Sea. Then the course followed the desolate shore of Arabia, bypassing Aden. Another rumor pursued Amelia. Someone "reliably informed" the *London Daily Telegraph's* representative at Aden that she would "be required to spend nine days in quarantine in India because she landed in a yellow fever area in Africa."[2]

Many wasteland regions had already passed beneath the Electra's wings, but few if any as grim as the southeastern Arabian shoreline. Amelia's map showed that beyond the coastal mountains lay "almost unbroken sandy desert." The prospect of a forced landing in this forbidding area was not pleasant. The geography alone was "pretty hopeless," and the attitude of any tribesmen they might encounter was decidedly questionable. Neither the appropriate officials nor the fliers relished these ideas, but they had to be faced.

Fred and Amelia carried with them a letter written in Arabic, presumably "bespeaking for us those things which should be bespoken." Amelia had mixed feelings about this document. In New York a linguist familiar with Arabia had read it and remarked that "it would be just too bad for us if such an introduction was presented to the wrong local faction." Amelia kept the letter beside her in the cockpit. They also carried such emergency items as a small land compass, water in canteens, concentrated foods, and heavy walking shoes. However, the Electra skirted Arabia without mishap.[3]

The plane landed at Karachi at 7:05 P.M. The flight had been fairly slow because the manual mixture-control lever had jammed. Unable to control the amount of fuel to the right engine, "which gulped gasoline unconscionably," Amelia feared she might run out of fuel, so she kept to a reduced speed. Once more Amelia, Fred, and the Electra had to undergo fumigation. They passed muster with the British medical authorities and met the welcoming handclasps of Jacques de Sibour, who had done so much to facilitate the venture. Greetings over, he said to Amelia, "There's a phone call for you."

Thinking it was probably from a local newspaper, Amelia gave Jacques an absent "Oh, yes."

"From New York," Jacques added. "G.P. on the wire."

In 1937 a long-distance call from New York to Karachi was no routine matter, and Amelia was thrilled, so much so that she recorded the conversation in full. The exchange is worth repeating:

▶ How do you feel?
Swell! Never better.
How's the ship?
Everything seems O.K. There's been a little trouble with the fuel flow-meter and analyzer but I think they'll cure that here.
How long will you stay in Karachi?
Probably two days. I want everything checked thoroughly. Wednesday, with luck, we'll shove off.
Where to?
Probably Calcutta.
How about this report you're going to be quarantined?
I don't think so. Everyone is being most awfully nice to us.
How's Fred?
Fine.
Are you the first person to fly from the Red Sea across Arabia to Karachi?
I hadn't thought of that. I'll try to let you know. [Pause] Jacques de Sibour is here and he says he thinks this is the first non-stop flight across to India. It was fun.
Having a good time?
You betja! It's a grand trip. We'll do it again, together, some time.
O.K. with me. Anything else?
Well, I'll cable tomorrow an estimate of when we should get to Howland. Good-bye. . . . See you in Oakland.[4]

This exchange contains a number of interesting touches. George, ever the entrepreneur, wanted to know if Amelia had set another record; Amelia hadn't given it a thought. She was in fine fettle, enjoying herself hugely, and looking forward to Howland, then home. And that casual sentence, "We'll do it again, together, some time," disposes of the divorce rumors.

In a letter to George, written in India, Amelia amplified this sentiment: "I wish you were here. So many things you would enjoy . . . perhaps someday we can fly together to some of the remote places of the world—just for fun."[5]

Amelia was finding her surroundings exotic enough to qualify for the Arabian Nights. Regretfully she declined an invitation to visit the Maharajah of Jodhpur, who had a private airport and a reputation for "boundless hospitality." But she could not resist riding a camel. Clinging to the animal as it arose reminded her of "the first symptoms of a flat spin." Fred called up to her, "Better wear your parachute!"[6]

Amelia visited the Karachi post office to have her cargo of "covers" canceled. The postal authorities were "very courteous and cooperative," permitting her to choose the stamp to be used. She selected the Karachi airmail type. The officials took her behind the scenes, and what was routine to them was fascinating to her—money orders being made out in rupees, and turbaned postmen sorting mail.

The Karachi airdrome, the largest of Amelia's acquaintance, was "the main intermediate point" for air traffic between Europe, India, and points eastward. Imperial Airways flew out of Karachi to Australia, KLM to the Netherlands East Indies. At the Karachi airport a most welcome box of Pratt & Whitney spare parts awaited the Electra. The fliers had experienced "no major mechanical troubles." But Amelia had found it difficult to discover the proper "little things." For example, differences in screw threads made interchange impossible.[7]

Amelia regretted that her and Fred's impressions of the fascinating locations through which they were passing were largely confined to the sights, sounds, and smells of airfields. Of "the delectable perfume of flowers, spices and fragrant countryside; the sounds and songs and music of diverse peoples . . . we clutched what we could." But much of this airport environment was pleasant to Amelia. She never tired of what she called "ground flying," the "tall tales of aviation in far places" told by the many pilots of various nationalities encountered along Electra's path. "Stout spinners of yarns . . . and generously friendly to a female of the species wandering in among them."

One such at Karachi gave her a real chuckle, handing her a Reuters dispatch advising, "All American Army airmen with false teeth have been ordered to take them out before flying" because "the violent motions of the machine in flight are likely to shake the pilot's false teeth down his throat and choke him." Amelia agreed with her new friend that this item was amusing but not necessarily true. She added that her own teeth were "originals."[8]

At 7:25 A.M. on June 17, Amelia and Fred left Karachi bound for Calcutta, 1,390 miles away. The weather was cloudy but cleared as they neared the Sind Desert. There wind flew the sand skyward, hiding the ground. As they proceeded, mountains began to loom through the sandy sky "like sharks through a yellow sea." Gradually the air cleared, and the fliers could make out landmarks.

Central India had been well mapped, so that rivers and mountains were easy to identify, and the many railroads offered navigation aids. But these advantages depended upon clear visibility, and on this day a thick haze veiled the view. An additional hazard developed. At five thousand feet, black eagles appeared. "They soared about us lazily, oblivious of the Electra and giving its pilot some very bad moments," wrote Amelia. "How they managed to miss the plane I do not know. I

never had such an experience. . . ." For the sake of both the birds and
the Electra, Amelia fervently hoped that for the rest of the way birds
would keep their distance.[9]

In contrast to the African landscape, that of central India gave evidence of long, close cultivation, with green, brown, and gold fields surrounded by irrigation ditches. The conditions aloft were not so favorable. Beyond the ancient city of Allahabad, mountains lifted up, with
heavy rainstorms above them. Amelia was trying to fly between them
when air currents sent the Electra hurtling a thousand feet upward,
despite her attempts to push the nose down. After that, she gave the
squalls a wide berth, but for miles rough air shook the Electra vigor-
ously. About one hundred miles from Calcutta, the sky cleared, and
Amelia could see below the approaches to a great city: fields blending
into towns, mills and factories, and at last the city itself.

Just before they reached Dum Dum Airport, the sky opened again.
Landing on the water-soaked field, the Electra threw up a spray that
completely screened it from the observer's view. This squall did not
last long. Soon ground crews were servicing the plane, while Amelia
and Fred enjoyed afternoon tea. Driving to the home of their host,
whom Amelia did not identify, she was intrigued by the white-clad people and the bulls that wandered about freely. Passing a theater, she
caught a glimpse of home: Shirley Temple in *Captain January* was
playing.[10]

Of course, Amelia knew that the monsoon season ran from June to
October, but, having reached India by mid-June, she hoped to "squeeze
through" before the monsoons reached full force. It was a gamble. As
Amelia admitted, "our course lay southwestward so that the monsoon
winds were full on our nose."

That night the rains came, although not at top strength, just enough
to soak the airport and make takeoff dangerous the next morning. Meteorologists advised that the fliers proceed. More rain was predicted;
they might slip through the intermittent deluges, but if they remained
the field might become unusable. So they took off at 6:42 A.M., a risky
business. Mud clutched at the wheels so strongly that Amelia barely
cleared the trees edging the field.

For a while it seemed that they had beaten the weather, despite the
dark clouds. The Electra sped over the mouths of the Ganges and
Brahmaputra rivers on the way to Akyab in Burma. In the rice pad-
dies below, tiny figures would glance up at the aircraft. Some waved
their hats; others simply returned to their tasks.

Amelia and Fred did not plan an overnight stay at Akyab; they
hoped to refuel, check the weather, and then move on to Rangoon.
They fulfilled the first part of this program before the forces of nature
took a hand. Amelia had experienced many rainstorms while flying,

but this exceeded them all. One could not improve on her own description:

▶   The wind, dead ahead, began to whip furiously. Relentless rain pelted us. The monsoon, I find, lets down more liquid per second than I thought could come out of the skies. Everything was obliterated in the deluge, so savage that it beat off patches of paint along the leading edge of my plane's wings. . . . The heavens unloosed an almost unbroken wall of water which would have drowned us had our cockpit not been secure.[11]

Amelia battled these impossible conditions for some time and then had to admit that the little aircraft was no match for the mighty powers of nature. She turned back to Akyab, heading out to sea and barely skimming the surface of the water. Visibility was so poor the fliers were afraid to "come low over land." Fred could see nothing but the waves below, and Amelia credited him with "uncanny powers" in returning the plane to the Akyab airport in safety. One might suggest that the pilot, too, had demonstrated uncommon skill.

Fred's reaction to this setback was disgust: "Two hours and six minutes of going nowhere!" Airport authorities could promise no improvement. What is more, they added that these conditions might prevail for three months.

During their brief stop at Akyab, Amelia and Fred wandered into a bazaar. There she saw some bright-colored bracelets that she bought and mailed to her niece Amy as a sixth birthday present. Fred bought a small silver bowl for his wife. This was the only souvenir they took aboard. On the Electra, every ounce had to serve a purpose. So Amelia reluctantly passed up the opportunity to buy lengths of beautiful sari cloth, although she wrote to Amy that these constituted a temptation.[12]

One can well believe that after some three weeks of slacks and shirts, Amelia, so responsive to beauty in all its forms, lingered over the idea of converting this lovely material into a gown or two suitable for gala occasions back home.

Chapter 24
Problems

*A*melia's last weeks contained so many setbacks that one is tempted to believe that Someone was trying to tell her something. But if she had called it quits, she would not have been Amelia Earhart.

In a brief article datelined Akyab, Burma, Saturday, June 19, the *New York Times* reported, "Amelia Earhart took off from Akyab today for the third time in an effort to reach Bangkok, Siam. . . . Bad weather had forced them back to Akyab earlier in the day. Yesterday they battled a monsoon for two hours and then returned here. The route to Bangkok is over about 700 miles of jungles and mountains."[1]

Monsoon weather, even worse than the previous day's, took over, so Amelia had to settle for Rangoon, "only 400 miles away." She took the Electra up to eight thousand feet to escape the mountains. "After two hours of flying blind in soupy atmosphere we let down. . . . Then we dodged about for fifty miles. . . ."[2]

Amelia's "first sight of Rangoon was the Shwe Dagon Pagoda." Naturally, she wanted to see the inside during their enforced visit to Rangoon. "To enter, one must be unshod, and plod up long flights of steps, worn by numberless feet before." Here Fred balked. He had stayed at her side over oceans, mountains, and jungles and through monsoons, but he refused to remove his shoes and socks and go inside. Amelia was glad that she made the effort, for there, to her great delight, "really was a woman smoking a 'whacking white cheroot.' . . . These are made of corn husks filled with leaves and some tobacco, and can be bought in a magnum size for weddings to last three days."[3]

The next morning they left Rangoon and, after refueling at Bangkok's excellent airport, took off for Singapore, over nine hundred miles away. On this leg the elements were so kind that Fred remarked, "I thought there was no more weather like this." They stayed briefly with U.S. Consul General Monnett B. Davis and his wife. "They had courage enough to take us for the night," wrote Amelia, "even after I explained our disagreeable habit of getting up at three in the morning and falling asleep immediately after dinner."[4]

True to this warning, they left Singapore at 5:57 A.M., headed for Bandoeng, Java. Early in the flight they crossed the equator for the third time "and definitely passed 'down under' into the nether world of Australasia." The flight took five hours and twenty minutes, during which they passed over the Java Sea, skirted Sumatra, and flew across a mountainous part of Java, landing at Bandoeng at 10:17 local time. According to the *New York Times,* "military planes went aloft to lead her to the landing field when she circled for fifteen minutes, apparently unable to see airdrome markers."

An hour after they touched down, Amelia had a telephone call from George. She did not record the conversation but was sufficiently in awe of modern technology to find it "slightly miraculous."

She decided to spend three days at Bandoeng as a rest for herself and Fred and arranged to have the Electra overhauled before going on to Port Darwin, Australia. She put the plane in the hangar and left it in the hands of mechanics of KNILM, the local sister of KLM.

Then she and Fred took off for a sightseeing break to the crater of an active volcano. Amelia's sensitive nose detected sulfur fumes well before they reached the crater. The volcano had last erupted in 1910, but the Dutch were taking no chances. A volcanologist lived nearby and took daily readings. For the first time on this trip, Amelia felt chilly. She and Fred slipped into their leather jackets "and liked them." That evening they dined at the home of a KLM pilot and stayed in a very good hotel. Amelia's room was "filled with flowers and everything was as neat and spotlessly clean as Dutch reputation prescribed."[5]

The field service representative of Glenn L. Martin Company, Francis "Fuzz" Furman, who was under contract to KNILM, offered his assistance. "Known as a diagnostician and problem-solver, he was an excellent mechanic." The "exhaust gas analyzer, the generator and its fuel flow meter" were the main problems, but none seemed serious enough to interfere with the flight plans.

Fuzz repaired the exhaust analyzer and at 3:34 A.M. on June 26 the Electra was warming up. Amelia planned on flying through to Australia; however, in her words, "When one instrument refused to function everyone present turned mechanic and set to work to help." Not until 2 P.M. was the plane ready to go. Once in the air, it became evident that they had been overoptimistic. "Certain further adjustments of faulty long-distance flying instruments were necessary." From Surabaya, which they reached that evening, Amelia phoned Fuzz that she was still having trouble. He recommended that she return to Bandoeng. So Amelia "had to do one of the most difficult things I had ever done in aviation" and flew back to Bandoeng. Both problems proved to be with one engine; the other gave no trouble.[6]

During their stay at Bandoeng, Fuzz saw a great deal of Noonan. He noticed that Fred was giving considerable thought to Howland Island. It would be a hard target to hit, and even a cloud could deceive them. Noonan also constantly checked his four watches against the chronometers at Bandoeng to be sure he had the accurate time essential in celestial navigation. Fuzz likewise recalled that he "never noticed any drinking problem" on Noonan's part.[7] This last comment is significant in the light of later tales.

Meanwhile, a reporter aboard the Coast Guard cutter *Itasca* sent off an AF dispatch dated June 25: "Preparations for the expected arrival within the next few days of Miss Amelia Earhart and her globe-girdling plane got under way today on Howland Island, tiny coral Pacific Ocean island 1,532 miles southwest of Honolulu." Surveying and marking three runways "and attempts to scare away thousands of birds" had been in progress, and on June 24 the first boat from *Itasca* had brought supplies to the island. This article noted that the Navy tug *Ontario* would "stand by at sea" to aid in this longest leg of Amelia's flight.[8]

Friends of Fred, the Faddens, who lived in Batavia, urged the travelers to visit them, so they drove the three-hour-plus journey. "Entrancing treasures" were available in Batavia, and again the fliers wrestled successfully with temptation. Amelia made one exception to her stern rule of no purchases. She bought "a lovely hand-wrought" sheath knife for the collection of John Oliver la Gorce of the National Geographic Society, her "favorite Geographer."[9]

The Electra finally departed Bandoeng on Sunday June 27. Amelia had hoped to push on to Port Darwin. "But the penalty for flying east is losing hours," she wrote. "Depending on the distance covered, each day is shortened and one has to be careful to keep the current sunset time in mind so as not to be caught out after dark." Arrival at Kupang, Timor, at about 1:30 P.M. meant that after refueling and checking out the Electra, it would be too late to continue safely to Darwin. So the travelers "settled down overnight in the pleasant government guest house."

Kupang's airport was "surrounded by a stout stone fence to keep out rooting wild pigs" with no facilities for aircraft beyond a small shed for storing fuel. So Amelia and Fred staked down the plane and put on the engine and propeller covers.[10]

The next morning at 6:30 they were aloft again and crossed the Timor Sea safely "against strong head winds," reaching Port Darwin after a flight of three hours and twenty-nine minutes. "We were pounced upon by a doctor as we rolled to a stop," wrote Amelia, "and thereupon were examined thoroughly for tropical diseases. No one could approach us or the airplane until we had passed muster." Amelia was sensible enough to approve because "if this work is done at all it should be thorough," although it did delay refueling. By way of lightening the ship, they left at Darwin their parachutes, "to be shipped home." As Amelia remarked, "A parachute would be no help over the Pacific."[11]

To the inevitable reporters, she spoke with her usual practical, optimistic good nature. "From Lae to Howland Island will be the worst section of the flight, but with Freddy Noonan navigating I'm confident we'll make it." She added, "It's been a very interesting flight. But for slight mechanical trouble which was remedied at Bandoeng, Java, we have experienced no hold-ups. We've been sitting down waiting for Australia to turn up and we'll push on to Lae, New Guinea. I'm not taking any risks, but am flying as fast as possible."[12]

At 6:49 A.M., June 29, Amelia lifted her Electra "without formally announcing her destination. She had said earlier, however, that Lae was her next goal." It was a long flight, some twelve hundred miles, most of it over water, and consumed almost eight hours, "against headwinds as usual." She described the landing field at Lae as "one long strip cut out of the jungle, ending abruptly on a cliff at the water's edge. It is 3000 feet long and firm under all conditions." She noticed that a number of metal planes had "to be hitched outside" the hangars. And there at Lae, as part of the regular service, was another Electra, "sister of my own."

She and Fred stayed at a hotel, and Amelia noted that "tomorrow we should be rolling down the runway, bound for points east. Whether everything to be done can be done within this time remains to be seen. If not, we cannot be home by the fourth of July as we had hoped, even though we are one day up on the calendar of California. . . ."[13]

The suggestion that much remained to be done is one of the few negative comments Amelia ever permitted herself in print. In fact, she had good cause to be concerned about two very important fields: communications and weather. Until some months later, there was considerable misunderstanding as to what her radio could and could not do.

Amelia's transmitter was, to quote Safford, a "Western Electric 13A 50-watt, 3-channel, crystal-controlled VOICE transmitter tuned to

500, 3105, and 6210 kilocycles, with 25-foot horizontal antenna from a king-post to the two vertical fins, powered by 24-volt, 50-ampere engine-driven G. C. generator. It had been purchased second-hand from Harry Richmond who had used it on a trans-Atlantic flight in 1935."[14] Harry Richmond was a popular singer-actor of the period.

Amelia was not happy with her transmitter, but the trouble with it was not lack of power, as she thought, but lack of frequency channels. In actual power it was equal to that of the Pan Am Clippers and more than that of most U.S. transport planes of the time. It was actually too big for its generator, and Amelia had to use it "rather sparingly" after it burned out "on the aborted East-West flight." Most American transport planes, however, carried a ten-channel or even a fifteen-channel apparatus, whereas the Electra had only three.[15]

When the plane was modified following its crack-up at Honolulu, instead of installing a new transmitter, George had

▶ arranged with the Bell Telephone laboratories, designers of the set, to make the same alterations they had made for Admiral Byrd and other trans-Atlantic flyers. The VOICE transmitter was modified to operation with CW (continuous wave) and MCW (modulated CW) as well as VOICE. The original 3105 and 6210 KC channels were retained, but the third was changed to 500 KC, the International Distress Frequency which is constantly guarded by ships and coastal radio stations all over the world. 3105 KC was the prescribed Calling Frequency for Itinerant Aircraft and was provided in practically all American transport planes. It was AE's best frequency for normal communications, day as well as night, but it was worthless as a "homing" or direction-finder frequency except at rather short distances. Both Amelia and Fred were ignorant of this fundamental fact of radio-navigation. . . .[16]

The only reason for including 6210 KC, in Safford's opinion, was its being the "second harmonic" of 3105 KC. He believed that an intermediate frequency, such as 1200 or 1500 KC, "would have been more useful at all times, and especially during the approach to Howland."

The Navy's San Francisco station had erroneously advised *Itasca* that the Electra could transmit on its three frequencies by both voice and telegraph and that both Amelia and Fred could handle Morse code up to fifteen words a minute. No one ever corrected this misinformation to *Itasca*, although this "would have made all the difference in the world."[17]

Amelia's real problem area was her receiver. The Electra carried a "Bendix (miniaturized) direction-finder receiver, covering frequency ranges of 200 to 1500 kilocycles and 2400 to about 10,000 kilocycles, with rotating-loop antenna only." This setup had three deficiencies: First, the loop antenna had "poor pickup," a problem that the discarded trailing antenna would have solved. Neither George, Mantz, nor the authorities at Miami informed those concerned that Amelia had removed the trailing antenna. Second,

> ▶ in order to achieve extreme ruggedness and compactness, and because the transistor was still several years in the future, the designer of the apparatus resorted to the notoriously inefficient "peanut tubes." . . . Third, in the attempt to provide an "all-wave" receiver, the designer provided for four frequency-bands, namely 200–500 KC, 550–1500 KC, 2400–4800 KC, and 4800–10,000 KC, with a "hand-selector switch." The 200–550 KC band was the only band of value for direction-finding or "homing" during her ocean flights. The two highest bands constituted a "booby-trap" for the ignorant and unwary.

In addition, an "all-wave" Western Electric telegraph receiver and a hand-power "emergency" radio-telegraph set—the latter Safford considered useless—had been removed when the plane was overhauled. This information was never passed to *Itasca* or any other search vessel.[18]

Some of the authorities at Lae were not happy about Amelia and Fred's lack of experience in radio. After the tragedy, District Superintendent James A. Collopy at Lae reported to the Civil Aviation Board at Salamaua, New Guinea, on August 28: "As the result of a talk with Mr. E. Chater and Mr. Balfour, the Lae radio operator, it is very apparent that the weak link in the combination was the crews' lack of expert knowledge of radio. Their Morse was very slow and they preferred to use telephony as much as possible." They told Balfour that they would change the wavelength at nightfall. He advised against this, as their signals were coming through satisfactorily, but they changed it anyway. Collopy thought "that had an expert radio operator been included in the crew the conclusion may have been different."[19]

By no means were problems confined to the Electra and its crew. *Ontario* was singularly ill-equipped for its assigned task, that of guard ship stationed halfway between Lae and Howland. It lacked both speed and endurance, and its radio equipment was inadequate. The transmitter range was 195 to 600 KC, the receiver's 100 to 1000 KC. So *Ontario* could not hear Amelia on 3105 KC and could not talk to her at all. The tug had no radio telephone, and neither Amelia nor Fred could understand Morse. *Ontario* was limited to transmitting on 375, 429, and 500 KC but was asked to send homing signals on 400 KC. And then nobody informed the tug when Amelia left Lae.[20]

Lieutenant True, the aerologist, had returned to Pearl Harbor instead of transferring to *Itasca*. Richard B. Black, the Department of the Interior field representative aboard *Itasca*, did not inform Amelia of this fact. Nor did he make the obvious arrangement to have True's weather reports sent direct from Pearl Harbor to Lae Aerodrome, "although the Navy transmitter on Oahu [NPM] was the largest and most powerful in the Pacific, if not in the entire world."

So one finds such messages as the following from Commander W. K. Thompson, skipper of *Itasca,* to radio Tutuila [NPU]: "If impossible to reach Lae with Fleet Air Base and Itasca weather request you forward same to Ontario to be forwarded to Earhart while in flight." It seems incredible that Thompson did not know that *Ontario* lacked a radio telephone and had no high-frequency transmitter and receiver.[21]

As George's personal representative, Black should have made arrangements for Amelia's communications, but an undated message—probably sent on June 19—addressed to San Francisco and NPM, among others, indicates that he expected her to do so after she reached Lae. Two days later, on June 21, Washington advised Black, quoting a message from George: "Retel TELL BLACK DIFFICULT CONTACT EARHART SATISFACTORILY BEFORE ARRIVAL DARWIN. FROM DARWIN SHE WILL COMMUNICATE ITASCA STIPULATING REQUIRED FREQUENCY ONTARIO STOP ITASCA CAN CONFIRM TO HER AT LAE STOP SHE WILL ADVISE FULLY VIA SAMOA BEFORE LEAVING LAE STOP WILL ADVISE WETHER [*sic*] HICKAM OR WHEELER UNQUOTE. It had not been determined yet on which Oahu airfield Amelia would land.

George was in the States; a quick telephone call to the Bendix firm or a chat with any radio expert could have determined what type of homing signal should be used with the Electra's Bendix direction finder. Instead, he dumped the responsibility on his wife, who had quite enough to do in preparing for the Lae-Howland leg of her journey.[22]

On June 23, Thompson sent his first message to Amelia, via Samoa:

▶ . . . REQUEST YOU ADVISE THIS VESSEL TWELVE HOURS PRIOR TO YOUR DEPARTURE FROM NEW GUINEA FULL INFORMATION YOUR DESIRES IN MATTER OF RADIO COMMUNICATIONS SCHEDULE PERIOD WE WILL CONFORM TO ANY FREQUENCIES DESIRED IMPORTANT ANTICIPATE YOUR DEPARTURE AS COMMUNICATION VIA PORT DARWIN VERY SLOW PERIOD ITASCA ON STATION HOWLAND ISLAND AT 2200 THIS EVENING PERIOD THIS VESSEL WILL CONTACT SWAN AND ONTARIO AND ADVISE THEM FULLY. . . .

Thompson later explained that he took this action because he realized that *Itasca* had the ultimate responsibility, "at least from a Coast Guard point of view," and also because "Black's government messages were burdening a Navy–Coast Guard network with undue traffic, which could be readily relieved by Navy–Coast Guard procedure." Obviously Thompson was fed up with having a civilian big shot on board cluttering up the lines with individually addressed items instead of using the more efficient multiple-address system.[23]

Nowhere in any of Amelia's books appears a hint of criticism of any of her colleagues. But she would have been indeed saintly had she not felt some impatience at the delay in resolving a relatively simple problem. As Safford expressed it, "After horsing around for ten days trying to learn what frequencies the ITASCA and the two navy ships intended to use, she finally took the bit in her teeth" and signaled Black from Bandoeng on June 27 via RCA Manila and NPM:

▶ SUGGEST ONTARIO STANDBY ON 400 KILOCYCLES TO TRANSMIT LETTER N FIVE MINUTES ON REQUEST WITH STATION CALL REPEATED TWICE END OF EVERY MINUTE STOP SWAN TRANSMIT VOICE NINE MEGACYCLES OR IF I (AM?) UNABLE RECEIVE (BE?) READY ON 900 KILOCYCLES STOP ITASCA TRANSMIT LETTER A POSITION OWN CALL LETTERS AS ABOVE ON HALF HOUR 7.5 MEGACYCLES STOP POSITION SHIPS AND OUR LEAVING WILL DETERMINE BROADCASTING SPECIFICALLY STOP IF FREQUENCIES MENTIONED UNSUITABLE NIGHT WORK INFORM ME LAE STOP I WILL GIVE LONG CALL BY VOICE THREE ONE NOUGHT FIVE KCS QUARTER AFTER HOUR AND POSSIBLY QUARTER TO BT EARHART.[24]

Amelia never pretended to be a radio expert, which is probably why she used the word *suggest*—which seems to invite countersuggestions—instead of *request,* which implies that this is what is wanted. But this message raised more questions than it solved. In Thompson's report of *Itasca*'s action, he pointed out that this was the tug's "first direct contact with Earhart prior to the anticipated flight." He considered it "the key message of the flight." He noted that the frequencies she cited "were high frequencies with the exception of the ONTARIO. This is contrary to the last message from Commander San Francisco suggesting 333 and 545 kilocycles." Moreover, 7.5 megacycles was "beyond the frequency range, that at least to our knowledge, of the plane's direction finder."

Safford believed the key words were Amelia's request, "If frequencies mentioned unsuitable night work inform me at Lae." Other than *Ontario*'s 400 KC, all were "too high even for day work and doubly unsuitable for night work. The only suitable frequencies for the *homing signals* were 333, 375, and 500 KC, all of which were within the 'DF' band of AE's receiver, and the transmitters of all three ships were calibrated to these three frequencies." Of these, the best for Amelia's purpose was 500 KC. The Electra could transmit on this frequency, "at least when 'close in,' and because 500 KC was monitored by all ships and coastal radio stations."[25]

On June 26, Thompson requested independence from Commander San Francisco, on the grounds that the existing relationship was "unsatisfactory and potentially dangerous to Earhart contacts and other vital schedules."[26] San Francisco granted this request and thereafter gave him no more directions. This was not too smart a move on Thompson's part, for it left him solely responsible in a potentially explosive situation. The next day he advised San Francisco of the current situation as he saw it:

▶ 6-27 SWAN ONTARIO ITASCA ON POINT STATIONS ASSIGNED AND COMMUNICATIONS FOR FLIGHT SATISFACTORY PERIOD DIRECTION FINDER INSTALLED ON HOWLAND PERIOD GENERAL OPINION HOWLAND AIR FIELD USEABLE PERIOD LARGE BIRDS APT TO BE PROBLEM PERIOD ITASCA LANDING ORGANIZATION SET IN CASE CRASH PERIOD FIRE COMMA SURF RESCUE COMMA ARRANGEMENTS COMPLETE PERIOD ORGANIZED FOR DAY OR NIGHT ARRIVAL BUT STRONGLY RECOMMEND DAYLIGHT ARRIVAL.

As we have seen, communications for the flight were a long way from "satisfactory." And unless George had mentioned it, this was the first time Commander San Francisco heard that Howland had a direction finder. In the area of rescue preparations, however, it is evident that Thompson was displaying the foresight and expertise to be expected of a Coast Guard commander.[27]

Amelia had addressed her message concerning frequencies to Black, but Thompson answered it on June 27, addressing her through the governor of Samoa:

▶ ITASCA TRANSMITTERS CALIBRATED 7500 6210 3105 500 425 KCS CW [continuous wave] AND LAST THREE EITHER CW OR MCW [modulated continuous wave] PERIOD ITASCA DIRECTION FINDER EQUIPMENT 550 TO 270 KCS PERIOD REQUEST WE BE ADVISED AS TO TIME OF DEPARTURE AND ZONE TIME TO BE USED ON RADIO SCHEDULES PERIOD ITASCA AT HOWLAND ISLAND DURING FLIGHT 0910.

In Thompson's report he merely remarked, "The above is the only information that Earhart received relative to available direction finder frequency on board ITASCA."

This reply left much to be desired. Thompson did not mention *Itasca*'s radio telephone or advise "which of the five calibrated frequencies the *Itasca* intended to use for the homing signals." And he neither approved nor disapproved Amelia's suggested frequencies. It is quite probable that Amelia and Fred assumed that, in the old expression, "Silence gives consent."[28]

It is difficult to understand why all these problems had not been resolved well before the Electra reached Southeast Asia, indeed, before departure from the United States. Surely George could have arranged for a representative of the Navy, the Coast Guard, and radio experts—perhaps from Bendix and Bell—to get together and spell out exactly the radio capabilities and limitations of *Itasca, Ontario, Swan,* and the Electra. Possibly neither George nor Amelia realized the importance of such a mutual understanding. Amelia had used radio on all her long flights, but this was the first time that plane-to-ship communication could literally spell the difference between life and death.

Chapter 25

Poised for Departure

*D*espite the cross fire of messages pertaining to radio frequencies, which practically ensured communications difficulties, no one appears to have been apprehensive about Amelia's venture. On the Pacific coast, George was knee-deep in the public relations aspects of the flight. On June 27 he had wired Black aboard *Itasca:*

> ... IF ARRANGEABLE PLEASE SEND ME BY EARHART SET NEGATIVES HOWLAND ARRIVAL ETC STILL PICTURES PERIOD IF MOTION PICTURE CAMERA ON BOARD PERIOD EARHART'S STORY TO BE SENT DIRECT TRIBUNE OAKLAND APPRECIATE YOUR COOPERATION PERIOD SUGGEST YOU EMPHASIZE DESIRE SHE SECURE AIRVIEWS OF ISLAND PERIOD IF POSSIBLE REMIND HER BRING AVAILABLE PHOTOS FROM LAE. . . .[1]

Amelia had had trouble with her direction finder on the flight to Darwin. Royal Air Force Sergeant Stan Rose, in charge of Darwin's direction-finding station, had corrected the problem—a blown fuse for the generator—in a few minutes.[2]

Amelia and Fred had every right to expect that they would find everything in order for the Lae-Howland hop; however, the weather forecast did not arrive until the next day. The routing of weather reports took a minimum of four hours and might lag to eighteen.

On June 29, Amelia sent off a message to "Commander USS *Itasca*" routed via Lae, Salamaua, Rabaul, Sydney, and Tutuila:

▶ PLAN MIDDAY TAKEOFF HERE PLEASE HAVE METEOROLOGIST
SEND FORECAST LAE HOWLAND SOON AS POSSIBLE IF REACHES
ME IN TIME WILL TRY LEAVE TODAY OTHERWISE JULY FIRST RE-
PORT IN ENGLISH [i.e., voice] NOT CODE [i.e., Morse] SPECIALLY
WHILE FLYING STOP WILL BROADCAST HOURLY QUARTER PAST
HOUR GC FURTHER INFORMATION LATER.[3]

Here, then, Amelia definitely requested that code not be used in contacting her.

Itasca's reply was less than helpful: ". . . REFERENCE YOUR MES-
SAGE HAVE NO AEROLOGIST ABOARD HAVE REQUESTED
FORECAST FROM FLEET AIR BASE COMMA PEARL HARBOR
FOR HOWLAND TO LAE THOUGH DOUBTFUL IF OBTAINABLE
WILL FORWARD HONOLULU HOWLAND FORECAST AS INDI-
CATED. . . ."[4]

The next day Amelia asked *Itasca,* in Safford's acid words, "to
do what it should have done on its own initiative seven days earlier,"
that is, to "contact Lae direct on 25 meters Lae or 46 meters so can get
forecast in time" for her planned takeoff time of 2330 GCT July 1. She
continued, "PARTICULARLY INTERESTED PROBABLE TYPE PER-
CENTAGE CLOUDS NEAR HOWLAND ISLAND STOP NOW UN-
DERSTAND ITASCA VOICING THREE ONE NOUGHT FIVE WITH
LONG CONTINUOUS SIGNAL ON APPROACH CONFIRM AND AP-
POINT TIME FOR OPERATION TO STAND WATCH FOR DIRECT
CONTACT."[5]

She had addressed this message to Black, but Thompson replied,
giving her the weather forecast and arrangements for trying to contact
Lae direct. The test times he set "gave a good example of night, twilight, and daylight conditions." However, he limited the tests to
twenty-five meters (12,000 KC) and omitted the suggested forty-six
meters (6522 KC). If it is true that the Electra's crew should have included a radio expert, at least for the two scheduled Pacific legs, it is
equally true that *Itasca* should have had a similar specialist aboard for
this mission. Such an expert—or any skilled radio amateur—could
have told Thompson "that although 12000 KC was ideal for spanning
the 3800 nautical miles between Howland and San Francisco, it was
much too high a frequency for the 2250 nautical miles between Howland and Lae, day or night. 46 meters would have been just about
right."[6]

Lieutenant True sent off his first weather report to Amelia at about
11 P.M. on June 29, Honolulu time, but it took fourteen-and-a-half
hours to go through the relay, so it was out of date by the time it was
delivered.[7]

The Electra received "a final overhauling" on June 30. Once more, all was not well. The plane had a break in the fuel line, and static "interfered with radio signals." The aircraft was poised for takeoff on July 1, "weighed with gasoline and oil to capacity. However," Amelia added, "a wind blowing the wrong way and threatening clouds conspired to keep her on the ground today.

"In addition," Amelia continued, "Fred Noonan has been unable, because of radio difficulties, to set his chronometers. Any lack of knowledge of their fastness and slowness would defeat the accuracy of celestial navigation. Howland is such a small spot in the Pacific that every aid in locating it must be available."

She and Fred had "had worked very hard in the last two days repacking the plane and eliminating everything unessential. We have even discarded as much personal property as we can decently get along without and henceforth propose to travel lighter than before. *I have retained only one brief case in which are my papers as well as my extra clothing and toothbrush*" (italics added).

This italicized sentence appears in the newspapers carrying Amelia's running account of the journey. But for some reason George omitted if from the book version, *Last Flight*. This was unfortunate because that sentence could have quashed at the outset several rumors based upon supposed Earhart relics.[8]

Amelia and Fred took the time for a sightseeing jaunt. Borrowing a truck from the manager at the hotel, they "set out along a dirt road" with Fred at the wheel and "turned into a beautiful coconut grove before a village entrance." To their amusement, they discovered that the natives trained pigs to act as watchdogs. "Fred said he would hate to come home late at night and admit being bitten by a pig!"[9]

Lieutenant True dispatched his second weather report some seven hours after his first:

▶ FORECAST THURSDAY LAE TO ONTARIO PARTLY CLOUDY HEAVY RAIN SQUALLS TWO HUNDRED FIFTY MILES EAST OF LAE WIND SOUTHEAST TWELVE TO FIFTEEN PERIOD ONTARIO TO LONGITUDE ONE SEVEN FIVE PARTLY CLOUDY CUMULOUS [sic] CLOUDS ABOUT TEN THOUSAND FEET MOSTLY UNLIMITED WIND EAST NORTHEAST EIGHTEEN PERIOD THENCE TO HOWLAND PARTLY CLOUDY SCATTERED HEAVY SHOWERS WINDS EAST NORTHEAST FIFTEEN PERIOD AVOID TOWERING CUMULOUS AND SQUALLS BY DETOURS AS CENTERS FREQUENTLY DANGEROUS. . . .

Amelia received this at about 5 P.M., July 1, Lae time. It was "the last forecast Amelia and Fred received from Pearl Harbor, and predicted headwinds which were ten knots less than those predicted for the next day."[10]

True tried again on July 1:

▶   . . . ACCURATE FORECAST DIFFICULT LACK OF REPORTS YOUR
VICINITY PERIOD CONDITIONS APPEAR GENERALLY AVERAGE
OVER ROUTE NO MAJOR STORMS APPARENT PERIOD PARTLY
CLOUDY SKIES WITH DANGEROUS LOCAL RAIN SQUALLS ABOUT
THREE HUNDRED MILES EAST OF LAE AND SCATTERED HEAVY
SHOWERS REMAINDER OF ROUTE PERIOD WINDS EASTSOUTH-
EAST ABOUT TWENTYFIVE KNOTS TO ONTARIO AND THEN EAST
TO EASTNORTHEAST ABOUT TWENTY KNOTS TO HOWLAND.

There is no evidence that Amelia ever received this message.[11]

That night, she waxed reflective: "Not much more than a month ago
I was on the other shore of the Pacific, looking westward. This evening,
I looked eastward over the Pacific. In those fast-moving days which
have intervened, the whole width of the world has passed behind us—
except this broad ocean. I shall be glad when we have the hazards of
its navigation behind us."[12]

With those words, Amelia's own detailed, good-humored account of
her last adventure closes. From here on, one must rely upon other
sources, some reliable, some not. Almost immediately, sensationalism
began to take over. An account of the night before takeoff is lurid
enough for the yellowest of yellow journals.

According to this tale, which originated with a man named Alan
Vagg, Amelia refused to stay at the "rather rowdy" local hotel and went
to a private home. Fred, however, stayed at the hotel. He had struck
up a friendship with Jim Collopy and complained to him that Amelia
had pushed him "every minute since they left Miami. Fred said he had
had a belly full and was going to relax a little."

Then, the story goes, the two men set out on a "real fling" that lasted
all night. It was 7:30 A.M. on takeoff day when they returned to the
hotel. Amelia knocked on Fred's door at 8:15, and Collopy told her that
Fred was getting dressed and he, Collopy, would bring him to the
airfield shortly. He managed to get Fred there in time for takeoff at
10 A.M.[13]

This canard has shadowed Fred Noonan's memory for years, despite
its self-evident incredibility. All too many writers and researchers have
accepted as given that Fred was badly hungover when he climbed into
the Electra that July morning. Fred had been a heavy drinker, but he
was not a fool. The last night of all nights that he would have picked
for a drunken spree was this one. The next day's hop would require
total alertness and every ounce of his skill. Even if by some miracle a
hungover navigator made a perfect landfall on an island virtually in-
visible at high tide, his career would nose-dive into oblivion. The flight
of the Electra had given Fred the sort of second chance of which most
men can only dream. If he blew it, that would be the end.

Fortunately, we need not rely upon logic alone because eyewitness evidence is available. According to Collopy, he and Fred did go on an impressive wingding, but not on the eve of the departure. The "night they first landed . . . was the night FN and I really got stuck into the social whirl. . . ." After "about twenty Scotches or thereabouts," Fred remarked, "She can fly—I can navigate—but we both are bum W/T operators."

Collopy and Fred had a drink or two the evening before takeoff. They had what Collopy believed to be "the last Scotch Fred ever enjoyed," adding, "I can say I could not have had the last Scotch with a nicer guy."[14]

In a letter dated May 26, 1968, Collopy assured Thomas E. Devine that Fred was in bed early, and sober, on the eve of takeoff. Collopy should know whereof he spoke because his, Amelia's, and Fred's rooms were adjacent. So the best possible evidence, that of his drinking partner, reveals that Fred had been guilty of foolishness in going on a bender, but not of the criminal insanity of doing so the night before heading off for Howland Island.

Oddly enough, Collopy got the impression that "there was no great love" between Fred and Amelia and that he was "somewhat scared of her."[15] Fred might well have been rather in awe of Amelia, who was in a position to control his future course, depending upon whether her reports of him were favorable or unfavorable. However, there is no evidence that their relationship was other than camaraderie and mutual respect. In support of this evaluation, we have Fred's own words from a letter to his wife, written on June 30, 1937, from Java: "Amelia is a grand person for such a trip. She is the only woman flyer I would care to make such an expedition with. Because in addition to being a fine companion and pilot, she can take hardship as well as a man—and work like one."[16]

On the day before departure, Amelia and Fred were "seriously thinking of making an offer" to Harry Balfour to accompany them. He was the radio operator in charge at Lae and also the electrician in charge, and occasionally on weekends he acted as flight engineer.

He first met Amelia when she sent for him to give her the weather and other messages. He recalled that she was "very nice to everybody . . . from a short distance she looked like a slim freckled faced youth. But to talk to she was very charming and seemed to take in all that was said to her, she was an excellent pilot and won the respect of our pilots for the way she handled that Lockheed."

In a conference with her and Fred, Balfour was shocked to learn that neither could use Morse code. Perhaps his dismay gave Amelia occasion to reconsider their radio arrangements because on the eve of takeoff she, in Balfour's words, "asked me if I would go along if they decided they could manage the extra weight." She added that if he lost his job as a result of accompanying her, she would see that he got a position with an American firm.

After checking with his wife, Balfour agreed to go. He did not consider the flight particularly dangerous, "because she had a good machine, good radio, a navigator . . . plenty of fuel, and up to date weather reports and an excellent forecast before takeoff." However, she decided against taking him because, as they would have to sacrifice his weight in fuel, she believed he would be of more use at Lae.[17]

This was one of those decisions that seem logical at the moment but prove to be unfortunate. The presence on board of a skilled radio operator would have more than compensated for the fuel and could have ensured the Electra a safe landing on Howland.

On July 1 Amelia radioed Black and Naval Radio Tutuila: "ASK ONTARIO BROADCAST LETTER N FOR FIVE MINUTES TEN MINUTES AFTER HOUR GMT FOUR HUNDRED KCS WITH OWN CALL LETTERS REPEATED TWICE END EVERY MINUTE STOP PLAN LEAVE BY TEN THIS MORNING NEW GUINEA TIME. . . ."

This was the last *Itasca* heard from Amelia until after she had completed half the flight.[18]

One wonders if Amelia had any realization of how heavily the dice were loaded against her. To begin with, there was the basic matter of fatigue. Had she undertaken the hops between Honolulu and Howland, Howland and Lae, at the beginning of the project, as originally planned, she and Fred would have been in top physical form to face the challenge. As it was, the Lae-Howland leg came after thousands of miles of flying, much of it under grueling conditions. Amelia was not the complaining type, so her own account and her newspaper interviews are upbeat, but she and Fred must have been exhausted.

In support of that assumption can be cited the record of the flight Ann Pellegreno made during the thirtieth anniversary year, 1967, in a Lockheed 10, following Amelia's course as closely as possible. Of course, there were many differences. The Pellegreno plane carried the most modern equipment and a crew of three besides the pilot. These were Bill Polhemus, an expert on navigation equipment and celestial navigation; Lee Koepke, an airline mechanic; and Colonel William R. Payne, a veteran pilot on leave from the U.S. Air Force. By Amelia's standard the Pellegreno flight was plush, but throughout Pellegreno's interesting account are many references to how very tired they were at various stops.[19]

If Amelia had received True's last weather report, would the reference to "dangerous local rain squalls" and "scattered heavy showers" have persuaded her to postpone the flight for another day? Or with her usual optimism would she have accepted the forecast of "generally average" conditions with "no major storms" as a green light? Perhaps she took all weather reports with the proverbial grain of salt. On both the *Friendship* flight and her Atlantic solo, the forecasts, provided by one of the best in the business, had proved at variance with the actual conditions.

The strip map of the Lae-Howland course Safford considered "the poorest of the set." It was printed in dark brown against a light brown background, giving less contrast than the usual blueprints. The distances on this ocean chart were given in land miles. Vital information was missing. "There was no indication of the dangerously high mountains on Bougainville, New Britain and New Guinea." Nauru, Ocean Island, the Gilberts, the Marshalls, Ellice, and the Phoenix Islands were all omitted. Several of the missing islands—such as Nauru, Ocean, Butaritari, and Tarawa—could have given the Electra beaconing signals, but the strip map ignored the actual islands, let alone their radio stations. Even Baker Island, only forty miles from Howland, was not shown. Howland itself was located five miles west of its true position. Moreover, "times for changing course were set in advance, under the assumption that AE would make good a ground-speed of exactly 150 miles-per-hour (130 knots) regardless of the winds of heaven." So rigid was the schedule that the postulated flight time was seventeen hours, one minute. This would be cutting it fine for a prime modern airliner; for a two-engine, two-crew Lockheed in 1937 it was absurd.[20]

Arrangements for monitoring the flight fell far short of what Amelia and Fred had a right to expect. Safford remarked tartly, "Richard Black's failure to made *adequate* provisions for sending weather forecasts to Lae had been duplicated by his failure to make *any* provisions for reporting the progress of AE's flight between Lae and Howland. . . . AE, *on her own initiative,* made arrangements for reporting her departure to Mr. Black, aboard the *Itasca,* and also to Mr. W. T. Miller in Washington . . ." (Safford's italics). The islands mentioned were not notified that the flight was under way. Neither was *Ontario.*[21]

By July 1, 1937, local time, Howland had completed its plan to receive Amelia. The three runways had been finished; marker flags and a wind sock were in position. Four boxes of engine spare parts and various tools stood by for emergency maintenance. Thirty-one drums of aviation gasoline and two barrels of lube oil would enable the Electra to refuel.

Itasca waited on the leeward (western) side of Howland, prepared to send up smoke and radio signals when the plane approached. *Itasca* had a radio-telephone operator on 3105 KC but not on 6210 KC. *Ontario* was on guard stationed midway between Lae and Howland; however, it could not communicate with the Electra, a fact Amelia did not know. *Swan* awaited halfway between Howland and Honolulu for the last leg of the flight. *Swan* could conduct two-way radio-telephone communications with the Electra on 3105 and 6210 KC.

Two Army officers and several enlisted men stood by to scare birds off the runways and assist in any way required. The Navy contingent included two aviation machinist mates and a photographer. It had also promised to provide Amelia with weather forecasts. She still believed the aerographer to be aboard *Itasca,* but as we have seen he was at Pearl Harbor.[22]

At first glance, it may seem that the government had gone to an inordinate amount of trouble and expense to assist one who, however famous and beloved, was after all only a private citizen. But actually the arrangements fitted in well enough with existing schedules and plans. The Department of the Interior wanted to establish U.S. sovereignty over Howland Island beyond cavil, so the opportunity to improve the facilities and reap a harvest of publicity attesting to the U.S. presence there could only be welcome. As for the Navy, *Ontario* and *Swan* were already in the general area; the trouble and expense of being at a particular location at a particular time were more than offset by the opportunity for on-the-spot training and the favorable publicity. The assignment posed no problem for *Itasca;* preparing for and participating in rescue at sea were among the Coast Guard's duties.

Perhaps it was the old story of "too many cooks." No one was in overall charge; there was no command post where all information to and from Amelia could be received and coordinated. In Safford's exasperated summation, "Commerce has constructed the runways but Interior has jurisdiction over the island. . . . The U.S. Government, with its neck stuck far out, has taken no part in the planning and has left that important matter to the amateurish efforts of unqualified private citizens. Above all, there has been a total lack of coordination between the various organizations involved."[23]

Chapter 26
Disaster

ae Aerodrome was an unlikely setting for the last appearance of a celebrity of Amelia Earhart's stature. Being unconcerned with glamor, she probably was well satisfied with Lae's facilities and capable personnel. Its principal business was to serve cargo planes "carrying machinery, supplies, and occasional passengers to the New Guinea goldfields." After dark the aerodrome was closed to air traffic. It was almost completely isolated except for its private radio station to the Amalgamated station at Salamaua. The runway was quite primitive. In 1937 it consisted of a dirt strip 1,000 yards long by 120 yards wide, running from a clearing in the jungle to an abrupt drop into the sea.[1]

Appropriately enough, a certain amount of confusion attended Amelia's takeoff. The *New York Herald Tribune* gave the time as noon on July 2 Lae time; this information reached *Itasca* from San Francisco. This newspaper further advised that George had "moved into San Francisco Coast Guard headquarters preparatory to giving out bulletins on the start and progress of the flight."[2]

A radiogram from Lae to Black advised that the Electra was leaving at 10 A.M. local time. A message from a Frank Griffin to Miller in Washington also gave the departure time as 10 A.M.[3] This was correct but was not confirmed to *Itasca* for several hours. This meant that Howland could not be sure just when to expect the Electra. The plane might show up at sunrise, but not until around noon Howland time could Amelia be considered overdue.[4]

According to the *New York Herald Tribune*, the Electra "made a difficult takeoff with ease, but it was only fifty yards from the end of the runway when it rose into the air."[5] This is putting the situation mildly. If purported eyewitness accounts are accurate, takeoff was a real cliffhanger. When Ann Pellegreno was in Lae, she heard the story from veteran pilot Bertie Heath: ". . . I saw her silver plane move slowly down the unpaved runway. . . . When her plane reached the road that had a high crest and ran across the runway near the seaward end, it bounced into the air, went over the drop off and then flew so low over the water that the propellers were throwing spray. . . . She continued straight out to sea for several miles before climbing on course slowly. . . ."[6]

Collopy's report confirmed the suspenseful nature of the event:

> ▶ The take-off was hair-raising as after taking every yard of the 1000 yard runway from the north west end of the aerodrome toward the sea, the aircraft had not left the ground 50 yards from the end of the runway.
>
> When it did leave it sank away but was by this time over the sea and continued to sink to about five or six feet above the water and had not climbed to more than 100 feet before it disappeared from sight.

Collopy added, however, that it was obvious the plane was well handled, and pilots of Guinea Airways who had flown Lockheed aircraft were "loud in their praise of the take-off" of such a heavily laden plane.[7]

The weight was the heavy load of fuel necessary because there were no refueling stops on this leg. According to Griffin's message to Miller, the Electra had aboard 1,100 gallons of gasoline and 75 gallons of oil.[8] Although the search vessels and various writers accepted these figures as accurate, Safford questioned them. First, ". . . NR16020 could take only 46 gallons of oil, even if the oil in the two engines be included." Second, while the fuel tanks had a total capacity of 1,170 gallons, calculations indicated that the Electra carried no more than 1,016. "The cabin tanks were full for the first time in the flight. The wing tanks with combined capacity of 162 gallons weren't full and held only 50 gallons of 100 octane fuel."

These lower figures make considerable sense; indeed, Polhemus (Ann Pellegreno's navigator) estimated that the Electra could not have become airborne under the current conditions if carrying more than 980 gallons.[9]

For many miles, at least a third of the total, the flight presented no difficulties to a pilot and a navigator as experienced as Amelia and Fred, respectively. Their courses kept them in sight of islands whose mountains and coastlines were clearly charted, enabling sight navigation.

Amelia broadcast the Electra's position every hour on the quarter-past, sometimes adding the altitude and speed, but never giving her course "so far as the record shows." Lae received these but, according to Safford, only one was forwarded to *Itasca,* delivered twenty-four hours late. This was timed at 0718 July 2 (GCT) and gave the plane's position as latitude 4° 33' south, longitude 159° 06' east. This was right on course toward Howland. Safford plotted this as 750 nautical miles from Lae with a ground speed of 103 knots. The carrier *Lexington,* which had been receiving Amelia's messages by radio from San Francisco, plotted 785 miles and 111 knots; the Hawaiian Sector "795 miles—on course to Howland." The local time was seven minutes before sunset, the position ten miles west of the Nukumanu Islands. "If the same course and ground speed were maintained," wrote Safford, "the plane should have arrived at Howland between 2100/2 GCT and 2145/2 GCT, or between 8:30 A.M. and 9:15 A.M. HST."[10]

Other potentially useful information from Amelia failed to reach *Itasca.* "An early report (probably at 0115/2 GCT) gave her speed as 140 mph, or 122 knots." The last broadcast from Amelia that Lae heard gave her altitude at 7,000 feet with speed of 150 miles per hour or 130 knots. At 0515/2 GCT she advised that "she was descending from 10,000 feet because of thick banks of cumulus clouds."[11]

At about 1030/2 GCT the Amalgamated Wireless station on Nauru Island picked up a voice broadcast on 3105 KC. Nauru had been receiving all of Amelia's broadcasts from 0630 to 1130 GCT and recognized her voice; however, the listeners could only distinguish the words "A ship in sight ahead."

This ship could only have been *Ontario,* whose log gave her 8 P.M. position as "Lat. 2°-59'-30" south; Long. 165°-20'-00" east." *Ontario* was right in position, 370 miles from the Nukumanus, and so was the Electra. There was no possibility of a mistake; the only other ship within 500 miles was the SS *Myrtle Bank,* headed for Nauru and a good 125 miles northeast of *Ontario.* Personnel on Nauru, who did not know of *Ontario*'s presence, assumed that Amelia had sighted *Myrtle Bank* and so advised Sydney, whence the American consul informed Washington.

To have reached *Myrtle Bank* Amelia would have had to be flying from the Nukumanus at a ground speed of 155 knots, "far beyond her scheduled base speed of 130 knots." Actually, she had been moving well under that speed. From her position reported at 0718 GCT to *Ontario* was 370 miles, yielding a ground speed of 116 knots by Safford's calculations, 345 miles and 108 knots by *Lexington*'s. Oddly enough, the important "ship in sight" message did not reach *Itasca,* although newspapers both in the United States and Australia published it.[12]

Another bit of information helps place the Electra in this time period. T. H. Gude, director of police on Nauru, "had just bought a new 12 valve Atwater Kent Radio Set" and was following Amelia's flight "with great interest." On the evening of July 2, the Gudes were entertaining guests at dinner. Much to his wife's annoyance, Gude "kept tuning in to pick up any messages" from Amelia.

Between 10 and 11 P.M. local time, he heard her calling Harold Barnes, the officer in charge of the Nauru radio station. "She called several times and said she could see the lights on Nauru. The lights she referred to were the flood lights strung out along the 2/1000 foot cableway situated on top of the island to permit mining at night." Barnes was not on duty at this time, but Gude believed one of the operators was. The Nauru radio station was "not on the air for 24 hours a day, but for specific periods only." Gude's receiver was much more suitable to receiving voice broadcasts than was Radio Nauru's telegraph receiver that "cut off the higher modulating frequencies and distorted the speech." Gude was quite sure that the Electra went down somewhere between Nauru and the Gilberts.[13]

Nauru was not on Amelia's strip map, but they knew about the island and its lights, thanks to Nauru officials' initiative. They had wired Lae: ". . . New Nauru fixed light lat. 0.32 S. Long 166.55 east five thousand candlepower 560 feet above sea level visible from ships to naked eye at 24 miles stop also there will be bright lighting 8 am baro 29.908½ therm 84 wind s e 3 fine but cloudy Sea smooth to moderate stop please advise time departure and any information re radio transmission with times."

The message also described an older light on Nauru: "A white light showing one flash every 8 seconds is exhibited from the wireless mast. The light is 530 feet above sea-level and is visible round the horizon to a distance of 15 miles in clear weather."[14]

As Safford remarked, "If the initiative, interest and common sense displayed at Nauru could have been duplicated at Lae, Howland, Samoa and Pearl Harbor, Amelia and Fred might have finished their flight in triumph!"

Gude picked up Amelia's broadcast between 1100/2 and 1200/2 GCT, about an hour after her "ship in sight" message. We do not know whether, after passing *Ontario,* Amelia and Fred continued on their direct course to Howland or detoured to the neighborhood of Nauru to check their position. However, it does not necessarily follow that because Amelia saw Nauru's lights she must have altered her course. The visibility distances cited in Nauru's message were for ships at sea; an aircraft, in that pure, unpolluted air, would have many times the seaborne visibility. "On the direct course from *Ontario* to Howland," Safford estimated, "the Electra would have passed Nauru abeam at about 1145/2 GCT, at a distance of 125 nautical miles. At 1130/2, Nauru would have been about 130 nautical miles away, and the 5000 candle-power fixed lights would have been visible from an altitude of 10,000 feet, or at least the loom of the light on the clouds overhead."[15]

Thus, while proof is lacking, we believe that in logic Amelia and Fred would have kept on the direct course to Howland rather than waste precious fuel on an unnecessary detour. Of one circumstance there can be no doubt: Up to this point in the flight, everything had gone well. The skill of pilot and navigator left nothing to be desired. The Electra was exactly where it should have been, when it should have been.

At 0630/2 GCT, several hours after Amelia's takeoff, *Itasca* received word of her departure. So the cutter "manned its second HF receiver . . . and sent radioman second class Frank Cipriani . . . ashore to man the loop direction finder on Howland." At midnight (1130/2 GCT), *Itasca* tried to reach the Electra for the first time: "KHAQQ DEN RUI HOWLAND AAAAAAA PSE GA 3105 NOW K." *Itasca* sent this by Morse on 7500 KC and by voice on 3105.

Amelia heard neither of these broadcasts. Anyone with a smattering of knowledge of radio frequencies could have predicted "that AE could not hear the 7500 KC signals at night; the closest they came to the plane was about 200 miles—directly overhead." Safford added with exasperation, "An orbiting rocket might have heard them." Some thirty-eight hundred miles away, NMC (San Francisco) picked up these signals, but instead of directing *Itasca* to use 500 KC, merely instructed the cutter to shift from fifteen words a minute to ten. This well-meant adjustment was no help at all, because in this instance the problem was not Amelia and Fred's ignorance of Morse but the too-high frequency.

Amelia could have heard the voice broadcast over 3105 KC, but she was using her single receiver for signals on 7500 KC, which Thompson had advised he would use initially, shifting to 3105 when the plane came fairly close to Howland. So Amelia did not expect any communication from *Itasca* on 3105 for several hours.[16]

From this point the situation deteriorated rapidly. The first of Amelia's hourly broadcasts heard at Howland came through at 1415/2 GCT on 3105 KC; however, the only intelligible words were "Cloudy and overcast." Her 1515/2 broadcast came in with "signals weak and fragmentary." *Itasca* did not hear the 1615/2 broadcast, and while it picked up the 1715/2 broadcast, it was unintelligible. Safford found this strange: "The foregoing broadcasts came during hours of darkness, when reception of radio signals is much better as a general rule than in daylight. After sunrise, which at Howland came at 1740/2 GCT, although the static was logged as stronger than the signals."[17]

At sunrise, 6:10 A.M. local time, the shore party left the cutter for Howland to make ready for the landing. Everything seemed to be under control. Black was in charge; Lieutenant Commander Baker of the Coast Guard would supervise the "emergency high-frequency direction finder"; two rescue boats were stationed on the windward and leeward sides of Howland. Captain Neilsen of the Engineer Corps and

Lieutenant David Cooper of the Army Air Corps, with three Army enlisted men, would refuel the plane "and render such other assistance as required." Two Navy aviation machinist mates landed, carrying special tools suitable to the Electra's engines and "four boxes of engine spare parts." Everything was ready, up to and including a photographer each from the Army and Navy, and two newsmen, respectively, from the Associated Press and the United Press.[18]

In short, Howland was well prepared to deal with a successful landing or even a splashdown. In contrast, unfortunately, radio communications were so inept as virtually to ensure disaster.

Itasca broadcast twenty times to the Electra on 7500 KC in Morse. Amelia heard only one, that of 0758-59. No broadcasts were made on 6210 KC, although Amelia radioed at 0845 HST, "Listening on 6210 kilocycles." Black knew that 6210 and 3105 were Amelia's frequencies and that she also had 500, but of "dubious useability." George had so informed him on June 16 through Black's secretary. *Itasca* made thirteen Morse broadcasts on 3105 KC "coupled with 7500 KC, but coupled with 3105 KC VOICE" every half hour from 0400 through 0600 local. "*The mutual interference on 3105 would guarantee that both signals would be completely unintelligible!*" (Safford's italics).

Five times *Itasca* asked Amelia to shift to 500 KC but broadcast on 500 KC only twice. Twenty-one voice broadcasts went out over 3105 KC, "generally coupled with 7500." Amelia heard not one of these voice broadcasts. In fact, of all *Itasca*'s transmissions, she received only one, and she could not get a bearing on it "because of sky-wave."

Safford's judgment that, "if it had been intentional, the *Itasca* could not have done a poorer job" may seem harsh, but it is not entirely out of line.[19]

One can imagine the frustration Amelia and Fred experienced with time speeding by and only one message—and it useless—from *Itasca*. Part of the problem may have been a too-narrow interpretation of his mission on Thompson's part. According to Don Dwiggins, Paul Mantz's biographer, from the beginning Thompson "wanted it made clear that the Coast Guard had *no intention* of navigating AE to Howland; the cutter had been ordered to the equatorial islands for guard duty only" (Dwiggins's italics). As Thompson saw it, that meant simply furnishing weather reports and forecasts. And when Black had offered to supply *Itasca* with "a staff of experienced Navy radiomen, Thompson's reply was a curt no."[20]

At the same time, personnel aboard *Itasca* were having their own problems trying to sort out the fragments being received from Amelia. Any messages she may have sent over 500 KC could not have reached *Itasca* or Howland because, as we have seen, Amelia had discarded her trailing antenna. By the same token, Amelia could have homed in with her loop antenna, except that *Itasca* was using 7500 KC instead of 500 KC when she tried to get a bearing on the cutter.[21]

At 0345 HST Amelia reported, ". . . OVERCAST WILL LISTEN ON HOUR AND HALF HOUR ON 3105. . . ." At 0453 HST the listeners heard her say, "Partly cloudy," and two minutes later "broke in on phone—unreadable." The radio logs did not always quote Amelia verbatim but showed the gist. Thus at 0614 the log recorded: "WANTS BEARING ON 3105 KCS ON HOUR/WILL WHISTLE IN MIKE." "On the hour" GCT was on the half hour Howland time. A minute later, "ABOUT TWO HUNDRED MILES OUT/APPROX/WHISTLING N W (Vol S-3)." After three minutes, "PICKED UP EARHART, USING LONG ANTENNA, S3, HARDLY ANY CARRIER, SHE SEEMS OVERMODULATED. SWITCHED OVER TO LOOP FOR BEARING, S1 TO S0. SHE STOPPED TRANSMISSION BEARING NIL."[22]

At 0630 Thompson's report noted, "Sending A's on 7500 (Asked her position) Listening through on 3105." At 0643, "KHAQQ CAME ON AIR WITH FAIRLY CLEAR SIGNALS CALLING ITASCA (VOICE)," and two minutes later, "KHAQQ REQUESTED—PLEASE TAKE BEARINGS ON US AND REPORT IN HALF HOUR I WILL MAKE NOISE IN MICROPHONE—ABOUT 100 MILES OUT (Earhart signal Strength–4 but on air so briefly bearing impossible.)"

And now, after about an hour had passed, *Itasca* picked up Amelia's broadcast of 0742. A note of desperation began to appear: "KHAQQ CALLING ITASCA. WE MUST BE ON YOU BUT CANNOT SEE YOU. RUNNING OUT OF GAS. ONLY ONE HALF HOUR LEFT. BEEN UNABLE TO REACH YOU BY RADIO. WE ARE FLYING AT ONE THOUSAND FEET." Radio log No. 2 added an anxious note: "CANT HEAR US AT ALL WE HEAR HER AND ARE SENDING ON 3105 AND 500 SAME TIME CONSTANTLY AND LISTENING IN FOR HER FREQUENTLY."

At 0758, Amelia radioed, "KHAQQ CALLING ITASCA. WE ARE CIRCLING BUT CANNOT HEAR YOU GO AHEAD ON 7500 EITHER NOW OR ON SCHEDULE TIME ON HALF HOUR." Homing signals would be in Morse. Amelia could recognize a single letter sent many times if she knew what to listen for. *Itasca* complied immediately, and at exactly 0800 (1930/2 GCT) she replied: "KHAQQ CALLING ITASCA WE RECEIVED YOUR SIGNALS ON 7500 BUT UNABLE TO GET A MINIMUM PLEASE TAKE BEARING ON US AND ANSWER 3105 WITH VOICE." The log noted, "Sent long dashes on 3105 for 5 seconds or so."

The last message *Itasca* received came in at 0844: "KHAQQ CALLING ITASCA WE ARE ON LINE OF POSITION ONE FIVE SEVEN DASH THREE THREE SEVEN. WILL REPEAT THIS MESSAGE ON SIX TWO ONE NOUGHT KILOCYCLES. WAIT. LISTENING ON SIX

TWO ONE NOUGHT KILOCYCLES. WE ARE RUNNING NORTH AND SOUTH." *Itasca* tuned one of its two high-frequency receivers to 6210 KCS but heard nothing further; the cutter did not tune its high-frequency transmitter to that wavelength.[23]

Radio Nauru had been covering Amelia's frequencies—3105 and 6210 KCS—whenever the station was operating. One of VKT's native operators heard and recognized her voice three times after the last *Itasca* reception, at 2031/2, 2043/2 and 2054/2 GCT, or 0901, 0913 and 0924 Howland time. Nauru informed Radio Bolinas, near San Francisco, of these receptions: "SPEECH NOT INTERPRETED OWING BAD MODULATION OR SPEAKER SHOUTING INTO MICROPHONE BUT VOICE SIMILAR TO THAT EMITTED IN FLIGHT LAST NIGHT WITH EXCEPTION NO HUM OF PLANE IN BACKGROUND." Radio Bolinas forwarded this to Coast Guard Headquarters in San Francisco, which immediately radioed it to *Itasca*. Thompson included it, without comment, in his official report.

There is no reason to doubt that these three broadcasts were authentic. As yet it was not widely realized that the Electra was in distress or had crashed, so the hoaxers—those sick creatures who seem to surface after every well-publicized disaster—had not yet made their appearance.[24]

Interpreting the record of the signal strength of Amelia's broadcasts, based on a scale of zero to five, Safford reached some interesting conclusions as to the Electra's position that no one aboard *Itasca* seems to have figured out. Her only intelligible message received during the night, at 0345 HST, came in on Strength–3. This was two and a half hours before sunrise, and Safford estimated the Electra was between 500 and 1000 miles from the cutter. An hour later, when the plane would have been roughly 110 nautical miles closer, reception was much fainter, indeed unintelligible. And her broadcast one hour later wasn't received. "In other words, the ship was *inside* the plane's *night* skip-zone." The hour following, and a half-hour after sunrise, she came in "with Strength–4, in Strength–5 static." Her last two broadcasts on 3105 KC "were logged as Strength–5, the strongest signal the human ear can tolerate. However, the loop DF on Howland was unable to get a minimum for a bearing; the *Itasca* was *beyond* AE's 3105 KC skip-zone" (Safford's italics).[25]

How, after covering the first half of their flight with expert navigation and pilotage, had Amelia and Fred become fatally lost?

Fred had planned on a system of navigation for use in the event he had only one star or only the sun for a fix. Safford pointed out that Polhemus, using this method, had hit Howland on the nose in 1967. But this system called for "a series of sun observations for the last three hours of flight," and Noonan had no available sun at that time, and no stars earlier. Shortly after the Electra passed *Ontario,* the skies darkened, and, by the time Fred should have been taking his sun observations, he could see nothing but water "and a black storm cloud which covered the entire sky and reached from an altitude of 2000 feet to about 18,000 feet."[26]

At first glance, it is difficult to accept that a change of weather could have made such a difference. Amelia had flown safely through many a storm but, as she noted more than once, she had been aiming for a continent. On her solo flight to Europe, she had hoped to land in Paris but had ended up in Ireland. That had not mattered; one landfall was as good as another. She had no such luxury now.

Thompson and others later argued that Fred was not depending on the direction finder on Howland, but really he had no viable alternative. Denied sun and stars, he had only dead reckoning and the D/F to rely on. Howland was much too small to provide a reasonable target for dead reckoning, even if he had had accurate estimates of the wind velocity. But, as we have noted, his latest information was ten knots less than a later estimate he never received. Nor did the Electra have the drift bombs that could have given Fred a check on his course. According to one source, he left them under his bed in Lae; according to another, they were left at Burbank. The latter is more likely; if the drift bombs had been a scheduled part of the Electra's equipment, a routine preflight check would have revealed their absence.[27]

Paul Mantz and many others have postulated that the 157-337 degree line of position Amelia had broadcast was a sun line, and on that basis Paul believed the plane had come down quite near Howland, and he so informed the Coast Guard at San Francisco.

Safford challenged the sun line theory, explaining, "At sunrise on July 2, 1937, in the vicinity of Howland Island, the sun bore 67-degree true, 58-degrees magnetic, and would change bearing to the north, that is, decrease in numerical value. Amelia was steering magnetic courses. . . . The maximum value a 'sun line' could have had was 148-328, magnetic. A discrepancy of nine degrees is too much to swallow."

Safford believed that the Electra's course at that time would have been 67 or 68 degrees magnetic. "When Noonan thought the plane had overshot Howland, he had AE circle for a few minutes and then fly at right angles to the original track on north-south courses, or 157-337 magnetic, to be exact."[28]

Based upon various factors, such as the plane's altitude, the wind strength, weather, and the inability of the Howland D/F to get any bearings on the Electra, Safford estimated the splashdown at about 325 miles west of Howland, "or in round numbers latitude 1 degree north, longitude 178 degrees east." He believed that there was "a 95%

probability that AE came down within 100 miles of this spot." He noted that Noonan, "an experienced aerial navigator," believed that he was over Howland at 1915/2 GCT, "so we must rule out Saipan, Mili Atoll, the Phoenix Islands, and other distant locations."[29]

These coordinates place the crash site in the vast open extent of ocean between the Gilbert Islands and Howland, about as desolate a spot as one could imagine. We cannot be sure Safford was correct, but his estimate has the virtue of being based upon logical and scientific considerations, which is more than can be said for many of the theories that arose and muddied the waters for years to come, and indeed continue to do so to this very day.

Chapter 27
The Early Searches

O ne can almost feel the change in atmosphere aboard *Itasca* once the perceived mission changed from guard ship to rescue ship. Amelia's "running out of gas" message convinced Thompson that the situation was indeed serious. At 8:00 HST he sent *Itasca*'s passengers off as an emergency shore party to assist the Electra if the message "proved to be a false alarm." At the same time, he recalled the on-the-spot shore party, advising them of his belief that the plane was down. He instructed Cipriani to stand by with the direction finder and to keep trying for radio bearings on the Electra.

This posed a problem. *Itasca*'s gun-firing batteries had been lent to Howland to power the D/F, and these had been reported weak at 7:45 A.M. By 9 A.M. they had run down completely. By a lucky chance, a radio amateur on the island had a charging set. Recharging occupied the remainder of July 2 and all of July 3; the D/F was out of operation until midnight that day. Cipriani and his assistants manned it continuously for the next thirteen days. They obtained only one bearing, at first believed to be the Electra, which turned out to be a Japanese station.[1]

The shore party came aboard *Itasca* at 9:12 A.M. Nothing had been heard from the Electra since 8:47, when Amelia's transmitter had failed. Every minute was precious, yet *Itasca* did not get under way until 10:40 A.M. An hour and a quarter had been lost while Thompson, Black, and others indulged in a futile argument. Black and Lieutenant Cooper agreed that Amelia was not yet lost, only overdue. *Itasca* should remain on station until noon. As for her "running out of gas" signal, that was "just to jog the ITASCA into greater effort." This is so fatuous as to defy belief. Amelia could make mistakes in judgment, but not to the extent of playing games with those on whom her and Fred's lives depended.

The Coast Guard men countered that time was essential; Black insisted otherwise. Probably 10:40 represented an uneasy compromise between noon and immediately.[2]

At about this time, *Itasca* advised the San Francisco Division and the Hawaiian Sector of the situation, and thus the first news of the disaster reached the outside world. The message ended that if the plane had not arrived by noon, *Itasca* would "commence search northwest quadrant from Howland as most probable area. Sea smooth visibility nine ceiling unlimited. Understand she will float for limited time."[3] The words "visibility nine" indicated that prominent objects would be visible for more than twenty miles.

Thompson conducted a tireless and meticulous search. Unfortunately, he made a number of understandable but mistaken assumptions. He either forgot, or never knew, that Amelia was flying by magnetic compass, hence "all her courses, bearings, and lines-of-position were magnetic, which differed by nine degrees from true courses, etc., in the vicinity of Howland." Therefore, *Itasca* was speeding on 337 degrees true, then changed to 67 degrees true. The cutter followed the latter course for one hundred miles, then resumed course on 337 degrees true. Moreover, Thompson assumed that because Amelia's final signal strengths had been so powerful, she must have gone down within one hundred miles of Howland. Thompson was by no means alone in that assumption; however, in view of the vagaries of radio reception it was not necessarily so.[4]

Early on, Thompson requested the Hawaiian Sector to procure help: ". . . SUGGEST CONTACT NAVY FOR SEAPLANE SEARCH PERIOD SIXTEEN HUNDRED GALLONS AVIATION GASOLINE NOW ON HOWLAND AND NINETYFIVE GALLONS OF LUBRICATING OIL."[5] The sector responded, asking for "full details" and "all information" that would be of value if the plane were dispatched. Somewhat unnecessarily it instructed Thompson to "broadcast data to all ships to be on look out."[6] The skipper did so immediately, or possibly had already done so.[7]

Apparently the SOPA (senior officer present afloat) was less than thrilled by the Coast Guard request for a patrol plane. He gave the chief of Naval Operations a brief rundown, including the fact that *Swan* had ten thousand gallons of aviation fuel on board. He continued nervously:

▶ PLANE OPERATION AT HOWLAND MUST BE CONDUCTED IN OPEN SEA ON LEE SIDE OF ISLAND NO ANCHORAGE FOR AIRCRAFT OR TENDER RETURN TRIP CANNOT BE MADE WITHOUT

REFUELING INVOLVING POSSIBILITY PLANE MAY BE FORCED TO
LAND HOWLAND UNDER UNSAFE SEA CONDITIONS OPERATIONS
THERE FEASIBLE ONLY DURING EXCELLENT WEATHER CONDI-
TIONS PERIOD PRESENT WEATHER FORECAST IS FOR CONTINU-
ING FAIR WEATHER VICINITY HOWLAND ISLAND FOR NEXT
FOUR DAYS PERIOD NOT PRACTICABLE TO SEND MORE THAN
ONE PLANE BECAUSE ONLY ONE CAN BE TENDERED AT HOW-
LAND PERIOD NAVIGATIONAL AND OTHER DANGERS OF THIS
LONG FLIGHT APPARENT PERIOD ADVISE.[8]

One wonders why, if the Navy was so conscious of all the perils lying
in wait for a young pilot fresh out of Pearl Harbor, it had not had some
inkling of what might happen to two people no longer in their first youth
who had already flown around most of the world. Thompson should not
have had to ask for a Navy patrol plane; the Navy should have stationed
Swan with at least three aircraft at Howland to be on the spot if circumstances called for an air search. As Safford observed, "It is true that
the Navy had furnished the exact assistance that Mr. Putnam had
requested, but the degree of foresight, imagination, and initiative exer-
cised by the U.S. Navy on this occasion was close to zero."[9]

While *Itasca* awaited word concerning the requested aircraft, furnished a stream of information to the Hawaiian Sector, and pursued its
conscientious but fruitless search, word that Amelia Earhart was missing crashed into the nation's newsrooms. *Itasca* had advised that she
was believed down shortly after 5 P.M. EDT. This meant that it was too
late for the story to break in the July 2 newspapers. But the next morning it hit the headlines and wiped every other news item from the public consciousness as with a giant squeegee.

The initial attitude was surprisingly upbeat. The New Zealand
Navy Cruiser HMS *Achilles* had reported at 3:30 A.M., July 2, New
York time, that shortly before that it had heard a signal from KHAQQ:
"Please give us a few dashes if you got us." This had come in "with good
strength" on both 3105 and 6210 KCs. This was about an hour and a
half after *Itasca*'s last reception. The *New York Herald Tribune* correctly reported *Achilles*' position as 10 degrees south, 160-50 degrees
west.[10] Interviewed at Burbank, Paul Mantz professed to believe that
the Electra could still land at Howland—Amelia might have mistaken
the amount of gasoline available to her. "Not all the gasoline reserve
shows on the gauges." And unless extremely rough weather developed,
the Electra "probably could remain afloat almost indefinitely."

This was sheer whistling in the dark. Later Paul admitted that he
thought Amelia and Noonan "had only 'one chance in ten thousand' of
making a safe water landing."

Paul had sat up the entire night of July 2 with a radio ham, Walter
McMenamy. At 10 P.M. EDT, the latter heard the letters "L-a-t . . . fol-

lowed by undecipherable figures." Then at midnight EDT, Carl Pierson, chief engineer of the Patterson Radio Corporation, picked up "erratic and indecipherable" signals. Both McMenamy and Pierson believed the signals came from "a hand-cranked generator." The *New York Times* added erroneously, "Miss Earhart carried one in her plane." Paul knew that Amelia had no hand-crank generator.[11]

Noonan's wife had telephoned the *Oakland Tribune* to ask if the plane had landed safely. Whoever took her call read her an Associated Press dispatch that the plane had probably been forced down at sea. Whatever she felt privately, she gallantly told reporters, "If they are forced down, I believe they will be saved by the *Itasca*." She would remain at work in the beauty shop she operated in Oakland "pending definite word."

George, too, tried to put a good face on the matter. "The plane should float but I couldn't estimate for how long, because a Lockheed plane has never been forced down before," he told reporters in Oakland. "The plane's large wing and empty gasoline tanks should provide sufficient buoyancy if it came to rest on the sea without being damaged."

He added, "There was a two-man rubber lifeboat aboard the plane, together with life belts, flares, a Very pistol and a large yellow signal kite which could be flown above the plane or the life raft." He further stated that Amelia "had planned to take emergency food rations and plenty of water."

George simplified this in a message to Washington requesting the Navy's aid:

▶ Technicians familiar with Miss Earhart's plane believe, with its large tanks, it can float almost indefinitely. With retractable landing gear and smooth seas, safe landing (on the sea) should have been practicable. . . .
The plane's large wing and empty gasoline tanks should provide sufficient buoyancy if it came to rest on the sea without being damaged.
There was a two-man rubber lifeboat aboard the plane, together with lifebelts, flares, a Very pistol and a large yellow signal kite. . . .[12]

As some newspapers pointed out, on occasion aircraft had come down at sea and their crews rescued after several days. But these instances had occurred fairly near shore or in well-traveled shipping lanes. Such instances were not comparable to a forced splashdown in an isolated area of the Pacific. Also, of the published statements about the plane's ability to float, not one that we have seen speculated about the fliers' ability to function under such conditions. Amelia had mentioned the intense heat when working inside the plane in Florida. Afloat virtually on the equator in a metal container, the heat would soon have been far above what the human body is programmed to withstand. If Amelia and Fred managed to scramble out onto the Electra's top, that would be no improvement. The direct tropical sun could kill within hours. The only real hope was that by some miracle the Electra had reached a scrap of land with some form of shade and potable water.

However hopeful a face George tried to show in public, he was exceedingly worried. One of his first actions was to hurry to Jackie Cochran, who was staying in her Los Angeles apartment. "He was extremely excited" and asked if she could "do something." Of course, Jackie tried, receiving clear and quite specific impressions: Amelia had run out of fuel and was floating "northwest of Howland and not too far away." Amelia was not hurt, but Fred had fractured his skull against the bulkhead and was unconscious. An American vessel named *Itasca*—of which Jackie had never heard before—was nearby and so was a Japanese fishing boat. At the time, she picked up its name, but by the time she wrote her memoirs she had forgotten it. She begged George to keep her name out of it, but to hurry planes and ships to "the designated area."

Jackie "spent three days in a hell here on earth." She phoned George on July 3 to tell him the plane was still afloat. But on July 4 she told him it was too late and went to the cathedral to light candles for Amelia's soul that "had taken off on its own long flight."

Grief-stricken and bitter, Jackie never used her gift again except very occasionally at her husband's urging. Of what use was it if it could not save Amelia?[13]

On July 5, an unnamed astrologer wired Edgar Cayce, arguably the dean of American psychics, asking for news of Amelia. His reading located the Electra northwest of Howland "less than a hundred miles out." There had been no physical injury; Amelia was "standing the conditions better than the companion"; they had "mighty little" of either food or water. Conditions were serious, but they might be located early the next morning.[14]

It is interesting that Cayce in Virginia, Jackie in California, and the responsible officers aboard *Itasca* all postulated that the Electra had come down in roughly the same area.

Meanwhile, *Itasca* continued the search on July 2, hampered by one more mistaken assumption. As Safford observed sourly but justly, "As has so often happened since the invention of radio . . . senior officers far removed from the scene of action and poorly informed as to existing conditions intervened and tried to conduct operations by remote control." In this case it was the Commandant, San Francisco, who advised:

▶ 8002 POSSIBILITY PLANE MAY ATTEMPT USE RADIO ON WATER AS RADIO SUPPLY WAS BATTERY AND ANTENNA COULD BE USED ON TOP OF WING PUTNAM AND LOCKHEED STATE POSSIBILITY OF

FLOATING CONSIDERABLE TIME EXCELLENT AND THAT EMER-
GENCY RUBBER BOAT AND PLENTY OF EMERGENCY RATIONS
CARRIED ON PLANE 0910.

In one important respect this was incorrect. Amelia's radio "operated from the generator on the right engine." Thus it would be
inoperable if the craft landed in the sea, and, as noted, she had no
hand-crank generator.[15]

In his official report, dated July 21, 1937, Thompson noted,

▶ This information formed the basis of the ITASCA's search at sea until information was contradicted by Lockheed on about 5 July. The ITASCA assumed the plane would float 9-hours or so. The ITASCA kept listening on
3105 and 500. The probability of the plane being able to use radio gave
credence ʋo numerous false amateur position messages. . . . As long as
radio use was possible search was not a hopeless affair. *The ITASCA
steadily called the plane* [Thompson's italics].

By late afternoon the press had gotten into the act, and the influx of
messages was maddening. "The period 1733 to 1748 was occupied with
commercial press requests and routine traffic pouring in during an
emergency situation," Thompson reported. These importunities from
the press and other irrelevant messages hampered *Itasca* throughout
the search period, as Thompson noted in no uncertain terms:

▶ Repeatedly commercial systems, photographers, and newspaper services
requested special consideration. Messages from these concerns interfered
with ITASCA listening to a marked degree. In one case . . . commercial
monitoring resulted in the release of inaccurate information and formed a
clear case of law violation. The efforts of amateurs and other stations to
hear Earhart's signals resulted in faked amateur messages and in the
diversion of the ITASCA from probable sectors of search to trace down
rumors.[16]

At about 8 P.M. Howland time, Thompson received orders from the
Commandant, Fourteenth Naval District at Pearl Harbor, to return to
Howland to rendezvous with Navy patrol plane 620, which was being
dispatched in accordance with Thompson's request. These orders not
only removed *Itasca* from the logical northwest sector but necessitated
recalibration of the cutter's transmitter to accommodate the Navy
plane's frequency. This, of course, hampered attempts to reach the
Electra. So, after about twenty-four hours, *Itasca* was back where it
had started.[17]

The patrol plane never arrived. The pilot, Lieutenant Warren W.
Harvey, reached *Swan* but not *Itasca*. The cutter had no trouble in re-

ceiving Harvey's transmissions that night. Two of them tell the story: "1003 WEATHER BECOMING UNFAVORABLE LOW BROKEN CLOUDS HIGH OVERCAST LIGHTENING TO WEST SOUTHWEST AND TO SOUTHWARD 0415." The second was much more specific:

▶ 2003 APPROXIMATE POSITION LATITUDE 0635 LONGITUDE 7200 PERIOD LAST TWO HOURS IN EXTREMELY BAD WEATHER BE-TWEEN ALTITUDE 2000 AND 12000 FEET SNOW SLEET RAIN ELEC-TRICAL STORMS PERIOD IN DAYLIGHT CONDITIONS LOOK EQUALLY BAD CLOUD TOPS APPEAR TO BE 1800 FEET OR MORE PERIOD AM RETURNING TO PEARL HARBOR NOW HAVE 900 GAL-LONS FUEL ON BOARD 0710.

So a storm sufficiently powerful to frustrate "one of the Navy's out-standing younger pilots"[18] ensured that there would be no air search at the very time when it represented the only realistic chance of locat-ing the Electra. These messages give a clue as to what Amelia and Fred had run into: a storm system with clouds too low to permit a wide panoramic view of their surroundings and too high to break through for sun sightings.

Expressions of hope and confidence continued in the stateside pa-pers. Lieutenant Commander Clarence S. Williams, who had prepared Amelia's strip maps, "expressed the belief that the plane landed on Baker Island, forty miles south of Howland Island." Paul Mantz claimed to believe now that Amelia might have landed on one of the Phoenix Islands, "a group southeast of Howland Island."

George's restless pacing indicated his agitation, but publicly he ex-pressed confidence that his wife would "pull through." He stressed, "She has more cool courage than anyone I know. I am worried, of course, but I have confidence in her ability to handle any situation."

He had the unenviable task of phoning the news to Amy Earhart. Soon reporters converged on her front door, asking if she thought Amelia was dead. "No, no, no! No, of course not," she told them coura-geously. "I know she's all right. I know she will be found soon. I know she is alive." Throughout the grueling search period, it was Amy who sustained "family and friends with her invincible display of courage and good faith," and she responded personally to the hundreds of sym-pathy letters she received.

George visited Beatrice Noonan, reaching her home just as she was leaving for the airport to look for him. "Everything is going to be all right," he assured her as he patted her shoulder. He reminded Beatrice that they had plenty of emergency food and water, and the plane, "if undamaged, should float for weeks."

At one point he let a touch of reality creep in. "It's this way, Bea. One of two things has happened. Either they were killed outright—and that must come to all of us sooner or later—or they are alive and will be picked up." He rose to go. "Keep your chin up, Bea," he exhorted her kindly.

"You, too, Mr. Putnam," she replied. Later that day she collapsed "and was placed under the care of a physician."[19] It was the first open crack in the wall of denial.

The Navy now came through with massive aid: the battleship *Colorado* with its three aircraft and the carrier *Lexington* with fifty-four planes aboard. The carrier was to have left San Pedro on the third to help Santa Barbara celebrate the Fourth of July. This trip was quickly canceled; officers and men of six squadrons were ordered to report at the Naval Air Station Pier at 6:30 A.M. on the fourth "prepared for a four weeks cruise." *Colorado* was at Pearl Harbor, much nearer the scene, but even so, it would take several days to cover the distance.[20]

Released from its aborted rendezvous with the Navy plane, *Itasca* returned to the search. Hoax messages began to come in and unfortunately could not be ignored because one just might prove authentic. The first came from San Francisco:

▶ 8003 FOUR SEPARATE RADIOMEN AT LOS ANGELES REPORTED RECEIVING EARHART VOICE THIS MORNING AND VERIFY QUOTE 179 WITH 1 POINT SIX IN DOUBT UNQUOTE POSITION GIVEN AS QUOTE SOUTHWEST HOWLAND ISLAND UNQUOTE ABOVE HEARD ON 3105 KCS AND CALL OF PLANE DISTINCTLY HEARD AND VERIFIED ACCORDING TO AMATEURS 2350

"This position placed Earhart nearly on the line of flight and about 200 miles south of Howland," reported Thompson. Although this meant leaving "the probable northwest sector" and steaming to the given location, Thompson felt he had no choice. As a result, *Itasca* "searched 2000 square miles on 4 July without result."[21]

Another message from San Francisco proved to be a hoax:

▶ 8004 UNCONFIRMED REPORT FROM ROCK SPRINGS WYOMING STATE EARHART PLANE HEARD 16000 KCS PERIOD POSITION ON A REEF SOUTHEAST OF HOWLAND ISLAND THIS INFORMATION MAY BE AUTHENTIC AS SIGNALS FROM MIDPACIFIC AND ORIENT OFTEN HEARD INLAND WHEN NOT AUDIBLE ON COAST VERIFICATION FOLLOWS 1510

"This message," wrote Thompson, "started the Phoenix Island Reef theory. It was logical due to sun line and reciprocal bearings . . . however, if on a reef the chances for safety were better than if drifting at sea and one ship could not cover the entire possible area of over

450,000 square miles." Later, *Colorado*'s planes searched the islands without result.

The next message of any importance came from the commander of the *Lexington* Search Group, advising the CinCUS, "LEXINGTON GROUP PROCEEDING ON DUTY ASSIGNED WILL REFUEL LA-HAINA ROADS EXPECT ARRIVE FOURTEEN HOURS EIGHTH 1910."[22]

Thus ended the Fourth of July, the day George had planned that Amelia and Fred would land triumphantly at Oakland to an enthusiastic welcome from Amelia's public. One hopes that George never fully grasped the terrible irony of the situation. He had loved publicity, courted it, and craved it. Now he had publicity, heaped up, pressed down, and running over, but it had come at the cost of losing his wife.

Chapter 28
The Last Search Phase

*T*he fifth of July was the sort of day guaranteed to drive a conscientious commander up the bulkhead. It began with a message from the Hawaiian Sector:

▶ 8005 FOLLOWING COPIES NAVY RADIO WAILUPE 1130 TO 1250 GCT QUOTE 281 NORTH HOWLAND CALL KHAQQ BEYOND NORTH DONT HOLD WITH US MUCH LONGER ABOVE WATER SHUT OFF UNQUOTE KEYED TRANSMISSION EXTREMELY POOR KEYING BEHIND CARRIER FRAGMENTARY PHRASES BUT COPIED BY THREE OPERATORS 0242.

If anyone had told Thompson that neither Amelia nor Fred could use Morse code, he would instantly have recognized this reception as the hoax that it was; *Itasca, Swan,* and the British steamer *Moorsby* would have been spared a "wild-goose chase;" and false hopes would not have been raised in the press. Thompson later decided it was "probably a faked message originating in the Hawaiian Islands."

At the time the message reached *Itasca,* the cutter was two hundred miles west of Howland, tracking down the "4 authenticated amateur reports." *Moorsby* was within one hundred miles, listening on 3105 KCs. *Swan* was northeast of the position "and was requested to stand to it." As darkness fell, the three vessels "converged on the position 281 north of Howland."[1]

Meanwhile, Thompson had sent Coast Guard Headquarters information for Secretary of the Treasury Henry Morgenthau Jr., who had asked to be kept advised of developments:

▶ ... INTERCEPTS OF RAGGED TRANSMISSION INDICATE POSSI-
BILITY EARHART PLANE STILL AFLOAT TWO EIGHTY ONE MILES
NORTH HOWLAND STOP BEARINGS RADIO DIRECTION FINDER
ON HOWLAND CONFIRMED APPROXIMATE POSITION WE WILL
ARRIVE INDICATED POSITION THIS AFTERNOON ABOUT 1700
PLUS ELEVEN AND ONE HALF TIME.[2]

As word reached the mainland, headlines sprouted: "THREE SHIPS
SEARCH SPOT NAMED BY EARHART RADIO MESSAGE 281
MILES NORTH OF HOWLAND"[3] and "SHIPS CONVERGING ON
SPOT LAST REPORTED BY AMELIA."[4] The accompanying stories
held few hard data but much speculation; however, every scrap of hope
was seized eagerly. The day before, Lieutenant Harvey had told reporters that in his belief Amelia and Fred "didn't have a chance" if they
had encountered the weather conditions that drove him back to Pearl
Harbor, "the worst storm I ever experienced in 11 years of flying." Nevertheless, he speculated that the Electra might not have flown sufficiently northward to run into it.[5]

Early in the day, a bearing reported from Howland complicated the
picture: "8005 AT 0035 HST OBTAINED BEARING ON A CONTINU-
OUS WAVE OF UNKNOWN ORIGIN INDICATING SOUTH SOUTH-
EAST OR NORTH NORTHWEST ON MAGNETIC COMPASS PE-
RIOD UNABLE TO OBTAIN UNILATERAL BEARING DUE TO
NIGHT EFFECT PERIOD NO CALL GIVEN PERIOD FREQUENCY
IS SLIGHTLY ABOVE 3105 KCS 0425."

This seemed to reinforce the growing theory that the Electra had
come down in the Phoenix Islands; however, as we have seen, the bearing proved to have been taken on a Japanese radio station.[6]

During the afternoon, an important message came in from the San
Francisco Division:

▶ 8005 OPINION OF TECHNICAL AIDES HERE THAT EARHART
PLANE WILL BE FOUND ON ORIGINAL LINE OF POSITION WHICH
INDICATED POSITION THROUGH HOWLAND ISLAND AND
PHOENIX GROUP PERIOD RADIO TECHNICIANS FAMILIAR WITH
RADIO EQUIPMENT ON PLANE ALL STATE DEFINITELY THAT
PLANE RADIO COULD NOT FUNCTION NOW IF IN WATER AND
ONLY IF PLANE WAS ON LAND AND ABLE TO OPERATE RIGHT
MOTOR FOR POWER PERIOD NO FEARS FELT FOR SAFETY OF
PLANE ON WATER PROVIDED TANKS HOLD AS LOCKHEED ENGI-
NEERS CALCULATE 5000 POUNDS POSITION BUOYANCY WITH
PLANE WEIGHT 8000 1525

Thompson reported, "This message changed the whole search problem and virtually eliminated all intercepted radio traffic ideas (unless

plane was on land)" (Thompson's parentheses). Until this time, *Itasca* had believed that the Electra had an emergency radio set capable of sending on water.[7]

Six hours later, San Francisco informed *Itasca* that Pan Am had reported bearings on a plane signal indicating a position in the Phoenix group. "These messages led to Mr. Putnam's request to the COLORADO to search the islands." Thompson later asked Pan Am "to test its bearings by taking them on the *Itasca*. The bearings were never received." He doubted that these signals came from Amelia. Neither *Itasca, Swan,* Howland, Baker, nor Samoa had picked them up. He also believed that if Amelia were broadcasting she would give "some useful information and not just call signs or dashes. (Both Earhart and Noonan could use code)" (Thompson's parentheses).[8] Once again, a logical assumption was based upon a false premise.

Near midnight on July 5 came a dramatic moment. The Hawaiian Sector sent out a signal: "8005 ITASCA SIGHTED FLARES AND PROCEEDING TOWARD THEM AT 2215 2243." This infuriated Thompson, who took this as evidence that "commercial or service stations" had been monitoring *Itasca*. No doubt this was correct because Mantz's biographer stated that "a commercial radio company in Honolulu" had been "monitoring the radio messages for pooled press services." Those same press services showered the bedeviled Thompson with "a deluge of commercial requests." In particular, they wanted pictures of the anticipated rescue, and two newspapers offered the captain of *Moorsby* liberal pay for his personal story.

What had happened, as Thompson reported, was that as *Itasca, Swan,* and *Moorsby* were converging on the 281 position, "two lookouts and the officer of the deck saw a distinct flare to the northward. It came up from and settled down to the horizon. Hoping the plane or boat could be afloat ITASCA headed for the flare and over radio asked Earhart if she was sending up flares. If so, send another one. A few seconds later another green light appeared bearing 75 degrees. . . ." There were twenty-five witnesses to this second sighting.

Listening at the radio in Los Angeles, Paul Mantz knew that the euphoria and press hunger were unfounded. Amelia had no flares aboard the Electra; she had left them in the hangar in Burbank.

The nearby *Moorsby* had seen no flares, but watchers on far-off Howland had done so and set afire three drums of gasoline as an impromptu lighthouse. *Swan* had seen the lights and correctly considered them to be meteors.[9]

Meanwhile, the U.S. Navy was sending in heavy reinforcements. The battleship *Colorado,* under the command of Captain W. L. Friedell, "bearing three navy planes with great cruising range," was headed south from Honolulu. It carried fuel and water for

Itasca, whose drinking water was running low and had to be rationed.[10]

For the search by the aircraft carrier *Lexington,* we are fortunate to have an eyewitness account written for Safford by Robert M. Stanley, president of Stanley Aviation Corporation in Denver. In 1937 he was a naval aviator. These men, although receiving the Navy's standard flight training, were not career men. They existed in a gray area between officers and ratings, eating in the officers' mess and with officers' club privileges but unable to sign for a message or see a Navy code book. And they could not even fly from ship to shore unless "'led' by an Annapolis graduate, regardless of his navigational or piloting abilities." Fortunately these young men were sufficiently self-assured to find these restrictions amusing. Some Navy actions were inexplicable to them. "For the life of us we couldn't understand why the Navy sent destroyers [*Drayton, Lamson,* and *Cushing*] all the way from the California coast to Hawaii, when Pearl Harbor had duplicate destroyers coming out of their ears."

These naval aviators approved the project in principle but doubted its practicality: "Though we savored the air of gallantry, none of us harbored any illusions about the prospects of our finding a drifting landplane, even should it remain afloat for the seven days that had intervened and the more delays that were to come before we could be on station, actually searching."

In view of the important role that radio played in the Earhart drama, Stanley's comments as to the state of the art in naval aviation at the time are worth repeating:

▶ In 1937, ours was . . . a Navy most of whose airplanes lacked radio of even the most primitive sort. . . . What little radio communication there was used Morse code, radiated from a long wire unrolled to trail behind the aircraft. Only the more senior officers rated radio-equipped airplanes, and even then did not communicate directly; they passed their written messages to a radioman sitting in the rear seat who sent and received all communications by key. . . . Aircraft radio in those days was in its earliest infancy. Small wonder that Amelia Earhart knew so little about it.[11]

While *Lexington* was steaming toward Hawaii, *Itasca*'s day on July 6 began with another message from San Francisco that narrowed down the possibilities:

▶ 8006 YOUR 8005 2010 PLANE CARRIED NO EMERGENCY RADIO EQUIPMENT EXCEPT ONE SPARE BATTERY IN CABIN PERIOD DYNAMOTORS ALL MOUNTED UNDER FUSELAGE WOULD POSITIVELY BE SUBMERGED IF PLANE WAS IN WATER PERIOD IN ABSENCE OF POSITIVE IDENTITY OF SIGNALS SUGGEST EVERY

EFFORT BE MADE TO OBTAIN DIRECTION FINDER BEARINGS HAVING IN MIND RECIPROCALS FROM HOWLAND PERIOD ROUGHNESS IN NOTE OF PLANE SIGNAL COULD BE CAUSED BY VIBRATION AND ALTHOUGH SET CRYSTAL CONTROLLED SOME SLIGHT DEVIATION DUE TO POOR ADJUSTMENT OF FRACTURED CRYSTAL 0115

One hour later San Francisco relayed a message from George. He noted that all the bearings thus far obtained plus Noonan's line of position passed through the Phoenix Islands. His message included a sound estimate: "WEATHER ANALYSIS INDICATED LIKELIHOOD HEADWINDS ALOFT MUCH STRONGER THAN NOONAN RECKONED WITH PROBABLY NEVER GOT 100 MILES FROM HOWLAND." This was the message that sent *Colorado* searching the Phoenix Islands.[12]

President Roosevelt told the press that he "was very much worried about the fate of the flyers," and "that he was anxious that the Navy search should cover as much territory as possible." On July 6 *Colorado* headed for Winslow Banks, "low, uncharted coral reefs" on the northern fringe of the Phoenix group. This was not a particularly realistic area to search. According to Navy charts, Winslow Reef was under thirty-six feet of water, and was shown as "PD" (position doubtful). Captain Friedell was much too experienced a seaman to risk a battleship in such dangerous waters. On two successive occasions he sent up his aircraft to comb the area. They never sighted Winslow, although Carondelet Reef, on the southern edge of the Phoenix Islands, was visible from ten miles out.[13]

On July 6, two Japanese ships joined the search. Prime Minister Koki Hirota had instructed Hirose Saito, Japanese ambassador to the United States, to offer the services of his country's navy. Hirota also instructed all Japanese ships in the South Seas to keep watch. The U.S. government gratefully accepted the offer, and the Japanese furnished the seaplane carrier *Kamoi* and the survey ship *Koshu*. The latter was no more suitable for the duty than was *Ontario,* but *Kamoi,* which carried sixteen long-range seaplanes, was much better equipped to search than was *Colorado* with her "three short range float planes." According to a report from Tokyo, *Koshu* was already "in the area around Howland Island," but *Kamoi* was in the Marshall Islands waters, far from the scene of action.[14]

In the afternoon of the sixth, *Colorado* received orders from the Commandant, Fourteenth Naval District, to "take charge of all naval and Coast Guard units" in the search area and to "direct and coordinate" the search pending arrival of the commander, Destroyer Squadron Two, with the *Lexington* group, who would then take charge.

Shortly *Itasca* received orders from San Francisco by way of the Hawaiian Sector to come under the Navy's command.

Itasca would continue to participate, after refueling from *Colorado* at 6 A.M. on the seventh, but from this point the cutter's role was simply to comply with the orders of the senior vessel. The little ship had done all that could be expected of it. As Safford noted, "Commander Warner K. Thompson's outstanding performance of duty during the Earhart Search was in marked contrast to his bungling of radio communications during the Earhart flight."[15]

Late on the sixth, San Francisco suggested that an "important area of immediate search of *Colorado* planes in Sector 320 to 350 degrees radius 250 miles from Howland." Friedell did not act upon this suggestion. He was sure there was no chance of finding the lost fliers alive unless they had reached land, and the nearest land from Howland in the 320/350 sector was the Kurile Islands or Siberia. So he kept *Colorado* searching in the Phoenix Islands.[16]

One notices a subtle difference in the press coverage on July 8. Radio signals and alleged voice receptions continued, but the press reported them perfunctorily. A good deal of coverage was devoted to recapitulation of past events. Admiral Orin G. Murfin, who as commandant, Fourteenth Naval District, was directing the search, announced that "it should be known by midafternoon Monday whether the round-the-world flier and her navigator were still alive." The dateline of the interview, July 7, fell on a Wednesday; Monday would be the twelfth.

Murfin explained that *Lexington* should reach the search area by Monday morning. "If it used all its planes, it would be able to scout thoroughly 36,000 square miles about the Phoenix Islands in six hours." If the initial search proved fruitless, "*Lexington* would continue the hunt as long as she had gasoline and fuel oil," which probably would last three days. Lieutenant Commander J. L. Reynolds, Murfin's aide, added that "in the absence of advice to the contrary, naval headquarters was taking it for granted the huge fighting ship carried a full complement of ninety eight aircraft," not fifty-seven, as originally announced.[17] Captain Leigh Noyes reported the next day that *Lexington* had sixty-two planes aboard.

Lexington arrived at Lahaina Roads at 11:10 A.M. local time on July 8, having provided such irreverent naval aviators as Stanley more cause for amusement. "We considered it hilarious that our arrival at Hawaii had been delayed due to our having to slow down so the California-based destroyers could catch up." They were astonished to discover that Lahaina Roads had no means of refueling the carrier. The tanker *Ramapo,* headed for Guam, had been ordered to Lahaina on the sixth, but had not yet arrived.[18]

Hawaii was the site of a brief flurry of excitement on the afternoon of the eighth. Navy Radio Hilo sent a startling message to Commandant, Fourteenth Naval District, with information to Navy Radio Pearl Harbor:

▶ 1908 MR. MANUEL FERNANDEZ OF HILO AIRPORT REPORTS HEARING AMELIA EARHART AND FREDERICK NOONAN CALLING ITASCA ON 1420 KCS AT 1615 AND ASKING THEM RUSH ASSISTANCE AS THEY CAN ONLY LAST SHORT TIME LONGER PERIOD ACCORDING TO FERNANDEZ HE ALSO SAID THE ITASCA ANSWERED AND TELL THEM TO HOLD OUT A WHILE LONGER PERIOD PLEASE CONFIRM IF ANY CREDENCE TO THIS REPORT AS LOCAL PAPERS REQUESTING INFORMATION 1715

This turn of events was an honest mistake, and the Navy immediately recognized it as such. Fernandez, a radioman employed by Inter Island Airways, had fallen victim to a realistic broadcast of *The March of Time,* a popular program presenting the news in dramatic form. In this particular broadcast, the producers had featured "an imaginary two-way conversation between Miss Earhart and the Itasca."[19]

Various other purported messages were received, one from a radio amateur, Ray Havens, of Great Falls, Montana. He claimed to have heard "All's well" at 5° south, 173° west. "That would be just west of Hull Island." A ham in San Francisco, Arthur Monsees, reported an SOS signal KHAQQ that mentioned "East Howland," "Lights tonight," "Must hurry," and "Can't find." Monsees said this came in on 6250 KCS, on which the Electra could not operate. Just how much hope such reports gave George is problematical. His son, David, had arrived by air from Miami to lend such support as he could give.[20]

After waiting twenty-seven hours for fuel, *Lexington* departed Lahaina Roads late in the afternoon of July 9, reaching the search area on the eleventh. The search commander selected Stanley to assist in preparing the plans. Expecting to be given "the total of all charts and maps aboard," he was dumbfounded to receive "a dog-eared, battered, small book on whaling published in 1841." That was it: "no other maps, no charts, no information of any sort, other than this one ancient volume. . . ." Moreover, the author was far from specific, listing "reefs, shoals, islands and atolls in a choice of positions." It was a disconcerting situation. In Stanley's words, "here we were on the biggest fighting ship in the world, faced with the need of high speed during the plane launch and retrieval, without knowing what reefs might be beneath us, or how close to the surface they might be."

The weather handicapped the search. "It was not stormy; merely the normal weather pattern of that part of the Pacific." A strong east wind and severe, frequent local rain showers "created high waves and whitecaps . . . effectively masking any debris, had there been any." The carrier passed within five miles of Howland Island without its being visible from the bridge.

The *Lexington* air search was well planned and conscientiously carried out. It concentrated on the area northwest of Howland as being the most probable if the lost fliers were adrift. Each search consisted of forty-two planes, twenty-one in each direction. They flew at a height of some seven hundred feet at eighty knots for about 120 miles. "Then they made a 50-degree turn to the left or right, flew 21 miles in the direction of the ship's course and then flew back directly toward the carrier." Each aircraft carried a pilot and an observer. Their daily flying time totaled about eight hours.

The *Lexington* search continued for six days, hampered by the continuing rainsqualls, any one of which could have concealed the missing fliers. "The texture of the ocean during our week of search was so turbulent," wrote Stanley, "so flecked with foam, and so changing in its lighting pattern that it would have been a major miracle to have seen the tiny speck of two humans in a boat against such a textured background." The *Lexington* fliers covered over 150,000 square miles of the Pacific, seeing no single reef, island, or atoll, "or any living thing other than the ubiquitous albatross." On the seventh day, the Navy called off the search, and *Lexington* headed home.[21]

During this time, press coverage began to wind down. Dispatches reflected an increasing sense of resignation. Such phrases as "naval searchers virtually abandoned hope for the rescue of Amelia Earhart today"[22] and "there is only a chance in a million for a rescue"[23] left little hope for a happy ending.

George still professed to believe that Amelia and Fred had a chance, but he ceased his long watch at the Coast Guard San Francisco Headquarters and went to his North Hollywood home to be with Amy.[24]

Inevitably, criticism arose in Congress. In those years of the Great Depression, prying out of Congress even the minimum necessary funds for the armed forces involved a major excavation, and any expenditure by the Army or Navy perceived as unnecessary was a sure target for a congressman eager to appear as the staunch defender of the public purse. On this occasion Representative Byron Scott, a Democrat from California and a member of the House Naval Affairs Committee, cut a swath that went beyond the Navy, demanding

> . . . that the navy, coast guard, and the bureau of aeronautics submit complete reports to him, on what the search has cost, whether it interfered with other naval duties, who issued permits to Miss Earhart and her navigator, and why they were issued. He said he probably would introduce

legislation which would prevent the use of Federal facilities in search for fliers who disappear while not on Government missions.

Representative Charles Faddis, Democrat of Pennsylvania, supported Scott, adding snidely, "If it had been some poor father of a family who had been blown into the Pacific in a fishing boat, do you think the Navy would be spending $250,000 a day searching for him?"

The Bureau of Aeronautics position, as stated by Assistant Secretary of Commerce Colonel Monroe Johnson, was this: "No more permits for 'stunt' flights will be issued. Miss Earhart's permit was allowed to stand because the department thought it would be unfair to revoke it, after instituting the new policy, in view of the fact that she had spent thousands in building the plane."[25]

This was a feeble excuse at best. Whatever funds Amelia had spent were irrelevant. If the Bureau of Aeronautics believed that the projected around-the-world flight was a "stunt" with no anticipated results to offset its danger, it should have refused a permit.

Roosevelt entered the fray, verbal battle-ax swinging in defense of his beloved Navy. He flatly denied that the search had cost the Navy "a large sum of money" and characterized a dispatch from Honolulu estimating the expenses at four million dollars "a plain prevarication." He explained that each Navy plane had to spend so many hours per year in the air, and the hours spent searching counted toward that total. Had they not been so occupied, they would have been up on maneuvers. The same reasoning pertained to fuel oil. *Lexington*'s speed had been no greater than it would have been during maneuvers. And the exercise, although sad because it had failed, had been excellent training. He ended with a comment probably aimed at Faddis: The Navy had done an excellent job "and would undertake a similar mission for any citizen, rich or poor."[26]

In fact, this was a teapot tempest. The estimate of $4,000,000 was way off base; official costs were slightly under $190,000, and this was "made up by economies within the fleet." The Navy requested no extra funds to cover expenses. And, as Safford commented, "The criticism would have been even stronger if the Navy had callously left Amelia and Fred to perish without making any effort to rescue them."[27]

George continued to explore every possible avenue. A friend, Sydney S. Bowman, offered a reward of two thousand dollars for information that would "definitely clear up the mystery"; the money came from George.[28] In New York on business at the end of July, he looked "tired and drawn. . . . He was pale, and seemed perplexed." But there was "hope in his eyes and voice" as he expressed the belief that the plane might have drifted at the rate of fifty miles a day and might still be found.[29]

He consulted the psychic community—a courageous act and perhaps a measure of his desperation, because in general people who did so were considered oddities. One he contacted was a young woman, Gene Dennis, married to J. Von Herberg, a Seattle theater operator. She had been born in Atchison, Kansas—Amelia's hometown. George, she said, "had appealed to her in a series of long distance telephone conversations." To aid her, he sent Dennis a pair of Amelia's stockings and a handkerchief belonging to Fred. She received the impression that the fliers were "alive and safe" on an island and would be rescued "possibly this weekend," just when the Navy called off the search. She picked up a name, "Gelbert," and the news item cautiously pointed to the Gilberts and to the "strong westward current in the Pacific."[30]

The anonymous astrologer who had contacted Edgar Cayce tried again on George's behalf on July 31. He could not personally come to Virginia Beach but would appreciate anything Cayce would do in his absence. "He has confidence in your work and any report will have much bearing on his future plans." Accordingly, Cayce gave a second reading on August 1. He sensed that Amelia had died on July 21, at roughly the same location he had specified in the reading of July 5. He added that she died alone, which indicates that Fred had perished earlier. And he made a brief comment: "Storm and heat."

The sympathetic astrologer wrote back, "I shall somehow get the news to George Putnam when I can although the man is so terribly stricken, yet trying very hard to carry on." He was having "almost nightly sessions" with psychics from the Psychic Research Society, and she believed that "the strain is bad for him."

It was a bitter experience for the unnamed lady. She had been sure that "Amelia would make a safe flight and told her so, and even advised her when to start on it. . . . I shall never again make a prediction with the same carefree attitude. . . ."[31]

Of course, the situation was ready-made for tests of psychic ability, many no doubt undertaken out of a sincere desire to be helpful. "During the period of the search," Admiral William D. Leahy confided to his diary, "literally hundreds of communications were received by the Navy Department from spiritualists, mediums, and other similar sources, giving the position of the lost plane." The consensus in the Navy was "that the plane was lost upon landing and that all messages reported as coming from the plane after it landed were either deliberate falsifications or garbled receipts from unknown sources."[32]

George must have realized that in all probability Amelia was lost, but he owed it to his wife and to himself to go the extra mile. He heard of a reef east of the Gilberts that the natives were accustomed to visit to gather sea turtle eggs. At George's request, the resident commissioner at Suva in the Fiji Islands sent a cutter to check on this rumor.

"Needless to say," commented Safford, "the cutter found neither eggs, turtles, nor the reef itself."[33]

George chartered two small ships to cruise south to Gardner and Phoenix Islands, north to Christmas and Fanning, then west "to comb again the myriad rocks and reefs of the Gilberts and the Marshalls." Again, there was no trace of either the Electra or a raft.[34]

On July 20 the *New York Times* paid tribute to Amelia in an editorial that was all her friends could have asked. It began by conceding that she was neither a Lindbergh nor "a scientific flier," and with "a little more careful preparation" might have come through.

▶ But the qualities which involved Miss Earhart and her companion in this last heroic failure were interwoven with her gay, luminous, self-confident personality. . . . She wanted to dare all that a man would dare. . . . She lost her life in the effort to get the final ecstasy out of it. . . .

And what was this vision? No man, perhaps, would ever wholly know, for . . . Amelia Earhart was wholly feminine. One remembers the outward symbols of what she was—the slender hands and wrists . . . ; the voice that was soft and beautiful; the rich inflections, the animation that would have made her an actress; the feminine dignity that melted into humor. . . . Perhaps in the vividness of her last glimpse of sun and sky and the curling tops of waves she knew that she had helped to make all women less afraid. . . .[35]

What a pity that the story could not end here, with an affectionate farewell to a beloved public figure.

Chapter 29
The Aftermath

George had received "hundreds of crank letters" since Amelia's disappearance and had paid no attention to them, but on July 31 an incident began that at first seemed that it just might have something in it. When he returned to his room at the Hotel Barclay in the evening of that day, he found a note written on the hotel stationery:

▶ Mr. Putnam:
  We have your wife on the ship. I will call Sunday at 2 o'clock.

Around midnight a man telephoned, asking George for an interview. He had "some very important information" about Amelia, but "he did not want to get into any trouble" and wanted George's assurance that he would not inform the police. George "assured this individual of his sincerity and desire to get this information." Nevertheless, he promptly called an old friend, Lieutenant Owens of the New York City Police Department, and arranged to have the man followed.

The man, who gave his name as Johnson, called on George as arranged at 2 A.M. According to "Johnson," he was a seaman aboard a vessel out of New Guinea when in early July it was passing near a coral reef at the edge of which was a wrecked plane. On it was a man barely breathing, who died almost immediately. The sailors buried him at sea. On the reef was a woman, "naked except for a pair of athletic shorts."

It was this detail that made George wonder if this story might contain a grain of truth. Amelia had, indeed, been wearing men's athletic shorts under her slacks when she started her journey, a fact that, as George said, "would not be available to anybody."

"Johnson" claimed that the woman was badly injured and out of her mind. A Chinese doctor aboard the vessel treated her. The seaman had been out of touch with the outside world and did not recognize her. When they cleared the Panama Canal, they heard the story, realized who she was, and "became panic-stricken" because, being engaged in "illegal activities," they wanted no publicity. The crew's wants, he assured George, were modest: just expense money and to get rid of the woman. But he was only a "contact man" and must consult with the ship's captain and crew. They arranged to meet again the next day.

Lieutenant Owens with two detectives followed "Johnson" and left him in a West Side restaurant. There Owens reported to George; he wanted to pick the man up and suggested "that if he applied some physical force to him that they could very likely get the true story." George refused, not, one suspects, out of any tender consideration for "Johnson," but because information obtained under duress would be tainted. Instead, he called upon the Federal Bureau of Investigation. Special Agent T. J. Donegan suggested that George ask a personal friend to be present at the next interview and that he ask "Johnson" to bring something with him that "would definitely identify Miss Earhart." When "Johnson" called to arrange the next meeting, he accepted these stipulations and advised that the crew agreed to having the woman placed in a hospital.

Donegan's idea had been that an agent pose as the friend, but George asked Eugene Vidal to be present, with Donegan posing as George's secretary. "Johnson" showed up at 4 P.M. on August 2, and the discussion lasted over two hours. He had not brought a lock of Amelia's hair and the shorts, as previously suggested, claiming that her head was bandaged and the pants dirty. But he did bring a brown-and-white scarf that he claimed was Amelia's. He wanted two thousand dollars in advance, upon receipt of which he would have Amelia taken to the designated hospital.

During this meeting "Johnson" waxed very graphic indeed, relating how Noonan's body had been gruesomely mutilated by sharks. He also described "horrible pictures as to the condition of Miss Earhart, practically causing Mr. Putnam to have hysterics."

The next day "Johnson" arrived to collect his money. He stuffed an envelope holding ten hundred-dollar bills in his shirt while Donegan, still in character as George's secretary, "held a check of $1000 with instructions to cash it and give the money to 'Johnson.'"

At the door of the building, Donegan revealed his true identity and arrested "Johnson." At the local FBI office, the prisoner rapidly deflated. His name was Wilbur Rothar; for the past four or five years he had been caretaker of a row of abandoned houses in the Bronx. There was not an atom of truth in his story. He had decided on this bit of extortion when he read that a two-thousand-dollar reward for information has been posted and because he had a scarf that he insisted had belonged to Amelia, having blown off her at Roosevelt Field on Long Island some years before. He had kept it as a souvenir. He did not explain the detail about the athletic shorts. It may have been a lucky shot in the dark, or at some time he may have heard somewhere that Amelia Earhart occasionally wore men's shorts.[1]

Some of the Earhart buffs, darkly suspicious of anything involving the government, thought there might be some truth in Rothar's story and went to considerable trouble seeking information about ships that had passed through the Panama Canal during the appropriate time. But it seems clear enough that this was one of the heartless attempts at extortion all too familiar to the FBI and other law enforcement agencies.

Harder to evaluate are the stories from various sources of individuals who claimed to have heard broadcasts either directly or indirectly from Amelia. Undoubtedly some meant well; in other cases the motives are more dubious.

Amy began to believe that Amelia was being held in Japan when, "a few days after Amelia's S.O.S.," an unnamed friend listening to a shortwave broadcast from Tokyo claimed to have heard that "they were celebrating there with parades etc. because of Amelia's rescue or pickup by a Japanese fisherman." The individual must have heard something because, as Amy wrote to Neta Southern, the former Neta Snook, who had taught Amelia to fly, "This young girl drove 27 miles at 11 o'clock at night and through a horrid part of Los Angeles to tell me."

Of course, the Japanese would have been pleased and proud to have rescued Amelia. But parades? Possibly she heard a garbled account of Japan's participation in the search or perhaps some ceremonies connected with the popular Star Festival, a happy occasion to be held on July 7. Patriotic fervor was running high in Japan, and July 8 would see the Marco Polo Bridge incident, usually considered the beginning of the Asian portion of World War II.

The next day Amy went to the Japanese Consulate, where she was received courteously. But when she returned two days later, the former consul had been replaced, and the new incumbent knew nothing about the matter. George came back the next day and telephoned the consulate. Getting no satisfaction over the phone, he "insisted on a personal interview, and saw the consul but got nowhere and came home angry and upset."

On this slim foundation, Amy based her belief that Amelia was in Japanese hands in Tokyo. From time to time, bits and pieces of rumors and theories reached Amy. Perhaps Amelia was being held prisoner "because of what she saw." Amy had spoken of this only to a few close friends, not even confiding in Muriel, having "no desire to start rumors which would worry Muriel as it often does me and Amelia's friends, whom I sometimes think includes most of the world."

This conviction that Amelia was alive sustained Amy for several years until World War II brought disillusionment. She wrote to Neta of this lost hope in words more touching in their dignity than any hysterical outburst would have been: "You know, Neta, up to the time the Japs tortured and murdered our brave flyers I hoped for Amelia's return, even Pearl Harbor didn't take it away . . . for I thought of them as civilized." Surely the Japanese would be more likely to hold her hostage to exchange "for some of their own they wanted," or perhaps after the war was over send her home unharmed and well, "just to show they were not the brutes we thought them—but when the story came out from our own men who had seen it all with their own eyes . . . I thought so no more. So the hope is only the finding out what happened. . . ."[2]

Nevertheless, according to Muriel, "For two years Mother kept a suitcase packed with a few simple clothes, cold cream for sunburn and scissors to cut her hair in case Amelia were discovered on a tropical island."[3]

Another example of an alleged shortwave pickup came from Charlotte Cooper, living in Arlington, Massachusetts, near Boston. Three or four days after Amelia's disappearance she had been unable to sleep, so around 3 A.M. "went downstairs and turned on the radio." She was "listening to band music coming in loud and clear. Suddenly there was a lot of static and then a complete silence. It was sort of scary.

"After a few seconds I heard a woman's voice speaking as if she was bone weary. She said, 'This is Amelia Earhart, this is Amelia Earhart. The weather is getting very wet. This is Amelia Earhart.'" Then came a man's voice, apparently giving latitude and longitude, but Cooper could not understand him because the static came back, then silence, then the band resumed playing. "The whole experience was eerie."

Cooper sensibly called a Boston newspaper to ask if a play about Amelia was being broadcast. The reporter knew of none "and became very excited." He wanted to send someone out to take pictures, but she refused.[4]

Obviously Cooper was not after notoriety, so her story deserves a bit of speculative analysis: This woman has been inviting sleep, listening to music at 3 A.M., an hour notorious for lowered resistance. Suddenly the music is replaced by the voice of a woman the entire United States had been hoping to hear. She gives a brief message, her companion tries to give their location, and then the sequence reverses itself. This scenario sounds very much like Cooper had drifted into sleep, had a short, vivid dream, and then woke convinced she had never been asleep and that the dream was real. Such events are by no means rare.

The third case we will consider is of a very different stamp. Mrs. C. B. Paxton of Ashland, Kentucky, did not object to publicity in the least. In fact, the local newspaper of July 9 carried an interview with her under the heading "ASHLAND LADY HEARS EARHART." Paxton claimed to have heard a distress message from Amelia at 2 P.M. on Saturday, July 3, preceded by Amelia's call letters, KHAQQ.

"The message came in on my short wave set very plain, and Miss Earhart talked for some time . . . I didn't understand everything Miss Earhart said because there was some noise." She understood Amelia to say, "Down in the ocean," either on or near "little island at a point near. . . ." After that, Paxton thought Amelia said something like "directly northeast." Then she heard, "Our plane about out of gas. Water all around. Very dark." Then came something about a storm and wind. "Will have to get out of here. We can't stay here long."

Evelyn Jackson, who did considerable local research on Paxton for such Earhart aficionados as John F. Luttrell and Charles N. Hill, appended to a clipping a skeptical note dated August 1, 1986: "There had appeared the standard Associated Press stories about Earhart in this newspaper for six days or so before Mrs. Paxton told her version of what she heard. Also, there had already appeared in the paper a detailed map of the area in the Pacific, showing many small islands around the Carolines, Howland, Solomons, and off the coast of New Guinea down to the Coral Sea."[5]

From this modest beginning, Paxton moved on to bigger and better things. On September 22, 1943, she wrote to famed gossip columnist and radio personality Walter Winchell, greatly amplifying the details she had given the press in 1937. Now she claimed that Amelia's message had "contained some 300 to 400 words—in which she described Mili or Mulgrave Atoll, Klee Passage, Knox Island and seemed to be located on a small island of 133 acres adjoining Knox directly NE of a part of Marshall Island." According to Paxton, Amelia "stated very plainly they had everything. . . ." She added that Amelia had said "the food supply was good" and presumed she meant their emergency provisions because there "was no habitation or life, but some vegetation. . . . She spoke of the Captain's injury." Also, Amelia had "described the damage to the plane and stated it was drifting."

Paxton explained to Winchell that she had assumed these calls had been received "by the proper authorities" and did not discover until quite recently that "nothing had been heard from Miss Earhart."[6]

By 1944 she was hearing another voice, usually on the same frequency on which she claimed to have heard Amelia. She informed Naval Intelligence that the names "Noonan" and "Amelia Putnam" came through clearly with the question "Can you bring them out?" The reply was not clear, but it was something like "not yet" or until permission had been granted.[7]

On June 14, 1962, Paxton repeated via the *Louisville Courier-Journal* some of her former statements, adding that she heard the call signal as KHABQ, not KHAQQ, and was convinced the latter had been wrongly made public.[8]

Charles Hill, an enthusiastic follower of the Earhart drama, took Paxton seriously enough to make inquiries of her local county government as to her reputation. The results were not encouraging. Her neighbors disliked her intensely. At least one "did not believe that Nina was 'playing with a full deck'. . . ." They knew of her claim to have heard Earhart broadcasts, "but they did not believe her." She was variously described as "everything from a 'screwball' to names that anyone with a sense of Christian charity would not repeat."[9]

John Luttrell was inclined to credit the Paxton material, having himself lit upon Mili Atoll as the probable site of Amelia's landing. He sent copies of the Paxton letters to the Australian Air Force, which dismissed them "as fairly typical of the 'crank' letters sometimes received in this office." The signer, a pilot named R. K. Piper, of the RAAF Historical Office, added a personal note of advice: "Never, never even waste your time on obviously ridiculous letters. People do it simply to attract attention."[10]

That seems to be true of the Paxton case, and it is rather sad. Here was a strange, bitter woman, widowed, virtually friendless, shunned by her neighbors, whose foster son went to jail blaming her for all his problems and threatening to kill her when he came out[11]—it would not be remarkable if such a woman craved recognition and approval to the point where fantasy took over.

With all the drama, the mechanics of human life had to be considered. On October 18, 1937, George petitioned the court to be named Amelia's trustee; permission was granted on November 2, 1937.[12]

In May of 1938, Paul Mantz requested help from Eleanor Roosevelt, whom he had met, in obtaining a copy of Thompson's report and a complete log of the operation. This request seriously upset Henry D. Morgenthau Jr., secretary of the Treasury. Talking by phone with Malvina "Tommy" Schneider, secretary to Mrs. Roosevelt, he protested,

▶ If we're going to release this, it's just going to smear the whole reputation of Amelia Earhart, and my. . . . Yes, but I mean if we give it to this one man, we have got to make it public; we can't let one man see it. And if we ever release the report of the Itasca on Amelia Earhart, any reputation she's got is gone. . . .

Now, I know what the Navy did, I know what the Itasca did, and I know how Amelia Earhart absolutely disregarded all orders, and if we ever re-

lease this thing, goodbye Amelia Earhart's reputation. . . . And we have
the report of all those wireless messages and everything else, what that
woman—happened to her the last few minutes. I hope I've just got to
never make it public, I mean—O.K.—Well, still if she wants it I'll tell
her—I mean what happened. It isn't a very nice story.

Turning to Assistant Secretary Stephen Gibbon, he said, "You [Gib-
bon] know the story, don't you?" And Gibbon replied, "We have evidence that the thing is all over, sure. Terrible. It would be awful to
make it public."

Elsewhere in this brief conversation Morgenthau seemed to resent
the suggestion that "people want us to search again those islands after
what we have gone through."[13]

In its report, the Coast Guard had had no qualms about dumping on
Amelia the entire blame for the disaster, so, knowing no better, Morgenthau had reason to be upset. But he was not the keeper of Amelia
Earhart's reputation; however, the Coast Guard came under the Treasury Department, so its reputation was of very immediate concern to
him. So disproportionate was his agitation that inevitably it aroused
suspicions. Luttrell even suggested to Goldstein that *Itasca* might
have run down the Electra during the search.[14] It is tempting to accept
this suggestion, which certainly would account for Morgenthau's near
panic, but such a horrendous circumstance would have been most difficult to keep secret all these years.

In any event, Paul received the material he asked for, and a note
from Eleanor Roosevelt dated May 14, 1938, assuring him that the
search had been very thorough and everything possible had been
done.[15]

A little over a month later, on June 26, 1938, Fred Noonan was declared legally dead, and Amelia was so declared on January 1, 1939. A
seven-year lapse is usual when there is no corpse, and Joe Klaas, in
his book *Amelia Earhart Lives,* suggests that this early declaration
might indicate dirty work at the crossroads.[16] It seems to us, however,
merely to reflect the court's feeling that the evidence of death was sufficient. The decision was a blessing for the families, who were left free
to continue with their lives.

Mrs. Noonan met and married a widower, Harry B. Ireland. She became an expert on cymbidium orchids. Evidently Ireland was well-to-
do, for Goerner spoke of "the Ireland mansion."[17] Certainly she deserved the good things of life after her long agony over Fred.

George remarried twice, in fairly short order. His third wife was
Jean Marie Cosigny, whom he married in 1939. He divorced her in
1944 and married Margaret Haviland. Probably Amelia would have
sympathized with George's efforts to find happiness, but we doubt if

she would have approved his administration of her estate. Her will had been straightforward: Her personal effects went to George. The rest went into a trust, its net income to go to Amy, and after her death the principal would be George's. If he should die first, after Amy the income could revert to Muriel, then to Muriel's children. "George persuaded the court that $125 a month was ample for an older lady living alone." By the time George died on January 4, 1950, the estate had almost vanished, and Amy was eking out a living on fifty to one hundred dollars a month. Fortunately, she had moved in with Muriel and Albert, whom Muriel called "Chief," in 1946. Amy lived to be ninety-five, dying on October 29, 1962.[18]

One event happened in 1940 that gave Paul Mantz considerable satisfaction. He received a letter from Captain Irving Johnson of the world cruise yacht *Yankee*. During the stay in the Gilberts, Johnson met a missionary who had tried to find out from the natives whether any airplane had been seen at the time of Amelia's flight. "He said that, in certain cases, it was hard to tell whether some ignorant native had actually seen an airplane or wished he had, but that *it was believed that the Earhart plane had flown eastward high up over the island of Tabiteuea*" (italics in original).

To refresh his memory, Paul checked his charts: Amelia's course had "passed directly through the little Gilbert Island of Tabiteuea!"[19] The Electra had been right on course as it covered the last group of islands on the way to Howland.

Chapter 30

The Rumor Mill

or several years, the Earhart story languished. In general, the public seems to have accepted the obvious solution: The Electra had run out of fuel and crashed in the ocean. Those, like Amy, who thought otherwise kept their doubts to themselves. It was not that Amelia had been forgotten; she would be remembered with affection long after many of the perceived greats of her generation had faded from memory.

But her countrymen had their own lives to live, and for many those lives were difficult. The Great Depression refused to release its grip on the economy and would not until the boom generated by World War II. The international front became increasingly ominous. Japan and China were locked in war; in Europe, Germany and its satellite, Italy, were obviously aiming at total domination of the continent. Many Americans fervently hoped to keep free from foreign problems, but would the belligerent regimes permit the United States that luxury? The disappearance of Amelia Earhart, however regrettable, was insignificant compared with the world picture.

The war in the Pacific and the occupation of Japan caused a gradual resurgence of interest in Amelia's fate. During the war, several servicemen on stateside leave took some of their precious time to visit Amy, bringing her reports gleaned from "English-speaking natives living on South Pacific Islands." These natives usually mentioned having seen a plane go down or occasionally something like " 'Boy see big bird (plane) hit water—go down under, no see more,' or 'Boy see bird float on water—two men hold wing—try swim—one not make it—other man—girl—bad hurt—dies,' or 'Get in Jap boat—die soon.'"[1]

Muriel mentioned an album filled with pictures of Amelia said to have been found on Saipan in September of 1944. This discovery was advanced as proof that Amelia's plane crashed on Saipan, approximately twenty-six hundred miles off course. Muriel added, "No one whom I know has ever seen this album, nor has any picture of it ever been published to my knowledge; however, it seems incredible that Amelia would give room to such an unnecessary and bulky object on the Electra when every pound had to prove its worth."[2]

The presence of such an album was not surprising. In the early 1900s, albums were a popular pastime. Some were just pleasant hodgepodges of bits of poetry, quotations, pictures, and the like; others centered around public figures the collector admired. We have seen that a Japanese girl sent one such album to Amelia to be autographed. The authors have a small album of contemporary Earhart items purchased from an antique shop.

Muriel recounted another story put forth by a "former service man, a Mr. Thomas G. Albright of New Jersey." In 1946, he had been one of an occupation detail on a small South Pacific island. One day "he saw an American woman living in a squalid fisherman's hut. She asked him for food, especially urging him to bring her some butter if possible. When he brought her sandwiches and part of a package of butter, she seized the heat-softened butter and ate it as if it were candy, licking the paper and her fingers like a child when she had finished."

Albright wrote to Muriel that he could not describe the woman in detail but remembered that "she was slightly above average height, slim in build, and having long unkempt blond and gray hair." He guessed her age at over forty-five and had no doubt "that she was Caucasian. We spoke in English, and, I might add, she spoke like a very well-educated woman."

When he told some of his shipmates about this encounter, one remarked in a joking manner, "Tom, maybe you've found Amelia Earhart!" Albright ignored this because he believed the woman was too old to be Amelia. But in 1959, "after seeing an unposed picture of Amelia facing the sun, and checking her death date, Mr. Albright became convinced that the middle-aged amnesia victim he had encountered in a Japanese fishing village in 1946 might be Amelia after all."

He informed Muriel that he had instituted a search for the "tiny nameless atoll," adding, "There are hundreds of villages like the one where I met the woman. Unfortunately most of them look alike." He visited many in the summer of 1961, but his vacation time and his money gave out. Although he received no help from "American officials in Tokyo" or from Red Cross personnel, he planned to continue the search and promised to keep Muriel posted. He warned, however, "against undue optimism in a situation in which a coincidental resemblance might mean nothing whatever."[3]

Now this story is very interesting, particularly for its striking resemblance to another one by another ex-serviceman, Thom Thomas, also of New Jersey. He described himself as twenty years old, attached to the Marine occupation force in Nagasaki, when one day he drove a platoon of Marines to a beach location for a picnic. Slightly inland was "a small, quiet fishing village. . . . It had no police force, newspaper, or any visible means of formal communication with the rest of Japan."

Noticing a group of Marines congregated in front of a house, he asked them why this interest. "'There's a white woman inside, 'putting out' for a buck!'" Thomas took his place in line but was soon summoned inside; the woman had asked for the driver. Thomas was stunned to see a naked Caucasian woman standing there. "She was tall, slim, rather well-shaped and pleasant-looking . . . she was light-haired, appearing to be in her middle forties and, unmistakenly, American." Speaking in English without a trace of accent, she asked if he had any food. She specifically requested butter.

In reply to Thomas's question, she told him that her husband was away fishing and would not return for several days. Thomas brought her food, which she quickly devoured. "The butter was coated with sand, having been loosely wrapped and tossed into the truck. . . . She began eating the butter . . . by itself, sand and all! Holding the lump of butter in both hands, she consumed it hurriedly, as a child would eat an ice cream cone on a hot summer day." He asked about her background, but she seemed "unable to answer rather than unwilling to do so."

Soon thereafter, Thomas returned to the States. While aboard ship, one of the men "mentioned the oddity of our having discovered an American woman living in a remote fishing village." A sergeant said jokingly, "Maybe you guys found Amelia Earhart!" Everyone laughed.

Thomas didn't think this likely; he was under the impression that Amelia had been lost in her mid-twenties, so she could have been no more than thirty-four in 1946. Then in 1958, back in Paterson, New Jersey, he related the story to someone who told him, "You're wrong. Amelia Earhart would have been near fifty in 1946." Startled, Thomas bought a copy of *Last Flight* and was sure he recognized her picture.[4]

He theorized that a Japanese fishing boat had picked up Amelia and that "as a result of the crash Amelia entered into a state of retrograde amnesia for the rest of her life."

He claims he offered his story to various magazines and was rejected. The narrative he wrote them was much less explicit. "In all due respect for such a great lady, I did not desire to reveal the sordid circumstances under which she had been forced to live. . . ." He returned to Japan in July of 1961 and again in July of 1962 to try to locate her, but was unable to find the village.[5]

So here we have remarkably similar tales: an amnesiac American woman, obviously well educated, living with a native fisherman in a very remote village, asking for food and with an unnatural craving for butter. The locale is different, and the South Sea version does not specify that the woman is a prostitute. Otherwise the stories are so close as to raise the suspicion that Thomas Albright and Thom Thomas are either one and the same, or else one cribbed wholesale from the other. Whatever the reason, the sameness of the two narratives reduces their credibility to approximately zero.

Another strange story came out of Japan. According to Thomas E. Devine, at the time of this incident he was a sergeant, the top NCO of the 244th Army Postal Unit on Saipan. He and his commanding officer, First Lieutenant Fritz W. Liebig, were driving in a jeep to Aslito Field when he noticed "a group of men, apparently Marine officers," gathered before the administration building, not far from a hangar where Devine pulled up. The leader of the group, who looked vaguely familiar to Devine, seemed to be military, yet he wore a white civilian shirt and carried no sidearms. This man stepped forward, saying "This is off-limits!" He suggested that Liebig report inside the administration building. Devine remained outside. When the white-shirted man walked away, a Marine officer shouted indignantly, "What do you mean it's off limits? We know Earhart's plane is in there! What are you trying to pull?"[6]

Devine went to check on the jeep and asked a nearby Marine guard, "Is it true that Amelia Earhart's plane is inside?"

"Yes," replied the Marine, "but for the love of God don't say I said so. I don't know why the hell they want to keep it a secret."

That afternoon, back at his base at Cape Obiam, Devine claimed to have seen "a large, twin-engine double-fin civilian plane" with the number NR 16020 clearly visible. Curious, Devine and a friend returned to Aslito later that evening. The plane was in front of the hangar, and the white-shirted man, carrying a bandolier of ammunition, was approaching. A photographer waved the two men away. They returned to their bivouac, where still later "a muffled explosion at Aslito Field erupted into a large flash fire." Devine crawled toward the airfield. "When I could see what was burning, I was aghast! The twin-engine plane was engulfed in flames!" About three weeks later, he realized that "the man in the white shirt" was Secretary of the Navy James V. Forrestal. Devine dated Forrestal's appearance on Saipan as being in July 1944.[7]

This is the sort of story, told by an alleged eyewitness, complete with incident and conversation, that can beguile the unwary. A little prodding, however, produces some notable holes. First of all, why would Forrestal be torching Amelia's Electra? Devine thought he had the answer. Forrestal ". . . was looking beyond the Second World War to postwar Japanese-American relations. The discovery of Amelia Earhart or her Electra could have hindered peace efforts and post-war international relations. . . . News of Amelia Earhart's plane, undamaged and in flying condition at Aslito Field, could have resulted in great ill-will toward Japan."[8]

The picture of the U.S. secretary of the Navy, in the summer of 1944, destroying evidence lest the American people think unkind thoughts of the Japanese severely strains credulity. And other circumstances break down Devine's story. There were no Marines at Aslito at the time. The 165th Infantry captured Aslito on June 18, 1944, and on June 22, the Army Air Force's 318th Fighter Group took over. The Second Marine Division that Devine named was far from Aslito, in "heavy action driving up the Saipan coast." What is more, Aslito's hangars had been reduced to skeletons and could not have concealed anything as large as an aircraft.[9]

It is unfortunate that Devine embarked upon this flight of fantasy because much of his book is well documented and checked out later as factual. But, like other Earhart fans, he tended to jump to conclusions on the basis of what someone told him. He was sure he knew where Amelia and Fred were buried on Saipan because an Okinawan woman, who had lived on Saipan since before the war, pointed out a grave site to him where, she claimed, two white people, one of them a woman, had been buried. They had "come from the sky." Devine took careful note of the spot, and the nearby cemetery had several readily recognizable features, so he was sure he could find it again. Devine recalled this incident as occurring in July of 1945.[10]

This was not the first time an alleged Earhart grave site had been— allegedly—discovered on Saipan. The initial find took place in the late summer of 1944 when Captain Tracey Griswold, USMC, assisted by Privates Billy Burke and Everett Henson, went on a detail that included excavating a grave. They discovered two skeletons that they packed in boxes Griswold had brought along. Henson asked Griswold what this was all about. "Have you ever heard of Amelia Earhart?" Griswold countered. Upon Henson's acknowledgment that he had, the captain answered, "I think, then, that's enough said."[11]

If this story is accurate, it strongly indicates that Griswold knew exactly what he was looking for and just where to find it. In a letter to Devine dated September 16, 1966, however, Griswold declared that in his initial conversation with Fred Goerner, author of *The Search for Amelia Earhart,* and in later correspondence with Goerner and his partner, Ross Game, he had

> flatly denied any part in the incident mentioned in their account. . . . I certainly do not recall any connection with the two enlisted men mentioned in the account.

I, of course, recall the "scuttle-but" that was rampant at the time of the initial invasion of Saipan. This involved many people and circumstances and most particularly Earhart and Noonan. However, I have no knowledge of any evidence, locations or other information pertaining to a grave site.

What is more, in a telephone conversation, Henson surprised Devine by declaring "he had never claimed that they had exhumed Earhart and Noonan" and had "brought this fact to Goerner's attention." Devine concluded that the bones were probably those of "two American servicemen."[12]

Throughout the forties, stories continued to surface indicating that Amelia and Fred had been in Japanese hands. A former prisoner of war related that before the conflict, in the Philippines, he had "overheard a conversation in English between two Japanese to the effect that Amelia Earhart was still alive and was being detained at a hotel in Tokyo." After he became a POW, on one occasion he found himself alone with a Japanese intelligence officer and asked, "Would you tell me frankly if my cousin Amelia Earhart is still alive?" The officer replied, "Don't worry about her. She is perfectly all right." Later the POW questioned "various Japanese guards at various POW camps and got various answers."[13]

Amy added considerable fuel to the fires of rumor by going public with her belief that Amelia had been a prisoner of Japan. The *Nippon Times,* an English-language newspaper, on August 29, 1949, published an interview Amy had given in Los Angeles:

▶ ... I am convinced she was on some sort of a government mission probably on verbal orders. ... I am sure there was a government mission involved in the flight because Amelia explained there were some things she could not tell me. I am equally sure she did not make a forced landing in the sea.

She landed on a tiny atoll—one of many in that general area of the Pacific—and was picked up by a Japanese fishing boat that took her to the Marshall Islands, then under Japanese control.

Amy also believed that Amelia was permitted to broadcast to Washington from the Marshalls and then was taken to Japan. "There she met with an accident—an 'arranged' accident that ended her life."

This same issue of the *Nippon Times* contained a refutation of information from Alvan Fitak, a former Marine lieutenant, who claimed to have heard from an islander named "Miki" that a "white lady aviator" had been taken prisoner and later apparently was taken to Japan.

The Japanese governor of the Marshalls in 1937 was Kenjiro Kitajima. He had "'absolutely no knowledge' of any white aviatrix—an aviatrix of any color for that matter—landing on the Islands at that time."[14]

Also, according to official Japanese information, Amelia could not have broadcast from the Marshalls to Washington because the South Sea Government did not begin radio broadcasting until the summer of 1941, when facilities were completed.[15]

Chapter **31**

An Open-Ended Case

*A*my's press conference stressed what had already begun to evolve as the next chapter of the Earhart story: Amelia had been on a secret spy mission for the U.S. government, probably at the request of Franklin D. Roosevelt. This last was not surprising. The revisionist school of thought that blamed Roosevelt for everything from the continuation of the Great Depression to Pearl Harbor was in full cry. It was only a matter of time before someone decided that he was behind Amelia's disappearance. The catalyst, however, was neither book, treatise, nor lecture—it was a movie.

Flight for Freedom, starring Rosalind Russell, Fred MacMurray, and Herbert Marshall, opened in the early 1940s. It concerned a famous aviatrix, "Toni Carter," who with her navigator played by MacMurray, embarked upon a flight across the Pacific. She was to land secretly on an obscure island named "Gull," while the U.S. military used the search for her as a cover for extensive photographing of the Japanese Mandates.

The Japanese, however, discovered the ruse, and a representative of Japan told "Toni" that she would be promptly rescued, so no search would be necessary. What could they do? The MacMurray character pointed out that the important thing was to be lost. Taking this to heart, "Toni" took off alone and deliberately crashed, giving the military its chance to photograph the area.[1]

Flight for Freedom was just one of many romance-propaganda films put out during World War II, no better and no worse than many others, but, despite the usual disclaimers, the parallel between "Toni Carter" and Amelia Earhart was obvious. This identification, given life by the always delightful Rosalind Russell, struck a chord. At least it hinted that Amelia's loss had had meaning and purpose and was not just random misfortune.

The script writer had been smart enough not to have "Toni" herself doing any spying. Others were not so discriminating. Soon the Amelia-as-spy theory sprang to full bloom: The Lae-to-Howland leg of her journey was but a cover for an aerial photography mission. How this concept gained such firm, long-lasting credence is a real mystery. Even the cynics who believe that the term "military intelligence" is an oxymoron would have blenched at the idea of entrusting such a mission to a woman who had never had an hour's training in intelligence gathering, had no experience in photography beyond wielding the equivalent of a Brownie, and who would not have recognized a military objective worth photographing if she tripped over it.

Moreover, such a project was technologically impossible. On the basis of his forty years' experience in the demanding field of aircraft technology, Robert M. Stanley declared it

> ▶ flatly impossible that a Lockheed Electra of any vintage would take off from the small airport at Lae, New Guinea, and fly a distance as great as that which would have been required for her to do espionage en route from Lae to Howland Island. It was nip and tuck whether she could even get the airplane off the ground with her heavy fuel load, and by flying in the most efficient possible direct course, her chances of reaching Howland Island before her fuel supply gave out were, indeed, thin. To have detoured far to the north to fly over Truk, Ponape, Kwajalein, Majuro or any of the other Japanese mandate islands would have entailed a fuel consumption far beyond her tank capacity and would, in short, have been a physical, technical impossibility.

Stanley could envision no conceivable value in any such detour:

> ▶ Remember, this was 1937. Radar didn't exist, electronic snooping had never been dreamed of. It is incredible to assume that an intelligent person could have been persuaded to undertake a mission which yielded so little hope of providing any useful information, and whose attempt would so drastically diminish the chances of success which already were minuscule.[2]

Francis X. Holbrook pointed out that, if one of Amelia's objects was to photograph Truk, the reversal of the route for the second attempt

> ▶ set up the worst possible route, because most of the permissions from foreign governments obtained by the State Department specifically prohibited the carrying of aerial cameras and some even prohibited the carrying of unsealed hand cameras. To hold that Miss Earhart carried aerial cam-

eras to Truk would involve belief in either a monstrous deceit on the part of the United States or a conspiracy to photograph the island of Truk involving not only the United States, but Venezuela, Brazil, England, the Netherlands, France, Italy, Burma, Siam and Australia as well.

Holbrook also noted that on all of her stops outside the United States local people serviced the Electra. Health and customs officials performed their necessary inspections.[3] At Karachi, Bandoeng, and Lae, considerable overhaul and mechanized work was performed. In fact, the Electra was open to inspection by dozens of people around the globe, and if evidence of intelligence-type hardware had been forthcoming, surely someone would have tipped off the local authorities.

Aside from the technological aspects, it is most difficult to imagine Amelia permitting herself to be conned into such a harebrained scheme. There is nothing to indicate that she was not a loyal American, but there is equally no evidence that she possessed the kind of mindless patriotism that would have permitted her to accept a mission that offered virtually no chance of coming out alive and promised no results commensurate with the risk. Then, too, Amelia was a convinced pacifist. She accepted and appreciated the help the armed forces gave her on her projects, but would she have reciprocated by collecting intelligence useful only in waging war? We doubt it.

As for the president, he extended such assistance to Amelia's project as was permissible, but to our knowledge no scrap of evidence has come to light hinting that he asked or expected her to engage in a foredoomed mission. Evidently the charge against her husband bothered Eleanor Roosevelt for years, because shortly before her death in 1962, she told Muriel, "Franklin and I loved Amelia too much to send her to her death."[4]

Considerations of logic and feasibility rarely, if ever, have any effect upon those whom a conspiracy bug has bitten. They got around the technological difficulties by a simple and perhaps foreseeable device: The Electra that Amelia flew out of Lae was not the original plane. She and Fred transferred to another Electra, souped up and equipped with all the necessary espionage hardware—all without attracting the attention of an airport full of knowledgeable workers. And, however modified, an Electra was still an Electra, capable of carrying just so much fuel. The spymongers claim that the new aircraft could reach greater speed than Amelia had been using, so the extended range was possible. In fact, the real Electra could have flown considerably faster, but Amelia's speed was closely calibrated to her fuel supply. Additional speed would have shortened, not lengthened, the plane's range.

Evidently intrigued by the theory of aircraft modification, on November 19, 1985, Charles N. Hill sent Fuzz Furman a long questionnaire about what, if any, changes had been made to the Electra. Fuzz replied by writing in his answers in ink.

There were no "indications of engine swapping en route." The cowlings were factory-fitted. Likewise, there were no "signs of nacelle modifications." Analyzer problems could not be traced to "jury rigging."

Hill asked what might be considered a loaded question: "Was Miss Earhart's major concern POWER or ECONOMY?" Fuzz fielded it neatly: "Making Howland."

The plane was not equipped with "an aerial camera." No part of the aircraft was "restricted as to access." No "major work or modification" was done at Bandoeng. He sized up Noonan as a good navigator-companion and advised Hill that there was nothing that Amelia or Fred would not discuss.[5]

The spy theory beguiled many intelligent people, among them Safford, who explained in his preface: "I have not distorted the evidence, Procrustean fashion, to fit a preconceived theory. In fact, I have reversed my own opinions completely, because at one time I believed that Amelia *had* been on a spy mission and that she *had* been shot down or otherwise captured by the Japanese as she flew over their Mandated Islands."[6]

Fred Goerner, the most persistent of the Earhart researchers, brought up a very big gun in support of his theory: Admiral Chester W. Nimitz. Goerner was a radio announcer and newscaster in San Francisco. He had been on the Earhart trail for about two years when, in late 1962, Commander John Pillsbury, the public information officer of the Twelfth Naval District, introduced him to the admiral. Toward the end of the conversation, Pillsbury mentioned Amelia Earhart, and Nimitz promptly made the connection. He said to Goerner, "So you're the man who refuses to give up. I thought your name was familiar. Several people from Washington have mentioned you, and I remember hearing you speak of the investigation on the radio." Goerner ventured a question: "Is there anything you can tell me, sir, about Amelia Earhart?"

"Not a great deal," Nimitz replied. "I remember hearing during the war that some things that belonged to her had been found on one of the islands. I don't remember which one, and I didn't actually see that material. Most likely it was channeled through Joint Intelligence at Pearl Harbor."

"Some people think I'm crazy for pursuing this thing so long," said Goerner. "Do you think I'm wasting my time?" Nimitz smiled. "You seem quite rational to me," he answered.

A few weeks later, some members of the media gave Pillsbury a dinner in honor of his retirement. Pillsbury took Goerner aside and said, "I'm officially retired now, so I'm going to tell you a couple of things. You're on the right track with your Amelia Earhart investigation.

Admiral Nimitz wants you to continue, and he says you're onto something that will stagger your imagination. I'll tell you this, too. You have
the respect of a lot of people the way you've stuck at this thing. Keep
plugging."[7]

There can be no question as to Nimitz's integrity. If he made a statement or offered an opinion, it was because he believed it to be true. But
he could be mistaken or misinformed. Safford believed this to be the
case. Out of the depths of decades in the U.S. Navy, he wrote,

▶ Clothing or other belongings believed to belong to AE had been found on
Kwajalein Atoll. Some eager beaver had reported the story to CINCPOA,
Admiral Nimitz, without bothering to verify the facts. Then, when it
proved to be false, the news never reached the Admiral. Things like this
occur frequently. This might have been a deliberate cover-up, but more
likely it was just Murphy's Law in operation.[8]

Pillsbury's comments require some discussion. His first sentence is
misleading. An officer's retirement does not mean that he has severed
his connection with the service and is free to speak on subjects hitherto taboo. He has merely gone off active duty, is still subject to military justice, and can be recalled if necessary. So either Pillsbury mis-
understood his position, which isn't likely, or he hinted at more than
he could produce. His message from Nimitz to Goerner raises questions. The admiral was getting along in years but was still very much
alert and quite capable of personally telling Goerner anything he
wanted him to know. And that "stagger your imagination" doesn't
sound like Nimitz. It sounds like a public information officer at home
with extravagant language. Holbrook expressed skepticism in this regard. "Even if she had been on a spy mission in 1937, that would
hardly 'stagger one's imagination' in the 1960s."[9]

Nimitz remained on friendly terms with Goerner and continued to
encourage him. Having had plenty of experience in sticking to his guns
in adverse circumstances, probably he had a fellow feeling for Goerner.
His characterization of Goerner as "the man who refuses to give up"
was right on target. In the attempt to prove Amelia's fate, Goerner
made four trips to the Pacific, each delivering setbacks that would
have squelched a man less dedicated or less sure of himself.

On his first visit, in the spring of 1960, he returned with a number
of taped interviews with natives of Saipan seeming to confirm the
story told by Josephine Blanco Akiyama of two American fliers, a man
and a woman, who had arrived by plane on Saipan in 1937, had been
imprisoned, and were later executed by the Japanese. He also brought
back pieces of wreckage from a downed plane that he and two native
divers had fished out of Tanapag Harbor.

Most unwisely, two of Goerner's sponsors, the *San Mateo Times* and the radio station KCBS, scheduled a press conference before the aircraft parts, notably a generator, could be definitely identified as coming from an Electra. Paul Mantz came to check it out, and to him it looked "exactly like" the generator he had put aboard Amelia's plane. But Bendix Aviation Corporation killed any chance that this was, indeed, Amelia's generator. Upon examination, Bendix reported that the generator was almost an exact copy of their model but that it had too many discrepancies in its details. It was of Japanese manufacture.[10]

Disappointed but not discouraged, Goerner went back to Saipan in September of 1961. This time he found an unmarked grave in what seemed to him roughly the location marked on a map Devine had given him. This was a cemetery called Liyang, lying about a mile south of what had been the outskirts of Garapan City. After some searching, Goerner and his associates found what appeared to be two skeletons "buried head to head in a common grave." After untangling miles of red tape—an experience that aroused Goerner's suspicions but was probably just the bureaucracy doing what came naturally—he received permission to take the bones off Saipan. Arriving stateside, he turned them over to Theodore D. McCown of the University of California.

After a week's careful examination, McCown announced his findings, which boil down to this: The bones came from a "secondary interment" of "a minimum of four individuals," all *Chamorros,* inhabitants of the Marianas. Goerner had counted heavily upon comparing the teeth with whatever dental records he could find of Amelia and Fred, especially as dentists on Saipan had expressed the belief that the teeth had fillings. They had mistaken "calcified dentine" for "zinc oxide."[11]

Despite this second crushing setback, Goerner returned to Saipan in 1962 for the third time. On this occasion his tangible finds near the cemetery consisted of "50 caliber machine-gun ammunition, clips of Japanese rifle-cartridges, rotted fabric, shirt buttons, combat goggles and broken sake cups . . . but no human remains." He did, however, acquire more "testimony" from various locals.[12]

Undaunted, Goerner returned to the Pacific in 1963. This time Tom Devine went along but was unable to find the grave site. At this time he told Goerner of the alleged destruction of the Electra. It was not until Goerner had returned home from this fourth visit that he learned of the Griswold-Burks-Henson incident. Convinced that the bones he had sought were somewhere in government hands, he hunted for them doggedly but with no success. At the end of his search he believed that Amelia and Fred came down at Mili Atoll in the Marshalls, were picked up by a Japanese fishing boat, were transferred to a Japanese warship, and were taken in turn to Jaluit, Kwajalein, and finally Saipan, where they were executed.[13]

Although Goerner was far too apt to swallow without chewing any story anyone told him, and to regard any bureaucratic block in his path as a sinister effort to thwart him and hide the truth, those interested in the fate of Amelia and Fred owe him a debt of gratitude. In Safford's words, "without Goerner's persistence, publicity, and political pull," the declassified documents vital to the story "would still be gathering dust in the classified files of the various departments of the U.S. Government."[14]

In March of 1968, yet another expedition visited Saipan bent upon finding the bones of Amelia and Fred. This group consisted of five men from the Cleveland area, and this was their second trip. Their leader was Dan Kothers, a former Navy man who had served on Saipan in 1946 and 1947. With the help of Anna Diaz Nagofna, they found the site they sought and commenced digging. They came up with 188 bone fragments, the largest of which was about two inches long and the only bone fragment that had not been incinerated. The other pieces ranged from one inch to one-tenth of an inch. Their finds also included a gold bridge and "some amalgam fillings."

The Clevelanders took their finds to Ohio for examination by Raymond S. Baby, an anthropologist at Ohio State University, who gave them a "long and thorough examination." He encouraged the excavators to believe that they had indeed uncovered the remains of Amelia and Fred and informed them that the "amalgam fillings" were "positive proof that a white person had been buried there." This was a non sequitur; Japan possessed excellent dentists. Dr. Baby was careful not to put in writing any definite identification of the two lost fliers, but his public statement skated close to the edge: "It is our opinion that the cremated remains are those of a female, probably white, between the anatomical ages of 40 and 42 years. Since the age changes are slight, an age of 40 is probably more correct. A single unburnt bone is not a part of or associated with cremated remains, but the remains of a second individual, a man."

Considering the paucity of the remains, this was sticking one's neck out with a vengeance. Actually, the fragments, in Safford's words, "were sweepings or debris from the nearby crematory (which had been demolished by gun-fire during the capture of Saipan by the U. S. Marines)."[15]

So far, granted their mind-sets, the investigators had avoided the sensational. The same cannot be said for others who dabbled in the Earhart legend. In fact, one has the bemused impression that, short of declaring that Amelia and Fred had been transported to another planet by a UFO, no theory was too bizarre to find adherents.

One claimed that she neither crashed nor was captured; she landed on Tabiteuea in the Gilberts, on an airstrip prepared for her under an agreement between Roosevelt and the British authorities. She and Fred flew to Hawaii, landing at Hilo on July 5, 1937, some time before noon. They proceeded to Oakland, landing at around 2 A.M. on July 8, 1937. Four other people in two other planes were shot down; two of the people were shot, the other two beheaded on Saipan. These were the real spy planes, each manned by a man and woman who closely resembled Fred and Amelia. This individual believed Amelia might have changed her identity to Irene Craigmile Bolam.[16]

This theorist never explained what could have been gained by this elaborate setup or how Amelia and Fred could have come through Hawaii and California without being spotted.

The Bolam-as-Amelia theory originated with Joe Gervais, an independent researcher who worked with author Joe Klaas. In brief, his theory was that the Japanese had captured Amelia and Fred and held them until after the war, when they released the two fliers on the condition that the emperor not be tried as a war criminal. The Americans brought them back and gave them new identities. William van Dusen, senior vice president of Eastern Airlines, displayed interest in Gervais's investigation, and Gervais promptly jumped to the conclusion that van Dusen must be Fred Noonan.[17] Photographs show a superficial resemblance, but van Dusen had been a fixture in the airline industry for years and was well known.

Gervais's prime instance of conclusion-jumping, however, was when he met Mrs. Guy Bolam, née Irene Craigmile, and immediately decided that she must be Amelia because she was wearing

▶ a silver medal that looked like Amelia Earhart's trans-Atlantic solo medal. Mrs. Bolam wore a major's oak-leaf insignia. Amelia Earhart had been made a honorary major in the Army Air Corps by a reserve squadron in San Francisco. Mrs. Bolam wore a miniature Distinguished Flying Cross ribbon, and Amelia Earhart had been awarded the DFC . . . for the solo flight across the Atlantic. Amelia Earhart was a member of Zonta Sorority and Ninety-nines, and so was Mrs. Guy Bolam.[18]

Apparently it never struck Gervais as odd that a woman who had established a new identity should thus festoon herself with artifacts reminiscent of the old. Safford attempted to set Gervais straight in a letter remarkably kindly in tone for a man who could be acerbic when confronted with what he considered stupidity:

▶ You might be able to get the finger-prints of AE and FN from the FBI or the FAA, but I would not advise it, as it would be only one more proof that Irene Bolam is not Amelia Earhart. Where you got off the beam was in "identifying" Irene as Amelia on the basis of certain decorations she was wearing when you first met her. Your reasoning was logical, so far as it went, but apparently you did not know that AE had willed all of her medals and decorations to Purdue U., and that all of them were on display at the time. A few were in Washington at the Air and Space Museum (I have seen them myself)—the rest at Purdue.[19]

Long before this letter was written, Gervais telephoned Irene Bolam to request another meeting. She asked why he wanted to see her, and he replied ". . . that if you put the names of the eight Phoenix Islands in a certain order and then crossed out certain letters, the name of her husband showed up—and that, furthermore, the numerical sequence of the letters in his name represented the exact longitude and latitude of Hull Island!"[20]

What Irene said to this masterpiece of logic, if she were not knocked speechless, is not recorded. The significance of "Hull Island" is that Gervais's theory postulated that Amelia had overflown Truk and the Marshalls, intending to become "lost" on Canton Island to give the U.S. Navy the excuse to search the Japanese islands. Somehow the Japanese forced her down on Hull Island. This scenario is so close to the Roz Russell movie, as is the resemblance between "Hull Island" and "Gull Island," that it requires no comment.[21]

Perhaps it was inevitable that from portraying Amelia as a spy for the United States, some visualized her as spying for Japan. The Luttrell files contain the copy of what seems to be an advertising poster for a lecture: "Secret Agent of Japan: Amelia Earhart." The lecturer, Jerome P. Steigman, was identified on it as a "forensic evidence consultant."[22]

One A. D. Gibson informed Gervais of an alleged State Department file dated September 7, 1946, referring to the wives of Japanese admirals, generals, and top government officials. Among eight photos was one of an American woman. Gibson continued that one part of this file read, "Mrs. Putnam wishes the U.S. government to henceforth consider her a national of the Nipponese Imperial Islands."

As if this was not lurid enough, Gibson claimed that Jiro Hirakoshi, a designer for Mitsubishi, had worked for Curtiss Aircraft

▶ at the Garden City, Long Island plant and he knew and talked with her many times in the early and mid-30's. She spoke Japanese fluently. In the spring of '36 they were together in Japan when they did the Zero wind tunnel tests, and she first flew the type 00 deck fighter at Kayunmayharu in July 1939. There is a picture of her next to a twin engine "Randy" which was never put into mass production in the file.

Gervais took this rigmarole seriously enough to ask the Tokyo Ministry of Justice if an Irene Craigmile or a Mrs. G. P. Putnam had been

naturalized in Japan. The reply asserted that "the record of naturalized persons" was "closed to the public."[23]

The most enduring legend in this category was that Amelia was
Tokyo Rose, the notorious English-language radio propagandist. So
persistent was this rumor that George, who was serving in the armed
forces, "made a dangerous three-day trek through Japanese-held territory to reach a Marine Corps radio station near the coast where the
broadcast reception was loud and clear." It took George less than a
minute to reach a conclusion: "I'll stake my life that that is not
Amelia's voice. It sounds to me as if the woman might have lived in
New York, and of course she has been fiendishly well coached, but
Amelia—never!"[24]

In recent years, the more tabloid-type versions of Amelia's disappearance have simmered down, but interest still remains. In the late
1980s and early 1990s, the International Group for Historic Aircraft
Recovery (TIGHAR) began a search based on their theory that the
Electra came down on McKean or more probably Nikumaroru (formerly Gardner) Island, about five hundred miles south of Howland. In
1989 the group was cautiously optimistic, having found several artifacts, including a cigarette lighter and case, a battery, and "a piece of
aluminum that could have come from an aircraft frame."[25]

In January 1991 the group announced that they had unearthed an
artifact they were sure had come from a civilian aircraft of the mid-
1930s period. This was an aluminum bookcase, 14 by 9 by 9½ inches,
of the type navigators used to store reference materials. Richard E.
Gillespie, TIGHAR's executive director, speculated that this plane
landed at low tide on Nikumaroru but later was swept off the reef, and
Amelia and Fred soon died of thirst, as the island had no fresh water.
The aluminum box was found "in a garbage dump left on the island."
The British colonized Nikumaroru in 1938 and abandoned the project
in 1963.[26]

In July 1991 Gillespie was in Washington trying to raise funds to return and hunt the Electra. Evidently he succeeded, for in September
they were planning the search. In February 1992, the expedition returned with "a 2 by 1½-foot sheet of aluminum aircraft skin found
October 18." Gillespie was almost certain that this was indeed a part
of the Earhart plane. Others, including several men who had worked
on Amelia's aircraft, were even surer that it wasn't. An assistant foreman at Lockheed, Ed Warner, compared the dimensions and shape of
the find with a duplicate of the Earhart Electra at the Western Aero-
space Museum. His verdict: Not even close.[27]

But Gillespie was confident enough to hold "a mobbed news conference at the National Press Club" in Washington in March 1992. In addition to the controversial piece of aluminum, he produced a bottle cap
and part of a woman's shoe, size nine. He admitted that some ques-

tions would always remain, but he added, "We're very confident that the Amelia Earhart case is solved."

There is no mention in the TIGHAR story of finding any bones or bone fragments that might have been identified, even tentatively, as those of Amelia and Fred. They did open a grave, which proved to be "that of a small child," apparently from the 1938–63 colony.[28]

As of this writing, Gillespie was awaiting the results of tests being conducted at the Aluminum Company of America (Alcoa) in Pittsburgh, Pennsylvania, on the aluminum fragment, tests designed to determine whether it could have come from an aircraft manufactured between 1930 and 1944. The manager of Alcoa's analytical services points out that any results would be inconclusive. "Unless Amelia signed it somewhere, there's no way we can be able to say the piece came from her plane. The best we can do is not negate what Rick Gillespie says." Verifying the date, however, would have a positive effect on Gillespie's efforts to raise five hundred thousand dollars in order "to book a research ship" for another expedition.[29]

It will be most interesting to see the results of this latest expedition. We cannot be optimistic about the chances for success. Searching for hard evidence of a specific aircraft that went down in the vastness of the Pacific is a task that makes the proverbial hunt for a needle in a haystack seem easy by comparison. Identifying bits and pieces would be almost impossible, as aircraft of that period were made of the same materials, and such items as flight jackets and briefcases were fairly standardized.

Nikumaroru is located more than three hundred miles due south of Howland, in the island republic of Kiribati, so Gillespie's theory is possible geographically although not very probable, because this location is a good 45 degrees off course. If Gillespie can produce incontrovertible proof that Amelia and Fred crashed on Nikumaroru, it will not disprove any suggestions we or our colleagues have made. We believe that the Electra went down en route to Howland, with the exact location open to question.

So we wish the TIGHAR team the best of luck. If they succeed, they will have solved a long-standing mystery and have absolved Amelia of the charges of espionage and treason. And if they fail, that will not be the end of the Earhart story, for her disappearance is one of those rare events, like Pearl Harbor and the assassination of President Kennedy, that refuse to die, and linger in the public consciousness for generations.

Thus over the years the investigators have reached varying conclusions and no doubt will continue to do so as long as Amelia's engaging personality issues its challenge: "Find me if you can!" Until the day— if ever—that incontrovertible evidence is forthcoming, we are free to choose our own ending to the saga of Amelia Earhart.

EPILOGUE

*W*hat really happened to Amelia Earhart and Fred Noonan? It would be highly agreeable to come up with a solution, complete and satisfying, buttressed by such incontrovertible evidence as the remains of a Lockheed Electra numbered NR16020 and two identifiable skeletons. Alas, we cannot pull such a rabbit out of the hat. Of course, we have our opinion, which is, prosaically, that the plane ran out of gas, and Amelia either crashed or ditched. The location may well have been quite close to *Itasca*'s estimate, that is, within a hundred miles northwest of Howland. Safford's suggestion of within a hundred miles of Latitude 1°N, Longitude 178°E, around 225 miles west of Howland, is also logical.

Understandably but unheroically, the Coast Guard laid the sole blame on Amelia for its failure to find her. The official report was explicit, and an even harsher judgment came from Lieutenant Commander Frank T. Kenner, who was aboard *Itasca* on temporary duty from the Hawaiian Sector. Kenner had been skipper of *Itasca* just before Thompson, and his protective instincts were still keen. He wrote to his wife,

> As to Amelia losing herself, she had only herself to blame. We all admired her nerve and pluck to attempt such a flight, but we cannot admire her good sense and judgment in her conduct of it. She was too sure of herself, and too casual. She devoted no effort to the details at all. When it was too late and she was going down she hollered for our aid, but that was too late. We did what we could. She never gave us any of her positions as we repeatedly requested of her, she never answered or acknowledged any of our messages. . . .[1]

284

This was a rush to judgment. As we have seen, Amelia had broadcast her positions hourly, but Lae forwarded only one to *Itasca*, and it was too late. And it never occurred to Kenner, apparently, that the reason she did not answer *Itasca*'s messages was because she never received them. Of all *Itasca*'s broadcasts, only one reached the Electra. Moreover, *Itasca* failed to broadcast on 6210 KCs, although Amelia had advised she was listening on that wavelength.

There was no need for the Coast Guard to make such haste to shunt all criticism onto Amelia; no one expected *Itasca* to accomplish the impossible. Any experienced seaman knew with what frightening suddenness a man overboard or a small boat could be lost to sight within a few yards of a ship. To locate a downed aircraft in the vast reaches and ever-changing swells of the Pacific would have been a feat bordering on the miraculous. Even if *Itasca* had had Amelia's precise splashdown coordinates, the ship still might have been unable to locate her.

That Amelia deserves a share of blame is undeniable. Stanley, who respected her memory, pointed out what he considered a major shortcoming. As a specialist in aviation technology, he believed firmly in the necessity for rehearsal, "testing and retesting, and exhaustively pursuing all possible avenues of failure." He cited the Apollo program, with its "countless rehearsals and countdowns. . . . Such are the ingredients of success."

This comparison is not quite fair. The situations were not analogous. Apollo was a government project, with almost unlimited time, money, and personnel at its disposal, not to mention the technology of the space age. In contrast, Amelia's venture was a private project, operating with limited means, resources, personnel, and time. The "countless rehearsals and countdowns" of which Stanley spoke were impossible. No one accused Amelia of lack of preparation after her Atlantic, Hawaiian, and Mexican flights, because they succeeded.

Stanley added, "Such is, however, the cautious path seldom followed by persons possessing an adventurous temperament. Miss Earhart had courage. She was intelligent. She knew the hazards and risks ahead of her. Had she been cautious, she would never have attempted the trip."[2]

One could stop right there and decide that the round-the-world trip in itself guaranteed disaster. But that would be an oversimplification. Before takeoff from Lae, Amelia had successfully overflown South American jungles—that sea of green as potentially deadly as any ocean—crossed the Atlantic, passed over the vast wastelands of central Africa, and fought monsoons in India before reaching Southeast Asia. There was no real reason to anticipate failure on the Lae-Howland leg. Everyone involved, including Amelia, knew this would be difficult and dangerous, but no one seems to have been pessimistic.

Were Amelia's piloting skills unequal to the final challenge? Commander H. M. Anthony of the Coast Guard wrote to Gervais of Amelia, "she was no flyer."[3] Then again, Clarence L. "Kelly" Johnson, who had worked with her as a flight engineer, denied that she was a poor pilot. "She was a good one when I knew her. She was very sensible, very studious, and paid attention to what she was told."[4]

It has recently become customary to downplay Amelia's skill as a flier. Perhaps this is a reaction against the admiration she commanded in her lifetime; perhaps it is a manifestation of that peculiar human instinct to cut prominent persons down to size. We submit that poor pilots do not solo across the Atlantic and from Hawaii to California in an aircraft of 1930s vintage. As far as we can determine, Amelia was a good flier but not as good as she could have been. In part, this was George's fault, in part Amelia's own temperament and approach to flying. From her return from the *Friendship* flight to the end of her life, George scheduled her on a full lecture circuit that left her no time to perfect her skills, to practice, and to become proficient in such vital areas as navigation and radio. Yet Amelia was no meek echo of her husband, to follow his bidding when it was against her better judgment. So we can only conclude that, as ardently as she espoused aviation, she did not take her own flying seriously enough.

This attitude went back to her childhood, when her agile mind jumped to the correct answers in mathematics while ignoring the steps to the solutions; she lost out on a mathematics prize to a less gifted but more thorough classmate. A certain impatience with detail seems to have persisted, as evidenced by her neglect to learn Morse code. It is unfortunate that in her formative years someone did not get across to her that inspiration without perspiration is superficial and can be dangerous. A gifted pianist may win a measure of fame without total dedication, but a great pianist practices daily. Talent is not enough; one must work at one's profession.

Amelia flew primarily because she loved it. Had she ceased to take pleasure in it, no doubt she would have moved on to something else, as she had several times in her early years. Some individuals did not understand this and resented her stress on having "fun" in one's occupation. An unidentified columnist in 1937 commented, "Amelia has fun. Yes, and has it her own way . . . she has flown every place and in every way that seems feasible for her, and the concerned face of her faithful husband as he tells her goodbye time and again, suffering apparently in silence, but undoubtedly suffering, touches the public sentiment. Enough fun, Amelia, enough fun."[5]

Whoever wrote that effusion obviously did not know George Putnam, who basked in the publicity of his wife's exploits.

Could a more serious attitude toward her responsibilities to herself have brought Amelia safely home? Perhaps not—but it would have helped. We have seen how dismayed and angry Paul Mantz was when she took off without having completed what he considered to be necessary indoctrination and training. The fact remains that she successfully fulfilled a large and demanding part of her schedule and was proceeding on a direct course toward Howland when whatever happened happened.

Was Fred Noonan the weak link? As with Amelia, opinions differ concerning his expertise. William van Dusen has been quoted as remarking that "Noonan could not navigate his way across my duckpond."[6] Yet the same Commander Anthony who had scornfully dismissed Amelia as "no flyer" wrote, "As far as I am concerned, Noonan, whom I knew, was a damn good navigator—air and surface. . . ."[7] Fuzz Furman agreed that Fred "was one of the best in the business."[8]

He operated primarily by celestial navigation, and for the portion of the flight beyond Nauru, a heavy storm system blotted out both sun and stars. This was hardly Fred's fault, and he was not to blame for the failure of communications between *Itasca* and the Electra. He may not have been in top form physically. Although he did not go on a bender on the eve of takeoff, as some have charged, he did overindulge while at Lae. This could have done his system no good, especially as both he and Amelia would have been superhuman had they not been exhausted and keyed up at this stage of their journey.

Quite aside from the abilities of either pilot or navigator, we believe that this flight was ill-advised. Had it taken place a few years earlier, it would have been an admirable pioneering adventure, probably productive of valuable data as to the capabilities of machine and crew. But by 1937 the scheme was irrelevant. Commercial aviation, of which Amelia could only dream in the 1920s, was a thriving reality. Passenger and cargo routes were being established all over the world. All Amelia could prove was that a woman could pilot a plane around the world, and that no longer was really questionable, thanks in large part to Amelia herself.

As to the "flying laboratory" aspect, Amelia may well have been sincere; scientific research had always appealed to her. Yet it is difficult to take this mission seriously in relation to the round-the-world flight. The only test Amelia mentioned in her account was the upper-air bug-catching experiment, and she and Fred made a joke of that. Certainly she and Fred were not suitable test subjects if the object was to observe the average human being's physical and psychological reactions to various flight conditions. Both were air veterans of long standing.

Monetary considerations may have existed. A successful globe-circling flight would generate publicity that, in turn, would lead to more and higher lecture fees and probably attract investors. We believe, however, that such considerations weighed very lightly if at all with Amelia, although they probably counted heavily with George. In our opinion, Amelia had fallen victim to what may be termed the "one more time" syndrome. Why do veteran politicians run for office again, although they know that they have seen their best days and a new generation has taken over? Why does an aging diva schedule another concert tour, when it would be wiser to let her admirers remember her at her best? This reluctance to admit that one has peaked and had best retire gracefully, to want to experience the joy of accomplishment one more time, seems to be deeply embedded in human nature. No wonder Amelia fell victim to it.

"It just seems as if I must try this flight," she told George. "I've weighed it all carefully. With it behind me life will be fuller and richer. I can be content. Afterwards it will be fun to grow old."[9]

Some have expressed the opinion that Amelia's death at age thirty-nine was a mercy, that she would have hated to grow old. This is a cliché with which survivors frequently comfort themselves for an untimely loss. We do not believe it does Amelia justice because it implies that she lived solely on a physical level, which is not the case. Amelia had much to make life after forty full, agreeable, and "fun." She could have continued to fly for pleasure for many years, and she had numerous interests such as books, art, music, and social and political causes that have little or nothing to do with years. She had a good if unconventional marriage; she had her mother and sister and a host of friends, including some of the most interesting people of her day.

Amelia left behind a thousand whys and ifs. Human beings usually like clear explanations and pat answers. But in this case they are not forthcoming, however probing the questions as to the cause of her disappearance. Was it pilot error, poor navigation, the communications mix-ups, the flight plan, the weather? Was it blind accident, fate, or a witches' brew of all these factors?

Amelia left another legacy—the memory of a personality so vivid, so glad to be alive, so interested in her chosen field that with all the reservations critics may have, it is difficult to imagine anyone who would have been more fun to know. Perhaps that is why it has been so hard for history to let her go.

NOTES

INTRODUCTION

1. Atlanta *Journal,* 11 August 1983.
2. Anne Morrow Lindbergh, *Hour of Gold, Hour of Lead* (New York: Harcourt Brace Jovanovich, 1973), p. 216.

PART I. TAKEOFF

Chapter 1. *Childhood Idyll*

1. Muriel Earhart Morrissey, *Courage Is the Price: The Biography of Amelia Earhart* (Wichita: McCormick Armstrong, 1963), pp. 11–12. Hereafter *Courage.*
2. Ibid., pp. 12–13.
3. Ibid., p. 13.
4. George Palmer Putnam, *Soaring Wings: A Biography of Amelia Earhart* (New York: Harcourt Brace, 1939), p. 7. Hereafter *Soaring Wings.*
5. *Courage,* p. 13; Amelia Earhart, *The Fun of It* (New York: Harcourt Brace, 1932), pp. 3–5. Hereafter *The Fun of It.*
6. *Courage,* pp. 13–14, 18.
7. Ibid., p. 14.
8. Ibid., pp. 14–15. (Muriel Earhart Morrissey obtained her information about the Earhart branch from a brochure titled *A Brief History of the Ancestors and Near Kindred of the Author and the Family and Kindred of His Wife. To Which Is Appended a Sketch of the Dangers and Customs of the Early Settlers of Western Pennsylvania and an Autobiography of the Author: The Rev. David Earhart* [January 1, 1898].)
9. *Courage,* pp. 14–15.
10. Ibid., pp. 15–16; *Soaring Wings,* p. 6.
11. *Courage,* pp. 16–17.
12. Ibid., p. 17; Muriel Earhart Morrissey and Carol L. Osborne, *Amelia, My Courageous Sister* (Santa Clara, Calif.: Aviation, 1987), p. 4. Hereafter *Amelia;* Jean L. Backer, *Letters from Amelia 1901–1937* (Boston: Beacon Press, 1982), p. 138. Hereafter *Letters.*
13. *Courage,* p. 17; *Soaring Wings,* p. 6.

14. *Courage,* pp. 17–18.
15. Ibid., pp. 18–20; *Amelia,* p. 5.
16. *Courage,* pp. 21–23.
17. These prices came from various newspapers of the day.
18. *Courage,* pp. 23–25; *Amelia,* p. 1; *Soaring Wings,* pp. 6–7.
19. *Courage,* pp. 25–26.
20. Ibid., p. 26; *Amelia,* p. 12.
21. *Courage,* p. 26; *Amelia,* pp. 11–12.
22. *Courage,* pp. 26–28.
23. Ibid., pp. 28–29; *The Fun of It,* pp. 6–7.
24. *Courage,* pp. 29–31; *Soaring Wings,* p. 5.
25. *Courage,* pp. 31–32, 52; *Soaring Wings,* p. 9; *The Fun of It,* p. 11.
26. *Courage,* pp. 51–52; *Soaring Wings,* p. 18.
27. *Courage,* pp. 49–50.
28. *Soaring Wings,* p. 26; *The Fun of It,* pp. 6–7.
29. *Courage,* pp. 55–57.
30. *Soaring Wings,* p. 11; *Courage,* p. 59; *The Fun of It,* pp. 5–6.
31. *The Fun of It,* pp. 5, 11; *Soaring Wings,* pp. 29–30.
32. *Courage,* pp. 64–65; *The Fun of It,* pp. 12–13; *Soaring Wings,* p. 11.
33. *Soaring Wings,* p. 24.

Chapter 2. *Shadow on the Sun*

1. *Courage,* pp. 68–69.
2. Ibid., pp. 69–71.
3. Amelia Earhart, *Last Flight.* Arranged by George Palmer Putnam (New York: Harcourt Brace, 1937), p. 5. Hereafter *Last Flight.*
4. *Courage,* pp. 71–73; *The Fun of It,* pp. 16–17.
5. *Courage,* pp. 73–76; *The Fun of It,* p. 9; *Soaring Wings,* p. 31.
6. *Courage,* pp. 76–78.
7. *Soaring Wings,* p. 33.
8. *Courage,* pp. 78–80.
9. Ibid., pp. 80–81.
10. Ibid., pp. 80–82; John Burke, *Winged Legend: The Life of Amelia Earhart* (New York: Berkeley, 1970), p. 28. Hereafter *Winged Legend.*
11. *Courage,* pp. 83–84.
12. Ibid., p. 84.
13. Ibid., pp. 85–87.
14. Ibid., pp. 87–88.
15. Ibid., pp. 89–90.
16. Ibid., pp. 90–95.
17. Ibid., pp. 95–97; *Soaring Wings,* p. 34.
18. *The Fun of It,* p. 18; *Soaring Wings,* p. 34.
19. *Courage,* pp. 97–99.
20. *Letters,* pp. 25–27. Amelia seldom dated her letters; Backer re-created many dates from external evidence.
21. *Soaring Wings,* pp. 34–35.
22. *Letters,* p. 27.
23. Ibid., pp. 29–30.
24. *Courage,* p. 99.
25. Ibid., pp. 99–100.
26. Ibid., pp. 100–1.
27. *Letters,* pp. 34–38; *New York Times,* 5 June 1928.
28. *New York Times,* 5 June 1928.
29. *Letters,* p. 39.
30. *Courage,* p. 102; *Letters,* p. 55.

Chapter 3. *Amelia Finds Wings*

1. *Letters,* p. 40.
2. Amelia Earhart, *20 Hrs., 40 Min.: Our Flight in the Friendship* (New York: G. P. Putnam's Sons, 1928), p. 31. Hereafter *20 Hrs., 40 Min.; Courage,* p. 102; *The Fun of It,* p. 19.
3. *20 Hrs., 40 Min.,* p. 33; *Letters,* p. 49.
4. *Courage,* pp. 102–3; *The Fun of It,* p. 20; *20 Hrs., 40 Min.,* pp. 33–34.
5. *Letters,* pp. 47–50.
6. *Courage,* pp. 103–5; *The Fun of It,* p. 20.
7. *Letters,* pp. 49–50; *The Fun of It,* pp. 20–21; *20 Hrs., 40 Min.,* p. 43.
8. *Courage,* pp. 105–6, 111; *The Fun of It,* p. 21.
9. *The Fun of It,* p. 21; *Courage,* p. 111; *20 Hrs., 40 Min.,* p. 44; *Letters,* p. 51.
10. *The Fun of It,* p. 21; *Courage,* pp. 106–7, 111; *Soaring Wings,* p. 37. The Earhart girls became acquainted with the Stablers that summer of 1919. The Stablers, a New York family, owned the next-door cottage.
11. *The Fun of It,* pp. 21–22; *Soaring Wings,* p. 36; *Courage,* p. 113.
12. *Courage,* p. 115; *The Fun of It,* pp. 23–24.
13. *Courage,* pp. 116–17; *Letters,* p. 53.
14. *Courage,* pp. 117–19; *Letters,* p. 55; *Amelia,* pp. 60–61; *Winged Legend,* pp. 30, 33.
15. *Winged Legend,* pp. 48–49; *Courage,* pp. 119–27.
16. *Courage,* p. 129; *The Fun of It,* p. 24; *Soaring Wings,* p. 38.
17. *20 Hrs., 40 Min.,* pp. 46–47; *The Fun of It,* pp. 24–25; *Soaring Wings,* pp. 38–39; *Last Flight,* p. 7.
18. *The Fun of It,* pp. 25–26; *20 Hrs., 40 Min.,* pp. 49, 67; *Soaring Wings,* pp. 38–39; *Last Flight,* p. 7.
19. *20 Hrs., 40 Min.,* p. 49; *Soaring Wings,* pp. 39–40; *Courage,* pp. 127–28.
20. *20 Hrs., 40 Min.,* pp. 53–54, 92; *Courage,* p. 129; *The Fun of It,* p. 28.
21. *Courage,* p. 128; *20 Hrs., 40 Min.,* p. 54; *The Fun of It,* pp. 26–27; *Letters,* p. 59.
22. *New York Times,* 5 June 1928.
23. *The Fun of It,* p. 28.
24. *Amelia,* p. 66.
25. *Courage,* pp. 128–29; *The Fun of It,* p. 27; *20 Hrs., 40 Min.,* p. 77; *Last Flight,* p. 8; *Amelia,* p. 66.
26. *The Fun of It,* pp. 48–49; *20 Hrs., 40 Min.,* pp. 77–81, 85; *Courage,* pp. 129–30.
27. *Courage,* pp. 130–31; *Soaring Wings,* pp. 44–45.
28. *Courage,* p. 131; *Letters,* p. 63; *The Fun of It,* pp. 49–52; *Last Flight,* p. 8; *Soaring Wings,* pp. 42–43.
29. *The Fun of It,* pp. 52–53; *20 Hrs., 40 Min.,* pp. 11–12; *Courage,* pp. 132, 138–39; *Soaring Wings,* p. 47.

Chapter 4. *"Ask for Amelia Earhart"*

1. *The Fun of It,* pp. 53–54; *Courage,* pp. 132–34; *20 Hrs., 40 Min.,* pp. 11–12; *Soaring Wings,* pp. 48–50.
2. *Courage,* pp. 134–35; *20 Hrs., 40 Min.,* p. 14; *The Fun of It,* p. 55; *Letters,* p. 66.
3. *20 Hrs., 40 Min.,* pp. 16–17; *Courage,* pp. 135–37. Amelia's poem, "Courage," has been reproduced many times. To the best of our knowledge, it first appeared in public print in the *New York Times,* 19 June 1928. It was made public on June 18 by the *Survey Graphic.*
4. *Courage,* p. 138; *The Fun of It,* pp. 56–57; *Letters,* p. 66; *Soaring Wings,* p. 51; Ann Hodgman and Rudy Djabbaroff, *Skystars: The History of Women in Aviation* (New York: Athenaeum, 1981), pp. 60–61. Hereafter *Skystars.*

5. *The Fun of It*, pp. 58–61; *Courage*, pp. 40–42; *20 Hrs., 40 Min.*, p. 15; *Last Flight*, p. 10; Paul L. Briand Jr., *Daughter of the Sky: The Story of Amelia Earhart* (New York: Duell, Sloan & Pearce, 1960), p. 5. Hereafter *Daughter of the Sky*.
6. Hilton Howell Railey, *Touch'd with Madness* (New York: Carrick & Evans, 1938), pp. 100–1. Hereafter *Touch'd with Madness; Soaring Wings*, p. 53.
7. *Touch'd with Madness*, pp. 101–2.
8. Ibid., pp. 102, 104; *Courage Is the Price*, p. 141.
9. *Touch'd with Madness*, pp. 102–3.
10. *20 Hrs., 40 Min.*, pp. 99–100; *Last Flight*, p. 10; *Courage*, p. 141.
11. *Courage*, p. 142.
12. Pete Hamill, "Leather and Pearls: The Cult of Amelia Earhart," *MS. Magazine*, Vol. 5, September 1976, p. 51.
13. *Courage*, pp. 140–42; *Daughter of the Sky*, pp. 66–71.
14. *Courage*, p. 142; *The Fun of It*, pp. 60–61; *20 Hrs., 40 Min.*, pp. 101, 126.
15. *20 Hrs., 40 Min.*, pp. 96, 101, 106; *The Fun of It*, p. 62; *Soaring Wings*, p. 61.
16. *New York Times*, 4 June 1928.
17. *Courage*, p. 144.
18. *New York Times*, 4 June 1928.
19. *Courage*, pp. 142, 146, 148; *The Fun of It*, pp. 62–63; *Soaring Wings*, p. 55.
20. *Soaring Wings*, p. 55; *Courage*, p. 146; *Touch'd with Madness*, p. 104.
21. *The Fun of It*, pp. 62–63; *New York Times*, 4 & 18 June 1928.
22. *Courage*, p. 143.
23. Ibid., p. 144; *New York Times*, 4 June 1928.
24. *The Fun of It*, pp. 64–65; *Soaring Wings*, p. 54; *Courage*, pp. 142, 145; *20 Hrs., 40 Min.*, p. 125; *New York Times*, 4 June 1928.
25. *Soaring Wings*, p. 59; *Courage*, pp. 145–47; *The Fun of It*, p. 66; *20 Hrs., 40 Min.*, pp. 115, 117, 126–27.
26. *Courage*, pp. 148–49; *New York Times*, 8 June 1928.
27. *New York Times*, 4 June 1928.
28. *20 Hrs., 40 Min.*, pp. 119–20; *The Fun of It*, p. 69.

Chapter 5. *The Flight of the* Friendship

1. *20 Hrs., 40 Min.*, pp. 142–49.
2. *Courage*, p. 150.
3. *20 Hrs., 40 Min.*, p. 147; *The Fun of It*, pp. 70–72.
4. *Courage*, pp. 151–52.
5. *20 Hrs., 40 Min.*, pp. 151, 155, 161.
6. *Courage*, pp. 152–53; *Soaring Wings*, p. 61.
7. *New York Times*, 11, 13, & 14 June 1928.
8. *Courage*, p. 153; *Soaring Wings*, pp. 61–62.
9. *20 Hrs., 40 Min.*, p. 171; *The Fun of It*, p. 72; *Courage*, pp. 153–54.
10. *Soaring Wings*, p. 65; *Courage*, p. 154.
11. *New York Times*, 18 June 1928; *20 Hrs., 40 Min.*, pp. 176–78.
12. *Courage*, p. 155; *20 Hrs., 40 Min.*, pp. 180–82; *New York Times*, 18 June 1928.
13. *The Fun of It*, pp. 72–73, 75; *Courage*, p. 155; *New York Times*, 18 June 1928; *20 Hrs., 40 Min.*, p. 179.
14. *New York Times*, 18 June 1928.
15. *The Fun of It*, p. 75; *20 Hrs., 40 Min.*, pp. 187–88.
16. *New York Times*, 19 June 1928; *Courage*, pp. 155–56; *The Fun of It*, pp. 75–79; *20 Hrs., 40 Min.*, pp. 188–92.
17. *20 Hrs., 40 Min.*, pp. 197–200; *The Fun of It*, pp. 80–81; *Courage*, pp. 156–57; *New York Times*, 19 June 1928.
18. *20 Hrs., 40 Min.*, pp. 200–1; *Touch'd with Madness*, pp. 105–6.

19. *The Fun of It,* p. 82; *New York Times,* 19 June 1928; *Courage,* pp. 157–58.
20. *20 Hrs., 40 Min.,* pp. 201–2; *Soaring Wings,* pp. 178–80, 184; *Courage,* pp. 157–58; *The Fun of It,* pp. 82–83.
21. *Courage,* p. 158.
22. *New York Times,* 19 June 1928.
23. *20 Hrs., 40 Min.,* pp. 200, 205–6.
24. Ibid., p. 206; *The Fun of It,* pp. 82, 84; *Soaring Wings,* p. 69.
25. *New York Times,* 20 June 1928.
26. *Touch'd with Madness,* pp. 106–8.
27. *New York Times,* 19 June 1928; *Soaring Wings,* p. 64.
28. *New York Times,* 19 & 21 June 1928; *Courage,* pp. 161–62; *20 Hrs., 40 Min.,* pp. 291–93.
29. *The Fun of It,* pp. 83–86; *Soaring Wings,* pp. 71–72; *20 Hrs., 40 Min.,* p. 207; *Last Flight,* p. 11; *Courage,* pp. 160–62; *New York Times,* 22, 25, & 27 June 1928.

Chapter 6. *Ticker Tape and Travel*

1. *20 Hrs., 40 Min.,* p. 209; *The Fun of It,* p. 86; *Courage,* pp. 162–63; *Soaring Wings,* p. 72.
2. *New York Times,* 7 July 1928.
3. *20 Hrs., 40 Min.,* pp. 210–11; *Courage,* pp. 164–65; *New York Times,* 7 July 1928.
4. *New York Times,* 10 July 1928.
5. *Courage,* pp. 165–66.
6. Ibid., p. 166.
7. *New York Times,* 12 July 1928.
8. *Courage,* pp. 167–68; *New York Times,* 18 & 20 July 1928; *Soaring Wings,* p. 229.
9. *20 Hrs., 40 Min.,* pp. 281–82; *Courage,* pp. 168–69.
10. *20 Hrs., 40 Min.,* pp. 281–82.
11. *Letters,* pp. 79–80.
12. *New York Times,* 1 & 15 September 1928.
13. *The Fun of It,* pp. 80, 93–94.
14. Ibid., pp. 94–96; *Letters,* p. 80; *New York Times,* 15 September 1928.
15. *Letters,* p. 80.
16. Ibid., pp. 81–82.
17. *New York Times,* 4 March 1929.
18. Ibid., 26 March 1929; *Courage,* p. 171.
19. *New York Times,* 29 March 1929.
20. *Skystars,* pp. 49–51.
21. *The Fun of It,* pp. 99–103.
22. *New York Times,* 20 May 1929.

Chapter 7. *Gain and Loss*

1. *Courage,* pp. 171–72; *Amelia,* p. 107; *Letters,* p. 83.
2. *Soaring Wings,* p. 226; *New York Times,* 2 July 1929.
3. *The Fun of It,* pp. 170–72; *New York Times,* 8 July 1929.
4. *Hour of Gold, Hour of Lead* p. 216.
5. *The Fun of It,* pp. 107–9.
6. Ibid., p. 106; *Letters,* p. 83.
7. *New York Times,* 23 & 24 July 1929.
8. *Letters,* p. 84.
9. *Last Flight,* pp. 14–15.
10. *Soaring Wings,* p. 231.
11. *New York Times,* 27 August 1929; *Winged Legend,* p. 104; *Skystars,* pp. 106–8; *The Fun of It,* p. 152.

12. *Skystars,* p. 108; *Winged Legend,* p. 105.
13. *Skystars,* pp. 109–10; *Winged Legend,* p. 105; *New York Times,* 27 August 1929.
14. *Skystars,* p. 108; *Winged Legend,* p. 106; *New York Times,* 27 August 1929.
15. *Skystars,* p. 109; *Winged Legend,* pp. 105–6.
16. *Skystars,* p. 110; *New York Times,* 27 August 1929. This issue lists Blanche Noyes as third with Amelia fourth. All other accounts that we have seen agree that Amelia took third place.
17. *New York Times,* 27 August 1929; *Courage,* p. 170.
18. *Skystars,* pp. 110–11; *Courage,* p. 171. As of this writing, Fay Gillis Welles is living in Alexandria, Virginia.
19. *Letters,* pp. 84–86; *Courage,* p. 175.
20. *Letters,* pp. 87–89; *Amelia,* p. 116.
21. *The Fun of It,* pp. 109–15; *Soaring Wings,* pp. 226–27.
22. *Letters,* pp. 91, 94.
23. *The Fun of It,* pp. 160–61.
24. *Letters,* pp. 94–96.
25. Ibid., pp. 96–97.
26. Ibid., pp. 97–98.
27. Ibid., pp. 97, 101–2.
28. *Courage,* p. 176.
29. *Letters,* pp. 99, 104.
30. *Boston Herald* and *New York Times,* both 8 February 1931.
31. *Soaring Wings,* p. 76.
32. *Letters,* pp. 105–6; *Courage,* pp. 176–77.
33. *Courage,* p. 177; *Letters,* pp. 106–7; *Amelia,* p. 118. Cornelia Otis Skinner's humorous essays make delightful reading.
34. *The Fun of It,* pp. 128, 131–34; *Automotive Daily News* (New York), 8 April 1931.
35. *Union Star* (Schenectady, N.Y.), 7 April 1931; *Intelligencer* (Wheeling, W. Va.), 8 April 1931; *Record Herald* (Helena, Mont.), 8 April 1931.
36. *New York Herald Tribune; Courier* (Evansville, Ind.); *Baltimore Sun,* all 9 April 1931.
37. *Baltimore Sun; Philadelphia Record; St. Louis Globe Democrat; New York Times,* all 9 April 1931. Amelia's feat received extensive coverage across the country.

Chapter 8. *Daughter, Sister, Wife*

1. *Letters,* pp. 107–11.
2. *Courage,* pp. 173–76.
3. *Letters,* pp. 110–11.
4. *New York Times,* 9 May 1931.
5. *The Fun of It,* pp. 134–36; *Courage,* pp. 172–73; *Letters,* p. 113; *Every Evening* (Wilmington, Del.); *Times–Star* (Bridgeport, Conn.); *Democrat* (Johnstown, Pa.), all 29 May 1931.
6. *New York Times,* 13 June 1931.
7. *The Fun of It,* pp. 136–37; *Letters,* pp. 113, 115; *New York Times,* 13 & 20 June 1931.
8. *Letters,* pp. 114–15.
9. Ibid., pp. 116–18.
10. Ibid., p. 117; *New York Times,* 13 September 1931.
11. *Soaring Wings,* pp. 209–10; *New York Times,* 13 September 1931; *Letters,* p. 117.
12. *The Fun of It,* pp. 136–37; *Letters,* p. 117.
13. *Letters,* pp. 116–19.
14. *Courage,* p. 178; *Soaring Wings,* pp. 81–84.

15. *Soaring Wings*, pp. 85–86, 211. A similar scrapbook found on an island in the South Pacific after her disappearance has been cited as proof that Amelia had been there. She was just about the last person to burden herself with a heavy scrapbook of her own doings on a flight where every ounce had to pay its way. It is much more likely that the scrapbook, if it really existed, was the work of some admiring youngster like Yamada.
16. *Courage*, p. 178; *Winged Legend*, p. 120.
17. *Soaring Wings*, p. 205; *Courage*, pp. 178–79.
18. *Letters*, pp. 120–22.
19. *New York Times*, 29 February 1932. A *workhouse* is currently defined as a "house of correction"—not quite a jail but almost.

PART II. HIGH FLIGHT

Chapter 9. *Vindication*

1. *The Fun of It*, p. 209; *Courage*, p. 181.
2. *Soaring Wings*, pp. 99–101; *Letters*, p. 123; *New York Times*, 22 May 1932; *Courage*, p. 179.
3. *Letters*, pp. 123–24; *Soaring Wings*, p. 102; *Courage*, p. 179; Bernt Balchen, *Come North with Me* (New York: E. P. Dutton, 1951), p. 196. Hereafter *Come North*.
4. *Letters*, pp. 123–24; *Daughter of the Sky*, p. 80; *The Fun of It*, pp. 210, 212; *Courage*, p. 180.
5. *Soaring Wings*, pp. 102–5; *Letters*, pp. 124–25; *Courage*, p. 180; *The Fun of It*, pp. 211–13; *Last Flight*, pp. 16–17; *New York Times*, 22 May 1932. *Soaring Wings*, *The Fun of It*, and *Letters* give her date of takeoff from Teterboro as May 20; however, *Last Flight* and *Courage* give the date of May 19. The latter is correct, being in accordance with the log published in the *New York Times* on 22 May 1932.
6. *Soaring Wings*, p. 105; *The Fun of It*, p. 213; *Courage*, pp. 180–81; *Letters*, p. 125; *New York Times*, 20 & 22 May 1932.
7. *Come North*, p. 197. According to the *New York Times*, 22 May 1932, Balchen told guests at a luncheon that "he had advised Mrs. Putnam not to fly at this time because of the danger of low temperature causing ice to form on the plane." There is no hint of this in his autobiography.
8. *New York Times*, 22 May 1932; *London Times*, 23 May 1932; *The Fun of It*, pp. 214, 216; *Soaring Wings*, pp. 107–8; *Courage*, pp. 181–82; *Last Flight*, p. 17.
9. *New York Times*, 22 May 1932; *London Times*, 23 May 1932; *The Fun of It*, pp. 215–16; *Courage*, p. 182; *Last Flight*, pp. 17–18.
10. *The Fun of It*, pp. 216–18; *New York Times*, 22 May 1932; *Soaring Wings*, p. 110.
11. *New York Times*, 22 May 1932; *Soaring Wings*, p. 114.
12. *Letters*, p. 126; *Soaring Wings*, pp. 110–11; *New York Times*, 22 May 1932; *London Times*, 23 May 1932.
13. *Soaring Wings*, pp. 110–11; *Letters*, p. 126; *Courage*, p. 182; *New York Times*, 23 May 1932; *London Times*, 23 May 1932.
14. *New York Times*, 22 May 1932.
15. Ibid.
16. *Skystars*, pp. 56–57; *New York Times*, 22 May 1932.
17. *New York Times*, 22 May 1932.
18. Ibid.; *Letters*, p. 127.
19. *Letters*, p. 127; *Courage*, p. 183; *Soaring Wings*, p. 111.
20. *New York Times*, 22 May 1932.
21. *Courage*, p. 183; *Soaring Wings*, pp. 90–92.

Chapter 10. *Europe Welcomes Amelia*

1. *Soaring Wings*, p. 111.
2. *Letters*, pp. 127, 129.
3. *New York Times*, 23 May 1932; *Soaring Wings*, pp. 111–12; *Letters*, pp. 127–28.
4. *Soaring Wings*, p. 112.
5. *New York Times*, 23 May 1932.
6. *London Times*, 23 May 1932.
7. *Manchester Guardian*, 24 May 1932.
8. *Letters*, pp. 127–28; *Courage*, p. 183.
9. *New York Times*, 25 May 1923; *Courage*, p. 183.
10. *New York Times*, 26 & 27 May 1932. From 1928 to 1948, this historic aircraft was on loan to the Science museum.
11. Ibid., 1 June 1932.
12. *Letters*, p. 128; *New York Times*, 31 May 1932.
13. *New York Times*, 2, 3, & 4 June 1932.
14. *Courage*, p. 183; *Soaring Wings*, pp. 115–16; *Letters*, pp. 128–29.
15. *New York Times*, 4 June 1932.
16. *Soaring Wings*, p. 118; *New York Times*, 5 June 1932.
17. *Soaring Wings*, pp. 116–17; *Letters*, pp. 138–39; *New York Times*, 7 June 1932.
18. *Soaring Wings*, p. 116; *New York Times*, 8 June 1932.
19. *Soaring Wings*, pp. 117–21; *Letters*, pp. 129–30; *Courage*, p. 184.
20. *Courage*, p. 184; *Soaring Wings*, pp. 120–21.
21. *Soaring Wings*, pp. 119–20.
22. *New York Times*, 9 & 11 June 1932.
23. *Soaring Wings*, pp. 121–22; *New York Times*, 14 June 1932.
24. *Soaring Wings*, p. 123; *Letters*, p. 129; *New York Times*, 14 June 1932.
25. *Courage*, p. 185; *Soaring Wings*, pp. 123–24.

Chapter 11. *The White House and Elsewhere*

1. *New York Times*, 17 through 20 June 1932.
2. Ibid., 21 June 1932.
3. Mary S. Lovell, *The Sound of Wings* (New York: St. Martin's Press, 1989), pp. 139, 143, 148. Hereafter *Sound of Wings*.
4. *New York Times*, 21 June 1932.
5. Ibid., 22 June 1932; *Courage*, p. 186.
6. *Soaring Wings*, pp. 125–26.
7. *Courage*, p. 186.
8. Ibid., pp. 186–87; *Letters*, p. 131; *New York Times*, 22 June 1932.
9. *Letters*, pp. 132–33; *Courage*, p. 187; *New York Times*, 22 June 1932.
10. *Soaring Wings*, p. 127.
11. *Courage*, pp. 187–88; *Letters*, p. 133; *New York Times*, 23 through 29 June 1932.
12. *New York Times*, 1 & 2 July 1932.
13. *Letters*, p. 133.
14. *New York Times*, 13 & 14 July 1932.
15. *Letters*, pp. 133–34.
16. *New York Times*, 26 August 1932.
17. Ibid.
18. *Skystars*, pp. 113–14; *New York Times*, 23 August 1932. The 1933 National Air Races scheduled only two events for women, and for 1934 no women were allowed to participate. The Ninety-Nines held their own meet that year for women.
19. *Letters*, pp. 135–36.

20. Ibid., p. 137.
21. *Courage*, pp. 187–88; *New York Times*, 12 December 1932.
22. *Letters*, p. 138.
23. See, for example, *New York Times*, 4, 14, & 17 November 1932; 5 & 6 January 1933.
24. Ibid., 21 December 1932.
25. *Soaring Wings*, pp. 90–91.
26. Ibid., pp. 131–32; *Amelia*, p. 174.
27. *Letters*, pp. 139–40.
28. *Soaring Wings*, p. 128.
29. *Letters*, pp. 140–41.
30. *Soaring Wings*, pp. 128–31.
31. Ibid., pp. 133–34; *Letters*, p. 141.

Chapter 12. *On the Ground and in the Sky*

1. *New York Times*, 22 April 1933.
2. *Letters*, pp. 141–42.
3. *Courage*, p. 188.
4. *Daughter of the Sky*, p. 76.
5. *Letters*, pp. 142, 144–45.
6. *Winged Legend*, pp. 139–40; *New York Times*, 2 July 1933; *Sound of Wings*, p. 203.
7. *New York Times*, 9 July 1933.
8. *Letters*, pp. 147–48; *New York Times*, 6 August 1933.
9. *Skystars*, pp. 81–83; *Letters*, p. 148; *Soaring Wings*, pp. 233–34; *New York Times*, 28 July 1933.
10. *New York Times*, 22 August 1933.
11. *Letters*, pp. 148–49.
12. Ibid., pp. 150–52.
13. *Soaring Wings*, p. 213.
14. Ibid., p. 93.
15. Ibid., pp. 213–14.
16. Ibid., pp. 214–15.
17. *Letters*, pp. 152–53.
18. *New York Times*, 18 December 1933.
19. *Letters*, pp. 153–54.
20. Ibid., pp. 155–57; *New York Times*, 21 March 1934.
21. *Soaring Wings*, p. 255.
22. *Courage*, pp. 188–89; *Soaring Wings*, pp. 94–95; *New York Times*, 13 January 1935; *Last Flight*, p. 21.
23. *Soaring Wings*, p. 96; *Letters*, pp. 157–60.
24. Don Dwiggins, *Hollywood Pilot: The Biography of Paul Mantz* (Garden City, N.Y.: Doubleday, 1967), pp. 2–4, 69, 76. Hereafter *Hollywood Pilot*.
25. *Letters*, p. 159; Jacqueline Cochran, *The Stars at Noon* (Boston: Little, Brown, 1954), pp. 42, 89–90. Hereafter *Stars at Noon*. This book contains an account of Jacqueline Cochran's early years, all the more poignant because it was written without self-pity.
26. *Letters*, p. 159.
27. *New York Times*, 22 November 1934.
28. Ibid., 19 December 1934.

Chapter 13. *West to East*

1. *Letters*, pp. 160–62; *San Francisco Chronicle*, 11 January 1935.
2. *Soaring Wings*, pp. 256–57; *Letters*, p. 164.
3. Quoted in *New York Times*, 30 December 1934.
4. *Letters*, p. 162.

5. *New York Times,* 30 December 1934.
6. *Letters,* p. 163; *Soaring Wings,* pp. 257–58.
7. *New York Times,* 7 January 1935.
8. *Courage,* pp. 190–91; *Letters,* p. 163; *Sound of Wings,* p. 208.
9. *Soaring Wings,* pp. 257, 260–61.
10. Ibid., p. 262.
11. Ibid., pp. 258–59; *Courage,* pp. 191–92; *New York Times,* 13 January 1935.
12. *Last Flight,* pp. 20–23; *New York Times,* 12 January 1935.
13. *San Francisco Chronicle,* 11 January 1935.
14. *Last Flight,* pp. 23–25; *Soaring Wings,* pp. 259–60; *San Francisco Chronicle,* 11 January 1935.
15. *Soaring Wings,* p. 260; *New York Times,* 12 January & 5 March 1935; *San Francisco Chronicle,* 11 January 1935.
16. *Last Flight,* pp. 25–27.
17. *Soaring Wings,* pp. 262–63.
18. *New York Times,* 12 January 1935; *San Francisco Chronicle,* 11 January 1935.
19. *Last Flight,* pp. 27–32; *San Francisco Chronicle,* 13 January 1935; *Honolulu Star–Bulletin,* 12 January 1935.
20. *New York Times,* 13 January 1935.
21. Ibid.
22. *Soaring Wings,* pp. 263–64; *New York Times,* 13 January 1935.

Chapter 14. *Mexican Venture*

1. *New York Times,* 14 January 1935.
2. Ibid., 15 January 1935; *Letters,* pp. 169–70.
3. *New York Times,* 17 & 20 January 1935.
4. Ibid., 20 & 21 January 1935; *Letters,* p. 170.
5. *New York Times,* 28 & 29 January 1935.
6. Ibid., 2 February 1935.
7. Ibid., 2 March 1935.
8. *Letters,* p. 171.
9. *Hollywood Pilot,* pp. 77–78, 92.
10. *Letters,* p. 172; *New York Times,* 17 March 1935.
11. *Last Flight,* pp. 34–35.
12. *Courage,* p. 193; *Letters,* p. 172; *New York Times,* 19 & 20 April 1935. *Mexico City Excelsior,* 20 April 1935.
13. *Letters,* p. 172; *Last Flight,* p. 38; *New York Times,* 21 April 1935; *Mexico City Excelsior,* 20 & 21 April 1935.
14. *New York Times,* 22 & 23 April 1935; *Letters,* p. 172.
15. *New York Times,* 24 & 27 March 1935; *Letters,* p. 172.
16. *New York Times,* 1, 3, & 5 May 1935.
17. Ibid., 9 May 1935.
18. Ibid.; *Last Flight,* p. 43.
19. *Soaring Wings,* p. 270; *Daughter of the Sky,* p. 130; *New York Times,* 9 May 1935.
20. *Last Flight,* p. 43.
21. *New York Times,* 9 May 1935.

Chapter 15. *Work and Honors*

1. *Hollywood Pilot,* p. 95.
2. *Letters,* p. 174.
3. *New York Times,* 10 & 11 May 1935.
4. Ibid., 24 May & 13 October 1935.
5. Ibid., 27 May 1935; *Soaring Wings,* p. 48.
6. *New York Times,* 28 May 1935.

7. Ibid., 26 May & 2 June 1935; *Courage*, p. 194.
8. *New York Times*, 8 June 1935.
9. *Letters*, pp. 174–75.
10. *New York Times*, 27 June 1935.
11. *Letters*, pp. 175–76.
12. Ibid., pp. 176–77.
13. *New York Times*, 7 August 1935.
14. *Letters*, pp. 178–80; *Courage*, p. 193.
15. *Hollywood Pilot*, pp. 93–94; *Letters*, p. 181; *New York Times*, 30 & 31 August 1935; *Winged Legend*, pp. 153–54.
16. *New York Times*, 31 August 1935; *Stars at Noon*, pp. 63–65.
17. *Letters*, pp. 182–85; *Courage*, pp. 194–95; *Last Flight*, pp. 46–49.
18. *Letters*, pp. 185–86.
19. Ibid., pp. 187–88.
20. *New York Times*, 10, 23, & 24 December 1935.

Chapter 16. *The Flying Laboratory*

1. *Letters*, pp. 89–90; *Daughter of the Sky*, p. 68. The former speaks only of "the two women" on this trip; the latter indicates that George was with them.
2. *Hollywood Pilot*, pp. 78–79, 95; *Letters*, p. 56.
3. *Hollywood Pilot*, pp. 132–33.
4. *Letters*, pp. 190–92.
5. *Last Flight*, p. 44; *Soaring Wings*, p. 272.
6. *Soaring Wings*, p. 272; *Last Flight*, p. 49.
7. *New York Times*, 20 & 26 April 1936.
8. Captain L. F. Safford, USN (Ret.), unpublished manuscript, *Flight into Yesterday: The Tragedy of Amelia Earhart*, pp. 121–26. Hereafter *Flight into Yesterday*. In *Hollywood Pilot*, p. 96, Dwiggins gives the total tankage as 1,202 gallons.
9. *Letters*, p. 192.
10. *Hollywood Pilot*, pp. 95–96. In *Last Flight* (p. 50), Amelia gave the gasoline capacity as 1,150 gallons and cruising range as 4,000 miles.
11. *Letters*, pp. 194–95.
12. *New York Times*, 2 May 1936.
13. *Letters*, pp. 196–97; *Courage*, p. 173. The double underlining and exclamation points are Amelia's.
14. *Letters*, pp. 197–99.
15. Ibid., p. 197.
16. *New York Times*, 20 November 1936.
17. Ibid., 28 May 1936; *Soaring Wings*, pp. 273–74.
18. *Hollywood Pilot*, p. 95.
19. *New York Times*, 8 June 1936.
20. Ibid., 15 June 1936.
21. *Letters*, pp. 200–1.
22. *Courage*, p. 173. Muriel mistakenly wrote that Amelia paid for this trip with money from her autogiro advertising. This would have placed Amy and Nancy in Europe in 1931 instead of 1936.

Chapter 17. *Plans and Warnings*

1. *Letters*, pp. 201–2; *New York Times*, 2 August 1936.
2. *Soaring Wings*, p. 274; *Letters*, p. 203.
3. *New York Times*, 30 August & 1 September 1936.
4. *Skystars*, pp. 114–16; *New York Times*, 1 September 1936; Jacqueline Cochran and Maryann Bucknum Brinley, *Jackie Cochran* (New York: Bantam, 1987), p. 128. Hereafter *Jackie*.

5. *New York Times,* 4 September 1936.
6. Ibid., 6 September 1936. For an account of Beryl Markham's career, see Mary S. Sovell, *Straight on Till Morning: The Biography of Beryl Markham* (New York, St Martin's Press, 1987).
7. *Last Flight,* p. 51; *Flight into Yesterday,* p. 21.
8. Courtesy of Safford.
9. Ibid.
10. *Hollywood Pilot,* pp. 94, 97–99.
11. Franklin D. Roosevelt Library, courtesy of Safford.
12. *Flight into Yesterday,* pp. 14–18, 22.
13. Ibid., pp. 23–24. The telegram is in the Franklin D. Roosevelt Library. Courtesy of Safford. The file copy had no signature.
14. *Letters,* p. 193; *Amelia,* p. 119.
15. *Last Flight,* pp. 51–52; *Letters,* pp. 193–94.
16. *Flight into Yesterday,* p. 143. Duplicates of these strip maps are available in the Map Room, Library of Congress.
17. *Soaring Wings,* p. 275.
18. *Amelia,* p. 184; *Letters,* pp. 193–94; *Courage,* p. 196.
19. *New York Times,* 20 & 27 September 1936.
20. *Letters,* p. 204.
21. *New York Times,* 6 & 16 November 1936.
22. Ibid., 22 December 1936.
23. *Stars at Noon,* pp. 88–89; *Jackie,* pp. 136–39.
24. *Stars at Noon,* p. 90; *Jackie,* p. 140; *Letters,* pp. 204–5. *Daughter of the Sky* mistakenly states that it was Fred Noonan whose navigation Jacqueline Cochran distrusted.
25. *Winged Legend,* pp. 166–67.

PART III. FLIGHT INTO MYSTERY

Chapter 18. *False Start*

1. *Letters,* pp. 206–7.
2. *Last Flight,* pp. xi, xii.
3. *Flight into Yesterday,* p. 25.
4. *Last Flight,* pp. x, xi.
5. *New York Times,* 12 February 1937; *Soaring Wings,* p. 276.
6. *Soaring Wings,* pp. 276–78.
7. *Courage,* p. 197.
8. *Last Flight,* p. 55.
9. *New York Times,* 13 February 1937; *Letters,* p. 207.
10. Courtesy of Safford.
11. *New York Times,* 17 February 1937.
12. Ibid., 18 & 22 February 1937.
13. Courtesy of Safford. See also *Flight into Yesterday,* p. 25.
14. *New York Times,* 10 & 13 March 1937; *Hollywood Pilot,* p. 99.
15. *Flight into Yesterday,* pp. 25–26.
16. *New York Times,* 13 & 15 March 1937.
17. *Letters,* p. 205; *Winged Legend,* pp. 173–74; *Last Flight,* p. 56; *New York Times,* 14 March 1937; *Sound of Wings,* p. 245.
18. *New York Times,* 15 March 1937.
19. *Hollywood Pilot,* p. 99; *Last Flight,* pp. 56–57.
20. *New York Times,* 17 & 18 March 1937.
21. *Letters,* pp. 209–10; *Last Flight,* pp. 56, 59; *Hollywood Pilot,* pp. 99–100; *Soaring Wings,* p. 280; *New York Times,* 19 March 1937.
22. *Last Flight,* pp. 59–62.

23. Ibid., p. 64; *Hollywood Pilot,* pp. 100–1.
24. *Hollywood Pilot,* pp. 101–2; *Last Flight,* p. 66.
25. *New York Times,* 19 March 1937; *Last Flight,* pp. 67, 69; *Honolulu Star-Bulletin,* 16 March 1937.
26. *Last Flight,* p. 67; *New York Times,* 19 March 1937; *Hollywood Pilot,* p. 102.
27. *Last Flight,* pp. 67–68; *Hollywood Pilot,* pp. 102–3; *New York Times,* 20 March 1937.
28. *Last Flight,* pp. 70–73; *Hollywood Pilot,* p. 103; *Soaring Wings,* p. 282; *New York Times,* 21 March 1937; *Pittsburgh Post-Gazette,* 22 March 1937.
29. *Soaring Wings,* pp. 283–84; *Last Flight,* pp. 73–74.
30. *New York Times,* 21 March 1937.
31. *Hollywood Pilot,* p. 103; *Last Flight,* p. 71; *Flight into Yesterday,* p. 9.
32. *New York Times,* 21 March 1937; *Last Flight,* p. 73; *Hollywood Pilot,* p. 104.

Chapter 19. *Entr'acte*

1. *Letters,* p. 217.
2. *New York Times,* 21 March 1937.
3. Ibid., 22 March 1937.
4. *Last Flight,* p. 68.
5. *New York Times,* 21 March 1937; *Hollywood Pilot,* p. 104.
6. *New York Times,* 21 & 28 March 1937.
7. Ibid., 21 March 1937.
8. Ibid., 26 March 1937.
9. *Jackie,* pp. 140–41.
10. *Courage,* pp. 198–99; *Letters,* pp. 217–18; *Last Flight,* pp. 75, 78. See chapter 6.
11. *Letters,* p. 217; *New York Times,* 24 April 1937.
12. *Amelia,* p. 212; *Courage,* p. 199.
13. *Letters,* pp. 218–20.
14. *Last Flight,* pp. 76–79.
15. Ibid., pp. 80–81.
16. *New York Times,* 4 May 1937.
17. *Letters,* pp. 220–21.
18. Courtesy of Safford.
19. Ibid.
20. *Jackie,* p. 141.
21. *Courage,* p. 199.
22. *Flight into Yesterday,* pp. 126–27. Safford's expertise in D/F is beyond question. He was an expert in both navigation and radio communications. From 1936 to 1941 "all the Navy's high-frequency direction finders (used for intelligence purposes) were under my cognizance and also the coastal intermediate-frequency D/Fs (used for navigating) until July 1941 when they were turned over to the Coast Guard. . . ." *Flight into Yesterday,* Preface, p. 7.
23. *Jackie,* p. 141.
24. *New York Times,* 22 May 1937.
25. *Last Flight,* p. 86.
26. *Letters,* p. 220.
27. *Last Flight,* p. 84.

Chapter 20. *Miami Takeoff*

1. *Hollywood Pilot,* p. 105.
2. *Last Flight,* pp. 86–87; *Soaring Wings,* p. 289; *Letters,* p. 224. According to the last, George left the flight at New Orleans and entrained for New York

to pick up his son, David. Neither George's account nor Amelia's gives that impression.

3. *New York Times,* 24 May 1937.
4. *Last Flight,* p. 87.
5. Ibid.
6. Ibid., pp. 87–91; *New York Herald Tribune,* 1 June 1937.
7. *Letters,* p. 225.
8. *Hollywood Pilot,* pp. 105–7.
9. *Flight into Yesterday,* pp. 127–28; *Letters,* pp. 221–22.
10. *New York Herald Tribune,* 31 May 1937.
11. *Courage,* p. 199.
12. *Soaring Wings,* p. 290; *Last Flight,* pp. 93–94.
13. *Soaring Wings,* p. 288.
14. *New York Times,* 1 June 1937.
15. *New York Herald Tribune,* 1 June 1937.
16. Ibid.; *Last Flight,* p. 91.
17. *New York Herald Tribune,* 1 June 1937.
18. *Letters,* p. 226.
19. *Soaring Wings,* pp. 290–91; *Last Flight,* pp. 95–96. Amelia gave the take-off time as 5:56 A.M., George 6:04 A.M., 1 June 1937.
20. *Last Flight,* pp. 96–100; *New York Herald Tribune,* 2 June 1937.
21. *New York Times,* 2 June 1937; *Pittsburgh Post-Gazette,* 2 June 1937.
22. *Last Flight,* pp. 101–3.
23. Ibid., pp. 105–6.

Chapter 21. *South America and South Atlantic*

1. *Last Flight,* p. 105; *New York Herald Tribune,* 3 June 1937; *Pittsburgh Post-Gazette,* 3 June 1937.
2. *Last Flight,* pp. 106–7; *New York Herald Tribune,* 3 June 1937; *Pittsburgh Post-Gazette,* 3 June 1937.
3. *Last Flight,* pp. 106–8; *New York Herald Tribune,* 3 June 1937.
4. *Last Flight,* pp. 108–10; *New York Herald Tribune,* 4 June 1937.
5. *Last Flight,* pp. 111–13; *New York Times,* 4 June 1937; *New York Herald Tribune,* 4 June 1937.
6. *Last Flight,* pp. 113–14.
7. Ibid., pp. 115–19; *New York Times,* 4–6 June 1937; *Pittsburgh Post-Gazette,* 5 June 1937; *New York Herald Tribune,* 5 June 1937.
8. *Last Flight,* pp. 120–22.
9. Ibid., pp. 122–26; *New York Times,* 7 June 1937; *Pittsburgh Post-Gazette,* 7 June 1937; *New York Herald Tribune,* 8 June 1937.
10. *Last Flight,* pp. 127–28; *New York Herald Tribune,* 8 June 1937.
11. *Last Flight,* pp. 128–35.

Chapter 22. *Across Africa*

1. *Last Flight,* pp. 135–36; *Flight into Yesterday,* pp. 143–44; *Pittsburgh Post-Gazette,* 8 June 1937.
2. *Last Flight,* pp. 137–39.
3. Ibid., pp. 140–41; *Pittsburgh Post-Gazette,* 9 June 1937; *New York Times,* 9 June 1937; *New York Herald Tribune,* 9 June 1937.
4. *Soaring Wings,* p. 87.
5. *Last Flight,* pp. 143–45.
6. *Pittsburgh Post-Gazette,* 11 June 1937; *New York Times,* 11 June 1937; *Last Flight,* pp. 145–48; *New York Herald Tribune,* 11 June 1937.
7. *Last Flight,* pp. 148–52; *New York Times,* 11 & 12 June 1937; *Pittsburgh Post-Gazette,* 12 June 1937; *New York Herald Tribune,* 11 June 1937.

8. *Last Flight,* pp. 153–55, 158; *New York Times,* 13 June 1937.

9. *Last Flight,* pp. 159–60; *Pittsburgh Post-Gazette,* 14 June 1937; *New York Times,* 13 June 1937; *New York Herald Tribune,* 13 June 1937.

10. *Last Flight,* pp. 161–65; *Pittsburgh Post-Gazette,* 14 June 1937; *New York Times,* 14 June 1937.

11. *Last Flight,* pp. 166–69.

12. Ibid., pp. 170–71; *Pittsburgh Post-Gazette,* 15 June 1937.

Chapter 23. *India and the Monsoons*

1. *Hollywood Pilot,* p. 107.

2. *Last Flight,* pp. 171–73; *New York Times,* 15 June 1937.

3. *Last Flight,* pp. 173–76.

4. Ibid., pp. 176–79; *New York Times,* 16 June 1937; *Pittsburgh Post-Gazette,* 16 June 1937; *New York Herald Tribune,* 16 June 1937. This conversation was mechanically recorded in the *Herald Tribune*'s New York office.

5. *Soaring Wings,* p. 87.

6. *Last Flight,* pp. 180–81; *New York Herald Tribune,* 17 June 1937.

7. *Last Flight,* pp. 181–82; *New York Herald Tribune,* 17 June 1937.

8. *Last Flight,* pp. 184–85.

9. Ibid., pp. 190–91; *Pittsburgh Post-Gazette,* 17 June 1937; *New York Times,* 17 June 1937; *New York Herald Tribune,* 18 June 1937.

10. *Last Flight,* pp. 191–93; *New York Herald Tribune,* 18 June 1937.

11. *Last Flight,* pp. 194–97; *Pittsburgh Post–Gazette,* 18 June 1937; *New York Herald Tribune,* 19 June 1937.

12. *Last Flight,* pp. 197–98; *New York Herald Tribune,* 17 June 1937; *Courage,* p. 200. *Last Flight* does not mention these purchases.

Chapter 24. *Problems*

1. *New York Times,* 19 June 1937.

2. *Last Flight,* p. 199.

3. Ibid., pp. 199–202.

4. Ibid., pp. 202–6; *New York Times,* 20 June 1937.

5. *Last Flight,* pp. 207–10; *New York Times,* 21 June 1937; *New York Herald Tribune,* 21 June 1937.

6. *Last Flight,* pp. 210–11; *Amelia,* pp. 220, 224; *New York Times,* 22 June 1937.

7. *Amelia,* pp. 225, 229.

8. *New York Times,* 26 June 1937.

9. *Last Flight,* pp. 212–13.

10. Ibid., pp. 213–15.

11. Ibid., pp. 216–17.

12. *Pittsburgh Post-Gazette,* 29 June 1937.

13. Ibid., 29 June 1937; *Last Flight,* pp. 219–22.

14. *Flight into Yesterday,* p. 152.

15. Ibid., p. 154.

16. Ibid., p. 155.

17. Ibid.

18. Ibid., pp. 155–56, 252–53.

19. Collopy report, 28 August 1937. Courtesy of Safford.

20. *Flight into Yesterday,* pp. 157–58.

21. Ibid., pp. 158, 162.

22. Ibid., p. 169; message 8019 courtesy of Safford.

23. *Flight into Yesterday,* pp. 170–71.

24. Ibid., pp. 171–72.

25. Ibid., p. 173.

26. Courtesy of Safford.
27. *Flight into Yesterday,* pp. 173–74.
28. Ibid., pp. 174–75.

Chapter 25. *Poised for Departure*

1. Courtesy of Safford. A slightly different version of this message appears in *Amelia,* p. 237.
2. *Sydney Sun,* 29 June 1937; report from OIC, Airdrome Darwin, to Consul General at Sydney, 3 August 1937. Both courtesy of Safford.
3. *Flight into Yesterday,* pp. 157–58.
4. Courtesy of Safford.
5. *Flight into Yesterday,* p. 159.
6. Ibid., p. 160.
7. Ibid., p. 161.
8. *Last Flight,* p. 223; *New York Herald Tribune,* 3 July 1937; *Pittsburgh Post-Gazette,* 30 June & July 1937.
9. *Last Flight,* p. 224.
10. *Flight into Yesterday,* pp. 161–62.
11. Ibid., p. 163; Courtesy of Safford.
12. *Last Flight,* p. 226.
13. Joe Klaas, *Amelia Earhart Lives* (New York: McGraw–Hill, 1970), pp. 9–10. Hereafter *Earhart Lives.*
14. Letter, Collopy to Gervais, 1 November 1965. Courtesy of Luttrell.
15. Thomas E. Devine, with Richard M. Daley, *Eyewitness: The Amelia Earhart Incident* (Frederick, Colo.: Renaissance House, 1987), pp. 14–15. Hereafter *Eyewitness.*
16. *New York Times,* 8 July 1937; *Last Flight,* p. 91.
17. Letter, Balfour to Gervais, 4 March 1961. Courtesy of Luttrell.
18. *Flight into Yesterday,* p. 176.
19. Ann H. Pellegreno, *World Flight: The Earhart Trail* (Ames: Iowa State University Press, 1972). Hereafter *World Flight.*
20. *Flight into Yesterday,* pp. 20, 142, 144–45. The Gilberts were under British jurisdiction at this time.
21. Ibid., p. 164.
22. Ibid., p. 27.
23. Ibid.

Chapter 26. *Disaster*

1. *Flight into Yesterday,* p. 29.
2. *New York Herald Tribune,* 2 July 1937.
3. *Flight into Yesterday,* p. 31; Griffin message courtesy of Safford.
4. *Flight into Yesterday,* p. 31.
5. *New York Herald Tribune,* 2 July 1937.
6. *World Flight,* pp. 143–45.
7. Collopy report, courtesy of Safford.
8. Griffin message, courtesy of Safford.
9. *Flight into Yesterday,* pp. 125–30.
10. Ibid., pp. 32–33.
11. Ibid., p. 33.
12. Ibid., pp. 34–37.
13. Letter, T. H. Gude to Frank Holbrook, 15 December 1969, courtesy of Safford; *Flight into Yesterday,* p. 35.
14. *Flight into Yesterday,* pp. 35–36.
15. Ibid., pp. 35–38.
16. Ibid., pp. 175–76. Times and direct quotations of messages are taken from *Itasca*'s radio logs, courtesy of Safford.

17. *Flight into Yesterday,* pp. 38–39.
18. Ibid., pp. 39–40.
19. Ibid., pp. 168, 178–79.
20. *Hollywood Pilot,* p. 109.
21. Ibid., p. 120.
22. *Flight into Yesterday,* pp. 40, 179–80.
23. Ibid., pp. 40–41, 180–81. For some reason, Thompson omitted the words "ON SEVENTYFIVE HUNDRED" from both his radio and written reports.
24. Ibid., pp. 42–43.
25. Ibid., p. 183.
26. *Hollywood Pilot,* pp. 118–40; *Flight into Yesterday,* pp. 134–37.
27. *Flight into Yesterday,* pp. 136–40, 150.
28. *Hollywood Pilot,* chart opp. p. 82; *Flight into Yesterday,* pp. 136, 149–50; Letter to Mr. Robert Stanley, Aurora, Colo., 29 June 1970, name of writer withheld, courtesy of Safford.
29. *Flight into Yesterday,* pp. 145–47.

Chapter 27. *The Early Searches*

1. *Flight into Yesterday,* pp. 44–45.
2. Ibid., p. 45.
3. *Itasca* message 6002-1015, courtesy of Safford; *Flight into Yesterday,* p. 46.
4. *Flight into Yesterday,* pp. 47–48.
5. Thompson's message 1018, courtesy of Safford.
6. COMHAWSEC message 6002-1401, courtesy of Safford.
7. *Itasca* distress broadcasts to all ships, 2 July 1937, courtesy of Safford.
8. COMBATFOR to OPNAV message 1002-1515, courtesy of Safford.
9. *Flight into Yesterday,* p. 51.
10. *New York Herald Tribune,* 3 July 1937; Message from *Achilles;* courtesy of Safford. All of the *Herald Tribune*'s statements were not this accurate. It quoted COMBATFOR at Pearl Harbor as saying that there were ten thousand gallons of gas "on Swan Island."
11. *Hollywood Pilot,* pp. 121, 127; *New York Times,* 3 July 1937.
12. *New York Times, Washington Post,* and *Pittsburgh Post-Gazette,* all 3 July 1937.
13. *Stars at Noon,* p. 91; *Jackie,* pp. 142–43.
14. Reading 1396-1, 5 July 1937, Edgar Cayce Foundation, Virginia Beach, Va.
15. *Flight into Yesterday,* p. 48; *Hollywood Pilot,* pp. 120–21.
16. Thompson report quoted by Safford, *Flight into Yesterday,* pp. 48–50.
17. *Flight into Yesterday,* pp. 48, 50, 52.
18. Ibid., pp. 52, 54; *Washington Post,* 4 July 1937.
19. *New York Times, New York Herald Tribune, Washington Post,* all 4 July 1937; *Letters,* pp. 231–33.
20. *New York Herald Tribune,* 4 July 1937.
21. *Flight into Yesterday,* pp. 54–55.
22. Ibid., pp. 56–57.

Chapter 28. *The Last Search Phase*

1. *Flight into Yesterday,* p. 50.
2. Message courtesy of John F. Luttrell. It is quoted in *Hollywood Pilot,* p. 122.
3. *Washington Post,* 6 July 1937.
4. *Pittsburgh Post-Gazette,* 6 July 1937.
5. *Washington Post,* 5 July 1937.
6. *Flight into Yesterday,* p. 59.
7. Ibid., pp. 59–60.
8. Ibid., pp. 60–61.

9. Ibid., pp. 61–62; *Hollywood Pilot,* pp. 122–24.
10. *Flight into Yesterday,* p. 79; *New York Times,* 6 July 1937; *Washington Post,* 6 July 1937.
11. *Flight into Yesterday,* pp. 69–72.
12. Ibid., pp. 62–63.
13. *New York Herald Tribune,* 6 & 7 July 1937; *New York Times,* 7 July 1937; *Pittsburgh Post-Gazette,* 7 July 1937; *Flight into Yesterday,* pp. 80–81.
14. *Pittsburgh Post-Gazette,* 7 July 1937; *New York Times,* 7 July 1937; *Flight into Yesterday,* p. 89.
15. *Flight into Yesterday,* pp. 64–66; message 0006-1505, courtesy of Safford.
16. *Flight into Yesterday,* pp. 65, 79–80.
17. *New York Herald Tribune, New York Times, Pittsburgh Post-Gazette,* all 8 July 1937.
18. *New York Herald Tribune,* 9 July 1937; *Flight into Yesterday,* pp. 70–71; *New York Times,* 7 July 1937.
19. Message courtesy of Safford; *New York Times,* 10 July 1937.
20. *New York Times,* 9 July 1937.
21. *Flight into Yesterday,* pp. 71–77.
22. *New York Herald Tribune,* 10 July 1937.
23. *Pittsburgh Post-Gazette,* 12 July 1937.
24. *New York Times,* 11 July 1937.
25. *Pittsburgh Post-Gazette,* 19 July 1937.
26. *New York Times,* 21 July 1937.
27. Report, CinCUS to CNO, 28 August 1937, courtesy of Safford; *Flight into Yesterday,* p. 89A.
28. *New York Times,* 25 July 1937.
29. Ibid., 30 July 1937.
30. *New York Herald Tribune,* 16 July 1937.
31. Reading 1396-2, 31 August 1937 and Allied Papers, Edgar Cayce Foundation, Virginia Beach, Va.
32. Diary of Admiral William D. Leahy, Library of Congress, Washington, D.C., courtesy of Safford.
33. *Flight into Yesterday,* p. 88.
34. *Courage,* p. 202.
35. *New York Times,* 20 July 1937.

Chapter 29. *The Aftermath*

1. FBI memorandum for the files, 2 August 1937, signed by Special Agent T. J. Donegan; statement of Wilbur Rothar, 3 August 1937; FBI memoranda for the Director, 2 and 3 August 1937. These are contained in FBI File No. 9-2984, Subject: George P. Putnam. Courtesy of Luttrell.
2. Letter, Amy Earhart to Neta Southern, 6 May 1944. Courtesy of Luttrell, who received a copy from Joe Gervais.
3. *Courage,* p. 202.
4. Letter, Charlotte A. Cooper to Joe Klaas, 27 December 1970. Courtesy of Luttrell.
5. Ashland (Ky.) *Daily Independent,* 9 July 1937, with a notation by Evelyn Jackson, 1 August 1986. Courtesy of Luttrell.
6. Letter, Mrs. C. B. Paxton to Walter Winchell, 22 September 1943. Courtesy of Luttrell.
7. Letter, Mrs. C. B. Paxton to U.S. Naval Intelligence, 23 February 1944. Courtesy of Luttrell.
8. *Louisville Courier-Journal,* 14 January 1962. Courtesy of Luttrell.
9. Letter, Evelyn G. Jackson to Charles N. Hill, 8 February 1986. Courtesy of Luttrell.

10. Letter, AF Office, Department of Defense, Canberra, Australia, to John F. Luttrell, 30 April 1986. Courtesy of Luttrell.
11. Letter, Evelyn S. Jackson to Charles N. Hill, 8 February 1986. Courtesy of Luttrell.
12. *New York Times,* 19 October & 3 November 1937.
13. *Hollywood Pilot,* p. 127; Diary of Henry D. Morgenthau Jr., 13 May 1938, Franklin D. Roosevelt Library, Hyde Park, N.Y. Courtesy of Luttrell.
14. Letter, Luttrell to Donald M. Goldstein, 12 June 1967.
15. *Hollywood Pilot,* p. 127.
16. *Earhart Lives,* p. 65.
17. Fred Goerner, *The Search for Amelia Earhart* (Garden City, N.Y.: Doubleday, 1966), p. 132. Hereafter *The Search.*
18. *Courage,* p. 211; *The Search,* pp. 41–42, 136, 258; *Letters,* p. 238.
19. *Hollywood Pilot,* pp. 126–27.

Chapter 30. *The Rumor Mill*

1. *Courage,* pp. 205–6.
2. Ibid., p. 204.
3. Ibid., pp. 208–10.
4. Thom Thomas, *My Search for Amelia . . . Alive!,* no publisher or publication date given, pp. 1–8.
5. Ibid., pp. 10–29.
6. *Eyewitness,* pp. 37–38.
7. Ibid., pp. 39–42, 47.
8. Ibid., pp. 45–51.
9. Francis X. Holbrook, "Amelia Earhart's Final Flight," *United States Naval Institute Proceedings,* February 1971, p. 55. Hereafter "Final Flight."
10. *Eyewitness,* pp. 51–61.
11. *The Search,* pp. 267–73.
12. *Eyewitness,* pp. 138–39.
13. U.S. government agency memorandum 27 December 1944. Courtesy of Luttrell. According to Paul Briand Jr. ("Requiem for Amelia," National Archives), this agency did not want this information attributed to it, so we are respecting this wish. The name of the POW is unknown to us because this agency had a habit of blacking out proper names on documents.
14. *Nippon Times,* 29 August 1949.
15. Department of the Army G20GHQ Interoffice Memorandum from Compilations to Deputy Chief, CI Division, subject, "Additional Information Amelia Earhart," 8 August 1949. This contained the translation of pertinent portions of a Japanese police report. Courtesy of Luttrell.

Chapter 31. *An Open-Ended Case*

1. The authors recall this film, along with the story that Horace McCoy wrote for *Women's Home Companion* based upon his movie script.
2. Stanley's Introduction to *Flight into Yesterday,* pp. 12–13.
3. "Final Flight," p. 52.
4. *Letters,* p. 237.
5. Letter with questionnaire from Charles N. Hill to Francis G. "Fuzz" Furman, 19 November 1965, with Furman's replies. Courtesy of Luttrell.
6. *Flight into Yesterday,* preface, p. 7.
7. *The Search,* pp. 260–61.
8. *Flight into Yesterday,* pp. 195–96.
9. "Final Flight," p. 55.
10. *The Search,* pp. 7–9, 60–71.
11. Ibid., pp. 97, 110–13, 176–77.
12. Ibid., pp. 225–26.

13. Ibid., pp. 265–66, 314.
14. *Flight into Yesterday,* p. 199.
15. Ibid., pp. 210–13; Joe Davidson, *Amelia Earhart Returns from Saipan* (Canton, Ohio: Davidson, 1969), p. 186; *Denver Post,* 3 March 1970.
16. J. D. Hadek, "Amelia Earhart Disappearance: A Condensed Summary," unpublished mss. Courtesy of Luttrell.
17. *Earhart Lives,* pp. 155–57; interview with Dan Wade, *Atlanta Journal,* 11 August 1983.
18. *Earhart Lives,* p. 174. Zonta International is an association of business and professional women.
19. Letter, Safford to Gervais, 8 March 1973. Courtesy of Luttrell.
20. Vincent Loomis, with Jeffrey Ethell, *Amelia Earhart: The Final Story* (New York: Random House, 1985), p. 77.
21. Ibid., pp. 76–77.
22. Courtesy of Luttrell.
23. Statement from A. D. Gibson to Gervais, undated; however, the covering envelope is postmarked 11 April 1972. Also exchange between Gervais, 11 June 1975, and the Japanese Ministry of Justice, 3 July 1975. Courtesy of Luttrell. If such a file of photos existed, it might have contained one of a Caucasian woman. Saburu Kurusu, a high-level diplomat, was married to an American.
24. *Courage,* p. 206.
25. Wilmington (Del.) *Sunday News-Journal,* 5 February 1989; *London Daily Telegraph,* 16 October 1989.
26. *USA Today,* 4 January 1991; *Pittsburgh Post-Gazette,* 4 January 1991.
27. *Washington Post,* 3 July 1991; Arlington (Va.) *Journal,* 12 September 1991; Wilmington (Del.) *News-Journal,* 6 February 1992.
28. *Washington Post,* 17 March 1992.
29. Wilmington (Del.) *News Journal,* 5 December 1996. Those interested in pursuing this subject further are referred to TIGHAR, Wilmington, Delaware, unpublished reports of Richard Gillespie.

EPILOGUE

1. Letter, Lt. Cmdr. Frank T. Kenner to his wife, 10 August 1937. Courtesy of Luttrell.
2. Introduction, *Flight into Yesterday,* pp. 10–11.
3. Letter, Cmdr. H. M. Anthony, USCG (Ret.), to Gervais, 21 August (?) 1967. The signature on this letter is cut off, but the handwriting is identical to another dated 30 November 1966, to Maj. Robert S. Dinger, USAF.
4. Clarence L. "Kelly" Johnson with Maggie Smith, *Kelly: More Than My Share of It All,* (Washington, D.C.: Smithsonian Institution Press, 1985), pp. 43–46.
5. *Letters,* p. 185.
6. Letter, Safford to Col. William L. Polhemus, 15 March 1971. Courtesy of Luttrell.
7. Letter, Anthony to Gervais, 21 August 1967.
8. *Martin Mercury,* 15 July 1960. House publication of Glenn L. Martin Co., Baltimore, Md.
9. *Last Flight,* pp. xi, xii.

GLOSSARY

aileron	A device near the trailing edge of an aircraft wing to control maneuvers.
Albright, Thomas G.	Claimed to have seen AE on a Pacific island.
Allen, Carl	Reporter for the New York *Herald Tribune*.
altimeter	A device for determining altitude, distance above sea level.
autogiro	A rotary-wing plane that uses a propellor for forward motion and a freely rotating rotor for lift.
Balchen, Bernt	Aviator and Arctic explorer.
Barnes, Peter	Friend of the Earharts in California.
barograph	An automatic recording barometer.
Black, Richard E.	Department of the Interior representative on Howland Island.
Boll, Mabel	Hoped to be the first woman to fly the Atlantic.
Byrd, Cmdr. Richard E.	Arctic explorer; helped prepare *Friendship* flight.
Campbell, Robert	Supervisor of runway construction on Howland Island.
Challis, Katherine "Katch"	A cousin of AE.
Challis, Lucy "Toot"	A cousin of AE.
Chapman, Samuel	Friend and ex-fiancé of AE.
Cochran, Jacqueline	Flier and friend of AE.
Collins, Paul	Veteran flier and business associate of AE.
Collopy, James A.	District supervisor at Lae.

Cooper, 1st Lt. David A.	Army Air Corps representative on Howland Island.
CW	Continuous wave.
Darrow, Dr. Louise deS.	College friend of AE.
Devine, Thomas E.	Claimed to have seen AE's aircraft destroyed.
D/F	Direction finder (by two separate radio stations).
Earhart, Amy Otis	AE's mother.
Earhart, David	AE's paternal grandfather.
Earhart, Edwin	AE's father.
Earhart, Helen	AE's stepmother.
Earhart, Mary	AE's paternal grandmother.
Earhart, Muriel "Pidge"	AE's sister.
EDT	Eastern daylight saving time.
Elder, Ruth	Flier and friend of AE.
Elliott, Edward C.	President of Purdue University.
ETA	Estimated time of arrival.
exhaust manifold	Tubes to channel exhaust gases from cylinders to the rest of the exhaust system.
Flight for Freedom	Film reminiscent of AE's disappearance.
Friedell, Capt. W. L.	Captain of BB *Colorado.*
Friendship	Aircraft in which AE first crossed the Atlantic.
Furman, Francis "Fuzz"	KNILM mechanic.
Gardiner, Florence	AE's governess.
GCT	Greenwich civil time.
Gervais, Joe	Researcher into AE's disappearance.
Gillespie, Richard	Executive director of TIGHAR, believes he found evidence that AE landed on Nikumaroru.
GMT	Greenwich mean time.
Goerner, Fred	Writer and researcher into AE's disappearance.
Gordon, Louis "Slim"	Mechanic on *Friendship.*
Gower, Louis	Standby pilot for *Friendship* flight.
Guest, Mrs. Frederick S. (Amy)	Sponsor of *Friendship* flight
gyroscope	Indicates true north when adjusted to latitude and speed of an aircraft.
Harres, Maria Grace	AE's maternal great-grandmother.
Hawks, Frank	Piloted AE on her first ride in an aircraft.
H/F	High frequency radio.
HST	Howland standard time.
KC	Kilocycles.
KHAQQ	Call letters of AE's Electra.
Kimball, Dr. James H. "Doc"	Weather expert, U.S. Weather Bureau.
Lindbergh, Anne Morrow	Author and wife of Charles Lindbergh.
Lindbergh, Charles A.	First to fly the Atlantic solo.
Luttrell, John F.	Researcher into AE's disappearance.

Manning, Capt. Harry	Liner skipper and navigator.
Mantz, Myrtle	Wife of Paul Mantz.
Mantz, Paul	AE's technical advisor and friend.
McKneely, Bo	AE's mechanic.
MCW	Modulates continuous wave.
Miller, W. T.	Department of Commerce representative on Howland Island.
Minor, Theresa	Paul Mantz's fiancée.
Morgenthau, Henry Jr.	Secretary of the Treasury.
Morrissey, Albert	Muriel Earhart's husband.
Nichols, Ruth	Flier and friend of AE.
Ninety-Nines	Organization of women fliers.
Noonan, Frederick J.	Navigator on AE's last flight.
Noyes, Blanche	Flier and friend of AE.
NR 16020	Number of AE's Electra.
NRUI	*Itasca* call letters.
Odlum, Floyd	Husband of Jacqueline Cochran.
Otis, Alfred	AE's maternal grandfather.
Otis, Amelia	AE's maternal grandmother.
Paxton, Mrs. C. B.	Claimed to have heard AE broadcasts.
Perkins, Marion	Head of Denison House where AE was a social worker.
Post, Wiley	Flier and friend of AE.
Putnam, David	AE's stepson.
Putnam, Dorothy	First wife of George P. Putnam.
Putnam, George Palmer	Promoter and husband of AE.
Railey, Capt. H. H.	Promoter of *Friendship* project.
Rogers, Will	Comedian and proponent of aviation.
Safford, Laurence F.	D/F expert and researcher.
Selfridge, Gordon	British businessman and friend of AE.
Sibour, Vicomte Jacques de	AE friend who helped arrange around-the-world flight.
Smith, Elinor	Flier and friend of AE.
Snook, Neta	Taught AE to fly.
Stanley, Robert M.	Naval aviator who participated in search for AE.
Stultz, Wilmer	Pilot of *Friendship*.
Sutherland, Abby	Headmistress of Ogontz School.
Thaden, Louise	Flier and friend of AE.
Thomas, Thom	Claimed to have seen AE in Japan.
Thomas, Wilbur	Aircraft motor expert.
Thompson, Cmdr. W. K.	Captain of *Itasca*.
TIGHAR	The International Group for Historic Aircraft Recovery.
True, Lt. Arnold E.	Aerographer, Navy officer specializing in meteorology.
Vidal, Eugene	Business associate and friend of the Putnams.
VKT	Nauru call letters.
Williams, Lt. Cmdr. Clarence S.	Prepared AE's strip maps.

BIBLIOGRAPHY

Books

Backer, Jean L. *Letters from Amelia 1901–1937*. New York: E. P. Dutton, 1958.

Brennan, T. C., and Ray Rosenbaum. *Witness to the Execution: The Odyssey of Amelia Earhart*. Frederick, Colo.: Renaissance House, 1988.

Briand, Paul L., Jr. *Daughter of the Sky: The Story of Amelia Earhart*. New York: Duell, Sloan and Pearce, 1960.

Brink, Randall. *Lost Star: The Search for Amelia Earhart*. New York: W. W. Norton, 1993.

Burke, John. *Winged Legend: The Life of Amelia Earhart*. New York: Berkeley, 1970.

Cochran, Jacqueline. *The Stars at Noon*. Boston: Little, Brown, 1954.

Cochran, Jacqueline, and Maryann Bucknum Brinley. *Jackie Cochran*. New York: Bantam, 1987.

Davidson, Joe. *Amelia Earhart Returns from Saipan*. Canton, Ohio: Davidson, 1969.

Devine, Thomas E., with Richard M. Daley. *Eyewitness: The Amelia Earhart Incident*. Frederick, Colo.: Renaissance House, 1987.

Donahue, J. A. *The Earhart Disappearance: The British Connection*. Terre Haute, Ind.: SunShine House, 1987.

Dwiggins, Don. *Hollywood Pilot: The Biography of Paul Mantz*. Garden City, N.Y.: Doubleday, 1967.

Earhart, Amelia. Arranged by George Palmer Putnam. *Last Flight*. New York: Harcourt, Brace, 1937.

Earhart, Amelia. *The Fun of It*. New York: Harcourt, Brace, 1932.

Earhart, Amelia. *20 Hrs., 40 Min.: Our Flight in the* Friendship. New York: G. P. Putnam's Sons, 1928.

Goerner, Fred. *The Search for Amelia Earhart*. New York: Doubleday, 1966.

Hodgman, Ann, and Ruby Djabbaroff. *Sky Stars: The History of Women in Aviation*. New York: Atheneum, 1981.

Johnson, Clarence L. "Kelly," with Maggie Smith. *Kelly: More Than My Share of It All*. Washington, D.C.: Smithsonian Institution Press, 1985.

Klaas, Joe. *Amelia Earhart Lives*. New York: McGraw-Hill, 1970.

Lindbergh, Anne Morrow. *Hour of Gold, Hour of Lead*. New York: Harcourt Brace Jovanovich, 1973.

Loomis, Vincent, with Jeffrey Ethell. *Amelia Earhart: The Final Story*. New York: Random House, 1985.

Lovell, Mary S. *The Sound of Wings: The Life of Amelia Earhart*. New York: St. Martin's Press, 1989.

Morrissey, Muriel Earhart. *Courage Is the Price: The Biography of Amelia Earhart*. Wichita, Kansas: McCormick-Armstrong, 1963.

Morrissey, Muriel, and Carol L. Osborne. *Amelia, My Courageous Sister*. Santa Clara, Calif.: Aviation, 1987.

Myers, Robert. *Stand By to Die: The Disappearance, Rescue and Return of Amelia Earhart*. Pacific Grove, Calif.: Lighthouse Writer's Guild, 1985.

Parlin, John. *Amelia Earhart*. New York: Dell, 1991.

Pearce, Carol A. *Amelia Earhart*. Berkeley, Calif.: Books Demand, 1988.

Pellegreno, Ann H. *World Flight: The Earhart Trail*. Ames: Iowa State University Press, 1972.

Putnam, George Palmer. *Soaring Wings: A Biography of Amelia Earhart*. New York: Harcourt, Brace, 1939.

Railey, Hilton Howell. *Touch'd with Madness*. New York: Carrick & Evans, 1938.

Rich, Doris L. *Amelia Earhart: A Biography*. Washington, D.C.: Smithsonian Institution Press, 1989.

Sloate, Susan. *Amelia Earhart: Challenging the Skies*. New York: Fawcett, 1989.

Snook, Neta. *I Taught Amelia to Fly*. New York: Vintage, 1978.

Strippel, Dick. *Amelia Earhart—The Myth and the Reality*. New York: Exposition, 1972.

Thomas, Thom. *My Search for Amelia . . . Alive!* No publisher or publication date given.

Thorpe, Elliott R. *East Wind Rain—The Intimate Account of an Intelligence Officer in the Pacific 1939–1969*. Boston: Gambit, 1969.

Ware, Susan. *Still Missing: Amelia Earhart and the Search for Modern Feminism*. New York: W. W. Norton, 1993.

Wilson, Donald M. *Amelia Earhart: Lost Legend*. Los Angeles, Calif.: Enigma, 1993.

Newspapers

Arlington (VA) *Journal*
Ashland (KY) *Daily Independent*

Automotive Daily News (NY)
Baltimore Sun
Bridgeport (CT) *Times-Star*
Denver Post
Evansville (IN) *Courier*
Helena (MT) *Record Herald*
Honolulu Star-Bulletin
Johnstown (PA) *Democrat*
London Daily Telegraph
London Times
Louisville Courier-Journal
Manchester Guardian
Martin Memory, Baltimore, Md.

Mexico City Excelsior
New York Review of Books,
    December 1985
New York Herald Tribune
New York Times
Nippon News
Philadelphia Record
Pittsburgh Post-Gazette
San Francisco Chronicle
Schenectady (NY) *Union Star*
St. Louis Post-Dispatch
Sydney Sun
Wheeling (WV) *Intelligencer*
Wilmington (DE) *Every Evening*
Wilmington (DE) *News-Journal*

Articles

Hamill, Pete. "Leather and Pearls: The Cult of Amelia Earhart." *MS Magazine*, September 1976.
Holbrook, Francis X. "Amelia Earhart's Final Flight." *United States Naval Institute Proceedings*, February 1971.

Unpublished Material

Paul Briand Jr. "Requiem for Amelia." National Archives.
Diary of Henry D. Morgenthau Jr. Franklin D. Roosevelt Library, Hyde Park, N.Y.
Diary of Admiral William D. Leahy. Library of Congress.
FBI File No. 9-2984, Subject: George P. Putnam.
J. D. Hadek. "Amelia Earhart Disappearance—A Condensed Summary."
Radio Logs, *Itasca*.
Readings 1396-1 and 2 and Allied Papers. Edgar Cayce Foundation, Virginia Beach, Va.
Report, District Superintendent James A. Collopy (Lae) to Civil Aviation Board (Salamaua), 28 August 1937.
Report, OIC, Airdrome Darwin to Consul General at Sydney, 3 August 1937.
Report to Cmdr. Warner K. Thompson, Cruise report of the *Itasca*.
Safford, Capt. Laurence F., USN (Ret.). *Flight into Yesterday: The Tragedy of Amelia Earhart*.

INDEX

ABOUT THE AUTHORS

DONALD M. GOLDSTEIN is a professor of public and international affairs at the University of Pittsburgh and a former Air Force officer.

KATHERINE V. DILLON, a retired Air Force chief warrant officer, collaborated with Dr. Goldstein and the late Dr. Gordon W. Prange on eight bestselling books, including *At Dawn We Slept* and *Miracle at Midway*.